'This engaging collection is a helpful foundation for exploring the use of ethnography in Christian ethics and theology. The authors provide thoughtful and probing challenges to how social scientists and theologians do our work-encouraging us to question and alter some of the basic assumptions of our work so that we do it with genuine rigor rather than with unexamined normative commitments or using the social sciences as lax sources for theological reflection. The challenge is genuine and I encourage us to read and learn from this fine collection.'

Emilie M. Townes, Yale Divinity School, USA

'Christian Scharen and Aana Marie Vigen have put together a remarkable book that fills many needs at once. The book surveys a wide range of ways scholars have engaged ethnography for the sake of theology and ethics. It consolidates a conversation. It then extends that conversation with a significant proposal for ethnography as theology and ethics. A series of examples begin to suggest the range and power of this vision. This book should become—immediately upon its publication—the generative center of one of the most important developments in contemporary theology and ethics.'

Ted A. Smith, Vanderbilt University, USA

'The turn to practice in Christian Theology and Ethics has made engagement with the social and cultural reality of the Church an urgent concern. Many talk about ethnography but few actually do it yet it is in doing of it that the theological force of 'practice' gains any kind of traction. it is the focus on actually doing ethnographic research that makes his book is a timely and significant contribution to the conversation around ethics and communal practices. In the introductory section the editors introduce key elements in ethnographic research. These are then illustrated through a series of studies. The result is a major resource for any one who wants to start to do ethnography as part of Christian Theology and Ethics.'

Pete Ward, Kings College London, UK

'A powerful affirmation of the human lives that animate theological reflection and practice. This timely and compelling book is a must read for all concerned with the creative interface of anthropology and theology.'

João Biehl, Princeton University, USA

'This volume pulls back the curtain on the ethnographic method of Christian theologians and ethicists who earn their living and scholarly reputations studying the lives of other people and offering truth claims about those realities. The collection is path breaking in the field of religion for its unflinching scrutiny of under-examined assumptions of white racial privilege embedded in method, careful delineation of the meaning of interdisciplinarity, as well as specific guidance on best practices for ethical research.'

Traci West, Drew University, USA

Ethnography *as*
Christian Theology and Ethics

Ethnography *as* Christian Theology and Ethics

Edited by
Christian Scharen
and
Aana Marie Vigen

continuum

Continuum International Publishing Group
The Tower Building, 11 York Road, London SE1 7NX
80 Maiden Lane, Suite 704, New York, NY 10038

www.continuumbooks.com

British Library Cataloguing-in-Publication Data
A catalogue record for this book is available from the British Library

ISBN 13: 978-1-441-19325-4 (hardback)
　　　　　978-1-441-15545-0 (paperback)

Typeset by Newgen Imaging Systems Pvt Ltd, Chennai, India
Printed and bound in the United States of America

To Nancy L. Eiesland, beloved teacher and mentor, 1964–2009, with my deep gratitude

—Christian Scharen

To Alison and Benjamin Gabriel, my family, for the infinite joy and grace you embody and for keeping me grounded in the particular

—Aana Marie Vigen

Contents

Part Three: Method

Foreword

So which part of the life of a Christian community is "theological" or theologically ethical? Is it the talk? The sermon? Or the recital of creeds? Is it the counseling done by the minister? Does "theological" only refer to certain things said in church space? If so, where does that leave those who do not understand Trinitarian dogma? Or those who live on the streets—whose major vocation is survival? What have the color of bodies and the status accorded different bodies in our cultures to do with "theology"? Unfortunately many expert definitions of "theological" do not offer ways to read these other spaces, practices and lives. Or they construe the dilemmas raised by these other spaces and lives as secondary "issues," not primary to normative theology. Given the continued prominence of such views I give thanks for the work of these authors for an alternative vision of the "theological." By interpreting the practices of ethnography as "theology and ethics" these worldly realities, in all their complexity, difference and messiness, are thereby granted status as places where the divine presence can and must be discerned and as central to real theology.

In short, the claim that ethnography can be understood as Christian theology and ethics is deeply important and timely, as well as provocative. It is deeply important for many reasons. Common sense tells us that attention to lived faith, or the lived situations of human beings everywhere is basic to Christian faith. What is the point of such faith if it is not about or relevant to life in all its complexity? How can theology matter if its content is not able to take seriously all the difference, ambiguity, beauty, horror and tragedy of created life? Christian theology and ethics must have some grasp of these messy realities, and participant observation is a marvelous way to initiate access to them. A second, more explicitly theological rationale for ethnographic work is, as the authors insist, the incarnational nature of Christianity. While differently narrated over the centuries such a defining theme as incarnation at its very minimum affirms the immanence of God, of the Divine—an immanence that requires the honoring of the finitely good creation, in all its ambiguity, brokenness and potential redemption. There is, as these authors make clear, no other place to look for God than as mediated through the messy place that is the world.

Ethnography and sustained participant observation are thus of enormous importance for those of us doing academic work in the fields designated as theology and ethics. And this project, the authors remind us, is not the first case to be made for research that attends to lived existence. Liberationist theologies have long argued for the context-driven character of all theology. Latin American liberationists, feminist, black, womanist, Latina/Mujerista, and, more recently, queer and disability theologies have argued not simply that theology is historically contextual, but that specific forms of social brokenness should be privileged as the generative sites of theological praxis/reflection. And for them "context" always entails not simply the cultural shaping of a theological worldview, but its embeddedness in (typically unacknowledged) power dynamics and social interests, insights that have been complicated further by postcolonial theories.

Practical theology, while not one single thing,[1] has also operated with the general assumption that all theological reflection is practical, or about lived faith.[2] Although not explicitly theological, congregational studies is obviously relevant, as is virtue theory for ethics as it provides another frame for attending to lived faith in theological thinking. Virtue theory's reappearance in the twentieth century, especially in the work of Alasdair MacIntyre, has impacted a shift to practices in theological ethics, a shift that has been enhanced for some through the works of Pierre Bourdieu and Michael de Certeau, which highlight the role of bodily habituations.

What makes *Ethnography as Christian Theology and Ethics* particularly timely, however, is not just that it provides further development of these important trajectories.

In addition, this project helps us to imagine alternatives to the false dichotomies that continue to plague the academy. Understanding how ethnography can be construed as *theological* provides a way to take seriously a thicker description of the realities of marginalized groups and do so without the constraints of the false opposition of the (ostensibly "secular") empirical research

---

[1] See Bonnie J. Miller-McLemore, "Practical Theology" in *The Encyclopedia of Religion in America* eds, Charles H. Lippy and Peter W. Williams (Washington, D.C.: Congressional Quarterly Press, 2010): 1735–1743.

[2] A related development is Edward Farley's classic analysis of the fourfold and its failure to make thematization of the "contemporary situation" key to theological education. Edward Farley, *Theologia: The Fragmentation and Unity of Theological Education* (Philadelphia: Fortress Press, 1982). He argues that theological education may be successful at teaching how to interpret texts, historical events and doctrines, but continuation of its classic fourfold structure problematically assumes that one can simply bring them to bear upon a context. Even as course in ethics and liberation theologies may offer examples of the latter, theological education still "bypasses most of the structural elements in the situation of the believer and, therefore, suppresses most of the acts in which communities interpret their own lives and situations." Edward Farley, "Interpreting Situations," *Practicing Gospel: Unconventional Thoughts on the Church's Ministry* (Louisville, KY: Westminster John Knox Press, 2003): 36, 38.

of social science and the normative theological. The project surfaces the value-oriented dimensions of social scientific research *and* the intersections between social science, both quantitative and qualitative, and the "theological." Furthermore, it *illustrates* rather than simply asserts their resonances and similarities.[3] This reading of ethnographic research opens to view how theology can and must benefit from the rich wisdoms of every imaginable *and* unfamiliar source.

Ethnography as Christian Theology and Ethics also offers an account of ethnographic research that surfaces its complex power dynamics. Now of course these power dynamics have been recognized in cultural anthropology for several decades. The ethnographer is not an objective recorder of empirical truths. However, this project goes further, reading the necessity for the professional "observer's" self-reflexivity and the recognition of privilege and bias that come with that position in a profoundly theological way. Without romanticizing its insights, the authors help us to see participant observation as a process that can serve as a kind of participant "witnessing" rather than participant "observing" in research that is theological.

Just as we are not called to simply read books about the "other"—the typical posture of the standard academic theological enterprise, ethnographic research is not about digging up empirical information that might serve as particulars for theology's *a priori* universal or divinely revealed truths. Expanding the mandatory self-reflexivity of the ethnographer, the authors show us how deeply responsible and lengthy exposure to the lived experiences of those in very different social locations is a profound gift. They even suggest, it seems to me, that this may be a kind of litmus for crucial and needed theological wisdom. Indeed according to these readings of ethnography as theology we are called to "receive from" the other, and the production of knowledge can be seen as a joint endeavor.

A radical claim is being made here, for the authors tell us that this process should affect a kind of "de-centering" of standard theological and ethical thinking. Now the authors are not rejecting the contribution of systematic thinking or the abstract paradigms that are inevitable to creative and faithful reflection. Nor are they romanticizing the "other." However, this de-centering is a humble recognition that if we confess that all knowledges are infused with the fallibility of experience, some overly privileged knowledges—like those of the "experts"—may well need some redemptive unsettling. Abstract paradigms inevitably require revisiting and sometimes redefining. And although she is

---

[3] Also refusing the theological position that rejects sociology, anthropologist/theologian Douglas Davies sees "a kind of family resemblance" between the work of the confessional theologian and the anthropologist's fieldwork. He says that each is, in a sense, a convert, because fieldwork has a kind of significant effect on the participant observer somewhat like church-life on the theologian. It "matches the religious experience that motivates the confessional theologian." *Anthropology and Theology* (Oxford, UK: Berg, 2002): 4, 7.

speaking specifically about the Roman Catholic Magisterium, I think author Reimer-Barry's claim that such work constitutes "the moral *obligation* of empathetic listening" (emphasis mine) should apply to all of us with the power to define normative theology and ethics.[4]

The gifts offered in this volume from examples of theological and ethical participant observation are quite rich. We learn about the role of African American wisdom for different master tropes of pastoral leadership. A fascinating ethnographic study of married Catholic women in Chicago who are AIDS positive leads to a very different account of the morality/immorality of condom use—an account apparently not on the screen of the Magisterium. Invoking "ethnography as revelation" one essay surfaces the crucial role class and ethnic status have on the "morality/immorality" of physician-assisted suicide. Other gifts include the way in which theological and ethical definitions of faithful life need revisiting if those of us who are predominantly white and privileged experts were to take street kids in Nairobi seriously; or the implications of Mayan culture for Catholic liturgy. While whiteness is an obvious marker requiring reflexive attention for participant observation, an account of its role in the reaction of Northern Ugandan populations to a Caucasian theologian/ethnographer offers especially striking revelations about this easy-to-ignore lens that shapes many "expert" interpretations. The complicated power dynamics identified in an incredibly inspiring model of intentional community with the homeless raise fascinating questions about the nature of ecclesial relationships and the problematic character of the paradigm for virtue ethics that ignores power.

What is provocative, then, about this project is the push to recognize how Christian theology and ethics have crucial stakes in places where they rarely if ever go. Indeed, it is precisely the failure to attend to such places that allows some theological work to continue to reproduce power differences even as it invokes high-minded doctrinal and ethical conclusions. Christian theology and ethics have never been—at least in the acknowledged sense—about simply repeating the past or had as their primary stated goal the reproduction of a religious institution, or the museum-like preservation of the past. The explicit end of Christian theological reflection at its best has been discernment of God's *living* presence in contemporary situations. *Ethnography as Christian Theology and Ethics* is a wonderful and provocative example of theologians' and ethicists' ability to discern this living presence. It invites us to discern this presence in new ways—theology cannot continue to just be "texts-about-texts"[5]—and

---

[4] Emily Reimer-Barry, "The Listening Church: How Ethnography Can Transform Catholic Ethics".

[5] Wesley A. Kort, *Bound to Differ: The Dynamics of Theological Discourses* (University Park, Pa.: The Pennsylvania State University Press, 1992). Todd Whitmore says that reading books about Africa, typically books by Western rather than African authors (i.e., Jeffrey Sachs

it challenges us to receive from the many wisdoms and challenges that are in (non-academic) places.[6]

Mary McClintock Fulkerson
Professor of Theology
Duke University Divinity School

preferred over Thandike Mkandiwive) is the preferred practice of most of us theologians and ethicists rather than participant approaches. Todd Whitmore, "Whiteness Made Visible: A Theo-Critical Ethnography in Acoliland."

[6] I am not suggesting that the academy is not a "real" place, or that it is not worth writing about. The workers who make academic life possible include housekeepers, ground-crews, and administrators as well as professors. Important wisdoms are not confined to the latter.

Preface: Blurring Boundaries

What is Theology? What is Christian Ethics? Who creates (or possesses the license to produce) them? What sources are central (and legitimate) to either task? These are among the first questions and lectures in any introductory course. They are ancient questions, explored since the time of Plato at least, that continue to be discussed and contested in contemporary scholarship. While some consider the basic definitions and boundaries around theology and ethics settled, this volume represents an intentional effort to muddy the waters a bit. A critical mass of scholars finds ethnography integral to their endeavors and this methodological shift is beginning to make important ripples in the academy. Indeed, a number of articles and books are emerging (including by many of the authors in this volume), as part of the blurring of boundaries between systematic and practical theology, theology and ethics, and the academic study of religion, religious participation, and prophetic critique.

Specifically, this volume grows out of a number of years of path-forging, ethnographic work done by several Christian theologians and ethicists. Initially, this kind of research was found only at a couple of doctoral programs in religion, but now it is spreading to more seminaries, divinity schools, and departments of religion. Especially since 2003, when a group of us held a panel on "Ethnography and Normative Ethics" at the Society of Christian Ethics, a growing number of scholars have been connecting at various academic meetings to share our respective work, learn from others exploring similar research trajectories, and discuss future possibilities. We regularly participate on panels, give papers, and meet in working groups at national conferences such as the Society of Christian Ethics, the American Academy of Religion, and the Association for Practical Theology, along with international networks (both informal and formal). Given these dynamic conversations and the number of recent or upcoming publications, it seems the right time to gather together select examples of ethnography as theology and ethics in one place. Thus, Part Two highlights what several scholars have been doing for a wider audience.

Yet, apart from featuring specific projects, this book aims to contribute focused reflection on matters of method. In other words, it wishes not only to encourage others to "go and do likewise," but to offer helpful insights into *how* to go about it and how to avoid problematic pitfalls. While it is not a pragmatic "step by step" handbook for designing an ethnographic study, readers will find recurring attention throughout to methodological qualities that we find essential to responsible and nuanced research.

Central Argument and Intention

Within theology and ethics, there is significant variety among scholars working with ethnography in terms of both content and subdisciplines. For our parts, while we both identify with Christian ethics, Scharen identifies particularly with practical theology, liturgical studies, and ecclesiology while Vigen roots herself in Christian social ethics. In the midst of such contrasts, a major theme that connects our scholarly concerns is the notion of moral and theological formation of persons and communities—how we understand ourselves to be in light of our faith in the divine informs our ethical commitments and responsibilities to others in creation. To explore this path, we have found that conversing with other academics and with texts is only one significant part of a larger research process. In this spirit, we—along with a growing cohort of scholars—resonate with the sensibilities of feminist ethnographer Ruth Behar as she reflects on why many anthropologists choose their particular vocational path:

> For many anthropologists, who enter the profession out of a desire to engage with real people in real (and usually forgotten) places, the literary critic, with "his" reading list of the great books of Western civilization, is a symbolic antithesis . . . Even today, we do not totally believe in books and archives; we believe somehow (still!) in the redemptive possibilities of displacement, of travel, even if, as happens lately, our voyages only return us to our own abandoned hometown or our high-school graduating class.[7]

While we do not disdain reading the "great books" and in fact often assign them in our classes, we share Behar's sense that engaging people can be just as important to learning, and we would add, to moral and theological formation. Indeed, to echo Behar's phrasing, there can be something redemptive—healing—about being displaced through ethnographic study. This theme of displacement or de-centering surfaces throughout the volume. For now, it is sufficient to note that in a similar vein as Behar's contention for anthropology, the overall argument of this book posits that in order to do theology and ethics well, scholars need to explore them through visceral ways, within embodied communities, and in particular contexts.

As it makes this case, the book serves three primary purposes. First, at the most fundamental level, we intend for the book to encourage the use of

---

[7] Ruth Behar, "Introduction: Out of Exile," in *Women Writing Culture*, Ruth Behar and Deborah A. Gordon (eds); (Berkeley: University of California Press, 1995), 10.

ethnography. We hope it assists graduate students to get started and that it deepens the work of scholars already working in these areas. The second and third goals may seem more provocative because they challenge scholars to think a bit differently about their work. Specifically, we intend the volume to challenge scholars in the social sciences to think through normative commitments they may bring (even if unwittingly) to their work. Third, and perhaps even more unsettling to some, we hope it will challenge scholars in theology to not merely "use" social science as non-theological knowledge, but to explore that work as part of the work of theology proper. Chapter Two and several chapters in Part Two explore this last claim in significant depth.

Basic Assumptions

For the sake of both clarity and transparency, we think it is important to touch upon four primary convictions we bring to this work as co-authors/editors. Together, they shape the theoretical framework within which we operate. They also appear in key places within the exemplary chapters of Part Two.

The interconnection of theology and ethics

We understand Christian theology and ethics to be integrally related, yet somewhat distinct disciplines. While, there are many areas of overlap (e.g., sources, themes, method), *theology* is often construed as "God-talk"—inquiring into the mysteries of divine being and doing and concentrating on elaborating formal, systematic categories (e.g., sin, salvation, revelation, ontology, Christology, atonement, eschatology) without making explicit or strong connections to human being, doing, and responsibility. For its part, *ethics*, also termed moral theology, explores human relationships, failures, and obligations in depth—grounded in an understanding that human action and accountability flow from who God is to and for creation. In all, there are both thematic and methodological differences in the formal training of theologians and ethicists along with strong points of connection. This reality is even more complicated in practical theology and other interdisciplinary sites for theological ethical work. While it is possible to work primarily in either systematic or ethical categories without much reference to the other, we find such formulations increasingly unsatisfying and offer this book as a contribution to a greater integration between these disciplines.

Therefore, while not all theologians may agree, for us, theology and ethics are necessarily bound up with one another. At least, the two ought not be divorced. As mentioned above, inquiry into the nature of God should also help us contemplate who we are—and what we ought to become and do—in light of divine being. This orienting assumption permeates the works and worldviews both of classical Christian thinkers (e.g., Augustine, Aquinas, Luther, Calvin) and many diverse modern theologians and ethicists.[8] In the way we conceive of our work, it is impossible to do good theology without Christian ethics and *vice versa*. Theology is both doxological and normative in nature. Consequently, with respect to terminology and in order to avoid tedious repetition, we may refer to "theologians" in certain places and "ethicists" in others; however, we have both in mind throughout this volume.

Confronting and contesting sites of privilege

This assumption will take a bit longer to explain because it deals with particularly thorny terrain—owning up to ways certain people and groups benefit from structured inequalities. There are numerous forms of privilege that scholars may embody *vis-à-vis* their ethnographic subjects (educational, religious, cultural, etc.). This possibility is intensified given the fact that many well-intentioned researchers are committed to working with, and learning from, communities who dwell on the margins of a given society. They, like we, see this commitment as a potential way to foster justice within their vocational endeavors. Many, including us, hope that this ethnographic work will raise insightful public awareness, engender respect and empathy among people, and perhaps even lead to transformation through what Behar calls "redemptive displacement."

Yet, potent dangers often lurk within the best of intentions. The category of race illustrates the point. Complex issues and potential problems arise whenever a white scholar does research that focuses on members of other racial-ethnic groups, including misunderstanding, misappropriation, and disrespect. Moreover, it is possible for the researcher to use whatever s/he learns for her/his own advancement and without sufficient accountability to those who teach her/him with their stories and insights.

Moreover, un-interrogated assumptions based on whiteness, socioeconomic class and ethnic/national identity found in much of Christian theology (and in public discourse) merit rigorous critical examination. As Black cultural theorist bell hooks knows all too well, "White scholars can write about black culture or black people without fully interrogating their work to see it if employs white western intellectual traditions to re-inscribe white supremacy, to perpetuate racist domination."[9] Put simply, white (especially affluent and/or well-educated)

---

[8] See especially various discussions of theological anthropology and its relation to ethics.

[9] bell hooks, *Yearning: Race, Gender and Culture Politics* (Boston: South End Press, 1990), 124. She adds that cultural studies (and we would add theology, ethnography, and ethics) can be an intervention, but only if certain conditions exist:
> Cultural studies can serve as an intervention, making a space for forms of intellectual discourse to emerge that have not been traditionally welcomed in the academy. It cannot achieve this end if it remains solely a privileged "chic" domain where, as Cornel West writes . . . scholars engage in debates which "highlight notions of difference, marginality, and otherness in such a way that it further marginalizes actual people of

an "ethic-of-white listening"

Anna Marie Vigen

persons must no longer be the frame of reference for understanding what it means to be human.

Consequently, to work toward justice in society and right relations among people, Jennifer Harvey, a white Christian ethicist, contends that those in positions of relative privilege (due to race-ethnicity, education, citizenship, socio-economics, religion, language, etc.) must actively interrogate and subvert these very sites in our advocacy, in larger structural and material relations, and in our scholarship. And in so doing, Harvey maintains, we also (re)form our own moral identities.[10] In this same spirit, Vigen elsewhere explores an "ethic of white listening" in which she articulates important methodological steps that can help hold white scholars accountable to darker-skinned communities.[11] These steps can also help produce self-aware and self-critical work that responds meaningfully to the realities and concerns surfaced by these communities.

Suffice it to say that ethnographic work is neither simple nor without significant risk. Given this fact, white theologians, ethicists, and researchers especially need to be nuanced in whatever research or dialogue we pursue that involves racial, socioeconomic class, cultural, or religious issues. It is important to note that the contributors to this volume are predominately white and that several work with darker-skinned communities. We include them as models of scholars and methods in which matters of privilege and inequality are taken seriously. Specifically, a recurring theme is reflexivity—explored in depth in Chapters 1 and 4 and also seen in the exemplary chapters in Part Two.

Ethnography as a fitting tool for embodied theology

Ethnography is a way to take particularity seriously—to discover truth revealed through embodied habits, relations, practices, narratives, and struggles. And as it is joined with a theological sensibility, our conviction is that each particular life, situation, or community is potentially, albeit only partially, revelatory of transcendent or divine truth. Undeniably, just as when scholars with significant privilege set out to learn from others with less, this assumption is not value- or risk-free. Indeed, it is possible, as critics note in Chapter 3, to reduce theology to anthropology. In other words, it could turn particular experiences into a

"human experience"

difference and otherness." When this happens cultural studies re-inscribes patterns of colonial domination, where the "Other" is always made object, appropriated, interpreted, taken over by those in power, by those who dominate. (Ibid., 125)

[10] Jennifer Harvey, *Whiteness and Morality: Pursuing Racial Justice through Reparations and Sovereignty* (New York: Palgrave Macmillan, 2007).
[11] See Aana Marie Vigen, "To Hear and To Be Accountable Across Difference: An Ethic of White Listening," in *Disrupting White Supremacy from Within. White People on What WE Need to Do*, Jennifer Harvey et al. (eds) (Cleveland: The Pilgrim Press, 2004) and Aana Marie Vigen, *Women, Ethics, and Inequality in U.S. Healthcare: "To Count Among the Living"* (New York: Palgrave Macmillan, 2006), xvii–xxiii, 87–110, 200–16.

kind of over-simplified, static, and idealized "stand-in" for a more complex, even infinite, reality. Our point is that while this is a potential pitfall, with methodological care and critical self-awareness, it is not a reason to rule out ethnography as theology.

Certainly, as Chapter 1 highlights, even within the history of secular anthropology, the possibility for creating simplistic and flat characterizations is evident. However, there has been a noticeable and significant evolution in how ethnography is done and in its basic assumptions. As anthropologist James Clifford explains in the introduction to *Writing Culture*, "Ethnography in the service of anthropology once looked at clearly defined others, defined as primitive, or tribal, or non-Western, or pre-literate, or nonhistorical—the list, if extended, soon becomes incoherent. Now ethnography encounters others in relation to itself, while seeking itself as other."[12] In other words, an uncritical ethnography (or we would add theology) is no longer intellectually viable. It now has to turn the spotlight on itself—its own assumptions, narrative, and depictions—even as it attempts to illumine a specific context.

To step back a bit, there are two distinct ways to conceive of the role of, and relationship between, ethnography and theology. In the traditional and predominant use of social science by theology, the central aim is to craft a "thick description" (Geertz) of what it is. The goal is decidedly not to confirm or prove a given hypothesis; rather it is to explore and describe as fully as possible what is—what is seen, heard, witnessed, experienced. And in such complex descriptions of a specific time, people, person or place, ethnography can help to keep researchers honest because before we can offer up any theological or normative conclusions about what ought to be, we must ensure that we adequately understand—perceive and appreciate—what is. And much is to be said for this use and goal.

However, especially as Scharen underscores here and elsewhere, there is a second way to conceive of the relationship between theology and ethnography that brings the two even closer together. Specifically, this view argues that the situation or context of study has embedded and embodied within its life substantive contributions to theology and ethics. And if this is the case, then the normative and/or theological conclusion cannot come solely from the researcher no matter how well s/he attends to the ethnographic data. Rather, what is normative is revealed through the partnership between the researcher and her/his collaborators. Said differently, rather than pairing ethnographic facts to universal theological truth, the ethnographer—through apprenticeship to the situation/people—aids in the articulation of those embedded theological convictions as primary theology itself. This perspective does not preclude

---

[12] James Clifford, "Introduction: Partial Truths," in *Writing Culture: The Poetics and Politics of Ethnography*, James Clifford and George E. Marcus (eds) (Berkeley: University of California Press, 1986), 23.

ethnography = embodied theology

bringing into the conversation other theological or theoretical materials, but the point is that they do not automatically have privilege over the local theological understandings operative in the lives of those studied. We find that this latter understanding of ethnography as embodied theology is a more accurate depiction of what really happens in the field. It is also the one that is emerging within the scholarship of the scholars alluded to above and is one we hope to foster through the publication of the present volume.

Ethnography as related to discipleship

A basic, and relatively uncontested, ethical dimension of social science is found in the accountability researchers have to ethnographic subjects. The fundamental requirements such as informed consent and freedom from coercion in terms of participating in the research reflect this concern. Yet, the responsibility goes further to include critical self-reflection (reflexivity) and transparency on the part of the researcher. Ethnographer James Spradley goes so far as to say that the choice of research topic ought to be informed by "community-expressed needs."[13] In other words, it is not only the scholar's research agenda that ought to set the course, but rather the project should be meaningfully related to the pressing issues and challenges faced by a particular community.[14] In short, it matters very much how the research is designed, what themes or issues are focused upon, how the researcher relates to the collaborators, and what is done with the fruits of the research.

Moreover, beyond being responsible to the subjects it explores, there is an additional aspect to the inherent moral character of social science. We contend that it is normative in the sense that in the descriptions it offers, there is often (implicitly if not explicitly) hope for certain outcomes.[15] Examples of such action-oriented research include hope for socioeconomic justice, the diminishment of poverty and human misery, improved health, better racial, cultural, and religious understanding across differences, etc.

Consider the work and scholarly convictions of Paul Farmer, both an M.D. and a Ph.D. in medical anthropology. In a passionate (at times prophetic) voice and with vivid description (backed up with weighty public health, sociological, and epidemiological statistics) Farmer explores the myriad ways "structural violence"

[13] James P. Spradley, *The Ethnographic Interview* (New York: Holt, Rinehart, and Winston, 1979), 14.
[14] Such a framing of research driven by local challenges animates Bent Flyvbjerg's strong call to social scientists in *Making Social Science Matter: Why Social Inquiry Fails and How It Can Succeed Again*, Steven Sampson (trans.) (New York: Cambridge University Press, 2001).
[15] See Robert N. Bellah, "The Ethical Aims of Social Inquiry," in *The Robert Bellah Reader*, Robert N. Bellah and Steven Tipton (eds) (Durham: Duke University Press, 2006), 381–401.

wreaks havoc on the lives of the global poor.[16] Millions of these people suffer acutely and needlessly from highly preventable and treatable diseases. Farmer lays out the bleak statistics: "Even if we consider only the big three infectious killers—AIDS, tuberculosis, and malaria—we are faced with tens of millions of preventable diseases slated to occur in our lifetimes. A recent document from the United Nations suggests, for example, that more than 80 million Africans might die from AIDS alone by 2025."[17] Yet, Farmer goes beyond reporting these disturbing facts to ask poignant questions—both of ethics and of methods of inquiry.

Specifically, he asks throughout his work how the rest of us can let these realities continue without doing more to abate them. It is not only a problem of resources, Farmer contends, but of moral imagination:

> [T]hese numbers have lost their ability to shock or even move us. What are the human values in question when we hear, and fail to react to, the news that each day thousands die of these maladies unattended? Where, in the midst of all these numbers, is the human face of suffering? Can the reader discern the human face in these reports? A failure of imagination is one of the greatest failures registered in contemplating the fate of the world's poorest. Can photographs and personal narratives play a role, even as rhetorical tools, in promoting those human values that might lessen the magnitude of these disasters?[18]

What do we do when horrific numbers are not enough to push those with the resources into action? Farmer employs an innovative strategy that combines vital statistics with poignant stories. He weaves evocative stories and select images throughout the reporting of stark, and often overwhelming, statistics. The resulting synthesis reveals not only the devastating inequalities and callous insults to human rights, but also witnesses to the profound humanity, courage, and resolve found in places such as Haiti, Rwanda, Russian prisons, Peru, and inner-city Boston.[19] Throughout, Farmer documents the impressive

---

[16] Farmer defines this term in his book *Pathologies of Power* and roots it in Latin American Liberation Theology's discussion of "sinful" social structures. See Paul Farmer, *Pathologies of Power: Health, Human Rights, and the New War on the Poor* (Berkeley: University of California, 2005), especially chapters 5 and 8. This book also makes his method clear—how he draws upon various kinds of sources and knowledge (biology, public health data, sociology, theology, anthropology, etc.).

[17] Paul Farmer, "Never Again? Reflections on Human Values and Human Rights," in *The Tanner Lectures on Human Values*, G. B. Peterson (ed.) vol. 25 (Salt Lake City: University of Utah Press, 2006, 144); online (accessed October 10, 2010):http://www.tannerlectures.utah.edu/lectures/documents/Farmer_2006.pdf.

[18] Ibid., 144–5.

[19] For a wonderful read on Farmer's work and results in global health, see: Tracy Kidder, *Mountains Beyond Mountains: The Quest of Dr. Paul Farmer, a Man Who Would Cure the World* (New York: Random House, 2004).

health and healthcare achievements possible when assumptions about what is "cost effective" are rigorously and scientifically challenged.[20]

Several scholars quoted in the pages that follow offer glimpses of the kinds of transformations for which many of us hope. As illustrated by Todd Whitmore among others, ethnographic work can even flow from a commitment rooted in the call of Jesus to "love the neighbor as yourself." In this sense, we can, therefore, consider our work as discipleship.[21] Many—both within and outside of the formal discipline of theology—are dedicated to the notion of pursuing knowledge for the sake of something—well-being, understanding, justice, or as we would put it, "to have life and to have it abundantly" (John 10.10). In these kinds of pursuits, there is a fundamental connection between theology and social science.

Outline of the Book

Before briefly outlining the basic structure of this text, it is worth mentioning how integral collaboration and co-authorship have been to the conceptual and writing process. Part Two of the book, obviously, was written by individual authors. However, as elaborated below, our work on the Preface, Chapters 1–4 and 12 emerged from our years-long conversations. Thus, even as we each took the lead on particular sections (Vigen on the Preface, Chapters 1 and 4; Scharen on Chapters 2, 3 and 12) we nonetheless shared the work—both conceptually and editorially—throughout the volume. While this particular way of working has been labor intensive, it has also been rather rewarding and has resulted, we think, in a high degree of integration within the text. We hope it gives readers a sense of the ongoing scholarly collaborations and conversations between us.

Part One (Chapters 1 through 4) is the Prolegomena. Pivotal methodological themes are integrated throughout. Its purpose is to sketch the main contours

---

[20] For a sharp, concise example of both his argument and method, see Paul Farmer, "New Malaise: Bioethics and Human Rights in the Global Era," *Journal of Law, Medicine, and Ethics*, 32 (2004), 243–51. To illustrate: Elsewhere, after showing the remarkable transformation in the life and health of a young Haitian man, Joseph, after receiving six months of effective therapy (infected with both AIDS and TB) Farmer remarks on the depth and kind of changes needed—one that moves beyond a "charity" or "pity" mentality:

> The medications that saved Joseph's life are commodities available throughout the global economy to those who can pay for them, and this is no less true in Kenya or any other place. The people who have died without a single dose of effective therapy over the past decade are, almost without exception, people who lived and died in poverty. In order to make sure that poor people dying from AIDS stop dying, it will be necessary to move beyond what Sontag referred to as the "unstable emotions" of compassion and pity, to more stable arrangements for all those afflicted with this and other treatable diseases. Translating compassion, pity, mercy, solidarity, or empathy into policy or rights is a difficult task. (Farmer, "Never Again?", 150)

[21] Todd Whitmore, "Crossing the Road: The Case for Ethnographic Fieldwork in Christian Ethics," *Journal of the Society of Christian Ethics* 27:2 (2007), 273–94.

of the territory—In Chapter 1, defining ethnography and elucidating pivotal moments in its history and then in Chapter 2 describing the turn to ethnography in theology. Next, Chapter 3 takes up debates among the critics of this turn and considers possible responses to them. With these concerns in view, it then makes a case for theological ethnography in Chapter 4.

With this orienting context and the tracing of theoretical and theological issues laid out, Part Two (Chapters 5 through 11) turns to specific and thought-provoking exemplars of theological and ethical work engaging in ethnography. These chapters offer concrete embodiments of possibility. We will briefly highlight the focus of each.

Jeffery Tribble writes out of his own experience as a pastor in the African Methodist Episcopal Zion denomination, tracing the trajectory of his research on transformative pastoral leadership as a means to do practical theology. Emily Reimer-Barry describes a project of empathetic listening to women living with HIV both in Chicago, USA and Kibera, Kenya suggesting that such attention to experience be a primary source for Catholic moral theology. Robert Jones did ground-breaking research among religious factions in the Oregon, USA Assisted Suicide debates as a means to show ethnography as revelation. Melissa Browning offers a careful depiction of the plight of street children in Kenya with remarkable attention to their faith and dignity despite achingly difficult circumstances. Andrea Vicini chronicles his work among indigenous peoples in southern Mexico where they sought shared power and communal dignity, experiences marshaled by Vicini as a contribution to ongoing discussions of worship and virtue ethics. Todd Whitmore takes his fieldwork in Ugandan refugee camps as a point of departure for a powerful reflection on the intersections of theology and white privilege. Finally, Peter Gathje reports issues of power, race, and community from his immersion in an intentional Christian community serving—and in part constituted and led by—the homeless. The complexity and subtlety of these chapters resists easy summary and thus these sentences must merely gesture towards the richness of their many contributions to our overall agenda in this volume.

Part Three elucidates a few central and pragmatic dimensions of method and offers benedictions—good words—for those who would like to head out and give ethnography a try. We offer some concrete advice, but with humility because all of us in this volume are working from the edges of our own competence, raising prospects for research pursuits we are only just getting adequate bearings for ourselves. In the introductory chapters we are in a sense a "thinking out loud" but in the context of readers who are, presumably, similarly grasping for something beyond the tidy confines of their disciplines and academic training. Our colleagues writing in Part Two share with us in seeking an apprenticeship in a space we have yet to build, or perhaps better, our continuing formation is coming largely through the process of construction of this new space in which we desire to work. The existence of the book and its multiple authors is evidence of this desire for new integrative spaces in which to carry out our theological and ethical work through ethnographic research.

Concluding Thoughts for Beginning

This book's origins can be described by charting two distinct paths: the direct route and the detours. Above, we briefly summarize the formal road taken through academic circles. Yet, in another sense, this book came about through a longer, winding, serendipitous, and somewhat unpredictable path of friendship. Much scholarship, whether explicitly acknowledged or not, comes out of collaboration (formal and informal) among two or more people.

In our case, we met in graduate school and soon discovered common scholarly commitments amidst somewhat differing backgrounds and thematic interests. We each took courses outside of the formal disciplinary boundaries of Christian theology and ethics at the University of California, Berkeley (Scharen in Sociology, Anthropology and Philosophy, and Vigen in Women's Studies, Postcolonial Theory, and Film Studies). During these years, we talked a lot about what we were learning from these diverse disciplines and on a couple of occasions we got to work together on a specific project. Yet, we did not then imagine then that our shared scholarly commitments and differing areas of expertise would lead us both to ethnographic methods. Nevertheless, through numerous geographic moves and stages of vocational development, the conversations (both within and between us) have continued—about how to do our work, what matters to us as scholars, and what we hope to create. These vocational and methodological explorations have progressed amidst detours and over bumps, and ultimately, have brought us to this crossing.

This book then, while offering up what we hope to be a useful thematic and methodological contribution, has also given us the additional opportunity to live out our friendship. In the writing, editing (and numerous conversations that preceded both) not only did this book take shape, but we have been able to realize again how central friendship and collaboration are to the creative process. And we have found this welcome gift to be true in terms of our learning from, and appreciation for, others in various streams of theology and ethics—specifically in this case, for those working with ethnography. So as we prepare to share this work with others, the predominant feeling is gratitude—for the contributors in this volume, for other colleagues who are integral to our scholarly lives, and for the opportunity to offer up these kinds of creative and collaborative endeavors as models for others to consider.

And in this spirit, we have specific thanks, most especially for our colleagues who have joined us in writing this book: Melissa Browning, Peter Gathje, Robert Jones, Emily Reimer-Barry, Jeffery Tribble, Andrea Vicini, and Todd Whitmore.

We also thank our home institutions, Luther Seminary and Loyola University Chicago, for the ongoing support and assistance. Colleagues at both institutions have offered support, as have the deans and division chairs: Roland Martinson at Luther and Susan A. Ross at Loyola. In addition, we are very grateful to Department Chair Susan A. Ross, Graduate School Dean Samuel Attoh, and the Office of Research Services at Loyola for awarding us special funding to assist with the costs of publication and indexing.

The volume would not exist without Continuum Press who said "yes." Sincere thanks to Thomas Kraft, our editor, for his ever-present patience, helpfulness, and graciousness. We also greatly appreciate other staff at Continuum and Newgen, especially Nicole Elliott, Molly Morrison, P. Muralidharan, and Anna Turton, who have been incredibly efficient and helpful at every stage.

We also benefitted from the technical assistance and expertise of three individuals. Grant Gholson, a doctoral student at Loyola University was very helpful in the initial research and writing stages. As the volume neared completion, Daniel Cosacchi, another Loyola doctoral student, plunged into compiling the bibliography and formatting the manuscript as soon as he arrived to campus. He was continually available and always helpful in his efforts. We also thank Judy Davis, a professional in every sense of the word, for creating a comprehensive and well-organized index.

For each of us, other conversation partners—some we have met and others we have not—have shaped our sense of these issues and they are scattered throughout the footnotes of this book. In addition, we are grateful to Mary McClintock Fulkerson for her theological leadership, her collegiality, and her encouragement of this volume. Chris Scharen especially gives thanks for one of his doctoral professors with whom he studied ethnography and alongside whom he carried out ethnographic research projects over a period of four years: Nancy L. Eielsand. Nancy tragically died of cancer in 2009 at the age of 44. The incandescence that she lived, he hopes, finds continued life in the work represented by this volume. He also thanks his family for all their love and support: spouse Sonja, son Isaiah, and daughter Grace.

Aana Marie Vigen continues to be grateful for mentors in ethnography and/ or Christian ethics from whom she continues to learn, especially Mindy Fullilove, Beverly Wildung Harrison, Karen Lebacqz, Emilie M. Townes, and Larry Rasmussen. She also sincerely thanks her extended family (the Vigens, Hemstads, and Stricklers) who always take a keen interest in her scholarly adventures and who offer much encouragement. A special nod to Y. Strickler for the many great years together. Finally, the completion of this (or any of her) work owes much to the constant, unconditional love and support of Alison and to the irrepressible, joyful, loving exuberance that is Benjamin.

About the Contributors

Melissa Browning is a Ph.D. Candidate in Christian Ethics at Loyola University Chicago. Her work centers on global ethics, particularly on issues surrounding sexuality and health.

Peter R. Gathje is Associate Dean and Professor of Christian Ethics at Memphis Theological Seminary. He is a co-founder of Manna House a place of hospitality for homeless and poor persons in Memphis and the author of *Sharing the Bread of Life: Hospitality and Resistance at the Open Door Community*.

Robert P. Jones is CEO and Founder, Public Religion Research Institute, Washington D.C., USA, and is a leading scholar in both academic and public policy circles. He is the author of two academic books, *Progressive and Religious* (Rowman and Littlefield, 2008), and *Liberalism's Troubled Search for Equality* (Notre Dame, 2007) as well as numerous articles on religion and public policy.

Emily Reimer-Barry is an Assistant Professor at the University of San Diego where she teaches courses in Catholic theology, fundamental moral theology, sexual ethics, and HIV/AIDS.

Christian Scharen is Assistant Professor at Luther Seminary, St. Paul, MN, USA where he teaches worship and practical theology. A leading scholar working at the intersection of ethnography and theology, he writes in the areas of worship, ethics, ecclesiology, and popular culture. He is the author of several books and scholarly articles, including the forthcoming *Broken Hallelujahs* (Brazos, 2011).

Jeffery L. Tribble, Sr. is Assistant Professor of Ministry at Columbia Theological Seminary where he teaches congregational studies, leadership, and practical theology. He is the author of *Transformative Pastoral Leadership in the Black Church* (Palgrave Macmillan, 2005). Recent ethnographic research published is "Embodying Sankofa: When Ancient Ways Inform the Future" in *Greenhouses of Hope: Congregations Growing Young Leaders Who Will Change the World*, ed. Dori Grienenko Baker (The Alban Institute, 2011).

Andrea Vicini, S.J. is Associate Professor of Moral Theology and Bioethics at the Faculty of Theology of Southern Italy: S. Luigi (Naples, Italy) and, currently, Visiting Professor at Boston College (MA, USA). His research interests include: biotechnologies, reproductive technologies, end of life issues, medical ethics, genetics, and environmental issues. He has recently published: *Genetica umana e bene comune (Human Genetics and the Common Good)* (Cinisello Balsamo: San Paolo, 2008).

Aana Marie Vigen is Associate Professor of Christian Social Ethics at Loyola University Chicago. Her scholarship brings ethnographic methods into conversation with medical ethics, feminist ethics, Protestant ethics, and white-antiracism commitments. In addition to various articles, she is the author of *Women, Ethics, and Inequality in U.S. Healthcare* (Palgrave, new edition forthcoming, 2011) and co-editor of *God, Science, Sex, Gender* (University of Illinois, 2010).

Todd Whitmore is Associate Professor of Christian Ethics in the Department of Theology at the University of Notre Dame. He is the author of several articles on ethnography and theological ethics, including, "'If They Kill Us, At Least the Others Will Have More Time to Get Away': The Ethics of Risk in Ethnographic Practice" (*Practical Matters: A Transdisciplinary Multimedia Journal of Religious Practices and Practical Theology*, Spring 2010), and "Crossing the Road: The ~~Role of~~ Ethnographic Fieldwork in Christian Ethics" (*Journal of the Society of Christian Ethics*, Fall-Winter 2007).

Part One

Prolegomena

Chapter 1

What is Ethnography?

What images come into your mind when you hear the term "research"?—A library, A lab? A river bed? A remote tribal village in Fiji? A microscope? An oncology ward? Many—probably most—formal theologians and Christian ethicists envision a desk, computer and keyboard—complete with books, electronic databases and web searches, and a cup of coffee. Unlike many scholars in the natural and social sciences, theologians generally don't do much standing or walking (unless they are pacing) while doing research. Instead, many associate their research with an intense—and often solitary—communion with texts. So, there is certain truth in the conclusion that theological methods of inquiry, along with those of other disciplines in the humanities (e.g. English, Philosophy, Classical Studies), are rather different from scientific ones.

However, there are at least a couple of problems with the view that theological methods are wholly distinct from those found in the natural and social sciences. First, it is oversimplified. Theologians learn (or have the ability to learn) as much from direct observation of natural and social events as any other human being. We are not a different species after all. Second, it is worth asking why some assume that certain methods are the sole property of specific disciplines and "off limits" to others in an age where academia continually praises "interdisciplinarity" and "connectivity" as the key to scholarly and pedagogical vitality. Third, the *telos* of a given research project, whether theological or scientific in nature, may be as important to explore as any methodological differences between them.

Perhaps what stands out most about Christian theology and ethics is that both are fairly bold in confessing that they are up to more than description; there is a normative dimension to the work. Christian theology and ethics are not content to describe reality as it is, but also how it ultimately *is* or *should* be. Theology is a discipline that allows human beings to advance particular descriptions and normative claims about what is most essentially real or true. In other words, it claims to provide a foretaste of ultimate truth yet to come or to be fully experienced.

Some natural and social scientists resonate with this aim in the sense that they intend their work to foster greater understanding, respect, and responsibility among human beings.[1] For example, many ecologists and other biological scientists hope that their work will lead to stronger attention to sustainability and a serious reckoning with global climate change; medical and biological researchers studying cancer or Alzheimer's hope their work will lead to more effective preventions and cures.

It is also important to note that there is a lot of variety within *both* theological and scientific methods. In order to appreciate the complexity and variety, we will briefly describe the difference between quantitative and qualitative research methods. In doing so, we wish to underscore that both basic method types are employed by scientists and theologians alike.

Contrasting Quantitative and Qualitative Methods

Most natural scientists, along with many social scientists, have a particular kind of enterprise in mind when they use the term "research." Specifically, they depend upon the methods of quantitative analysis that are rooted in presumptions of objectivity and large, generalizable findings—resulting in irrefutable, conclusive "hard" evidence. Similarly, they exemplify methods that utilize the testing of a hypothesis, double-blind trials, control groups, uniformity in sampling, etc.

Such quantitative research methods are essential to many kinds of important work: clinical drug or medical treatment trials; national polling samples; demographic and census statistics; economic data; biological and ecological studies of species, climates, habitats and the corresponding effects human beings have upon each. In short, findings that hold up across specific regions (large sample sizes), that demonstrate statistical accuracy and validity, and whose methodological purity is above reproach (making sure all but one variable is controlled for) are all prized.

In terms of theological pursuits, a method similar to quantitative research is found in the works of those scholars who carefully track the number and kinds of usages of specific terms in scripture or other theological writings. It is also glimpsed in the familiar efforts to use the ancient scriptures or doctrines of a faith in the lives of concrete, contemporary communities. While we do not generally favor such a deductive interpretative approach,[2] it is important to note this common element found in both scientific and theological methods. Specifically, the shared assumption with secular, quantitative method here is that

---

[1] Bellah, "The Ethical Aims of Social Inquiry," 381–401.
[2] Having said this, we wish to emphasize that we certainly recognize the need to put the scriptures and core beliefs of a community into use within concrete lives and situations. Sacred scriptures and faith claims must somehow be visible and active within embodied contexts or else they cease to "live" or be relevant.

there is an "objective" truth that can be discovered through observation of the phenomena in question. In other words, good scientific or theological inquiry depends on the proper deduction of facts derived from careful reading, reflection, interpretation and recording of data. Thus, whether the pursuit is theological or scientific in nature, the method is deductive, meaning that general, *a priori* principles are discovered in sources of information (e.g. sacred texts, nature, philosophical writings) that hold true in concrete situations across time and space and thus can be applied in specific contexts and hold universally.[3]

In strong contrast to quantitative protocols and reports, ethnography values a very different kind of data—often discovered through disciplined attention to a few research sites or participants. Consequently, some researchers who prize quantitative data find its methods too narrow and its findings too anecdotal to be of any real scientific value. They may dismissively liken it to the quaint storytelling of a well-intentioned, perhaps tiresome, relative who yammers away at the family gathering about times long past—at first amusing, but ultimately of little interest or insight. For their part, and as Scharen discusses in greater depth in Chapter 3, some theologians (Hauerwas, Milbank) are skeptical of qualitative methods because they think they import secular theologies implicitly under the guise of "neutral" or "objective" social science. Instead, they favor theological inquiry that starts with scripture and other primary theological texts that give a faith community its distinctive identity.

Yet, as we discuss elsewhere,[4] scientists of various kinds use qualitative methods and find substantial value in them. For our parts, we contend that both quantitative and qualitative methods have important places in numerous kinds of research. Indeed, both are vital to research and understanding. Rather than cast them as necessary competitors that demand an "either/or" allegiance, we see them as complimentary methods, but with distinct aims and objectives. Moreover, we question the undervaluing of qualitative methods and find that they merit more respect and serious consideration than they sometimes receive—from scientists and theologians alike.

The Origins and Meanings of Ethnography

A personal account

Before sketching a succinct history of the evolution of ethnography, it is important and integral to our particular method to be located. In this brief section,

---

[3] The classic move in philosophical ethics is Kant's, although Stephen Toulmin argues for Descartes' turn to the universal as a response to the horrors of subjective religious belief that funded the bloody "wars of religion" in the seventeenth century. See Stephen Toulmin, *Cosmopolis: The Hidden Agenda of Modernity* (New York: The Free Press, 1990).
[4] See Vigen, *Women, Ethics, and Inequality*, 84–98.

I (Vigen) describe—what is at stake for me in using ethnography, how I came to it, and the tensions and challenges that have arisen in doing this kind of research. During graduate studies and needing to connect what I had been reading with other domains of knowledge, I sought out concrete experience in medical ethics by working as a hospital chaplain and serving on a hospital bioethics committee. At times, I found reading theological and ethical texts—along with abstracted medical ethics case studies without sufficient, real-life context—tedious and unsatisfying. I yearned to learn about, and talk through, various theological and medical quandaries with people who did not identify as academics.

Persistent questions interrupted my contemplation of the traditional scholarly sources: "So what? What resonance (if any) might a given theological or ethical claim have for people in the pews and/or those living with a serious illness? Would they agree or disagree with it? What more might they see or know? How might they perceive and articulate the central issues and questions at stake?" Even more urgently, I wondered: "How can I as a scholar connect what I think and write to what others live, especially those too often ignored both in scholarship and in the public square? How might their knowledge correct mine? How is my work in dialogue with them?"

A previously untapped part of my scholarly identity came alive as I talked with patients and participated in clinical bioethics case discussions. Here were vital faith questions and ethics in action. Theological musings about life after death, human responsibility and sin were no longer hypothetical. Each day at the hospital, the rubber hit the road with force and urgency. Similarly, questions about quality care played out in palpable, sometimes tragic, ways along the hospital corridors and in the daily (even routine, seemingly mundane) decisions, conversations, and unspoken actions.

To briefly illustrate one example of my learning, a chaplaincy internship made me acutely aware of the fact that many patients felt ill-at-ease not only because of their medical condition, but because of a lack of common language, understanding, and respect between them and their care providers. As a part-time intern in California during 1995–96, I was the only non-Latino staff person who spoke Spanish with any degree of efficacy at the hospital. When I was not on duty, the hospital called an AT&T operator or a family member translated. On other occasions, a member of the housekeeping or food service staff was called to translate. Such realities question claims and procedures regarding informed consent.

Proposition 187, later found unconstitutional, was in effect at this time. While in force, it mandated that undocumented immigrants were to be denied medical care.[5] Consequently, many Latinos (regardless of their immigration

---

[5] Even as it is no longer California state law, the basic sentiments and ethos of Proposition 187, can be glimpsed in some of the legislation being debated in other states (e.g. Arizona, Florida) in 2010. See for example: Randal C. Archibold, "Judge Blocks Arizona's

status) felt viewed with suspicion and were uncomfortable in the hospital environment. For example, as a chaplain it was my responsibility to discuss Advance Directives with all patients for whom there was nothing on file. Since I spoke Spanish, I was asked to do this especially for these patients. I noticed that when I spoke with white patients (who were predominately upper-middle class or affluent and insured) they were eager to fill out the paperwork, noting sometimes that they did not want to end up as a "vegetable."

In glaring contrast, when I went over the same information in my functional Spanish, patients would look at me more guardedly and very few filled it out while I was there. While no one said this exact comment to me, their expressions and reserve gave me the sense that they thought filling out the paperwork would give hospital staff an excuse to not do everything to save their lives. What was clear is that the level of trust and rapport between many of the Spanish-speaking patients and their providers was not nearly as high as it was between many of the white and English-speaking patients and providers.

In all, working in two different hospitals and on a bioethics committee often contributed significant understanding as it also interrogated what I thought I knew as an emerging scholar. Furthermore, as I describe elsewhere, working with the Rev. Dr Annie Ruth Powell and witnessing her struggle with cancer made my own shortcomings and outright failures—as a listener, as a white person, and as a well-intentioned, lay caregiver—all too apparent.[6] Thus, before I knew anything about the formal discipline of "ethnography" per se, I instinctively knew I needed to incorporate into my ongoing research method some kind of substantial dimension that would enable these kinds of dialogues, self-critical analyses, and interruptions.

What I did not fully understand then is that my desire to engage the wisdom and insights found outside the common domains of academic Christian ethics, and within embodied persons very different from myself in key respects, would involve not only learning through conversation with such people, but that it also necessitated an even great *conversion* on my part—a conversion to the other, to learn and labor with others. And implicit in this desire was a budding sense that as a scholar, I needed to do more than simply advance a thesis. Instead, I felt called to seek (or at least strive and hope for) transformation in society, in practices, and importantly, in my own heart and way of being in the world. Yet, I don't think I realized at first how I would be changed by the research—or how important it was that I be open to such change. I also don't know if I fully comprehended the degree and complexity of self-critical awareness that would be required.

Immigration Law," *The New York Times* (July 28, 2010), online (accessed October 15, 2010): http://www.nytimes.com/2010/07/29/us/29arizona.html

[6] Vigen, *Women, Ethics, and Inequality*, xviii–xxiii.

In the years following my ethnography with Black and Latina women with breast cancer and with healthcare providers, I continue to reflect especially on the experience of learning from these women and I feel disquieted by the fact that this work has benefited me in tangible ways (completion of a Ph.D., an offer of an academic position, tenure) while they have not benefited in any obvious way. At least one of the women with cancer has died. One other (maybe more) has faced a recurrence. Perhaps telling their stories was cathartic for them. I hope I succeeded in making them feel heard and respected. I hope they left the interview period knowing how much I cherish their stories and insights. Yet, even assuming these positive outcomes, the overall imbalance of benefits remains. They gave me a gift that has changed my life in important ways. And yet I cannot say that my work has had as dramatic or even tangible an impact on their lives, let alone on the state of healthcare quality or provider–patient relations.

Such inequality disquiets me; it works to keep me clear-eyed on what my life's work needs to be about. As a white, presently healthy and well-insured academic, Christian, and US citizen, I have discerned that my vocational calling entails learning from and advocating for those who are uninsured, darker skinned, undocumented, in ill health, at risk of being ignored and/or mistreated. And as I listen, I need to reflect critically on my own assumptions, privileges, "good intentions," and awkward missteps lest I misunderstand or misappropriate the sacred gift that is the stories, lives, experiences, and truths of others.

My particular history with ethnography is a microcosm of a much larger history within the field. Given that this book intends a resounding call to theologians and Christian ethicists to take seriously ethnography as an important dimension to our work, it is crucial that it is accompanied by a sharp understanding of pitfalls and limits as well. We reject a romanticized, naïve posture that sees ethnography as substituting for other forms of knowledge or as consisting of simply "talking to folks, recording what they tell us, and publishing it." The history of ethnography itself shows how anthropologists, cultural theorists, sociologists, and others have questioned and critiqued ethnography as a way to complexify its assumptions, methods, and practices.

A condensed history: three key moments in ethnography's evolution

As a method of scientific inquiry, ethnography was born within the disciplinary home of anthropology. Since the mid-twentieth century, it has become a major subcategory within qualitative research methodology and is used not only in anthropology, but increasingly in sociology, and across many fields including religious studies, medicine, and so on.[7] Yet, given our commitments to self-critical reflection and to white antiracism, it is important to highlight three central moments in its history prior to elaborating our working understanding of the term and method. Specifically, it is imperative for us as white scholars to address the reality that modern anthropology has often been intertwined with colonialism, imperialism, and racial prejudice.

The first moment comes at the turn of the twentieth century. Histories of anthropology commonly identify its modern beginnings in the notable legacies of anthropologists and ethnographers such as Franz Boas, Bronisław Malinowski, and E. E. Evans-Pritchard. In the late nineteenth century, while some careful work was being done in areas related to modern anthropology, there were many more individuals who used their travels, diaries, and anecdotal observations to justify western colonial projects, cultural and religious imperialism, Christian missionary ventures and racial discrimination and subjugation. Sensational accounts were published in both scholarly and popular venues telling tales of the "savages," "cannibals," and "primitive man," that reinforced stereotypes and prevalent western views of the "superiority" and "civility" of Europe and the United States. At the same time, these voyeurs, voyagers, and thrill-seeking adventurers ransacked indigenous societies and filled European and US museums with their art, valuables, tools, symbols and textiles.

In contrast to many of their contemporaries, Boas, Malinowski, and Evans-Pritchard were among the first western scholars to use sustained, empirical methods of study to explore cultures outside their own. They spent extended periods living among indigenous people in Africa, the South Pacific, and the Americas—taking detailed field notes, learning indigenous languages, and building relationships with their informants. They developed contextual theories about how cultural symbols, traditions, social patterns, intimate relations, and so on functioned in particular cultures through intensive study and observation of various facets of daily living. In the course of this work, they not only attempted to communicate with people in their native languages, they developed complex relationships with members of the communities they observed.

For example, Malinowski is honored by many as the "father" of social anthropology and is recognized for trail-blazing ethnographic studies of people in New Guinea, Australia, and the Trobriand Islands. His meticulous ethnographic work, along with that of Franz Boas, is often signaled as a pivotal break both with "armchair" theorists and untrained travelers whose methods they critiqued for their respective overreliance on grand generalizations accompanied by cursory anecdotes as support for them (e.g. Lewis Henry Morgan and

[7] A beautiful example from medical anthropology is João Biehl, *Vita: Life in a Zone of Social Abandonment* (Berkeley: University of California Press, 2005); from religious studies, David Mellott, *I was and I am Dust: Penitent Practices as a Way of Knowing* (Collegeville: Liturgical Press, 2009).

Sir James Frazer) and their lack of care, time, and detailed analysis as part of their research. Malinowski is seen by many anthropologists as contributing critical innovations to fieldwork (e.g. participant observation) and as one of the first anthropologists to give significant attention to studying all aspects of daily living—not ruling any part out as too ordinary or mundane.[8]

Boas is commonly thought of as the "father" of both modern and also American anthropology.[9] He started the first US doctoral program in anthropology (Columbia University) and he contributed richly to anthropology's theoretical underpinnings. Furthermore, Boas left a legacy of students, many of whom shaped the emerging field for the next decades and became its preeminent scholars in the early- and mid-twentieth century (e.g. Benedict, Herskovits, Kroeber, Lowie, Mead, Sapir, Spier).

In particular, Boas is credited with making cultural relativism, empiricism, and rigorous, intensive field study (living with a society being studied for an extended time, learning indigenous language(s), taking detailed field notes) all standard norms for anthropology. Unlike many of his academic contemporaries, Boas did not see western civilization as superior to others. Cultural and racial bigotry masquerading as scientific observation were commonplace in anthropology and Boas sought to keep such bias in check by placing greater authority in making careful, sustained, detailed observations of what was actually found in the field. In doing so, he developed a theoretical and practical method for anthropological research, modeled partially after the one used by Darwin and in the natural sciences more generally. In short, his idea was that rigorous field research and scrupulous methods would test, correct, and necessarily revise any theory or hypothesis found lacking. Unfortunately, much of European and US history testifies to the fact that this is not always the case— that biases and unchecked presumptions are more pernicious and self-fulfilling than we would like.

Nonetheless, in addition to establishing distinctive theoretical and methodological base points for anthropology and educating a leading generation of scholars, Boas blazed public activist trails as well. For example, he is remembered

---

[8] See Michael W. Young, *Malinowski: Odyssey of an Anthropologist, 1884–1920* (New Haven: Yale University Press, 2004). For central examples of Malinowski's work, see *Argonauts of the Western Pacific* (1922), *Crime and Custom in Savage Society* (1926), *Sex and Repression in Savage Society* (1927), *The Sexual Life of Savages in North-Western Melanesia* (1929).

[9] See: Norman F. Boas, *Franz Boas 1858–1942: An Illustrated Biography* (Mystic: Seaport Autographs Press, 2004); Douglas Cole, *Franz Boas: The Early Years, 1858–1906* (Seattle: University of Washington Press, 1999); Regna Darnell, *And Along Came Boas: Continuity and Revolution in Americanist Anthropology* (Amsterdam: John Benjamins, 1998); Adam Kuper, *The Invention of Primitive Society: Transformations of an Illusion* (London: Routledge Press, 1988). For central examples of Boas' own work, see: Franz Boas, *The Mind of Primitive Man* (1911); *Anthropology and Modern Life* (1928); *Race, Language, and Culture* (1940). See also this collection of his works: George W. Stocking, Jr (ed.), *A Franz Boas Reader: The Shaping of American Anthropology, 1883–1911* (New York: Basic Books, 1974).

for passionately and publically confronting racial inequality and "scientific," essentialist arguments related to racial superiority/inferiority. Indeed, he may have been the first white scholar in the United States to publish the view that whites and Blacks were essentially equal.[10] He is also credited with training some of the first anthropologists and folklorists of color (e.g. Gilberto Freyre, Manuel Gamio, Williams Jones, Zora Neale Hurston). Moreover, Boaz came under scrutiny himself when he publically denounced peers who used anthropology as a cover for spying on behalf of the US government.

While giving due credit to what was revolutionary given the larger historical contexts in which they are situated, subsequent anthropologists point out that, even if unacknowledged, Boas, Malinowski, Evans-Pritchard—along with their contemporaries and students—nonetheless used unexamined filters through which they viewed and interpreted the cultures and peoples they observed. They understood an integral part of their work was to catalogue and categorize the objects, symbols, roles, and activities they studied. They assumed they were simply "reporting objective facts." Instead, they created systems of meaning with their interpretations that could never exhaustively describe or "capture" the self-understandings and worldviews of the people they studied. And they too collected a treasure trove of artifacts for display, study, and enjoyment in western museums.

In summary, a problematic lack of self-criticism accompanied by the gaze of the colonialism/colonizer infused much of anthropological scholarship through the early- and mid-twentieth century.[11] White and predominately male scholars created the categories and typologies that "made sense" of others' realities for western understanding and consumption. Yet, for the most part, they did not fully acknowledge the subjective nature of their interpretations and characterizations.[12]

---

[10] Vernon J. Williams, Jr, *Rethinking Race: Franz Boas and His Contemporaries* (Lexington: University of Kentucky Press, 1996); George W. Stocking, Jr, *Race, Culture, and Evolution: Essays in the History of Anthropology* (New York: Free Press, 1968); Thomas Gossett, *Race: The History of an Idea in America* (New York: Oxford University Press, 1963).

[11] See for example: Talal Asad (ed.), *Anthropology & the Colonial Encounter* (Atlantic Highlands: Humanities Press, 1973); Frederik Barth, Andre Gingrich, Robert Parkin, and Sydel Silverman, *One Discipline, Four Ways: British, German, French, and American Anthropology* (Chicago: University of Chicago Press, 2005); Stocking, Jr, *Race, Culture and Evolution*.

[12] To be fair, the writings of Boas along with later, detailed studies of his work and life reveal that he thought of the indigenous people he studied as his teachers and that he had some awareness of the contextual, contingent, subjective nature of his findings and descriptions. Yet, Boas and his contemporaries never followed these insights as far as they might have. See: Herbert Lewis, "Boas, Darwin, Science and Anthropology," in *Current Anthropology* 42:3 (2001), 381–406; Matti Bunzl, "Boas, Foucault, and the 'Native Anthropologist,'" in *American Anthropologist* 106:3 (2004), 435–42. James Clifford comments that the 1967 publication of Malinowski's Mailu and Trobriand diaries "publically upset the applecart" that took objectivity for granted: "Henceforth an implicit mark of interrogation was placed beside any overly confident and consistent ethnographic voice."

This provocative insight is part of the fundamental and ground-breaking point of the collective essays in *Writing Culture* (1986) and constitutes a second key historical moment. Of particular note, collectively this text emphasizes and critically analyzes the process of writing integral to ethnographic study. James Clifford contends that the above forerunners took the process of writing about culture for granted—as the transparent recording of observed, objective facts. In contrast, Clifford underscores that the contributors to *Writing Culture* begin

> not with participant-observation or with cultural texts (suitable for interpretation), but with writing, the making of texts . . . The fact that [writing] has not until recently been portrayed or seriously discussed reflects the persistence of an ideology claiming transparency of representation and immediacy of experience. Writing reduced to method: keeping good field notes, making accurate maps, "writing up" results.[13]

Starting especially in the 1960s, scholars in fields such as cultural studies, critical theory, history, and anthropology (e.g. Barthes, Bourdieu, Clifford, Foucault, Geertz, Marcus, Rabinow, Said) critically interrogate the view that writing is a mere tool in the objective task of creating accurate description. Clifford makes the contrast with earlier anthropology plain:

> [The contributors to *Writing Culture*] see culture as composed of seriously contested codes and representations: they assume that the poetic and the political are inseparable, that science is in, not above, historical and linguistic processes. They assume that academic and literary genres interpenetrate and that the writing of cultural descriptions is properly experimental and ethical. Their focus on text making and rhetoric serves to highlight the constructed, artificial nature of cultural accounts. It undermines overly transparent modes of authority, and it draws attention to the historical predicament of ethnography, *the fact that it is always caught up in the invention, not the representation, of cultures* (emphasis ours).[14]

Thus, a hallmark of both ethnographic and critical theory beginning in the 1970s is the radical explorations of the historical and social processes involved in the construction of knowledge.

> Anthropology no longer speaks with automatic authority for others defined as unable to speak for themselves ("primitive," "pre-literate," "without history")

What desires and confusions was it smoothing over? How was its 'objectivity' textually constructed" ("Introduction," *Writing Culture*, p. 14).

[13] Clifford, "Introduction," p. 2.
[14] Clifford, "Introduction," p. 2.

> . . . Cultures do not hold still for their portraits. Attempts to make them do so always involve simplification and exclusion, selection of a temporal focus, the construction of a particular self-other relationship, and the imposition or negotiation of a power relationship.[15]

The curtain concealing the wizard is pulled back. Omniscient vantage points are discovered to be limited in their scope after all. If subjective, partial visions in a given ethnography try to mask themselves as objective and/or complete, they are quickly exposed in scholarly exchanges.

In all, *Writing Culture* made a significant intervention in the assumptions and practices of ethnography. It prompted a series of vigorous discussions and debates related to race, gender, privilege, and class. Indeed, it was quickly followed by another key development—both critical and creative.

Two years after its publication, feminist theorist Deborah Gordon[16] published the first response to *Writing Culture* and bell hooks contributed a substantive and provocative critique in 1990.[17] Ruth Behar and Deborah Gordon subsequently published a thought-provoking collection of essays entitled *Women Writing Culture* (1995) partly as a response to its shortcomings and blind spots. All call attention to the lack of serious engagement with feminism (even as this is weakly justified in the introduction) and with white privilege.

Behar begins her rigorous critique by first acknowledging the weighty significance of *Writing Culture*. She credits its publication with demolishing the realist tradition and setting off a wave of debates that forever changed American anthropology: "[N]ever before had the power of anthropological rhetoric been subjected to such keen and sophisticated textual analysis, extinguishing any remaining sparks of the presumption that ethnographies were transparent mirrors of culture."[18] This self-awareness is a major contribution and one that we carry forward as fundamental to efforts to represent others faithfully within the domains of theology and Christian ethics.

However, as Behar and others explore in greater depth, it is both ironic and disappointing that Clifford and Marcus failed to acknowledge both the contributions of feminism to anthropology and the way *Writing Culture* re-inscribes

---

[15] Clifford, "Introduction," p. 10.

[16] See Deborah A. Gordon, "Writing Culture, Writing Feminism: The Poetics and Politics of Experimental Ethnography," in *Inscriptions* 3/4 (1988), 7–24. See also: Frances Mascia-Lees, et al., "The Postmodernist Turn in Anthropology: Cautions from a Feminist Perspective," in *Signs* 15 (1989), 7–33.

[17] hooks, *Yearning*, 123–33.

[18] Behar, "Introduction," 4. Behar continues:

> At the same time, the "new ethnography" was also expected to reflect a more profound self-consciousness of the working of power and partialness of all truth, both in the text and in the world. The "new ethnography" would not resolve the profoundly troubling issues of inequality in a world fueled by global capitalism, but at least it would seek to decolonize the power relations inherent in the representation of the Other.

authority and inequalities along the very gender and racial lines that it seeks to undermine. *Writing Culture* gives only a cursory reference to Margaret Mead, a prolific scholar, considered by many as the most famous anthropologist of the twentieth century. And just as—if not more—troubling, it completely ignores the rich contributions to the history and practice of modern anthropology made by women such as Ruth Benedict, Zora Neale Hurston, and others along with male anthropologists of color such as Gilberto Freyre and Williams Jones. Thus, even as it acknowledges that social thought and culture are constructions, it continues long history of building it in male, mostly white and/or European, terms. Behar sternly challenges the erasure of women by patriarchal canons[19]:

> Why is it that the legacy of what counts as social theory is traced back only to Lewis Henry Morgan, Karl Marx, Emilie Durkheim, Max Weber, Michel Foucault, and Pierre Bourdieu? . . . Why is the culture concept in anthropology only traced through Sir Edward Tylor, Franz Boas, Bronislaw Malinowski, Claude Levi-Strauss, and Clifford Geertz? Could the writing of culture not be traced . . . through Elise Clew Parsons, Ruth Benedict, Margaret Mead, Ella Deloria, Zora Neale Hurston, Ruth Landes, and Barbara Myerhoff to Alice Walker?[20]

The irony is that had Clifford and other contributors explored this history, they would have found that lighter and darker skinned women along with a few men had begun to question and resist realist assumptions back in the era of Boas, Malinowski, and Evans-Pritchard. Moreover, these early scholars had long experimented with creative blendings of genres (e.g. personal diaries, fictional novels, poetry, ethnographic field notes, autobiography) long before it became *en vogue* within mainstream academic anthropology to question the rigid divisions among them.

Another level of serious critique shifted attention away from words as representation to zero in on the power of image. Specifically, both Gordon and hooks take Clifford and Marcus to task for their choice of cover image that makes a white male ethnographer (one of the contributors to the book working in the field) the center with a darker skinned man off to the side, possibly observing the ethnographer writing. In addition, the cover text literally writes over the image of a darker skinned woman and small child relegated—nearly obscured—at the edge of the frame. hooks pointedly asks: "Why does this cover

---

[19] See also the searing challenge to the traditional anthropological canon by Kamala Visweswaran, "Defining Feminist Ethnography," in *Turning Points in Qualitative Research: Tying Knots in a Handkerchief*, Yvonna S. Lincoln and Norman K. Denzin (eds) (Walnut Creek: AltaMira Press, 2003), 73–94.

[20] Behar, "Introduction," 12. See also ibid., 17–20.

doubly annihilate the value of the brown female gaze, first by the choice of picture where the dark woman is in the shadows, and secondly by a demarcating line?"[21] For Gordon and hooks, the cover image visualizes blind spots found in the written text, meaning the relative absence of perspectives of darker skinned people and the general lack of robust engagement with feminist insights and contributions.[22] Hooks laments:

> Despite the new and different directions charted in this collection, it was disappointing that black people were still being "talked about," that we remain an absent presence without voice . . . [The editors] give no attention . . . to anthropologists/ethnographers in the United States who are black . . . . [This collection] in no way challenges the assumption that the image/identity of the ethnographer is white and male.[23]

In short, hooks and Gordon, while acknowledging that the contributors problematize ethnographic authority, expose colonialization, and call attention to the textual form of ethnography and its inherently constructed and subjective nature, they identify important limits. Even as it makes a vital contribution to scholarship, taken as a whole, *Writing Culture* nonetheless reflects and reinforces common engendered and racial presumptions embedded within western academic notions of authority, authorship, and scholarship.

Critical theories—found in both white feminism along with scholarship by darker skinned theorists (e.g. Collins, Conquergood, hooks, Pui-Lan, Trinh, Spivak, West)—not only deconstruct others' efforts who fail to take gender, race, and colonialism seriously, they break new ground from which all scholars stand to benefit. For example, the essays collected in *Women Writing Culture* and in *Turning Points in Qualitative Research* exemplify the rich and renewing theoretical and practical insights that are needed to keep ethnography (and even theology and ethics) relevant and accountable. In particular, they concretize what self-critical awareness and collaboration mean for ethnography. These contributions are discussed below following a brief explanation of how we employ the term ethnography in this volume.

---

[21] hooks, *Yearning*, 127.

[22] Only one woman (white) contributed to the volume and she did not draw upon feminist analyses. Two darker skinned men contributed to it. Deborah Gordon, bell hooks, and Ruth Behar all note, and then roundly criticize, Clifford's acknowledgment of the lack of engagement with feminism in his introduction—offering a weak justification for this fact. However, hooks goes on to explain how disconcerting it is that the editors think to offer an explanation for a lack of feminist contributions, but do not even think to comment on the lack of scholarship and contributions by Black anthropologists and other dark-skinned scholars. See hooks, *Yearning*, 126–7. To be fair to the editors and contributors of *Writing Culture*, much of their subsequent work shows they took the critiques seriously and continued to reflect on them.

[23] hooks, *Yearning*, 126.

A Working Definition of Ethnography

Countless works in anthropology and sociology, along with a few pioneering works in Christian theology and ethics, unpack the root definition of ethnography as writing culture: *ethno* (culture) and *graphy* (writing). Rather than compare and contrast them, we wish to share the sense of the term that has come to inform our work. In doing so, we want to underscore two things: First, the active, necessarily imperfect and yet potentially revelatory process of meaning-making; and second, ethnography as a process with distinct and disciplined aspects that together contribute its particular character.

To begin, it is helpful to conceive of ethnography less as a tool, product, thing, or even research strategy and more as a dynamic process of meaning-making that is inherently intertwined with power dynamics. Clifford contends: "Ethnography is actively situated between powerful systems of meaning. It poses its questions at the boundaries of civilizations, cultures, classes, races, and genders. Ethnography decodes and recodes, telling the grounds of collective order and diversity, inclusion and exclusion. It describes innovation and structuration, and is itself part of these processes."[24] Ethnography does not stand wholly outside that which it explores—it itself and its narrative is also part of the inquiry. Thus, it and the ethnographer, need to interrogate themselves as much as they seek to learn from the people with whom a study is undertaken. There is an inescapable dimension of vulnerability—often most acutely felt on the part of the people being studied. Yet, if it is done well, the researcher or academic will be vulnerable as well.

For the purposes of this volume, we understand ethnography as a process of attentive study of, and learning from, people—their words, practices, traditions, experiences, memories, insights—in particular times and places in order to understand how they make meaning (cultural, religious, ethical) and what they can teach us about reality, truth, beauty, moral responsibility, relationships and the divine, etc. The aim is to understand what God, human relationships, and the world look like from their perspective—to take them seriously as a source of wisdom and to de-center our own assumptions and evaluations. By de-centering, we mean that while it is impossible (and not desirable) to cast off completely our own views and values as researchers and as people of faith, it is both possible and helpful to put them off to the side in order to focus on the stories, perspectives, and lived realities of others—who may or may not share the lenses we bring.

Said differently, and in contrast to quantitative research, ethnography primarily utilizes an inductive method, which means rather than apply a broad principle to a concrete situation, it seeks to discover what truth or valuable

---

 [24] Clifford, "Introduction," 2–3.

insight is found within specific locations—discovered in communal and individual stories, cultures, practices, and experiences. Ethnographic methods provide a path *by which* truth emerges, rather than a way to apply truth. The researcher assumes the posture of a learner who wants to be taught rather than that of an expert who possesses the crucial theory for analyzing what is going on or what is really real.

Tools and Values

Ethnographers draw upon multiple research tools in their work (e.g. participant observation, focus groups, individual interviews, extended immersion within a particular culture or community). We will not attempt to outline all of the possible ones to utilize; others have described these in detail and we commend them to interested readers as logistical and strategic guides.[25] At the most basic level, we urge all considering ethnographic projects to do a thorough literature review of research methods so that one has a clear sense of the times, resources, collaborators, and particular tools that will be most helpful and needed. And it goes without saying that Institutional Review Board (IRB) approval will almost always be needed so time to work through the exams, protocols, and approval process must also be figured into the equation.

What we wish to do here is highlight four central features of ethnographic methods that are integral to responsible research. These qualities are glimpsed in four adjectives: humble, reflexive, collaborative, and audacious. What follows is a succinct discussion of what is most important to us in understanding and incorporating ethnography—its value and the qualities that ought to be embodied in any ethnographic research endeavor.

Humility amidst sustained, attentive and careful observation

The first, and perhaps most fundamental, ingredient necessary for successful and enlightening ethnographic research is a genuine spirit of openness to what other others know and live. Much has already been said about this quality in the Preface. Here we will simply emphasize that a posture of humility and friendly curiosity are crucial character traits of a skilled and responsible ethnographer. As James Spradley knew so profoundly, the ethnographic researcher must not come into the work assuming he or she is the expert; rather, the person needs

---

[25] See for example: James P. Spradley, *The Ethnographic Interview* (New York: Holt, Rinehart, and Winston, 1979) and John Swinton and Harriet Mowatt, *Practical Theology and Qualitative Research* (London: SCM Canterbury Press, 2006).

an ardent desire to learn and to be taught by others who often possess very different kinds of knowledge and expertise. It is noteworthy that all of the contributor chapters in Part Two, each in its own way and style, embody this commitment.

Such a posture can be challenging to assume for academics and professionals who are understandably invested in their identities as "scholar, Ph.D., MD, leading authority, Reverend" etc. Indeed, we spend significant years and financial resources precisely on becoming experts! Similarly, many pursue our professions because we enjoy, and have discernable gifts for, teaching others. So, it makes sense if the idea of relinquishing this status of teacher and expert—or at least loosening our grasp of it (after we have worked so hard to achieve it)— chaffs a bit.

To be clear, we do not wish to suggest that a scholar or professional renounces or erases what one knows or has endeavored to master through study and training. Central pieces of this learning become part of who we are and it would be both impossible and foolish to attempt to divorce ourselves from it. Ethnographic work involves both subjective and objective dimensions and also inductive and deductive modes of inquiry. This observation means that researchers cannot become (nor need to be) completely "blank slates." We may well bring some (relatively limited) assumptions, understandings, and particular commitments to the ethnographic field. The critical question is whether we are both honest and transparent about them *and also* genuinely willing to test them—open them to being altered and even disproved by what we learn through the research. In other words, we need to identify in a self-conscious way the subjective posture we bring with us to the field.[26] And we need to test our subjective convictions and responses by what we learn—especially that which catches us off guard. In short, new breakthroughs in understanding can happen when we put to the side "what we think we know" in order to discover what we do not. Being open to surprises and complications enriches both our knowledge base as researchers and subsequently any analyses or prescriptions we may offer up for public consideration.

Scholarly humility is also needed in terms of the scope of what we claim to know or describe. Even with intensive and prolonged ethnographic research, we never arrive at full or complete understandings of a particular situation or the lives of others. Clifford remarks on the liberation possible once we acknowledge our limits in knowing or discovering the truth:

---

[26] Clifford remarks: "Since Malinowski's time, the "method" of participant-observation has enacted a delicate balance of subjectivity and objectivity. The ethnographer's personal experiences, especially those of participation and empathy, are recognized as central to the research process, but they are firmly restrained by the impersonal standards of observation and 'objective' distance" (Clifford, "Introduction," 13).

In cultural studies at least, we can no longer know the whole truth, or even claim to approach it. The rigorous partiality I have been stressing here may be a source of pessimism for some readers. But is there not a liberation, too, in recognizing that no one can write about others any longer as if they were discrete objects or texts? And may not the vision of a complex, problematic, partial ethnography lead, not to its abandonment, but to more subtle, concrete ways of writing and reading, to new conceptions of culture as interactive and historical?[27]

While Clifford is speaking in terms of cultural theory and anthropology, we see a connection to theology. For us, all theology represents human (and thus inherently finite) attempts to know the infinite. Moreover, human beings, albeit imperfectly, are incarnate images of God (*imago dei*). Consequently, just as we cannot ever claim to know completely the transcendent God, we cannot ever claim final or complete knowledge of one another.

Both divine being and human being are knowable, are revealed in powerful ways, but as soon as we claim to command a mastery, we have turned our understanding of this truth of the other (human or divine) into a static, reified idol. We can discover real and relevant truth—about God, creation, human beings—through ethnographic study and in many cases this truth is transformative. But it is never perfect or all encompassing. Thus, even as we will hopefully gain significant insight through ethnographic study, we never come to "own," "possess," or "master" the subjects or material. Rather, it is more apt to say that we continually deepen in our awareness and awe of all that we do not know *and also* of our profound indebtedness to those who teach and collaborate with us.

Reflexivity: self-critical awareness and accountability

Intimately related to the virtues of humility and sincerity in learning from the lives and wisdom of others is the courageous willingness to being changed by what one sees, hears, learns, and observes. Reflexivity means that the researcher is willing to look honestly at one's self—location, biases, etc. Critical self-reflection involves taking a hard look at one's own assumptions. And as mentioned earlier, it means that the research is genuinely open to being surprised by what one is hearing and seeing. Simply put, ethnographers must be profoundly committed to learning from research collaborators and informants. Doing so may very well mean altering one's research to take into account what one is learning and candidly reporting data—especially when it does not line

---

[27] Ibid., 25.

up with what one expected to find. This self-critical and reflexive process is ongoing and continues well beyond the point of the research project itself. Works by Fulkerson, Vigen, Spradley, among others, all underscore this point. This theme also surfaces in several places within this volume, especially in Chapter 4 and in Chapters 6 and 10 by Reimer-Barry and Whitmore.

Reflexivity is of paramount significance as a way to guard against violating those from whom we seek to learn. Unfortunately, is all too possible for careless ethnographic work to become "pornographic" in that it serves only to objectify and profit from the act of narrating and exposing isolated parts of others' lives and personhoods. When this happens, it does textual, symbolic, and quite tangible (financial, social status, etc.) violence to the persons/communities it narrates because it does not do justice to their lives, views, experiences, or to the meanings of events. These works often fall in the gap between ethnography and journalism. The book *Methland* by Nick Reding is a case in point. He studied a town in Iowa and its meth problems and published his work without showing it first to the people he had interviewed. The town was horrified.[28]

Other, sadly more common and very popular, media forms are even more egregious. They are found in sensationalistic pseudo-journalism and problematic amalgamations of "news" and entertainment found in many popular magazines, newspapers, and television. For example, some "exposé" programs and "reality" shows claim to show the "true" lives and stories of people, unsolved mysteries, crimes, etc. In actuality, they often (re)produce dangerous stereotypes (racial, socioeconomic, cultural) and amount to little more than a circus show of gawking at the misfortunes, imperfections, and struggles of others. Meanwhile and notably off-camera, producers and directors tend to rake in the profits from these shows that are fairly cheap to produce, since they don't have to pay trained actors. In all, these examples so ubiquitous in popular culture raise our hackles because of their callous commodification (and profits) at the expense of the people featured in them.

In summary, when ethnographic research lacks rigorous and sustained self-critical analysis it fails on at least two key levels: First, it does not approach a complexified and multidimensional picture of "what is going on" and instead uses the ethnographic data simply to confirm its own assumptions (tautology). Simply put, the quality and depth of the research suffers. For example, theologian Mary McClintock Fulkerson acknowledges that initially she did not grasp the intricacy of the dynamics at a congregation, Good Samaritan, because her "frame for thinking about what mattered was too intellectualistic to capture

---

[28] Nick Reding, *Methland: The Death and Life of an American Small Town* (New York: Bloomsbury Press, 2009). The town's reaction is summarized online (accessed September 10, 2010): http://www.dailyiowan.com/2009/07/22/Arts/12162.html.

what seemed important to the community."[29] Her theoretical framing concealed more than it revealed.[30]

Second, it fails to hold the scholar accountable because it does not demand
that the researcher locate him/herself in the work or reflect on missteps,
assumptions, surprises that foster new awareness and perspective. Moreover,
without reflexivity, often there is no feedback loop in which the research wres-
tles with the person's or community's subsequent response to the work—as
evidenced in Reding's mistake referenced above. Indeed, offering up what we
write to those who have been so instrumental in the writing is imperative not
only for the credibility and substance of the work itself. Doing so is crucial
because scholars can make or advance careers on the basis of what others live.
For example, renowned ethnographer and cultural theorist, Paul Rabinow,
calls for critical explorations into the academic contexts in which texts and
truth claims are written and published. He urges scholars to tease out explicitly
in our scholarship the larger conditions in which knowledge is produced.[31]

In all, as researchers and scholars—by definition privileged—we need to be
up front about the inequalities and sites of privilege that are present in any
room where formal academic(s) come together with research subject(s). Moreover, we need to reflect deeply about how the scholarship is disseminated,
shared, used—who reads it, what kinds of effects it has, and how the benefits
might be shared beyond the scope of an individual's career/tenure record.
Because we are the ones to publish others' accounts and gain materially from
them, robust and multidimensional accountability is absolutely essential.

Collaborative: pushing the notion of authorship

At its best, ethnographic work embodies a conversation among numerous and
varied voices. Rather than simply presenting an individual's scholarly reflection

---

[29] Mary McClintock Fulkerson, *Places of Redemption: Theology for a Worldly Church* (New York:
Oxford University Press, 2007), 10.

[30] The same thing happened with Renato Rosaldo and his effort to understand Ignot head-
hunting. See: "Grief and a Headhunter's Rage: On the Cultural Force of Emotions" *Text
Play, and Story: The Construction and Reconstruction of Self and Society* (Long Grove: Waveland
Press, 1988), 178–95.

[31] Paul Rabinow writes:
My wager is that looking at the conditions under which people are hired, given tenure,
published, awarded grants, and feted would repay the effort . . . How are careers made
now? How are careers destroyed now? . . Whatever else we know, we certainly know
that the material conditions under which the textual movement has flourished must
include the university, its micropolitics, its trends. We know that this level of power relations exists, affects us, influences our themes, forms, contents, audiences. We owe these
issues attention—if only to establish their relative weight. Then, as with fieldwork, we
shall be able to proceed to more global issues. (Rabinow, "Representations are Social
Facts," in *Writing Culture*, 253–4)

or observations, it reflects an engaged dialogue with others.[32] In other words, it is <u>participatory</u> on a fundamental level. The ethnographic subjects are not objects of study, but rather <u>collaborators</u>—experts in their own right who have valuable knowledge that the ethnographer needs.[33]

This recognition points out the degree of respect and consideration owed to ethnographic subjects. They are not resources to be mined and then abandoned. Nor are they unreflective works of art to be interpreted and revealed by the scholarly gaze. Instead, they are, in a real sense, co-authors. Anthropologist Kamala Visweswaran comments on the significance of such a move in the way scholarship is conceived: "[W]hen the 'other' drops out of anthropology, becomes subject, participant, and sole author, not 'object' then . . . we will have established a 'hermeneutics of vulnerability' and an 'anthropology which calls itself into question.'"[34] Realizing intellectual and hermeneutic vulnerability exemplifies the kind of genuine reflexivity we value so highly.

Moreover, when this happens—when those who speak to ethnographers are no longer considered simply resources to be explored (or worse exploited)— then, as Clifford notes, all kinds of new questions emerge. "Once 'informants' begin to be considered as co-authors, and the ethnographer as scribe and archivist as well as interpreting observer, we can ask new, critical questions of all ethnographies."[35] For example, what might it mean for ethnographers not to narrate or represent others, but instead create a space for collaborators and informants to speak in their own voices—represent themselves? Visweswaran rightly notes: "If we have learned anything about anthropology's encounter with colonialism, the question is not really whether anthropologists can represent people better, but whether we can be accountable to people's own struggles for self-representation and self-determination."[36]

When the scholar divests a bit from being the "author" and "expert," those from whom they learn are more likely to be rightly regarded as full human subjects, rather than as research objects. And when this happens, they do not

---

[32] Clifford explains:
> Dialogical modes . . . need not lead to hyper self-consciousness or self-absorption . . . . [D]ialogical processes proliferate in any complexly represented discursive space . . . . Many voices clamor for expression. Polyvocality was restrained and orchestrated in traditional ethnographies by giving to one voice a pervasive authorial function and to others the role of sources, "informants," to be quoted or paraphrased. Once dialogism and polyphony are recognized as modes of textual production, monophonic authority is questioned, revealed to be characteristic of a science that has claimed to *represent* cultures (emphasis in the original). (Clifford, "Introduction," 15)

[33] See Spradley, *The Ethnographic Interview* and Mindy Fullilove, unpublished handbook for qualitative research for classroom use, *The Little Handbook*, Mindy Thompson Fullilove (ed.), created for the use of the Qualitative Research Methods (QRM) 101 class, Mailman School of Public Health, Columbia University, New York, NY, 2001.

[34] Visweswaran, "Defining Feminist Ethnography," 89.

[35] Clifford, "Introduction," 17.

[36] Visweswaran, "Defining Feminist Ethnography," 89.

merely inform the researcher about specific facts of their lives, they can become witnesses to truth on a much more profound level. Similarly, ethnographers are not simply passive observers, they take on a witnessing role as well. Interestingly, as Gordon highlights the distinctive connotations of identifying ethnographers as "participant witnesses" rather than "participant observers," she invokes explicit theological language:

> Carrying a host of conflicting associations, including informant, litigant, function of the Holy Ghost, and spectator, a witness is less an observer than a teller—that is, one who translates what s/he sees and hears for an audience . . . As an informant, the witness purposely informs or tells, with all of the potential for betrayal implied. Yet witnessing in the context of the Americas also brings to mind the long-standing indigenous tradition of personal testimony, with the witness calling up a broken humanity to redeem it. Characteristically, American traditions of African American preachers, Latin American human-rights activists, and the advocates for the poor continually reinvent stories of redemption through suffering to challenge social injustice . . . In participant witnessing, the lines between ethnographer and informant blur as each hears the other in a way that encourages self-representation.[37]

Gordon's comments highlight two important things: First, ethnographic witnessing on the part of both ethnographer and collaborator/informant can take on a normative quality in the sense that witnessing to human struggles can implicitly or explicitly carry an imperative to transform suffering into healing and well-being. Second, this kind of collaboration means that all involved attend to one another—hear one another into a fuller sense of being—and all participate in the resulting representation. The ethnographer is not the sole authority.

Gordon takes the notion of collaborative writing to a concrete level as she discusses specific projects that directly link academic with other community needs and goals. She lifts up the example of El Barrio, "a community-based program of action research initiated by the Center for Puerto Rican Studies at Hunter College" which operated from 1985 to 1989 in New York City.[38] This program combined an ethnographic, oral history project with empowering Latina women through literacy education.

The work of El Barrio testifies to the ways in which power and identity can shift through dialogue, joint-writing, collaborative education, and the teaching of one another throughout. And even when joint writing is not desired or

---

[37] Deborah A. Gordon, "Border Work: Feminist Ethnography and the Dissemination of Literacy," in *Women Writing Culture*, 383.
[38] Gordon, "Border Work," 377.

possible, research subjects and collaborators can offer vital insights and corrections through critiques of what the academic writes. Through this kind of partnering, while the power dynamics and inequalities between researchers and collaborators were real and tangible, they were also dynamic (not static).

In all, authentic collaboration means that ethnographers are accountable to those from whom they learn and that they ought to show them what they write, or discuss their writing and conclusions with them. There ought to be some kind of feedback loop so that informants and collaborators know what becomes of their stories—what is written, discussed, produced. They may not like or agree with the researcher's narrative, but they should at least have some kind of opportunity to know what it is and to respond to it. The researcher may or may not amend what s/he creates, but regardless has a responsibility to be aware of it and to acknowledge areas of (dis)agreement.

Audacity: efforts at pragmatic solidarity

Undeniably, there is a danger—and a visible track record—of white, western academics (wittingly or unwittingly) aiding colonialist and/or patronizing forces as they naïvely attempt to "save" or "liberate" pepole whose intellect, religious and cultural commitments, and agency they under-estimate (and often disrespect). The methodological steps related to humility, reflexivity, and collaboration help to avoid such problematic outcomes and processes. Attending seriously to these safeguards, theologians and ethnographers might then find a measure of appropriate audacity. Illuminating ethnography often requires that the researcher be bold enough to claim that the work reveals truth—albeit partial—but nonetheless real and significant. Even more, this kind of revelation is not only theoretical or abstract, it is embodied in practices and in tangible interventions in the way things are. In other words, speaking truth involves pragmatic solidarity with those who suffer or are too often rendered invisible by the power structures of the world. Put simply, research that hopes to be both relevant and to speak to truth needs to consider the priorities and needs of the communities with which it hopes to work.

Behar comments that the kind of dynamic, illuminative work such as that in El Barrio shows how "collaborative texts can be created when ethnographic research takes place within community agendas. Sharing privilege, sharing literacy, sharing information—which in our world is power—is one way for feminist relationships in postcolonial conditions of inequality to bridge the gaps between women in the academy and women in ethnic communities."[39]

---

[39] Behar, "Introduction," 21.

This kind of endeavor exemplifies what we mean by pragmatic solidarity.[40] A genuinely humble, reflexive, and collaborative process means that research agendas ought to be integrally linked to tangible, visceral needs within a given community engaged through ethnography.

To illustrate, Gordon puts the success and significance of El Barrio in these terms:

> The centerpiece of the El Barrio project, one critical in any discussion of feminist ethnography, is research that attempts to redistribute educational privilege. That redistribution is centered in teaching critical rather than function literacy . . . Life histories were collected by teaching women participants to write in a way that changed their sense of self and led to collective empowerment. For example, as women reinterpreted their lives through the life-history process, they become more willing to resist welfare workers.[41]

While it is not always so, research can be transformative—perhaps even redemptive. Put more modestly, it can be at least a vehicle for positive change.[42] With careful methodological attention and accompanied by appropriate humility, it can contribute to the material, psychological, spiritual, and social flourishing of an individual or community. On the other hand, it may not realize such goals (and at worst, if done carelessly, it could obstruct them). Yet, regardless of any practical outcomes, the point is that a scholar's research agenda ought to connect with, perhaps even prioritize, the "on the ground" needs and challenges a community faces. This commitment is poignantly expressed in the chapters by Browning, Gathje, Jones, and Whitmore.[43]

---

[40] Gordon explains why pragmatic solidarity is of such great importance:
[O]riginal ways of conceiving experimental ethnography may be lost if feminist ethnography simply means more academic books rather than material dispersion of authorship. Feminist experimentalism with ethnography will be impoverished without sustained reflection on how to mix sociological, political-economic, and historical analysis as well as policy recommendations such that women historically excluded from higher education gain from its material resources. (Gordon, "Conclusion: Culture Writing Women: Inscribing Feminist Anthropology," in *Women Writing Culture*, 432)

[41] Gordon, "Border Work," 378.

[42] The tradition of "action research" is but one specific means towards this end. See, for example, the cutting-edge work on display in Helen Cameron et al., *Talking About God In Practice: Theological Action Research and Practical Theology* (London: SCM Press, 2010); Peter Reason and Hilary Bradbury (eds), *Handbook of Action Research: Participatory Inquiry and Practice* (Thousand Oaks: Sage Publications, 2001); and Beverly Haddad, "Living It Out: Faith Resources and Sites as Critical to Participatory Learning with Rural South African Women," *Journal of Feminist Studies in Religion* 22:1 (2006), 135–54.

[43] See Melissa Browning's ethnographic research focusing upon women and HIV/AIDS in sub-Saharan Africa in forthcoming anthologies and journal issues (2011 and 2012).

Conclusion

Pragmatically, these four qualities translate into significant time and effort spent listening, looking, and taking detailed notes—without coming to conclusions prematurely. The initial stages, that can last several months or longer, involve writing down and reflecting on as much as possible—before knowing fully what will evolve into central insights or pivotal turning points. Thus, the ability to ask good—evocative—questions is essential. Sometimes ethnographers grope for questions—stumble around to find the right phrasing that gets at the matter, speak to the person's experience, and cultivate a sense of rapport and shared understanding with the informants and other collaborators. This awkwardness is necessary because it can be a way for the researcher to demonstrate humility and imperfection and for her/him to find the key to understanding what she/he previously did not. When others witness the researcher being a human being, rather than an expert—complete with flaws and humor—they are often more likely to trust the person and share more of what they have come to know.

Indeed close, attuned observation and the meticulous recording of data are the bread and butter of both quantitative and qualitative methods. The difference in ethnographic/qualitative methods is that the researcher does not stand as far apart from the research subject or assume the same kind of objectivity. Rather, the ethnographer owns his/her assumptions, biases, hopes, and concerns as part of the process. This quality is discussed above in terms of reflexivity.

It takes significant patience and discipline to get past the surface of things in ethnographic research. Ethnographers who are in too much of a hurry often frustrate their own efforts—people don't like to be pressured into self-revelation and they have little reason to trust those who seem only interested in "getting the goods" and moving on. Moreover, there is often significant uncertainty over what "the goods" are. It takes time (sometimes a year or more) to learn what the key issues, questions, and themes are. Seeking to explicate this dimension of the "untimeliness" of ethnography, Paul Rabinow has recently compared journalism, investigating and writing on a publishing deadline, to the open-ended practice of ethnographic research.[44]

Being in a hurry often means that the researcher only wants confirmation of what he thinks she knows—of the themes and issues already chosen as foundational. Proceeding in such a way leads to a tautological circle where one's assumptions substitute for the evidence needed to support them. The aim of ethnography is not merely to confirm or prove false one's hypothesis or

---

[44] Paul Rabinow and George E. Marcus et al., *Designs for an Anthropology of the Contemporary* (Durham: Duke University Press, 2008).

theoretical claim. Rather, it is to learn from the scene itself—to let the questions and knowledge bubble up from the situation—to get a deep reading of what is there—on its own terms.

Of course, at the outset, the research will likely need some kind of map. We do not recommend that anyone begin research with no sense of the central questions and issues. What we wish to underscore is that the map probably needs to be written in pencil rather than indelible ink. It demands flexibility because ethnographers cannot fully predict where the research will take them. Working with modeling clay may be an apt metaphor—as long as it keeps moist so that it does not become hardened and brittle, you can shape and reshape it as often as required in order to capture as accurately—and with as much vivid detail as possible—the scene you are attempting to know and describe.

This is our sense of the history, purpose, significance, and key features of ethnography as a research method. In Chapter 4, we make a particular case for why and how ethnography can be at home within theology and ethics. But before we make that case, we need to trace two other histories. Chapter 2 charts the turn to ethnography in Christian theology and then Chapter 3 engages, and responds to, some criticisms of such a move to depend upon social science theory and methods.

Chapter 2

The Ethnographic Turn in Theology and Ethics

Privileging particularity

In response to a variety of critical intellectual currents, scholars in Christian theology and ethics are increasingly taking up the tools of ethnography as a means to ask fundamental theological and moral questions and to make more compelling and credible claims. Privileging particularity, rather than the more traditional effort to achieve universal or at least generalizable norms in making claims regarding the Christian life, echoes the most fundamental insight of the Christian tradition—that God is known most fully in Jesus of Nazareth. Echoing this "scandal of particularity" at the heart of the Christian tradition, theologians and ethicists involved in ethnographic research draw on the particular to seek out answers to core questions of their discipline: who is God and how do we become the people we are, how to conceptualize moral agency in relation to God and the world, and how to flesh out the content of conceptual categories such as justice that help direct us in our daily decisions and guiding institutions.

This perspective does not deny the possibility or credibility of larger moral claims that can cross contexts. Yet, it does argue that in order to have anything like generalized claims of what ought to be, Christian theologians and ethicists ought to start with the particular as integral to their methods of inquiry. In other words, before such scholars can state what is normative, they need to cultivate a "thick description" (Geertz) of what is real to and within concrete congregations and communities. Parallel circumstances in theology and social science have forced a new attention to particularity. Movements such as postcolonialism and postmodernism have expanded the breadth of acceptable sources for doing Christian theology and ethics and the desire to be accountable to those beyond the academy, especially the church—in terms of describing faithful discipleship—and those on the margins—in terms of listening to their voices rather than simply speaking about them or on their behalf.

Numerous avenues might be pursued that begin to show how scholars are responding to the shift to particularity, especially to those on the margins. Of course, the seven scholars whose work is featured in Part Two of this volume represent one avenue. However, they primarily show their work in action rather than telling about the reasons and routes they followed in coming to such an ethnographic approach to theological and ethical research and writing. In this chapter, we point to a few trajectories that bear within them some of the reasons and persons relevant to the "turn" to ethnography in theology.

Trajectories

Mary McClintock Fulkerson, a professor of theology at Duke University Divinity School whose gracious foreword begins this book, exemplifies this turn to ethnography in her own professional evolution. Her first major book, *Changing the Subject,* drew on critical social theory to elaborate a critique of feminist theology's "universalist" claims regarding women's experience. Arguing that the "female subject" is multiply constructed and plural, embodying complex and competing discourses, she seeks to "change the subject" so that such multiple subject positions are the basis for further theoretical work on difference and identity.[1]

Fulkerson's initial work in feminist theology and social and cultural theory led to her participation in a conference at the University of Chicago in 1997 seeking to articulate more explicitly the ways theologians were turning from philosophy or the history of ideas to culture as a primary conversation partner for their work. Fulkerson brought her ideas of complexity and hybridity to the study of the culture of a local congregation, Good Samaritan, where she had spent "two years of interviewing and observing participants."[2] Here, drawing on anthropologist Pierre Bourdieu, she emphasizes the creative habituation of values of inclusion at the heart of the church's interracial identity. Yet rather than agree on some simple movement from belief and ritual to the formation of habits, she argues for a more open and contested notion of a "repertoire" available for the persons and community as they act out their life together.

By the time of Fulkerson's book-length analysis of this congregation, published in 2007 as *Places of Redemption,* she explicitly describes her fieldwork as ethnography, and begins the book recalling her ethnography class in which she gained the fieldwork practices by which she sought to "bring something fresh to theological reflection on ordinary Christian community."[3] She aims

---

[1] Mary McClintock Fulkerson, *Changing the Subject: Women's Discourses and Feminist Theology* (Minneapolis: Fortress Press, 1994).
[2] Mary McClintock Fulkerson, "'We Don't See Color Here': A Case Study in Ecclesial-Cultural Invention," in *Converging on Culture: Theologians in Dialogue with Cultural Analysis and Criticism,* Delwin Brown, Sheila Greeve Davaney, and Kathryn Tanner (eds) (New York: Oxford University Press, 2001), 140–57.
[3] Fulkerson, *Places of Redemption,* 3.

not for an "objective" analysis of the community (having, along with the postmodern anthropology she had read, given up on such an idea). Rather, she tried to do research and writing "adequate to the full-bodied reality that is Good Samaritan, one capable of displaying its ambiguity, its implication in the banal and opaque realities of ordinary existence, even as it allows for testimony to God's redemptive reality."[4]

While we can make some sense of this turn to ethnography in the trajectory of Fulkerson's public career, we can show with even more particularity how this turn took shape in our own lives drawing for the moment on the genre of autobiography. We describe how one of us (Scharen) became disaffected with theology and "crossed over" to be doubly trained—in social science as well as theology; how by doing so I hoped to correct the too idealized pictures theology consistently drew of church and the Christian life; and yet under the tutelage of mentors in sociology and anthropology, began a series of comparative ethnographic studies of worship and social ethics in urban congregations that took theology with great seriousness. These studies were eventually written up in a stuttering theological voice, a voice struggling to unite the conflictual pair I had grappled with from the start: theology and ethnography.[5] While my early work did not fully accomplish the hoped-for integration of the two, it did lead to developing a theological counterpart to the enormously fruitful proposal for, and embodiment of, an ethnographic approach called "carnal sociology" in the work of Pierre Bourdieu developed further in important ways by his student, Loïc Wacquant.

Positing that Bourdieu is right that "we learn by body" I pursued studies that position the worshipper and, in a broader sense, the congregation as a whole not merely as object to be understood, as perhaps a part of the burgeoning sociology or theology *of* the body, but also *from* the body, requiring submitting myself to the painful apprenticeship in context that allows forging the corporal and mental dispositions that make up the competent worshipper within the crucible of congregational life. A bodily submission, then, to the rigors of apprenticeship *in situ* becomes both the object and means of inquiry, opening, as Merleau-Ponty shows, access to sensory-motor, mental, and social aptitudes—a corporal intelligence that tacitly guides "natives" to a particular "familiar universe."[6] It is, as Wacquant argues, a "mutual molding and immediate 'inhabiting' of being and world, carnal entanglement with a mesh of forces pregnant with silent summons and invisible interdictions that elude the scholastic distinction between subject and object as they work simultaneously from

---

4   Fulkerson, *Places of Redemption*, 7.
5   Christian Scharen, "Lois, Liturgy, and Ethics," *The Annual of the Society of Christian Ethics*, 20 (2000), 275–305; Scharen, *Public Worship and Public Work: Character and Commitment in Local Congregational Life* (Collegeville: The Liturgical Press, 2004).
6   M. Merleau-Ponty, *Phenomenology of Perception* (New York: Routledge, 1947/1962).

within, through the socialization of cognition and affect, and from without by closing and opening viable paths for action."[7] Such a "carnal sociology" transfigured into a "carnal theology" illumines dynamics at the heart of Christian faith one might gesture toward in a preliminary way through categories such as God's "in-dwelling," or perhaps better, "in-carnation."

On Crossing Hearst Avenue

Drawing on the genre of biography interspersed with elements of theory, theology and reports from ethnographic fieldwork, we begin here with a brief version of how I came to the academic study of theology and social science. Prior to arriving in Berkeley California for masters studies in theology, I had been actively engaged for five years in homeless ministries in impoverished urban areas. This work began as part of a religious intensification during undergraduate studies, one that through a powerful experience of the college chapel life initiated me to a way of living the Eucharist as deeply intertwined with questions of worldly justice. However it took on full weight in a year spent as part of the Lutheran Volunteer Corps (LVC) sharing life and ministry with a Franciscan-based ministry to the homeless near Philadelphia. In the late 1980s, homelessness had burgeoned under the weight of Reagan-era policies of deinstitutionalization of the mentally ill along with the scourge of crack cocaine that ravaged lives and spiked US incarceration rates. Nightly vigilance was required to keep the crack dealers off of the front steps.

During the year working in LVC, I was learning skills of liturgical leadership at a local Lutheran parish located in the city but as distant from the realities of my work in the homeless shelter as might be imagined. The intricacies of chant tones and properly assisting the Lavabo after the offering, for example, seemed ridiculous at the time—examples of ritual for its own sake deeply disconnected from the context and its broken, plaintive cries. In part in an effort to cope with the screaming disjuncture of my daily existence, I began keeping a notebook of observations, reactions, and suppositions related to the daily occurrences, the coming and going of the men, the activity in the neighborhood, and my oscillation between the Lutheran congregation and the Franciscan house that served as home for two brothers and up to 14 homeless men. The liturgy of dignity eating hearty meals together around a dining room table, cooked and presided over by Fr Hilary, seemed a much more profound embodiment of Eucharistic hospitality than the stilted distribution of wafers and a small glass of overly sweet wine on Sunday mornings.

---

[7] Loïc Wacquant, "Carnal Connections: On Embodiment, Apprenticeship, and Membership," in *Qualitative Sociology*, 28:4 (Winter 2005), 466.

The initial move into seminary education then sought to interpret and understand the disjuncture between these various ritual experiences, some seeming to be springs of a way of understanding and action deeply connected to the cries of suffering and injustice in the world, and others seemly asleep with dreams of individual peace and eternal reward. My sense then was that the world was on fire, that God was implicated deeply in the suffering, and the story of Jesus' body and blood "for us" meant our incorporation into the shape of that suffering love, working in solidarity with those most broken and in need as indeed God already was doing.

The influence of liberation and feminist theologies were also important, playing a role for those who desired to break out beyond the confines of cloistered classroom education to engage the life of the streets, neighborhoods, and lives of the Bay area. However, as I progressed in my theological studies, simultaneously investing myself in a local congregation as an apprentice to a mentoring pastor, I found myself quite without tools for understanding the distinctiveness of what I was experiencing, or how to speak of the yawning gap between the thrilling intersection of vibrant communal worship and work for justice and the frankly boring recital of dry biblical, historical, and theological data seemingly hovering above history. This abstract theological material felt as if it was required for professional hazing; that is, required as much for its inscription of distinction—a class marker painfully achieved for those ascending to the pulpit and altar—as for any practical use in ministry.[8]

So I crossed over Hearst Avenue to study social science at U. C. Berkeley. One key intersection was with Robert Bellah. Trained at Harvard under Talcott Parsons during the late 1940s and early 1950s, Bellah had by 1970 established himself as one of the leading sociologists of religion in the United States. His important collection of essays, *Beyond Belief,* was a sociological watershed on many fronts including classic arguments about civil religion in America and about religious evolution, the topic on which he is currently writing a major book.[9] *Beyond Belief* especially impressed me for its eloquent description of the "religious implications of social science" and Bellah's hoped-for "integration" or "open interchange" between the two leading to a much more powerful understanding of ourselves and the realities in which we live.[10] In the trajectory of his work, from early books on the role of religion in Japan's modernization to his major study of individualism in American culture, *Habits of the Heart,* the religious element of social science has mostly been evidenced in a

---

[8] Pierre Bourdieu, *Language and Symbolic Power* (Stanford: Stanford University Press, 1991), 123.

[9] See for example this preliminary essay that is part of that larger forthcoming work: Robert N. Bellah, "What's Axial about the Axial Age?" *European Journal of Sociology* 46 (2005), 69–89.

[10] Robert N. Bellah, *Beyond Belief: Essays in Post-Traditional Religion* (New York: Harper, 1970), 244.

powerful normative agenda funded by faith.[11] The appendix to *Habits*, titled "social science as public philosophy," argues that for social science to be good in a technical sense it must also be good in a moral sense, that is, seek to do good.

The other very significant early encounter in the social sciences was with anthropologist Paul Rabinow. Rabinow is widely known for his early works introducing Michel Foucault to a broader English-speaking audience (and hosting Foucault as a visiting scholar at U. C. Berkeley in the early 1980s).[12] Yet within anthropology Rabinow has participated in nothing less than a refashioning of the field, pioneering new forms of the ethnographic practices that are more or less constitutive of anthropology. Classically trained in anthropology at the University of Chicago under Clifford Geertz, Rabinow did the requisite field studies abroad in rural Morocco but by the early 1980s had joined in a dramatic challenge to the practice of ethnography captured in the jointly authored classic *Writing Culture*.[13] We put this watershed volume in perspective relative to the developments in anthropology in Chapter 1 above.

Rabinow's seminal work at the intersection of philosophy and social science depends upon critiques of modern epistemology (Wittgenstein, Heidegger) and offers an alternative, through Foucault and Pierre Bourdieu, that claims the place of knowledge is embedded in forms of life, or to put it simply, in practice; as Rabinow puts the point: "thought is nothing more and nothing less than a historically locatable set of practices."[14] Claiming anthropology needed to turn its gaze upon the modern west, Rabinow developed lines of research into the anthropology of reason but also the anthropology of the contemporary leading to entirely novel ethnographic studies, for example, of biotechnology laboratories both in the United States and in France.[15]

Rabinow shares Bellah's deep commitment to social science as practical ethics, yet his work is not theological. Despite little help making the connections to the life of faith and the practices of congregations, I entered doctoral studies at Emory University in Atlanta with a substantial repertoire of perspectives for studying congregations. In my research in Atlanta, guided by Steven Tipton (himself a student of Bellah) and Nancy Eiesland, another sociologist of religion, I focused on the logic of lived theological identity and the embodied

---

[11] Robert N. Bellah, *Tokogowa Religion: The Cultural Roots of Modern Japan* (New York: The Free Press, 1957); Robert N. Bellah et al., *Habits of the Heart: Individualism and Commitment in American Life* (Berkeley: University of California Press, 1985).

[12] Paul Rabinow and Hubert L. Dreyfus, with Michel Foucault, *Michel Foucault: Beyond Structuralism and Hermeneutics* (Chicago: University of Chicago Press, 1983); Paul Rabinow (ed.), *The Foucault Reader* (New York: Vintage, 1984).

[13] See Paul Rabinow, "Representations are Social Facts," 234–261.

[14] Ibid., 239.

[15] Paul Rabinow, *French DNA: Trouble in Purgatory* (Chicago: University of Chicago Press, 2002); Rabinow, *Making PCR: A Story of Biotechnology* (Chicago: University of Chicago Press, 1997).

shape of moral commitment. I focused on worship or liturgy as the nexus where such interplay between theological identity and moral commitment could be found. However, as Martin Stringer has pointed out in his similarly placed ethnographic studies of congregational worship in Manchester and Birmingham (England), very little literature existed in the late 1980s and early 1990s at the intersection of theology, worship, and ethnography.[16]

Much of the relevant literature was just emerging during the 1990s. Of use were both virtue ethics approaches that argued worship formed Christian character, on the one hand, and practical theology and congregational studies that argued ritual had a formative power shaping congregational identity, on the other. In this vein, the work of theologian Stanley Hauerwas was pivotal. Yet his allergic reaction to social science generally and ethnography in particular made his self-described "naïve" observations of congregational life both embarrassingly self-serving and descriptively weak (see Chapter 3 below for this critique). On the congregational studies side, the work of Nancy Ammerman has been pivotal, yet as with most work in congregational studies, her work has remained solidly within its domain as a subdiscipline of sociology of religion and thus had little engagement with theology.[17] Within practical theology, Don Browning's labors to introduce a "descriptive theological" moment to the overall task of theology moved beyond most congregational studies literature in seeking to bring to explicit focus implicit normative claims present in particular situations.[18]

For those seeking to integrate ethnography and theology, it was a gift to be entering graduate school at a time when practical theology was going through something of a revival in part, as noted in the case of Don Browning, drawing on congregational studies and ethnographic fieldwork as a key way to approach such study. The intersection of practical philosophy, theology, and ethnography clearly rode the wave of the "turn to culture" so prominent across the disciplines in the 1980s and 1990s, a trajectory masterfully unfolded in Kathryn Tanner's book, *Theories of Culture*.[19] There she offers a sharp critique of George Lindbeck, Stanley Hauerwas, and others whose appropriation of the "turn to culture" issued in a relatively holistic notion of culture formed through worship and existing as a counter-community and story over against the dominant culture and story of modern liberal democratic society. Her critique pointed to the need to understand congregations as particularly shaped *by the world* in

[16] Martin D. Stringer, *On The Perception of Worship: The Ethnography of Worship in Four Christian Congregations in Manchester* (Birmingham: The University of Birmingham Press, 1999).

[17] Nancy Ammerman, *Congregation and Community* (New Brunswick: Rutgers University Press, 1997); Penny Becker, *Congregations in Conflict: Cultural Models of Local Religious Life* (New York: Cambridge University Press, 1999).

[18] Don Browning, *A Fundamental Practical Theology* (Minneapolis: Fortress Press, 1996).

[19] Kathryn Tanner, *Theories of Culture: An Agenda for Theology* (Minneapolis: Fortress Press, 1997).

order to see how their formative power worked *over against the world*.[20] Help in articulating such a complex understanding also emerged from sociological and liturgical writings on ritual, including the fruitful approach to ritual practice in the work of Pierre Bourdieu.[21] With these conversation partners, I was able to move from studying, as I put it then, "the Church" to studying "churches," or as theologian Nicholas Healy puts it, from "idealized" to "concrete" ecclesiology.[22]

Over the course of a few months I visited multiple downtown churches in Atlanta, walked the streets and learned some of the history of the center city. I settled on three churches that had been founded along with the city itself 150 years prior, and represented the oldest Catholic, white Protestant, and African American Protestant congregations: The Shrine of the Immaculate Conception, Central Presbyterian, and Big Bethel African Methodist Episcopal. By way of procedure, briefly, I planned to spend a season of the year that made internal sense to each fully immersing myself in the life of the congregation, including all ordinary worship, education and social activities but also staff meetings. I interviewed clergy and staff, older members who served as volunteer or informal congregational historians, and a wide variety of members. I read archives, anniversary booklets and whatever else of the congregation's life and ministry I could find to deepen my sensibilities. Most importantly, however, was simply becoming a church-goer as fully and as enthusiastically as I could in each place, feeling what it was to be there.

Looking for a "Eucharistic Self"

Plunging into fieldwork in these urban congregations required qualitative sociology and ethnography in particular as means for understanding rather than explaining the church's public life, seeking immersion in "primary" or "lived" theology observed, heard, seen close at hand, and portrayed by articulation of its practical logic—the wisdom embedded or embodied in practice. David Ford's writing played an important roll, especially what he called "a worshipping self" or perhaps more particularly "a eucharistic self."[23] In the book *Self and Salvation* Ford posed a basic question "about the formation of the self through the Eucharist. What happens to the self shaped through that

---

[20] This is one of the key arguments in Scharen, *Public Work and Public Worship*.

[21] Catherine Bell, *Ritual Theory, Ritual Practice* (New York: Oxford University Press, 1992); Pierre Bourdieu, *Outline of a Theory of Practice* (New York: Cambridge University Press, 1977).

[22] Nicholas M. Healy, *Church, World and the Christian Life: Practical-Prophetic Ecclesiology* (New York: Cambridge, 2000), 150.

[23] David F. Ford, *Self and Salvation: Being Transformed* (New York: Cambridge University Press, 1999), 137.

worship?"[24] Drawing on Timothy Jenkins' creative deployment of Bourdieu for ethnographic study of local congregations and communities, Ford outlined four aspects of such inquiry into actual practice.[25] These aspects of ethnographic investigation guided me as I sought means in each congregation to participate, pay attention to, listen for, and begin to understand those characteristics of a social, religious, and cultural competency through which God was animating their worship and work in the world.

Such practical modes of knowing are gotten at, Ford begins, through first clearly stating that these are "nonverbal and habitual." He points to the absolutely basic fact that Christian identity is constituted in and through worship, through a practice, and not through many other things, from law and ethics to an alternative worldview or set of doctrines. Here he introduces Bourdieu's concept of *habitus*, briefly summarizing it as "the durably installed generative principle of regulated improvisations."[26] The ritual of the Eucharist, Ford suggests, is in its many variations "a condensation of the Christian habitus." Yet it is not the words nor the confessed theological understandings but rather the "patterns" of "how and why" these particular patterns of gathering are "rooted in distant or recent history" and so on.[27] Secondly, and implicit in the first, Ford argues, such embodied knowledge comes by "the apprenticeship undergone by all actors."[28] Noting the "synoptic illusion" that allows supposing a map to be what people follow in traversing the paths of their daily lives, Ford describes the parallel for the Eucharist that requires apprenticeships in practical mastery rather than overviews based on ritual texts or doctrine. Rather, the Eucharist incorporates participants, and distinctively, particularly, in ways not easily articulated in scholastic terms favored by the theologian.

Third, the nature of apprenticeships is intensified by the multiple apprenticeships within each life that overlay each other creating complexities of many sorts, all coexisting within what Bourdieu calls the "socially informed body" with all its senses.[29] A final ethnographic point follows in that this complex embodied mastery is not easily given representation in language and in doing so its best path for offering a similarly rich conception of human and divine action comes through being itself diverse. Eucharistic language, Ford argues, includes many genres: "praise, lament, confession, exclamation, narrative, proclamation, petition" as well as "the oral and the written" but both are performed and "resist discursive overview in a somewhat similar way to

---

[24] Ibid., 138.
[25] Timothy Jenkins, "Fieldwork and the Perception of Everyday Life," *Man, New Series* 29:2 (1994), 433–55; Timothy Jenkins, *Religion in English Everyday Life: An Ethnographic Approach. Methodology and History in Anthropology, Vol. 5* (Oxford: Berghahn Books, 1999).
[26] Bourdieu, *Outline of a Theory of Practice*, 78.
[27] Ford, *Self and Salvation*, 140–1.
[28] Ford, *Self and Salvation*, 141; see also Jenkins, *Religion in English Everyday Life*, 444.
[29] Bourdieu, *Outline of a Theory of Practice*, 124.

good drama."[30] This kind of diverse "telling" of what is learned through ethnographic research is explicitly what Wacquant achieves in his account of learning boxing in South Chicago. In Wacquant's book, *Body and Soul*, he draws upon "sociological analysis, ethnographic description and literary evocation."[31]

Finally, in a theological mode, Ford highlights the way the logic of Trinitarian "creativity and abundance" giving way in Christ to a radical singularity in the incarnation offers a way to understand Christian faith as true to itself only in "becoming freshly embodied in different contexts." Life "in Christ," Ford argues, is a matter of what Bourdieu calls "necessary improvisation" showing "the distinctive and different realizations of the eventfulness of God" and exacting "ways beyond any overview the truth of the doxology: 'Heaven and earth are full of your glory.' " Especially here, Ford can press on the fact that the habituation of a "eucharistic self" is not primarily about forming a self for its own sake but to be "responsive to Jesus Christ and other people, and coping with their responses in turn."[32]

Ironically, his turn in the chapter disappointingly is to biblical interpretation rather than attending closely to formation in particular communities and communion rituals. Despite Ford's own choice to avoid the difficult process of submitting himself to ethnographic research in order to have exemplary portrayals of actual apprenticeships, he "longs to find a full anthropological study of Eucharistic practice along the lines suggested by Jenkins and Bourdieu above. That, if it were theological informed, could be a most helpful accompaniment." He means by "theological" that the practice be oriented to Jesus Christ and to others.

In order to show with more fullness here the fruit of the ethnographic turn, and how that trajectory sketched above led to ethnographic "field work," I can highlight briefly an experience in one of my case congregations: Big Bethel AME. Immediately, however, Ford's language of a "eucharistic self" begs the question of such a life "in Christ" becoming "freshly embodied in different contexts" in some of which—as in this case—such language is not even used. But the distinctiveness of their particular practices and the apprenticeships enacted display this diversity in no uncertain terms. It is important to first introduce the context of Atlanta, in the southern state of Georgia, before moving to a particular gathering of the congregation as an example of "eucharistic practice." This narrative description is excerpted from my longer study of these congregations published in the volume *Public Worship, Public Work*.[33]

---

[30] Ford, *Self and Salvation*, 144.
[31] Loïc Wacquant, *Body and Soul: Notebooks of an Apprentice Boxer* (New York: Oxford, 2004), 7.
[32] Ford, *Self and Salvation*, 165.
[33] Scharen, *Public Worship and Public Work*, 111ff.

Context

By far the most imposing building along this stretch of Auburn Avenue in Atlanta, Georgia, Big Bethel's grey granite spire rises high above the modest two-story brick buildings housing businesses and church offices on the rest of the block. As telling for the church's membership, however, one block to the east cars zoom by on the "Downtown Connector," a merger of two interstate highways that curl through downtown Atlanta. The freeway both hastened the out-migration from the neighborhood 40 years ago and now provides the ease of access important for helping members drive in to the church from such suburban Atlanta communities as Smyrna and Marietta, 15 miles to the north-east, Riverdale, 20 miles south, and Stone Mountain, a similar distance straight east. Walking up to the church Sunday morning, signs of such suburban suc-cess are present as Mercedes and Lexus automobiles pull up to park alongside the many more moderate sedans and sport utility vehicles.

As I noted after my first visit in the September 1999, the congregation on a Sunday morning is predominately African American and comprised of all ages. While the congregation is weighted slightly toward middle aged to elderly, there are a significant group of younger adults (30s and 40s) and many chil-dren. As a rule, dress is very formal with men in suits and women in dresses. A few women had large flowing and pastel colored hats. While the church has long been home to a fair share of educated professional members, its older members still remember days of working as domestics and in other low-end service jobs. Each younger generation, however, grows in the diversity of its work affiliation; the largely public-sector and self-employed work of the civil-rights generation (baby boomers) has given way to much more private-sector employment in the post-civil rights generation (generation x, or the "busters"). Rev. James Davis, the pastor at that time, had especially tried to draw this youngest group into leadership, "planting the seeds now for Big Bethel's future." One evening, he told his Steward Board that, "when we have young professions working at major corporations and IBM trusts them, when Broad-cast companies trust them, then the Church has to trust them."

The impressionistic description of the church thus far helps bring to the fore why, when asked for one word to describe the church, members often said, "diverse." In the face of changing demographics in its membership, one of the biggest challenges Big Bethel faces is being more than an historic elite church on Auburn Avenue. On the one hand, its historical status does give it a unique visibility in the city. Often referred to as "the old landmark," its cache of his-torical importance for the African American church in Atlanta is only rivaled by Ebenezer Baptist church, the home church of Rev. Martin Luther King, Jr, located just two blocks to the east. As the first Black church in Atlanta and the mother church of African Methodism in the region, Big Bethel certainly deserves its designation as a "historical landmark." Its landmark status and many distinguished members make its historical importance central. During the Fall of 1995, while worshiping across town so that Bethel could undergo a $1.6 million interior renovation, Rev. Davis said, "This is a tried and proven facility. We're committed to restoring it because it has a place in history." Featured prominently on its website, its mission statement, the church's 150th anniversary brochure, and on the sidebar of the thank you letter sent out to visitors, Bethel's historical consciousness embodies the spirit of the A. M. E. church as an institution that knows the "stony road" it has trod.

On the other hand, however, the fact that the membership lives nearly everywhere in the city *but* in the surrounding neighborhood means the church has had to foster an identity that draws its metropolitan membership downtown. As one member, a middle-aged banker who lives in southwest Atlanta, put it:

> We're an urban church and it's difficult to get people to drive all the way in here from the suburbs. They have to drive by nice big churches with easy, flat parking lots, where people can just stroll out to their cars talking on Sunday morning. It's a challenge to keep professional people coming all the way down here—there has to be a draw, there has to be excitement.

While members gave many responses to the question about what they like at Big Bethel, the "red thread" stitched through all the responses boils down to spirituality. Mr Clark, a middle-aged man and trustee at the church, remarked that at his previous church, "I was drying up." At Bethel, however, he had found a spiritual leader who would inspire and nurture him. "That's what I get here, and it goes back to Rev. Davis." Another noted: "Before Rev. Davis, this was not a tithing church, and not a Word-based church it *should* be. Before Rev. Davis, bible study was only on Wednesday night, and wasn't well attended." Typical of many members, the renewed spiritual depth in the life of the congregation is credited to Rev. Davis' dedication, energy, and vision.

Love Feast as Communion

Come along on one particular morning a few months into my time at Big Bethel. I took the subway downtown and walked the few blocks to Big Bethel through the early morning chill. As I hurried down Butler Street, I could see the looming steeple of the church bearing the famous neon blue "Jesus Saves" sign. I was headed to a "Love Feast," a traditional Methodist ritual that John Wesley learned from Moravians on his boat trip across the Atlantic some two centuries before. Big Bethel holds the "Love Feast Prayer Service" at 7.30 a.m. on the first Saturday before the first Sunday of the month, the Sunday when they celebrate Holy Communion. I walked through the side doors of the imposing granite building and down into the Fellowship hall where chairs were set up in two rows of five with a middle aisle, six rows deep for a total of 60 chairs. I found a chair near the rear and waited, noting that in front a table was set up, draped in white linen cloth covering trays.

People steadily streamed in and when the prayer service began, there were nearly 40 people, giving the space a cozy, well-filled feel. For the most part people wore sweatsuits, casual clothing such as jeans and sweaters, and only a few people wore dress clothes. The service was coordinated by the Married Couples' Ministry and consisted of an Opening Hymn (Blessed Assurance), Invocation prayer ("Dear heavenly father, we just thank you that you allowed us to gather in your house once again . . . ") a scripture reading, and then alternating prayers and hymns. Jacques, the energetic Minister of Music, was there to play the old upright piano in the corner. Each section of prayers had three parts, each prayed by a member in his or her own style, from the heart, and regarding a given topic. For instance, the various sections focused prayer on spiritual maturity and Christian discipleship, on national and local government, schools and school officials and teachers, and on the hungry and homeless everywhere. While some prayers were quiet meditations guiding us in our "supplication before the Lord," others built a crescendo plea, boldly approaching "the throne of grace."

As this pattern of prayer and hymn-singing (we always sang two verses of hymns, never more) continued, more people streamed in and before long, the place was packed with nearly 100 people, including at least ten children of varying ages. As the prayers concluded, Rev. Davis moved to the front of the room and offered some words of greeting and asked how many had not been to a love feast before, and I joined about ten people who raised their hands. To this, he and other regulars said, "Praise God!" He noted that it is important for members to keeping reaching out, to keep getting to know others. As if to make his point, he asked, "Alright, somebody raise their hand if they know every person in the room." No one did. Then he asked, "Somebody raise their hand if you see three people you don't know." Nearly the whole room raised their hands. He took a moment to have each person find three people they didn't know and introduce themselves—it was an upbeat and friendly break of about five minutes with people milling around, talking, and hugging.

We moved into a large circle and Rev. Davis asked Rev. Streator to explain what would happen next. While Rev. Davis and Wood-Powe stepped around the circle with silver communion trays, handing each person a clear plastic communion cup filled with water, Rev. Streator described the "symbolism of the water." Because of the water's transparency and purity, one is encouraged to let go of grudges that prohibit interpersonal transparency. And if one bears a grudge, before going to the altar for communion the next day during Sunday morning service, you should go to them and make amends. He stated that, "the purity of the water symbolized that 'transparency of love' that should mark the community." As if drinking the promise of purity, the others and I tipped back our glasses in unison. Then, each person was given a piece of white bread, about a third of a slice lengthwise. I thought we would then eat it in unison as we drunk the water. Actually, however, no one eats the bread. Each person gets a piece of everyone else's bread. This happens in the following way, and it is, according to Rev. Streator, "intended to build fellowship, to be a symbol of oneness."

Starting with Rev. Davis, the process began; he gave a piece of bread to the person to his left, and they took a piece of his bread, and they hugged and exchanged God's blessing by saying, "God loves you and so do I." Each subsequent person pealed off and followed Davis, forming a second inner circle moving around the outer circle until everyone had exchanged bread and greetings in a similar way with every other person in the room. I noticed in the process that people stuffed the tidbits of bread they received from others into their little communion cups and I followed suit. The greetings were sometimes strong hugs and others offered tentative pats on the shoulder, but always faces met, eyes glancing into one another, and smiles. At the end, as if in a collective "*eucharista*" for the communion we had just shared, all the cups of bread were placed upon the altar table and we sang a stirring rendition of the old gospel hymn, "Amazing Grace." Before closing, Rev. Davis introduced Mother Theodora, who stood hunched over her cane near the altar. He reported that she is one of the oldest members and, he said, "she has adopted Love Feast and comes every time, even today when she doesn't feel well." People applauded and Rev. Davis commented that this might have been the most successful love feast yet.

Woven in and through the process of the bread and greetings, I chatted with Ms. Green, a member since 1948, and a stewardess, the ministry group that hosts the "Love Feast." She noted that this ritual was new for Big Bethel, even though it had deep roots in Methodism generally. In a later interview, she credited this to Rev. Davis being "a deeply spiritual man, and a visionary." Indeed, the "Love Feast" and Rev. Davis' enthusiasm for it go to the root of this old church, and account in large part for its current revival. Such a circle ritual has deep roots in the slave "ring shouts" related to me by another old member, Mrs. King.[34] And out of the solace of such song, prayer, and common spirit, gatherings in this fellowship hall have given birth to schools, financial institutions, local civil rights actions, and many programs of social uplift for members and beyond.

---

[34] Ring Shout was a dance-like form of Christian worship done by African American slaves, mostly before the Civil War. It involves moving in a counterclockwise circle, singing, clapping, stomping, and beating on the floor rhythmically with a stick or broom. See Art Rosenbaum, *Shout Because You're Free: The African American Ring Shout Tradition in Coastal Georgia* (Athens: The University of Georgia Press, 1995).

Yet, the storied history of first Black church in the city could not alone keep the church vibrant and engaged today. A downtown church whose membership left the neighborhood decades ago faces a peculiar problem of attracting membership and building community. The Love Feast symbolically connects to the purity and unity represented in Holy Communion to be solemnly enacted the next morning. But here as Rev. Davis well knew our very bodies enacted communion, facing each other "in Christ" and "as Christ." As he noted at the minister's meeting held directly after the Love Feast, "we need to work on fellowship, for commitments to do don't *start* with doing–they start with family. We need to put all our commitments down, take time to become brothers and sisters, and then together go and do." The Love Feast is also, however, about doing. Fellowship serves the agenda of "kingdom building." As Rev. Davis often says in his charge to the neophyte Christians who answer the "Invitation to Discipleship" after the sermon on Sunday morning, "Salvation is not a feeling, it's faith; now believe and live like a saved person ought." The church that proclaims "Jesus Saves," through programs that reach all over the city and beyond, finds its taproot in becoming a fellowship of disciples, gathered to feast on love given in abundance in order to become love given for others.

Theology *from* the Body

In my research I was not actually after the Eucharistic self, or worshipping self, but the congregation as "particular case of the possible" in relation to the world, a variety of distinct lives, a living tradition all of which gives way to a complexity of multiple formations.[35] I was able to gain proximity to these congregational worlds and the worshipping selves they produce through a kind of ethnographic apprenticeship, through placing myself in the "vortex of action in order to acquire, through practice, in real time, the dispositions of the [worshipper] with the aim of elucidating the magnetism proper to the [doxological] cosmos."[36] I have come to see in retrospect, through the ethnographic writing of Loïc Wacquant on the world of boxing,[37] what he was doing in his research that went beyond typical "participant observation." It was less "observation" and more a throwing oneself into the life of the congregation as far as was possible, seeking as full a "participant" role as possible.

---

[35] Gaston Bachelard, *Le Nouvel Esprit Scientifque* (Paris: PUF, 1949), 58; see also Pierre Bourdieu and Loïc J. D. Wacquant, *An Invitation to Reflexive Sociology* (Chicago: University of Chicago Press, 1992), 75.

[36] Loïc Wacquant, "Habitus as Topic and Tool: Reflections on becoming a prizefighter," in *Ethnographies Revisited: Constructing Theory in the Field*, William Shaffir, Antony Puddephatt, and Steven Kleinknecht (eds) (New York: Routledge, 2009).

[37] Wacquant, *Body and Soul*.

Many fieldworkers in practical theology speak of their research position as "participant observation." But further specification might help us to be very clear about what ethnographers are doing and how it is that the body does or does not play a significant role as a source of data in the research process. For example, James Stevens in his book on charismatic churches in England notes that his 1987–91 tenure as curate at St. John the Evangelist in Welling, Kent allowed him to experience elements of a Vineyard charismatic culture that had been set in motion some years prior to his coming to the parish. This pastoral experience there, he says, accounted for the "initial stage" of research giving him "in-depth example of" his research topic and preparing him for the main period of research, 1993–95. At this latter stage, he writes, "I was simply re-entering the research field in which I had already, unintentionally, completed three and a half years of ethnography."[38] While of course being a priest in a charismatic congregation ought to give one some aid in subsequent research on charismatic congregations, it is dangerously confusing to retroactively describe a pastoral tenure as "ethnographic" research.

When Stevens does describe his research role proper, he offers four positions within the range of options for participant observation:

a. The "complete participant"—sustained participation, observation concealed
b. The "participant-as-observer"—sustained participation, observation acknowledged
c. The "observer-as-participant"—contact is brief, formal, observation acknowledged
d. The "complete observer"—eavesdropping, little contact with informants' views

His study in six case studies of churches was brief, and hosts regarded him as one who had come to "look at" their worship, so his work fits closest to the "observer-as-participant" model. He reports "following what was expected of congregational participation in its various forms: standing, sitting, kneeling, singing, greeting, and receiving the sacrament." How was his participation different? He writes, "Whilst others were worshipping, and 'letting themselves go' in singing and acts of devotion, I was working, maintaining an analytical frame of mind that was anathema to the situational ethos."[39]

Wacquant offers another possibility, one that makes sense of my attempt to learn "from the body" and seems near to what Mary McClintock Fulkerson

---

[38] James H. S. Stevens, *Worship in the Spirit: Charismatic Worship in the Church of England, Studies in Evangelical History and Thought* (Carlisle and Waynesboro: Paternoster Press, 2002), 39–40.

[39] Stevens, *Worship in the Spirit*, 42.

engaged in as well during her two and a half years at Good Samaritan. This is to push the logic of participant observation to the point where it becomes inverted and turns into observant participation. The typical warning, and one Bourdieu gave to Wacquant during his immersion at Chicago's Woodlawn Boxing Club, is "don't go native." Wacquant's position, in turn, is to "say 'go native' but 'go native armed,' that is, equipped with your theoretical and methodological tools, the full store of problematics inherited from your discipline, with your capacity for reflexivity and analysis."[40] The idea, to revise Stevens' description, is to indeed enter into the worshipping, to "let oneself go" in the singing and acts of devotion and exactly in and through those experiences attend to the ways the apprenticeship "enables us to pry into practice in the making and to realize that the ordinary knowledge that makes us competent actors is an incarnate, sensuous, situated 'knowing-how-to' that operates beneath the controls of discursive awareness and propositional reasoning."[41]

The point is, as Wacquant puts it, that meaning-making in such bodily worlds as the boxing gym and the worshipping congregation "is not a mental affair liable to an intellectualist reading, as the hermeneutic tradition, trapped in the scriptural metaphor of social action as text, would have us believe."[42] A carnal sociology, and, we want to suggest, a carnal theology, that

> seeks to situate itself not outside or above practice but at its "point of production" requires that we immerse ourselves as deeply and as durably as possible into the cosmos under examination; that we submit ourselves to its specific temporality and contingencies; that we acquire the embodied dispositions it demands and nurtures, so that we may grasp it via the prethetic understanding that defines the native relation to the world—not as one world among many but as "home."[43]

As I noted earlier, early on in my training and career I was critical of theology in its scholastic forms because of its relative lack of connection to lived experience in particular communities and persons. But in and through the careful attending ethnographic practice required I slowly gained a sense that this was constitutive of a way of doing theology that both allowed me to merge theology and social science (what Nick Healy is after in commending "ecclesiological ethnography"[44]), and to articulate the substance of such theology as an emerging form of formal or secondary theology but much more immediately responsible to the practical contexts of life and faith from which it spoke.

---

[40] Wacquant, "Habitus as Topic and Tool," 7.
[41] Wacquant, "Carnal Connections," 466.
[42] Ibid.
[43] Ibid.
[44] Healy, *Church, Word and the Christian Life*, 174.

A full accounting of what ethnography as theology would look like is the task of this whole volume, and beyond it, the work of those who share its aims and practices. However, perhaps we might briefly conclude by returning to David Ford's concluding frame for "a Eucharistic self" in which he hopes for "a full anthropological study of Eucharistic practice, theologically informed." To do such would, he argues, embody an approach that takes with utter seriousness the "radical singularity of the incarnation" as a theological support for claiming the Christian faith as true to itself "only in becoming freshly embodied in different contexts."[45]

Presumably, the "love feast" at Big Bethel AME offers such "fresh embodiment" of the church. In my apprenticeship amongst them, however, he not only learned that the rite of the Eucharist is not celebrated—or even known in those terms—but that the ritual of the love feast enacted the day prior to communion carries their practice of holy communion in the sense that communion is enacted through the love feast in the laborious process of sharing oneself with another, one by one, as thread stitches cloth, offering and receiving greetings, prayer, confession, reconciliation, singing, cups of water, broken bread, and thanksgiving.

Conclusion

We have come a long way toward making sense of the shape and character of the "turn to ethnography" in this chapter, partly through more tentative general reflections and through the risk of telling a particular tale of formation in scholarly disciplines. While each person's trajectory has its distinctive elements, there are cultural and intellectual currents that have prevailed over the last decade that have helped bring ethnography to the fore. In summary, we wish to simply state those more clearly. First of all it is necessary to situate the rise of ethnography as a means for doing theology and ethics within the larger rise of the study of culture as a major grounding discourse for theology. Second, it is a way for theology to have broader relevance within the academy (it is tied to the social sciences and broadly practiced—in the humanities and professional schools as well as social science). Yet that very relevance is also clearly compelling to the practical interests of ordinary people and the organizations and communities they inhabit.

Ethnography is also an effective tool for doing certain kinds of work and it bears noting how it does this. Historically, as we describe in the first chapter, ethnography has tended to be a way to understand a people, community or culture "other" than one's own. While this has often meant some exotic locale,

<hr />

[45] Ford, *Self and Salvation*, 144.

it can mean a nearby locale with which one is not familiar (as in Fulkerson's Good Samaritan or Big Bethel). On the other hand, the work of Paul Rabinow among others has shown how ethnography might be used to offer an "untimely" and therefore rich and suggestive view of a familiar site.[46] Rabinow has done this with science laboratories both in the United States and in France. Later in this volume, Jeffery Tribble follows this trajectory of ethnography, more deeply exploring pastoral leadership in his own denomination. Finally, ethnography—in part because of its "untimeliness"—can offer a way to test out the truth of particular claims, something for example that I have done with theological ethicists claiming some simplistic unidirectional formation of the self through ritual participation. From the perspective of one's office, the idea that "worship forms Christians" has an attractive self-evidence that serves certain claims about the distinctiveness of Christian identity and witness (as Kathryn Tanner pointed out above). Ethnography, however, takes time to show the complexity of how such formation happens, when and how it works, and the various ways such a view is complicated by the formative power of participation in other institutions humans inhabit). We pick up this last point in the next chapter as a weak spot in some of the critiques of the use of ethnography and social science generally in theology and ethics. To that discussion we now turn.

[46] Rabinow and Marcus, *Designs for an Anthropology of the Contemporary*, 59ff.

Chapter 3

Critiques of the Use of Social Science in Theology and Ethics

Thus far, we've outlined an understanding of ethnography and described some of the terrain involved in the turn to ethnography in theology and ethics. It is clear by this point that we believe ethnography ought to be a means of doing theology. We've explained what we mean by ethnography as "writing culture" and that we assume it includes some level of direct, qualitative observation and participation *in situ* using a combination of practical disciplined methods of attending as well as theoretical frames and insights. Yet even as ethnography has risen in visibility among theologians and ethicists, its use—as part of a whole range of social science methods and theories—has come under strong critique.

In order to describe and evaluate this critique, the following chapter takes stock of debates set in motion by John Milbank's influential 1990 book, *Theology and Social Theory*, and perhaps equally as influential, by Stanley Hauerwas in a series of books and articles. While attempting to take their critiques seriously, we argue that by the logic of Milbank and Hauerwas' own positions, ethnography provides the most robust response to the sorts of work they themselves argue is needed to understand the church and the daily lives of Christians in the world.

The chapter proceeds by way first of questioning Milbank and then Hauerwas regarding their critiques of the use of social science in theology. Each has distinctive points yet they have learned from one another and considerable connection exists between their respective positions. Secondly, we answer these critiques by examining Robin Gill's argument for, and use of, social science in theological ethics but find his dependence on broad social survey method limited. Then we engage theologians Nicholas Adams and Charles Elliott who argue for the use of ethnography in theology. Such a position offers the most robust response to Milbank and Hauerwas, opening the way for us to then move to ethnography as Christian theology and ethics.

Questioning Milbank

John Milbank's *Theology and Social Theory* dazzles most scholars with its immense learning and broad-ranging discussions in contemporary social theory.[1] He soundly trounces theological dependence on social science, describing this phenomenon of modern theology with the strong and memorable term "policing the sublime."[2] He means by this that through generating its own theory of society, sociology ensures that "religion is kept, conceptually, at the margins—both denied influence, and yet acclaimed for its transcendent purity."[3] The standpoint from which social science positions and describes the phenomena of religion, Milbank argues, is not objective. It is, rather, a "positivist theology" that continually rediscovers the "religious" as one aspect of society.[4] Although his book is long, and beyond adequate summary here, as Fergus Kerr has put it, its argument is "simplicity itself": there is no need, as has become commonplace, to bring social theory and theology together, for social theory is already theology, and theology already a social theory.[5] As theology, Milbank shows, modern social theory tends to colonize and compartmentalize religion, effectively turning it into spirituality.

Kerr, whose summary of Milbank's complicated book received approval of the author himself, recommends a reading strategy that begins with the last chapter. Here, under the title "The Other City: Theology as Social Science," Milbank's Augustinian intentions become obvious. In particular, he wants to argue for theology itself as a social science, an aid and guide for the "inhabitants of the *alterna civitas*, on a pilgrimage through this temporary world." When theologians depend on particular analysis of social scientists, in doing so they import functional explanations of events and actions that effectively bracket the agency of God (in Milbank's classical framing, "efficient" rather than "final" causes).[6] As Milbank puts it, theology has

> frequently sought to borrow from elsewhere a fundamental account of society or history, and then to see what theological insights will cohere with it. But it has been shown that no such fundamental account, in the sense of something neutral, rational and universal, is really available. It is theology

---

[1] John Milbank, *Theology and Social Theory: Beyond Secular Reason* (Cambridge: Blackwell, 1990); by way of response, see the various review articles and Milbank's response in the special issue of *New Blackfriars* 73 (June 1992).

[2] See Milbank, *Theology and Social Theory*, 101ff.

[3] Ibid., 109.

[4] Ibid., 140.

[5] Fergus Kerr, "Simplicity Itself: Milbank's Thesis," in *New Blackfriars* 73 (June 1992), 306–10.

[6] Michael J. Baxter, C.S.C. shows how this point is lost on some who critique Milbank's basic thesis in "Whose Theology? Which Sociology? A Response to John Coleman," in *Theology and the Social Sciences*, Michael H. Barnes (ed.) (Maryknoll: Orbis, 2001), 34–42.

itself that will have to provide its own account of the final causes at work in human history, on the basis of its own particular and historically specific faith.[7]

Why? Because Christian social theory derives from and has as its task the explication of a Christian mode of action, a Christian practice, and thus such a theory of this "other city" must also be ecclesiology. In this sense, then, ecclesiology is also "sociology." But, Milbank contends, "This possibility only becomes available if ecclesiology is rigorously concerned with the actual genesis of real historical churches, not simply with the imagination of an ecclesial ideal."[8]

Rowan Williams picks up Milbank's claim that a "Christian sociology" must "articulate Christian difference" as a description of society grounded in its own distinct society, the church. As Williams argues, Milbank positions the church against (especially) the Roman sacralization of dominion and the Jewish commitment to law as the defining good, Williams suggests that Milbank is "fusing historical narrative with "essentialist," diagrammatic accounts of ideological options."[9] Williams, in other words, worries that Milbank's desire to have a Christian meta-narrative defining of the present church's difference obscures in his telling the ways in which this difference was achieved through crisis and conflict. Thus, on Williams' judgment, "the risk Milbank's exposition runs is, paradoxically, of slipping into a picture of history as the battlefield of ideal types."[10]

While oblique, in his response Milbank seems to accept Williams' critique. While he first notes that the place where he finds the church most clearly is not a "place" at all, nor an identity achieved through crisis and conflict. Rather, the church is a gift "given, superabundantly, in the breaking of the bread by the risen Lord, which assembles the harmony of the peoples then and at every subsequent Eucharist."[11] Yet, argues Milbank, despite no intention to make his "formal" descriptions exhaustive, he also sees an important role for "judicious narratives of ecclesial happenings which would alone indicate the shape of the Church that we desire." And the need for this, he sees, is sharpened by the tension between his formal and ideal descriptions of the Church and his own "rather minimal attempts at 'judicious narrative.' "[12]

Among the challenges emerging from substantial engagement with Milbank's work is how one might learn from and incorporate aspects of sociology into the

---

[7] Milbank, *Theology and Social Theory*, 380.
[8] Ibid., 380.
[9] Rowan Williams, "Saving Time: Thoughts on Practice, Patience, and Vision," *New Blackfriars* 73, 319–26.
[10] Ibid., 321.
[11] John Milbank, "Enclaves, or Where is the Church?" in *New Blackfriars* 73 (June 1992), 341–52.
[12] Ibid., 343.

work of theology so as to achieve more robust examples of wise stories of Christian life and community. Our arguments in this volume propose, in response, that ethnography can be drawn upon as a fairly "theory-free" practice of sociology able to incorporate the full range of the theological imagination in taking stock of the world's life. Yet our extension of Milbank in this way seems rather of the sort one would call not throwing out the baby with the bath water. Generations of social science researchers have learned practices of research—including ethnography and its attendant methods—that ought to aid the work of theologians attending to the world. Similar mild critique and amendment emerge from dialogue with another theologian who is tempted to throw out the social science baby with the bathwater: Stanley Hauerwas.

Questioning Hauerwas

Hauerwas' understanding of the church offers another angle for critically examining the use of social science by theologians and ethicists—and as part of that discipline, the practice of ethnography. Hauerwas is known for a strong claim that the church's first task is to live the truth of its identity in God through Christ, thus helping the world to know it is the world.[13] His hope and vision for the church is that it be a counter-society, a community living the story of Jesus. Such a community is "God's gesture on behalf of the world to create a space and time in which we might have a foretaste of the Kingdom."[14] The world can, in a sense, see how it really ought to be through its encounter with how the church really is.

Moreover, for Hauerwas, if the church has as its first task to make the world the world by being its contrast, the church has as its essence a social and political task.[15] Worship and the things that constitute it such as prayer, preaching, baptism and the Eucharist, among others, fold Christians into God's life as Christ's body. By one's participation in the body of Christ, one's life includes baptism and Eucharist, but also "immersion in the daily practices of the Christian church: prayer, worship, admonition, feeding the hungry, caring for the sick, etc." Hauerwas concludes, "By these we are transformed over time to participate in God's life. So we become full members in a city ordered to peace."[16] This participation in the body is a political reality produced and maintained through sacraments as political rituals. Sacraments, writes Hauerwas, "are not

[13] Stanley Hauerwas, *Christian Existence Today: Essays on Church, World, and Living in Between* (Durham: The Labyrinth Press, 1988), 102.

[14] Ibid., 106.

[15] Stanley Hauerwas, *In Good Company: The Church as Polis* (Notre Dame: University of Notre Dame Press, 1995), 249, n12.

[16] Stanley Hauerwas and Charles Pinches, *Christians among the Virtues: Theological Conversations with Ancient and Modern Ethics* (Notre Dame: University of Notre Dame Press, 1997), 69.

just 'religious things' that Christian people do. They are the essential rituals of our politics."[17] Therefore, the "liturgy is not a motive for social action, it is not a cause to effect. Liturgy *is* social action."[18] The church in Hauerwas' vision is an alternative public, a society constituted by its own distinct practices, goods, and modes of life.[19]

In defending his view of liturgy *as* social action against the charge that such churches are idealized, and as such, not actually able to engage in meaningful ways in public life, Hauerwas takes on the task of attempting a careful description and interpretation of the significance of an administrative board meeting at his church at that time, Broadway United Methodist, in Notre Dame, Indiana. In so doing, he avoids speaking only about an ideal church. But rather than work from what he understands to be an "objective" sociological perspective, he argues that his "telling of the story" is normative in intent; it serves "not just as an example but as an argument for how Christian ethics ought to be done."[20] Such a telling is informed by, and attempts to test, his constructive theological and ethical positions. At stake was whether in fact his understanding that liturgy *is* social action could escape the charge that it merely an ideal, and an ideal that counsels withdrawal from the world rather than engagement in it.[21]

Through the example of his congregation, Hauerwas aims both to show that actual churches do act the way he thinks the church "should" and that the critiques miss the sort of "responsibility for the world" his view of liturgy *as* social action implies. Hauerwas describes a board meeting where two issues—repairing the leaking roof and moving to weekly Eucharist—took center stage in discussions. Given the impoverished neighborhood surrounding the church, Hauerwas interprets the commitment of large sums of money for roof repair as a theological-ethical stance to be a witness of God's presence in and for that neighborhood. Weekly Eucharist, Hauerwas argues, subsequently led the congregation to propose not a soup kitchen for the needy, but rather an after-church lunch shared among the members and all who wanted to come from the neighborhood. Again, this action held powerful symbolic and actual power for Hauerwas in that it embodied the church's calling to be a witness to the kingdom come near in Jesus Christ, and a concrete symbol to the neighborhood that all was not lost. While their first concern was not city politics, Hauerwas notes, their commitment to be a presence in the neighborhood included concern "about what was happening in the politics of the city."[22]

---

[17] Hauerwas, *The Peaceable Kingdom: A Primer in Christian Ethics* (Notre Dame: University of Notre Dame Press, 1983), 108.

[18] Hauerwas, *Christian Existence Today*, 107. A nearly identical phrase is found in *The Peaceable Kingdom*, 108.

[19] Hauerwas, *In Good Company*, 6–8.

[20] Hauerwas, *Christian Existence Today*, 113.

[21] See Whitmore, "Crossing the Road," 273–94.

[22] Ibid., 122.

Hauerwas' empirical analysis of the church permitted him to develop a theological ethic that helps people "appreciate the significance of their worship." In Broadway, he

> saw a congregation formed and disciplined by the liturgy that made possible an extraordinary social witness. That congregation's life belies distinctions between theology and liturgy, ethics and liturgy. The meal they prepare every Sunday for the neighborhood is not the way they express their social ethical commitments in distinction from their liturgical life. Rather, the meal they prepare and liturgical life are for them parts of a single story. The theological task is first and foremost to help us and them understand why that is the case.[23]

Hauerwas wants his description to take up the ordinary experiences of the congregation, but told with their significance. Thus, his theological task begins by the admission that:

> we have not paid enough attention to how difficult it is to understand the common things we do as Christians: pray, baptize, eat meals, rejoice at the birth of a child, grieve at illness and death, re-roof church buildings, and so on. If we cannot describe theologically the significance of these activities, we will distort what we do by having to resort to descriptions and explanations all too readily provided by our culture.[24]

What our culture provides us, he says, are social scientific accounts of the life of congregations. He does not mean to "deny the value of sociological, psychological, and general social-scientific accounts of the life of congregations." Yet, he continues, "the issue is the uncritical use of the social-scientific paradigms which often, if applied rigorously and consistently, methodologically preclude the theological claims necessary for the church's intelligibility."[25] Harkening back to Milbank's claims that social-scientific paradigms limit themselves to efficient causes, Hauerwas means the church must draw on final causes, especially THE final cause, God, in order to make any proper sense of itself. In short, Hauerwas fears that in the translation of theological claims to publically intelligible claims, the church implicitly takes for itself the role of national handmaiden, blessing and supporting the secular civil order.

Yet, we claim that Hauerwas' rejection of social science limits his work in two ways. First, Hauerwas defeats his own aim of grounded theological work because he does not go far enough, carefully enough, in his attending to congregational life. For example, Hauerwas emphasizes the importance of the

---

[23] Ibid., 125.
[24] Ibid., 123–4.
[25] Ibid., 130n.

liturgical practices of congregations generally, as well as how important Eucharistic practices were at Broadway, but does not offer any description of those practices. He asserts that such practices were done and meditates on their theological meaning at length. This approach seems at best to minimally fulfill his own call to understand everyday practices of congregations, practices that are at once theological, liturgical, and ethical, but maybe also utilitarian and self-serving, shallow, or even explicitly unjust in one way or another.[26] Our advocacy of a critical, yet empathetic ethnographic inquiry does not repeat the external and causal critiques, nor the "spiritualization" of the church that worries Hauerwas, but instead calls for critical work that can understand and articulate the many practices located in various spheres of social life formative of church members, including but clearly beyond the church.

Second, it follows that Hauerwas' polemically driven theological framework, "liturgy as ethics," does not include a view of culture nuanced enough to capture the significance of cultural pluralism forming contemporary Christians and their congregations. Whereas Hauerwas' rhetoric draws a simple church–world distinction necessary for discussing a Christian culture and its practices contrasted to the world and its practices, actual modern people, including Hauerwas, have commitments to work, family, citizenship, and leisure, in addition to religion. All of these are legitimate commitments for contemporary Christians, commitments Kathryn Tanner and Mary McClintock Fulkerson, among others, frame much more adequately in terms of the problem of complexity in identity formation. This problem cannot be ignored, as Hauerwas does, because American society, like all societies that have passed through the painful process of modernization, is constituted by differentiated yet interrelated and interconnected spheres of activity, each with potentially significant tensions with theological commitments. While critical use of sociology is not the only way to understand such complicated interconnections in the Christian moral life, it is one viable and sophisticated way to accomplish such a view. While the next two sections begin to pay down on this claim about the potential role of social science, and especially ethnography, the whole volume intends this as well.

Answering Milbank and Hauerwas: Robin Gill

Robin Gill, in a powerfully argued book titled *Churchgoing and Christian Ethics*, critiques Milbank along the lines indicated by Rowan Williams. Gill places

---

[26] Susan A. Ross develops these issues in relation to the question of women religious who are required to have a priest, who is always a man and thereby an outsider to their community, come to preside at celebrations that include the Eucharist. See her "Like a Fish without a Bicycle?" in *America* 181/17 (November 17, 1999), 10–13; "Liturgy and Ethics: Feminist Perspectives," in *Annual of the Society of Christian Ethics* 20, (2000), 263–74.

Milbank within the broad revival of virtue ethics begun by Alasdair MacIntyre and Stanley Hauerwas that sees theology's task not as deducing from ideas a set of actions to follow, but reflection upon a Christian mode of action, a Christian practice that forms an alternative society. Gill takes a first appreciative step with such theologians, for he fundamentally works out of a virtue ethics model as well. Yet, as Gill maps out the arguments of Milbank and Hauerwas, he balks at what he perceives as their strong rhetorical position that the church is the sole repository of Christian virtues and that the church exists as a strong contrast society over against the world. The problem is, Gill notes, that Milbank and Hauerwas speak mainly of an idealized church, but especially Hauerwas, by his investment in a character ethics approach, depends on the actual church for schooling Christians who will be the citizens of this alternative society constituted by a "given" Eucharistic peace.[27]

The difficulty in such an argument, depending on an idealized understanding of the church, Gill argues, is that actual church people look rather a lot like everybody else! He makes the argument that Hauerwas' and Milbank's claims of Christian culture and practices forming a distinctive alternative social life are quite testable. Along the way, he dismisses sociologists who consider churchgoing as an epiphenomenon, instead arguing for a "cultural theory" which posits that churchgoing and especially communal worship shape and reinforce Christian beliefs and behavior. Thus, he argues that a decline in churchgoing should precede declines in Christian belief and behavior, while active churchgoing should evidence increases in Christian belief and behavior.

The center of Gill's argument, chapters 4 through 7, consists of detailed statistical analyses of the annual British Household Panel Survey that includes questions about churchgoing as well as a variety of beliefs and behaviors. Gill's original analysis of this survey data focuses on three general areas–indicators of Christian beliefs (faith), indicators of seeing life as worthwhile (hope), and indicators of altruism (love). He concludes that churchgoing is strongly correlated with certain values and virtues, beliefs and behaviors, not unique to churchgoers but more distinctive of them than of non-churchgoers.

Gill then asks the obvious question: how does churchgoing have such an influence? If, as Gill argues, a cultural theory of churchgoing states that people learn these beliefs and virtues in church, how is this so? By way of an answer, Gill engages in a long discussion of various worship practices central to traditional Protestant (Presbyterian, Anglican) and Roman Catholic churches. These, he argues, are the constitutive practices of "the distinctive culture of churchgoing and act as crucial carriers of Christian identity."[28] He goes to

27. Robin Gill, *Churchgoing and Christian Ethics*, New Studies in Christian Ethics 15 (New York: Cambridge University Press, 1999), 13–30.

28. Gill, *Churchgoing and Christian Ethics*, 226.

great lengths to show that they together contain the values his survey analysis found more strongly present in churchgoing people. He concludes:

> Significant traces of faith, hope, and love have been detected amongst those most exposed to the culture of churchgoing. The staple ingredients of this culture—hymns, sermons, intercessions, public confessions and, above all, readings of Scripture and celebrations of the Eucharist—all act as carriers of this distinctive culture. Together they continue to shape lives—however imperfectly—of faithful worshipers.[29]

In this conclusion, Gill makes clear resonance with a character ethics approach—by going to church and engaging its practices, one's habits and thus character is formed.

It is ironic, however, that in trying to escape claims for an idealized church, Gill ends up with another sort of idealized church—his churchgoers don't go to any actual church but are generic Christians who go to generic churches. Depending on survey data, Gill individualizes the question of churchgoing and then makes a pseudo-communal claim about churchgoing itself, aside from the character of the particular local church. Because his measures of Christian belief and behavior are so general (faith, hope, love), this fact does not matter as much as it could. Still, the fact that he brushes over denominational, cultural, racial, and other differences within and among churches limits the real resonance his churchgoers can have for the reader, and limits the clarity his analysis has regarding exactly how parishes have such formative effects.

Such preference for a generic-real church may be understandable given his dependence on survey data yet it feeds a second problem that Gill shares generally with those working in the Aristotelian tradition of virtue ethics: his conclusions still depend on a "simple" cultural view of church and world as distinct.[30] Theologically speaking, such a distinction can be attractive. But without a means to directly account for cultural pluralism and the complicated, bifurcated social-structural worlds shaped by and shaping Christian people and their communities, one may miss the ways real communities of faith are Christian in ways that tightly interrelate with what I refer to as their congregational "communal identity." Without this more complex understanding of culture and community, it is difficult to account for the identity "given"

---

[29] Gill, *Churchgoing and Christian Ethics*, 229.

[30] And they have good Augustinian and Pauline reasons for doing so (to a point). But too strong a version of this division opens one to the charges Aidan Nichols puts to Milbank ("hermeticism") and James Gustafson puts to Hauerwas ("sectarian"). See Aidan Nichols, "Non Tali Auxilio: John Milbank's Suasion to Orthodoxy," in *New Blackfriars* 73 (June 1992), 326–32; James Gustafson, "The Sectarian Temptation: Reflections on Theology, the Church, and the University," in *Catholic Theological Society of America Proceedings* 40 (1985), 83–94.

through eucharistic participation, never "generic" but always particularly incarnate within the life of this or that Christian community.

Answering Milbank and Hauerwas: Adams and Elliott

To be fair, Robin Gill knows that more is required; his deep and substantial work in sociology has taught him exactly the limitations of survey research. Thus, he writes "there is indeed something very crude about reducing beliefs and moral attitudes to such collectable and measurable forms."[31] In the words of Steven Tipton, the problem with survey research is that "opinions are like noses, in short, or at length, if you will: everyone has one and everybody's is a little different. All you can do is count them up in polls and check for the sociological equivalent of family resemblances."[32] Seeing this problem, Gill concludes his book calling for "more qualitative research to be done on local congregations and parishes."[33]

This is not an unproblematic call, however, especially given how Hauerwas has cautioned against the hidden agendas disguised within apparently neutral description. According to Hauerwas, here giving a disclaimer before attempting his own description of his church in North Carolina, "'description' is, of course, anything but innocent. The methodological assumptions that often shape the 'sociology' governing such descriptions reproduce the kind of 'spiritualization' of the church for which I am trying to provide an alternative."[34] In lieu of whatever he thinks a sociological description might be, Hauerwas offers his own "naïve" description, an odd adjective for an approach equally freighted with assumptions as any sociological approach would bring.[35]

Milbank, by way of a corrective of his own work, calls for "supplementation by judicious narratives of ecclesial happenings." In other words, prudence in the use of description; I take it, he intends something like what Nicholas Adams and Charles Elliott have recently called for in their programmatic article "Ethnography is Dogmatics."[36] By merging Barth's dictum that ethics is dogmatics and Michel Foucault's understanding that ethics is ethnography, they propose an approach recommending "that theologians take ethnographic description at least as seriously as dogmatics: indeed, the latter (if it concerns 'the real') is,

---

[31] Gill, *Churchgoing and Christian Ethics*, 43.
[32] Steven Tipton, "A Response: Moral Languages and the Good Society," in *Soundings* 69 (1986), 165–80.
[33] Tipton, "A Response," 262.
[34] Stanley Hauerwas, *Sanctify Them in Truth* (Nashville: Abingdon, 1998), 160.
[35] Ibid.
[36] Nicholas Adams and Charles Elliott, "Ethnography is Dogmatics: Making Description Central to Systematic Theology," in *Scottish Journal of Theology* 53 (Autumn 2000), 339–64.

and should be, the slave of the former."[37] Hardly objective or neutral observers, they simply argue a full metaphysically shaped eye is all anyone has to look with, and for a theologian, theism simply implies a God-shaped eye.

Therefore, Adams and Elliott provocatively suggest ethnography as dogmatics ought to be descriptive and eschatological; that is, it ought to teach Christians how to see the world as it is, and in the light of how it shall be. While strongly suggesting that theologians learn from social anthropology and sociology about the skills of ethnography, they do not reduce theology to social anthropology. Adams' and Elliott's ethnographic work in Northern India portrays "powerless people" who nevertheless find "the capacity to change radically" the circumstances of their lives. In one case, a forest-dwelling community faced massive deforestation by aggressive logging companies. Another details the conflict between the World Bank and local communities over the construction of a huge dam. The resistances offered in each case are described in great detail, and are summarized as "miracles," examples of the escatological exultation promised for the humble and meek. In arguing thus, they break the disciplinary divide, calling for theologians to be better students of the real exactly as they see it: both now and not yet. Such a call offers another approach to the dilemma of narrative theology and its too ideal portrayal of the church.

Ethnography, although dominated by the domain of anthropology and sociology today, in fact has been and should be a skill available to the theologian as theologian. What, after all, was Tertullian up to in his classic critique of the Roman games in *Spectacles*? It was ethnography as ecclesiology, in the sense that he intended it for use in baptismal catechesis. Such descriptive work shows the world as it is and as it should be. The work of those contributing to this volume offer examples to and a challenge for theological work that would speak of the "real" church, and not simply a formal or ideal one.

"Judicious narratives," it seems to us, are prudent or wise exactly here: that they show us who we are just now as *this or that part* of the one, holy, catholic, and apostolic church, so that we know what we must do to be faithful to that identity. In such work, ethnography is the right sized tool to build a complex enough understanding of culture and community to account for the sorts of hybrid identities and complex communities actually lived out today. In the following chapter, we seek to more carefully articulate theological justifications for the disciplined practice of ethnographic inquiry.

---

[37] Adams and Elliott, "Ethnography is Dogmatics," 363.

Chapter 4

Theological Justifications for Turning to Ethnography

Do You Belong Here?

In 1929, Virginia Woolf dared to carve out a place for women—both as writers of and central characters in—fiction.[1] Defying a crushing wall of patriarchal publishing houses and assumptions about what constituted "good literature," Woolf pursued her creative impulses. And in so doing, she opened numerous vocational rooms in which subsequent generations of women could work and publish. Fast-forward 50 years to 1987: Gloria Anzaldúa publishes a rich exploration of the multilayered (geographical, spiritual, cultural, linguistic, sexual, racial) borderlands she experienced as a woman who grew up on Texas-U.S. Southwest/Mexican border. In evocative language, Anzaldúa explores how she (along with thousands of Mexicans and Mexican-Americans) managed to create a home and identity that straddled numerous boundaries simultaneously. We share her sense that one's home (culturally, academically, religiously, etc.) is not found one side of the border or the other. Rather, it is found at the creative, albeit uncomfortable, place of the intersection itself—where differing disciplines, ways of knowing and being come together—in Anzaldúa's words, on a "thin edge of barbwire."[2]

Undeniably, aspects of the life stories of both Woolf and Anzaldúa speak to the personal costs of questioning and chipping away at culturally fortified academic and disciplinary boundaries. Living and working on such a sharp,

---

[1] Virginia Woolf, *A Room of One's Own* (Orlando: Harcourt, 1929).

[2] Gloria Anzaldúa, *Borderlands La Frontera: A New Mestiza* (San Francisco: Aunt Lute Books, 1987), 13. Earlier in the Preface, she elaborates:

> The actual physical borderland that I'm dealing with in this book is the Texas-U.S. Southwest/Mexican border. The psychological borderlands, the sexual borderlands, and the spiritual borderlands are not particular to the Southwest. In fact, the Borderlands are physically present whenever two or more cultures edge each other, where people of different races occupy the same territory, where under, lower, middle, and upper classes touch, where the space between two individuals shrinks with intimacy.

toothy edge is precarious and inherently involves multiple risks. One's professional identity can be called into question—by others and by one's own self doubts. It is possible to be overwhelmed by the complexity of the work and to get stuck indefinitely. Sometimes researchers are not emotionally or intellectually prepared for what they hear or discover and have no way of knowing how to respond. Then, even when the work is complete, writing in unconventional ways or with new methods does not necessarily lead to academic milestones such as a Ph.D., a first job, or promotion and tenure.

In terms of the carrying out ethnographic research, as Scharen reveals in Chapter 2, it is a risk to go where "one does not belong"—is an outsider and does not know exactly what to do, what to ask, or even how to "be" in the space. Anyone who has done ethnographic work knows of the awkwardness felt in one's bones when it is painfully apparent how much the researcher "sticks out"—in terms of the various, often simultaneous privileges a researcher may embody (e.g. race, education, gender, socioeconomic status, nationality, religion). On top of these tenuous inequalities, ethnographers often stumble as they grope to learn about the distinct contexts and lives of others.

In fact, it may well be that the missteps are needed in order for nuanced learning to happen. Without them, the researcher may not realize sufficiently that s/he did not know all the right questions and could not guess the answers at the outset. Making gaffes, fumbling, looking silly—even embarrassing one's self—can lead to crucial epiphanies for researchers in that previously subconscious assumptions come to the surface for critical reflection. Indeed, such instances often teach, or at least remind, academics what it means to be human.

Yet, for as awkward as it can be to feel out of place, the dangers associated with this work go deeper to extend into the far more serious concerns of invading the lives of others. It can be all too easy to take what we hear/learn for selfish gain; to manipulate the stories and insights so that they fit into the researcher's predetermined frames; to violate the privacy and the integrity of others by treating what they offer the research as something cheap rather than as sacred. In short, ethnographers are often asked—*should* be asked—and need to ask themselves if they belong where they are. Do they have a good enough reason to impose upon the lives of others for a time in order to learn from and with them?

In all, rigorous interrogation—coming from various quarters—while vexing and frustrating at times, can be integral to the overall quality of the work. Responding to questions—both friendly and less so[3] in nature—constitute an ongoing part of the research process. As Chapter 3 makes clear, not all welcome this attempt to create more of a home at the crossroads of theology,

---

[3] Vigen encountered this lesson during an intensive Institutional Review Board (IRB) process. See: Vigen, *Women, Ethics, Inequality*, 102–9.

ethics, and ethnography. The use of the social sciences in the doing of theology and ethics has been met with strong resistance by some prominent theological minds. In a sense, they ask: "Why seek theological insights through illegitimate theological sources, ones that at best bracket faith and at worst deny it?" In a similar vein, social scientists raise their own critical questions. "What do theologians and Christian ethicists know about qualitative research? What right do they have to venture into this terrain given their lack of formal training?" As theologians and Christian ethicists cross disciplinary boundaries, a valid concern is that they will run "fast and loose" with the methods of ethnography and, minimally, do shoddy work, and of even greater concern, put others at risk or expose them to "discomfort, pain, or risk" with "harm."

For example, one significant concern rightly raised by social scientists revolves around what one "does with the data." Sociologists and anthropologists who use ethnography emphasize the central tasks of in-depth, accurate observation and reporting of life, people, and events. The aim is decidedly *not* to over-interpret or issue claims of "ultimate meaning" or what "ought to be" based upon what is seen, heard, understood, etc. So asking the kinds of questions that theologians and ethicists might tend to ask such as, "what does this practice indicate about atonement" or "how is this liturgical move reflective of a particular ecclesiology?" or "what normative implications flow out of the facts as observed in this ethnography case study?" may strike a sociologist or anthropologist as precisely the *wrong* questions to pose. This complex disciplinary disconnect may be one reason why theologians and theological ethicists sometimes face prolonged and arduous Institutional Review Board (IRB) processes. It takes time to explain the goals and rationale and to translate terms and methods across distinct disciplines.

Thus this endeavor—ethnography as theology and ethics—encounters resistance from two different academic borders/sides: from theological ones that want to safeguard the purity and preeminence of traditional theological sources and methods from the "muddiness" of secular, experiential modes of inquiry; and from social scientific ones that take issue with an ethnographic project done by disciplinary "outsiders" and/or that would have the audacity to make theological or normative claims out of such research. In light of these concerns, two important questions surface for theologians: (1) *Why* attempt ethnography? and (2) *How* ought a Christian theologian or ethicist go about it responsibly? The latter question is the subject of the concluding chapter in Part Three.

Here, in what follows, we discuss three basic reasons why ethnography has a place in Christian theology and ethics—and even more—how it can be an expression of/vehicle for them—what it contributes. Throughout what follows, while we do not presume—or even hope for—monumental shifts in how theology and Christian ethics are done, we hope the analysis is provocative enough to give practitioners of both a little nudge. The moment has come for Christian theology and ethics to grow in a somewhat novel direction. And ethnography may both be a pathway for such work and also a representation of a particular kind of theological and ethical enterprise.

Considering How Ethnography Is Properly Theological: Source, Substance, Self-Critique

Embodied knowing

Epistemology is a big word that denotes the realm of ideas and theories that explore how we as human beings know what we claim to know. It asks not *what* is true, but rather, *how* do we know truth? How do we arrive at it? Traditionally, theologians are formally trained to draw especially upon the disciplines of religious doctrine, biblical studies, and theological and ecclesial history in their quests for truth. In Christian ethics, the four commonly cited sources of moral knowledge are scripture, reason, tradition, and experience. While we affirm the centrality of each of these sources, this volume represents a sustained case for giving more attention and weight to the realm of human experience. And ethnography is an invaluable tool in revealing its profound and complex wisdom.

Notions around what constitutes an adequate method in the doing of formal theology and ethics have been earnestly discussed and hotly debated by Christian scholars, institutions, clergy, and laypersons for centuries. In particular, a focal point of contention has been differing takes on the role and category of human experience. While most theologians and ethicists acknowledge it as valid source, it also often viewed with suspicion and or dismissed as overly subjective, personal, and emotional. In a nutshell, the persistent fear is relativism—in belief and in ethics. The argument can be summarized this way: If experience is given too much weight in the analysis, claims to transcendent or universally normative truth will degenerate into biased, or at least problematically limited visions, based on one's own preferences and encounters. Experience cannot be given too much authority in efforts to know the divine or the good because it is not rooted in an objective or transcendent ground—it is too vulnerable to individual dispositions, filters, interpretations, and blind spots. Consequently, taking experience as a central source will lead to "anything goes" in theology and ethics, meaning that there will be a lack of objective criteria by which to measure more or less adequate descriptions of God, God's relation to humanity, or of human responsibility in the world in light of this relationship.

In contrast to such views, the authors in this volume understand that experience is a multidimensional source and is accessed through varied disciplines and mediums (not only anthropology, sociology, or personal narrative).[4] Indeed, a rich understanding of human experience is cultivated through the critical use and interpretation of multiple and mutually corrective sources, among them: sociology, natural sciences, anthropology, literature, storytelling, the arts, history, sacred scriptures, autobiography, ethnography, ecclesial doctrines, and theological accounts. When described in this manner, many Christian scholars are more amenable to the category because they see that experience includes a range of disciplines and sources that put an individual experience into a larger context. It is not simply "my experience," but rather the experiences of individuals and communities—in history, over time, and as discovered through the careful study of texts, artifacts, embodied practices, living traditions, etc. Thus, by the term "experience" we do not have in mind a simplistic "my personal experience tells me" kind of thinking. Rather, our understanding of the category triangulates experience *with* experience—integrating ethnographic, sociological, economic, cultural, theological, biblical, and other sources of knowledge along the way.

Professing to have a repository for sacred traditions, doctrines, texts, ritual or other practices is not sufficient to keep theology "relevant and real" in a particular context. These sources of theological and moral wisdom and identity must be accompanied with an interpretive competence that resonates within a given community. The process of moral and spiritual formation is complex and ongoing. Does the practice still mediate identity? How is a given community interpreting texts, rituals, practices, doctrines—which ones are they actively engaging and which are sidelined? How are they using these resources? How are they (re)interpreting these sources and thus how does the interpretative process shape them—read and constitute the sources themselves?

While so much concern around "identity" (religious, denominational, etc.) centers around the question, "Is the community holding fast?" (a.k.a. interpreting and using the sacred deposits of the tradition faithfully), Mary McClintock Fulkerson asks a very different question. She asks not if a community is being faithful, but "*how* is it faithful?" What holds meaning for community members as they express that meaning in many different ways (verbal and nonverbal; textual and visual)? Pivotal community practices and rituals involve not only bible studies or formal worship, but also the full range of activities and projects engaged by members of a faith community (soup kitchens, second-hand stores, shelters, homeless youth accompaniment, public policy advocacy and so on).

- Is it faithful?
- How is it faithful?

[4] For elaboration on this point, see Aana Marie Vigen, "Conclusion: Descriptive and Normative Ways of Understanding Human Nature," in *God Science Sex Gender: An Interdisciplinary Approach to Christian Ethics*, Aana Marie Vigen and Patricia Beattie Jung (eds) (Urbana: University of Illinois Press, 2010), 241–58.

empirical principle (handwritten)

In a related vein, giving the category of experience priority can create a lively space for interaction and reflection among *all* of the sources—traditions, sacred scriptures, doctrines, the sciences, etc. It can inspire and support inter-disciplinary conversation and reflection. Appreciating the complexity and rigor of experience helps us see the ways human beings are both shaped by all of these sources and then in turn shape them and reinterpret them. Such awareness can lend to the vitality of faith traditions and communities, rather than working to dismantle them, because this study can reveal inadequacies in academic theological and ethical reflection and also suggest ways for correcting them that are both rigorous and grounded. Giving more weight to experience shows respect *both* for the traditions and scriptures we inherit *and* for the lives and events we create and encounter.

Furthermore, we make another claim regarding experience, shared by several Womanist and feminist theologians and ethicists who contend that experience is not simply a source for theology and ethics—it is the primary lens through which human beings access any and all scientific, moral, or theological knowledge.[5] This argument is more controversial than making the case that experience is discovered in a variety of sources and disciplines. Here, experience functions as a "type of truth claim"—in itself, it contains moral knowledge.[6] As Scharen contends elsewhere:

> While many disagreements over the proper balance of [reason, scripture, tradition, and experience] exist in the scholarly literature, I wish to point out that experience is never simply just one among the four sources. Rather, it infuses all the others, as a sort of founding source or means of knowing. So, for example, Holy Scripture records people's experience and reception of God and God's revelation in Jesus Christ; the church's traditions represent the collective experiences of God's pilgrim people over time; and it is now common to assume scholarly work to be influenced by the experiences of the scholar her-or himself. In addition, our experiences deeply influence how we interpret the data drawn from sources: how and what we draw from Scripture, tradition, and the secular disciplines.[7]

[5] See M. Shawn Copeland, *Enfleshing Freedom: Body, Race, and Being* (Minneapolis: Fortress Press, 2009), Margaret Farley, *Just Love: A Framework for Christian Sexual Ethics* (New York: Continuum, 2006), Carter Heyward, *Touching Our Strength: The Erotic as Power and the Love of God* (San Francisco: Harper and Row, 1989), Emilie M. Townes, *Womanist Ethics and the Cultural Production of Evil* (New York: Palgrave Macmillan, 2006), Traci C. West, *Disruptive Christian Ethics: When Racism and Women's Lives Matter* (Louisville: Westminster John Knox Press, 2006).

[6] See Susan L. Secker "Human Experience and Women's Experience," in *Dialogue about Catholic Sexual Teaching: Readings in Moral Theology vol. 8*, edited by Charles E. Curran and Richard A. McCormick (Mahwah: Paulist Press, 1993), 577–99.

[7] Christian Scharen, "Experiencing the Body: Sexuality and Conflict in American Lutheranism." *Union Seminary Quarterly Review* 57:1–2 (2003), 101.

In other words, experience is not simply a category among others; it is the interpretative vehicle. We mediate all moral and theological knowledge through our flesh—inclusive of bones, hearts, emotions, conscience, and embodied minds. Certainly for some Christians, this view threatens a sense of the transcendent divine presence in creation (that is uniquely revealed in scripture and tradition). To this concern, we respond that such an understanding is instead a way to take God's incarnation in the world seriously.

Fulkerson's work is instructive with respect to the depth and breadth of the category of experience. *Places of Redemption* explores a complex matrix of multifaceted materials[8] in an attempt to get at the richness of experience within a particular congregation. Her model shows the density of experience and how, in order to do justice to it, an ethnographer must take into account an expansive range of material—including bodies, visceral ways of knowing, daily practices, desires, various kinds of power, liturgies and ways scripture or formal theology is incorporated and interpreted. All of these dimensions help develop a multivalent description of the situation—of the life of a community.

In pursuing this rich account, Fulkerson takes seriously postmodernist deconstructions of presumed neutrality and objectivity. There is no completely impartial "view from nowhere"—all claims to truth—including those made by theology—are situated within particular convictions and stances. As part of a larger and thoughtful discussion of the significance and meaning of "place," which she redefines places as "a structure of lived, corporate and *bodied* experience," Fulkerson remarks: "When understood as *bodied ingression into the world*, place is truly fundamental in generating knowledge . . . The world *takes shape through our bodies*."[9] All knowing is embodied knowing.

Consequently, rather than fearing subjectivity in theology and ethics, we find that acknowledging its presence is the most honest and authentic theological and ethical response. All truth claims—even as they grasp and reach toward the transcendent, come from specific positions, perspectives, and bodies. Even as they may very well reveal some of the truth, none is exhaustive—they are always partial in scope. Thus, they continually merit reexamination and critical reflection to see both what they reveal and also what they miss or conceal. Jones' work in Chapter 7 is instructive on this point.[10]

If this insight seems jarring, historical perspective can be helpful. Throughout human history, a particular truth is discovered in light of prior limits of

---

[8] Fulkerson attends to a wide spectrum of elements such as, hidden inheritances, habituated bodies with desires, local and political powers, rituals, behaviors, kinship relations, and all kinds of beliefs that are present at various levels. See Fulkerson, *Places of Redemption*, 11–12.

[9] Emphasis hers. See Fulkerson, *Places of Redemption*, 25; pages 24–31 offer an in-depth discussion of place.

[10] A key source for these ideas is developed by Jones in Chapter 7, drawing on H. Richard Niebuhr's *The Meaning of Revelation* (New York: Macmillan, 1941).

human thought and then becomes overemphasized in its own time and thus needs to be corrected with an opposite polarity in the next. For example, consider the revolutionary notion of human autonomy that came out of the Enlightenment and owes much to thinkers such as Hume, Locke, Kant, and Jefferson. The notion that all individuals (at least white, male, landowners)—regardless of social stature or economic standing—were ordained with equality and had equal rights was absolutely revolutionary in the context of feudalism. Yet, many theologians and ethicists (among others) have argued that in the late twentieth and early twenty-first centuries of US society, autonomy and negative rights have been overvalued to the detriment of positive rights and the common good. In light of this predominant cultural view, they conclude that a refocusing of priorities and conceptions of the human person and the good are desperately needed—for both human and larger ecological survival and well-being.[11]

"Recognisably real" theology and ethics

Several scholars included in this volume (Browning, Reimer-Barry, Whitmore) and elsewhere emphasize the integral role that human experience plays in the cultivation of theological and moral knowledge. Yet, a few such as Scharen and Fulkerson take an additional methodological step to make the case that ethnography is a way to access *both* human experience and knowledge of the divine. Thus, it can be more than a mere tool in the doing of theology; it in itself can be an *expression* of theology. As Chapter 3 discusses, John Milbank and others view such a claim with significant suspicion. Yet, Milbank accepts the critique of his own work in *Theology and Social Theory* that his elaboration of the church is too idealized. To this, we have suggested in Chapter 3 that ethnography can offer the most robust corrective to the problematic of too formal an ecclesiology. It can, therefore, offer just the sort of "judicious narratives" called for by Milbank that can make such ecclesiology more "recognisably real." In other words, ethnography can help us create theology that is relevant—that attends meaningfully to living and historically rooted traditions, the Gospel, and to contemporary human events, practices, and needs. In a similar vein, Fulkerson argues that theological reflection "does not begin with a full-blown doctrine of God or of the church. Such a method misses that strange, often unremarked thing that *compels* a theological response—how it is

[11] See Lisa Sowle Cahill, *Theological Bioethics: Participation, Justice and Change* (Washington, D.C.: Georgetown, 2005); Allen Verhey, *Reading the Bible in the Strange World of Medicine* (Grand Rapids: Eerdmans Press, 2003); Larry L. Rasmussen, *Moral Fragments and Moral Community: A Proposal for Church in Society* (Minneapolis: Fortress, 1993), and Rasmussen, *Earth Community Earth Ethics* (Maryknoll: Orbis Books, 1996).

that theological reasoning is provoked at all."[12] Theology does not emerge from a vacuum; concrete dilemmas and encounters inspire its creation.

Elaborating upon the insights of Charles Winquist and Walter Lowe, Fulkerson poignantly describes theology as a "response to a wound," meaning that it arises in direct response to our most intimate and urgent hurts, crises, and questions:

> Wounds generate new thinking. Disjunctions birth invention—from a disjuncture in logic, where reasons is compelled to find new connections in thought, to brokenness in existence, where creativity is compelled to search for possibilities of reconciliation. Like a wound, theological thinking is generated by a sometimes inchoate sense that something *must* be addressed.[13]

In its most primary sense and purpose, theology is not a system of thought; it is not a static or perfect elaboration of divine being and doing. It is a visceral and sensual response to hurts and harms. It strives to respond to the disconnect between the love and right relationship human beings sense is possible—even taste in some of their experiences—and yet is not completely fulfilled in them. At its best, theology and ethics represent intentional and nuanced efforts to make sense of suffering *and* to do something (e.g. prophetic, pastoral, constructive, hope-filled) about it—to create "places of redemption."

As support for this provocative claim, Fulkerson cites the example of Karl Barth's theology of the Word responding to the wound of "idolatries of the German Church" and James Cone's Black theology calling white theology to account for its false claims to universality and for its "deeply entrenched racism."[14] Dietrich Bonhoeffer's theology also comes to mind, but so does the theology of earlier theologians as well. Certainly St Augustine's and Martin Luther's theological visions were rooted in the concrete, enfleshed, and practical questions and crises of their days—whether in the particular political and doctrinal controversies and violence of Hippo in fifth-century North Africa or in those of sixteenth-century Saxony.

So too it is with theological and ethical endeavors in the twenty-first century. For theology to remain vibrant, it must resonate with pressing issues and it must attentively and thoughtfully address the wounds of embodied, dynamic communities of faith. And to do this, it cannot simply be applied to situations; it must, at least in part, take flesh within them. Ethnography can be an illuminating way to take seriously God's incarnation in the world. For her part, Fulkerson hopes that such theological responses will create a space for

---

[12] Fulkerson, *Places of Redemption*, 13. Emphasis in the original. She cites Walter Lowe, *Theology and Difference: The Wound of Reason* (Bloomington: University Press, 1993), 9–10.
[13] Fulkerson, *Places of Redemption*, 13–14. Emphasis in the original.
[14] Ibid., 14; fn22.

"appearing," meaning that those previously lost to ignorance, apathy, and as she puts it, "obliviousness" will be finally seen, heard, and attended to.[15]

In this way, ethnography can serve as an intervention that calls into question antagonistic "Church or theology vs. world" kinds of thinking. Rather than a sectarian sense of faithfulness as setting one's self or religious community apart from the world, exploring "worldly theology" through the use of ethnography invites scholars and others to see how intertwined faith, theology, church, culture, and the larger societies are. Acknowledging how utterly enmeshed these domains are does not rule out the need for critique among them. Indeed, at times, faith communities can be prophetic in their calling governments, common practices, and predominant values into question. For their part, democratic institutions, the natural and social sciences, and secular humanism can all, in their distinctive voices and methods, starkly reveal the limits of particular theological perspectives. To say that these ways of knowing and being are mixed up with one another does rule out mutual correction and critique.

Rather, it means that no one domain ever truly exists in a "pure" or isolated state. While we profess a guiding, normative role for scripture in Christian theology and ethics, we also acknowledge its enactment is interpretative and therefore contested. Cultures, the sciences, historical events, theology and ethics, are all in a dynamic spiral—informing, revising, reinforcing, critiquing, and responding to one another. Rather than seeing theology or the church as set apart from secular society, we follow Jesus' teaching that Christians and Christian communities are called—created by God to be—persons and entities that are "in the world, but not wholly of it" (e.g. the Gospel of John, chapters 17–18).

With specific regard to the task of ethics, we contend that Christian ethicists have a duty to test what we claim normatively against what others live. For ethics to offer constructive insights and norms for shaping social relations and values, it has to demonstrate that it has first taken the complexity of reality and lived experience into account. Moral claims lack force if they jump too quickly into prescription without taking a full enough view of the complexity of the issues at stake. Key sources of information and moral knowledge are not only those found online and in texts, but in embodied lives of people and communities.[16] The turn to ethnography in Christian theology and ethics, then, makes the bold claim that what non-academics think, live, know, practice, do, and experience matters in a *fundamental* (not merely illustrative) way. Poignant examples of such nonacademic contributions to moral knowledge can be

---

[15] Ibid., 18–22.
[16] For a fuller argument on this point, see Vigen, "Conclusion," 245–55.

found in many disciplines.[17] Furthermore, we contend that this kind of wisdom matters not only as source of moral knowledge *but also* as part of theology proper.

For example, in Vigen's work in medical ethics, the central conviction that runs throughout is this: If ethicists want to understand what justice and right-relationship mean in healthcare contexts, we need to explore the needs and experiences of those who are most often marginalized by structural inequalities. At its best, theology offers the insight that to understand what it means to be human, one has to think concretely, relationally, and contextually.

Roman Catholic Womanist theologian M. Shawn Copeland argues that the only viable conception of what it means to be human must take seriously as its frame of reference the concrete bodies of the most despised, namely, "the exploited, despised, poor woman of color."[18] Theological and ethical definitions of what it means to be human will only approach adequacy if they include explicit, substantive respect for these actual persons. What it means to love the neighbor as one's self only becomes real in the particular—discovered in large part inductively. The poetic command to "love one another as one's self" needs to be enfleshed—surrounded—by the knowledge that comes out of concrete relationships, especially with those who are in some way vulnerable—those who have to fight to live, to be seen, heard, understood, and to be loved in as an end in herself.

Ethnography is one possible means by which to make the above theological commitment concrete. Publicizing the principles,[19] goals, and mission of a hospital on every wall by the elevators does not ensure that they are lived out in the practices, sensibilities, cultures, and bodies of healthcare providers. Qualitative research may help to expose problems in perception—for example, how care providers' perception may be impaired by socioeconomic class and racial assumptions and the consequences these assumptions have on patient lives and well-being.[20]

---

[17] For example, see texts in medical anthropology, sociology, illness narratives, and medical ethics: David Moller, *Dancing with Broken Bones* (Oxford: Oxford University Press, 2004); Arthur Kleinman, *Illness Narratives* (New York: Basic Books, 1989); Margaret Mohrman, *Attending Children* (Washington, D.C.: Georgetown University Press, 2006); Arthur Frank, *The Wounded Storyteller* (Chicago and London: The University of Chicago Press, 1997); João Biehl, *Will to Live* (Princeton and Oxford: Oxford University Press, 2007). See also *Subjectivity*, João Biehl, Byron Good, and Arthur Kleinman (eds) (Berkeley: University of California Press, 2007).

[18] M. Shawn Copeland, "The New Anthropological Subject at the Heart of the Mystical Body of Christ," *CTSA PROCEEDINGS* 53 (1998), 30.

[19] Tom L. Beauchamp and James F. Childress, *The Principles of Biomedical Ethics* (New York: Oxford University Press, 2001, 5th edition).

[20] See Vigen, *Women, Ethics, Inequality* for an in-depth discussion of these and related themes.

Critical self-reflection: the imperative of reflexivity

As Reimer-Barry lifts up in Chapter 6, adequate and responsible ethnographic scholarship must be profoundly self-aware. It must reflect back upon itself—examining the scholar's preconceptions and assumptions that s/he brings to the study. As discussed in Chapter 1, various postmodern and postcolonial critiques have soundly trounced any naiveté that would purport that ethnographers simply "report" facets of reality. To be credible observers, researchers must acknowledge the filters through which view that which they study and own up to their inherent limits and subjective quality.

A self-aware stance helps to guard against creating a purportedly perfected system of theological or ethical thought. In other words, it protects against the idolatry of one's one theological and ethical creations. Part of nuanced theological and ethical reflection is the acknowledgment of the limits and frailties of one's creations. No theological statement fully conveys divine being and action. Our understandings of revelation are never final or complete. At best, we glimpse transcendent truth in partial, yet illuminating fragments.

For its part, ethnography ought not attempt to tidy the messy contradictions it may find or create a false sense of unity, homogeneity, synthesis. Instead, it is necessarily open to finding disconnects, ruptures, and paradox—indeed, it expects them. Put simply, ethnographers, theologians, and ethicists alike do not need to be "all-seeing" or "all-knowing" in order to offer up relevant and illuminating insights about what is true or relevant. Instead, they can offer up as valid the partial—but no less true or significant—perceptions they gain through situating themselves in particular contexts, listening thoughtfully to others, and reflecting upon their own lives, emotional responses, and even (or especially) internal biases.

Thus, researchers have to be gutsy enough to check our own assumptions and to be open to being surprised, wrong, and changed by what we learn in the ethnographic field. Such a posture is not only essential for methodological credibility, it is also a way to model intellectual and spiritual humility. In a word: transparency. Scholars need to confront and own the subjective stances they bring to their work and be willing to subject them to critical examination—both by their own reflection and by others engaging their work.

In an effort to practice self-disclosure, some ethnographic models combine ethnography with autobiography. There can be dangers in doing this—the work can amount to little more than glorified "navel-gazing." Yet, if it is done with care and a degree of restraint, it can help reveal the (mal)formations and transformations within the person who writes the narrative, rather than only shining a spotlight on others while remaining hidden. In other words, it is one possible way to enact self-disclosure for the sake of intellectual honesty and authenticity.[21]

ethnography + autobiography

---

[21] See, for example, works that tell one's own story of professional moral and spiritual formation: Mohrmann, *Attending Children*, Frank, *The Wounded Storyteller*, Kleinman, *The Illness*

Fulkerson models this kind of humility in acknowledging the discomfort and awkwardness she felt on her first visit to a congregation very unlike those to which she was accustomed. Her candor is instructive:

> While I am expecting a mixed-race group, I am surprised at my own response to all the dark skin in the room. A black woman approaches me. Extending her hand with a bulletin, she introduces herself and welcomes me warmly. I find myself aware of the paleness of my skin as I respond, trying to hide any signs that I am not used to worshipping with more than a few token black people. The overeager sound of my voice tells me I am probably failing. A good three-fourths of the people gathering to worship are black, or rather ebony, dark tan, bronze, and shades of color for which I have no names.
>
> Next I notice a thin white man sitting twisted in a wheelchair parked next to a short man who looks like he has Down syndrome. As I approach the man in the wheelchair my body feels suddenly awkward and unnatural . . . My height feels excessive and ungainly. I tower over this pale man strapped in his wheelchair. Do I kneel down? Bend down to be face level to him? Speaking to him from above feels patronizing. Or is it the crouching down that would be patronizing? My hand moves to touch his shoulder, as if to communicate, "I care about you, despite your mildly frightening, contorted body and guttural gurgling sounds." But I withdraw my hand quickly, wondering if this, too, would be a sign of condescension. What was it like to be unable to command a safe space with your presence, to be vulnerable to the groping of other peoples' hands?[22]

It takes a more than a little courage to show the places where we do not "shine" as stellar individuals or communities—to be honest about how we often grope, fumble, and misstep in our relationships. And for those whose identities are tied up with notions of "expertise, intellect, scholarship," and professional titles, it can be especially threatening to admit how little we really know and how awkward we can feel around people dissimilar to our accustomed ways of being. It can feel a bit like we are naked—the robes, lab coats, and professional garb in which many of us wrap ourselves is stripped away (or at least cast in a chair for the moment). Some fear a loss of authority or credibility. Others seem to be unsure of who they are without the security of the professional cloaks.

Narratives, and Jerome Groopman, *How Doctors Think* (Boston and New York: Houghton Mifflin, 2007). Though none of these are categorized as formal ethnography per se, they offer up models for theologians and ethicists to think about how they might more transparent in their scholarship. Vigen and Scharen's work also attempt to model critical self-reflection combined with some personal storytelling, but neither fits within categories of autobiography or personal narrative.

[22] Fulkerson, *Places of Redemption*, 4–5.

Undeniably, it can be uncomfortable and risky to reveal our own humanity in the research and work. Yet, finding the wherewithal to do so is vital—not only for the quality for the work, but for the intellectual and moral formation of the scholar. Critical self-reflection provides not only a way to check for pre-conceptions and blinders, it helps teach us to be human—imperfect, embod-ied, a member of a larger community that calls us to accountability, to relationship. And in this reckoning, there is not only embarrassing revelation of our shortcomings as people, there is also grace, forgiveness, reconciliation, compassion, and even perhaps, approximations of justice. It is for these rea-sons that we have tried to reflect consciously and conscientiously on our identi-ties and sites of privilege as a white, western, Christian, educated, employed (tenured and tenure track) woman and man. And in order to do so, we have had to relate stories where our actions fall short of the ideals to which we aspire.[23] Doing so helps us not only be better scholars, but to learn to be more human—both worthy of love and also fallible.

Moreover, it is not just Fulkerson's or our story at play here. Individual stories can reveal larger social, political, economic, cultural, and racial dynamics that are too often hidden or silenced. For example, as Fulkerson's reflects on her own visceral experience described above, she makes connections to larger societal dynamics:

> My feeling of strangeness in response to the unaccustomed "blackness" of the place and the presence of people with disabilities at that first visit sug-gests that my conscious commitments to inclusiveness were not completely correlated with my habituated sense of the normal . . . This tacit sense that surprised me when I became self-conscious of my whiteness and my able-bodiedness suggests forms of occlusion operating in my own internalized sense of the world. Evidence of a broader social "unaccustomedness" to black and disable bodies, this discomfort has significance far beyond my own sense of dis-ease. It is an unaccustomedness and obliviousness with widespread parallels, not only at Good Samaritan, but in the larger society as well. It is an obliviousness that comes with dominance, and it foreshadows fracture in the smooth veneer of welcome and Christly inclusivity in the church as well.[24]

Fulkerson's story shows that there was a disconnect between her intellectual assent to inclusiveness and her habituated and embodied sense of what is con-sidered by many in society as "normal." The problem is that it can be far too easy for certain groups (based on race, socioeconomics, and physical/mental

---

[23] Vigen, *Women, Ethics, and Inequality in U.S. Healthcare*, xviii–xxiii; Scharen, "Experiencing the Body."
[24] Fulkerson, *Places of Redemption*, 15.

abilities) to not truly see others—in Fulkerson's terms to remain oblivious to them. Obliviousness is not only a personal character flaw; it is also operative at social and structural levels as well—most clearly seen when one considers education, neighborhood demographics, health indicators, etc. Indeed, Fulkerson goes on to discuss related scholarship and statistics that helps see the layers of segregation present among sectors of the US population—how seemingly invisible yet palpable lines divide differing racial, socioeconomic, and (dis)abled communities from one another.[25]

As an intervention to interrupt social obliviousness, Fulkerson, drawing on the work Kimberley Curtis, focuses on ways to cultivate a "shared space of appearance." Profound changes in consciousness are needed—changes in rational thought, but also accompanied by changes in hearts and concrete practices as well. Those changes which primarily receive lip service or even those codified (e.g. through legislation) are not complete if they do not penetrate hearts and the daily rituals of a society. Change must be registered at embodied levels for it to take full root in the mindset and habitual ways of being in a society.

Fulkerson draws on Bourdieu's elaboration of *habitus* and MacIntyre on practices to show these limits and to get at the dynamic combination of understanding and action that is needed for transformation or conversion in worldview and in the way a person or community lives it life:

> Just as books about boxing are not enough to make a good boxer, a *habitus* of justice is not adequately defined by knowledge of principles (or stories) of love, or of what the church or even Jesus have said in the past. Any such *habitus* requires a feel for and grasp of the "items, events, and power" of an environment and how they "gather", to use the earlier language of a situation; *situational competence* is fundamental to the successful continuity of a practice.[26]

---

[25] Fulkerson cites relevant scholarship on the persistence of racial segregation and inequality in various arenas of US life (religion, schools, neighborhoods, etc.); see for example: The Civil Rights Project at Harvard University Report, "Race in American Public Schools: Rapidly Resegregating School Districts" (2002); Michael Emerson and Christian Smith, *Divided by Faith: Evangelical Religion and the Problem of Race in America* (Oxford and New York: Oxford University Press, 2000). For data on racial-ethnic disparities in health and healthcare, See the Commonwealth Fund Report: *Racial and Ethnic Disparities in U.S. Health Care: A Chartbook* (2008) and The Kaiser Family Foundation Report, "Key Facts: Race, Ethnicity and Medical Care, 2007 Update." For additional incisive social and philosophical analysis, see: Iris Marion Young, *Justice and the Politics of Difference* (Princeton: Princeton University Press, 1990), Glenn C. Loury, *The Anatomy of Racial Inequality* (Cambridge, MA and London: Harvard University Press, 2002), Ellis Cose, *Color-Blind: Seeing Beyond Race in a Race-Obsessed World* (New York: Harper Perennial, 1997). For analysis of disabilities, stigma, and inequality, see works by Nancy Eiesland, Rosemary Garland-Thomson, and Erving Goffman.

[26] Fulkerson, *Places of Redemption*, 46. See also her earlier discussion of Bourdieu and MacIntyre on pages 35 and 38–9. She continues this point on p. 47: "The point here,

On its own, intellectual assent or commitment will not suffice—too often that means people say what they think they are supposed to say, and keep their authentic beliefs, feelings, and concerns beneath the surface. All dimensions of human being and doing need to be integrated through words, deeds, embodied senses, thoughtful reflection, prayer, and various rituals of daily existence.

Furthermore, people (especially those of us who benefit from one or more sites of privilege in society) have to confront our fears and sites of dis-ease—focusing on releasing the anxiety or discomfort so that visceral reactions and daily practices are more consistent with our stated beliefs. We concur with Fulkerson that such transformation is not only important for political and social life, but bears on the spiritual dimensions of our existence in a fundamental way:

> What is needed to counter the diminishment and harm associated with obliviousness is a *place to appear*, a place to be seen, to be recognized and to recognize the other. Being seen and heard by others, being acknowledged by others—these are said to be essential to the political life; my point is that they are also essential to a community of faith as an honoring of the shared image of God.[27]

Ethnography is one way to work toward such appearances and to give flesh and bone to the theological concept of *imago dei* (image of God).

To be even more explicit theologically, ethnography can be both radically related both to divine creation and incarnation. By paying strong attention to what exists—in creation, in a community, in embodied practices, it offers a method for heeding Martin Luther's call to "honor God's handiwork."[28] Similarly, and as poignantly expressed by Whitmore in Chapter 10 and elsewhere,[29] theo-critical ethnography can provide a way to take up Christian discipleship. In immersing itself in the depths and complexities of suffering in the world, ethnographic methods can become a way both to witness to, and to express solidarity with, those who are hurting and in need. In this sense, ethnography can be a way to testify.

---

however, is that the wisdom suggested by the *habitus* requires a shift away from a rule- or content-driven model for normative thinking about traditioning. The kind of "knowledge" at stake here combines flexibility with identity in a way best described as improvisational."

[27] Fulkerson, *Places of Redemption*, 21.

[28] Martin Luther, "The Estate of Marriage"(1522). *Luther's Works, American Edition, Volume 45*, translated by Walther I. Brandt (Philadelphia: Fortress Press, 1965), 17.

[29] Whitmore, "Crossing the Road," 273–94. Here, he draws on William C. Spohn, *Go and Do Likewise: Jesus and Ethics* (New York and London: Continuum, 2007), chapters 2–3.

Conclusion

In one sense, these three contributions of ethnographic methods offer a some-what novel, and perhaps unnerving, way of thinking about the task of theology and Christian ethics. Indeed, Fulkerson's description may unsettle some: "Theological reflection is not a linear form of reflection that starts with a cor-rect doctrine (or a 'worldly' insight) and then proceeds to analyze a situation; rather it is a situational, ongoing, never-finished dialectical process where past and present ever converge in new ways."[30] Yet, what Fulkerson describes is what faith communities have been doing for centuries—these dynamic processes did not begin with post-modernity. Indeed, they are as ancient as the faith traditions themselves—for they are part of the perennial quest to make mean-ing, discover truth, and remain relevant amidst complexity and thorny challenges.

Speaking specifically as ethicists and with Part Two in view, we would take Fulkerson's insight even a step further: The ethical questions of our day demand that we leverage the very best information from all possible sources and to appreciate the complex degrees of interpretation happening within each one. Put simply, Christian ethicists don't have the luxury of turning our noses up at sociology or anthropology any more than we can ignore economics when addressing the financial crisis or what biological experts on climate change are discovering when we address the ecological crisis.

Put even more bluntly, if we want what we write about AIDS prevention, end of life care, sexual ethics, economic ethics, bioethics, ecological ethics, democ-racy and capitalism, poverty, or the prison industrial complex, and produce work that speaks meaningfully to these situations, we have to work with all of the pertinent data. And doing so may very likely mean talking with people or observing groups at work who deal daily with these issues or who have faced direct personal confrontations with them. Otherwise, why should anyone—in academia, public policy, or the larger society—listen to what we have to say? The burden of demonstrating credibility and relevance is on our shoulders. With this set of methodological and theological commitments and rationale sketched out, we now turn to see examples of theological ethnography in the making.

---

[30] Fulkerson, *Places of Redemption*, 234.

Part Two

Exemplars

Chapter 5

Ethnographic Research on African American Pastoral Leadership and Congregations

Jeffery L. Tribble, Sr

Ethnography as Ministry

My ethnographic research of pastoral leadership in the context of ministry departs from the methodological perspective that critical and constructive research is conducted by a dispassionate researcher. My use of ethnography is an extension of my vocation in ministry. I engage in this research because I care about the ministry of pastors and other Christian leaders. I wonder with others how persons and congregations might be transformed themselves and thus foster transformation as instruments of God's mission in the world. Margaret Ann Crain and Jack Seymour articulate a perspective of ethnography as ministry as they write the following:

action research

> Ethnographers take seriously the dual commitments of understanding and serving human needs. Ethnographic research in the context of ministry is for education and empowerment. To speak theologically, our research seeks to build up the communities of faith and extend God's call for wholeness and justice.[1]

More particularly, my ethnographic research is motivated not only by the pursuit of knowledge, but also by a desire to serve the communal well-being of people who are marginalized and oppressed.

During the course of my doctoral studies, I recall a congregational researcher remarking in the introduction of this text something like the following: "My research is limited to white North American mainline congregations and does not begin to explore the rich depth of African American congregational life and other racial ethnic faith communities due to the difficulty of my gaining social access to these communities." I saw this as a "call" to help fill a needed gap

[1] Margaret Ann Crain and Jack L. Seymour, "The Ethnographer as Minister: Ethnographic Research in Ministry," in *Religious Education* (Summer 1996), 310–11.

in the literature and address a particular community through my research and writing. More fundamentally, my being born and raised in the hyper-segregated environs of the South Side of Chicago and a product of positive family, church, and educational experiences in the Black community had convinced me of the worth and value of a people striving for equality, full humanity, excellence, and freedom. Raised by hardworking parents who broke into the middle class, members of my family and I were never far from Black poor and working-class people. My ethnographic research on African American pastoral leadership and congregations is further shaped by my vocation as an African American ordained minister and practical theologian. Congregational studies and ethnography are research methodologies of choice as I believe strongly that normative claims of what religious leaders "ought to do" need to be formulated in relationship with particular contexts of resource and constraint.

The incarnation of God in Jesus Christ is the theological touchstone for the conviction that the ethnographic work of describing social reality and human experiences of life with God in faith communities is theological work. In this chapter, I reflect methodologically and practically on what I have done in field research of African American pastoral leadership, how and why I did it, and what I learned that may be of significance to other researchers. In this chapter, I will reflect on my quest to define and describe through grounded theory research the concept of "transformative pastoral leadership in the black church."

By comparing the similarities and differences of pastoral leadership of an exemplary female pastor and exemplary male pastor in two ministry contexts, the project evolved into my efforts to describe and explain a new concept, "transformative pastoral leadership in the Black church" and generate theories of the praxis of transformative pastoral leadership relevant to the nature and mission of the Black church entering the twenty-first century. Growing out of my nearly ten years of pastoral experience in one of the historically Black Methodist denominations, the African Methodist Episcopal Zion Church (A. M. E. Zion), I had become interested in questions of how church leaders both foster transformation and conserve traditions within the congregational and denominational systems of my own denomination. Practical questions growing out of reflections on my pastoral experiences and observations were the starting point of a practice-theory-practice model of congregational research. Utilizing congregational research methods, I bridged theories of practices of ministries, biblical and theological reflection, and the sociological study of the Black church.

Reflecting back on my use of the practice-theory-practice model in this practical theological research, I was not as explicit as I should have been about its affinity to the method of Black theology. Dwight Hopkins describes the "rhythm of black theology" as follows:

The rhythm of black theology starts from faith in, commitment to, worship with, and work for the poor in the African American community . . . .

Because the spirit of comfort, hope, and liberation exists among the least in society even before the theologian works with them, the theologian has to be connected to this dynamic between the poor and a liberation spirituality. From a relationship with the poor and their concerns, theology follows as a second step within the rhythm of black theology. In fact, theology is self-critical thinking about the practice and faith of liberation of grassroots people within the church and the nonchurch. The third dimension of black theology's methodological rhythm is the return of theology to the practice of faith to further the pastoral, ethical, political, cultural, economic, linguistic, and everyday way of life of the African American poor trying "to make a way out of no way" with their liberator God.[2]

Broadening of a Research Idea through Practical Theological Reflection

Critical and constructive reflection on the diverse experiences, understandings, and activities of two pastors in their congregational, communal, and denominational contexts was done with the aim of sharing practical wisdom. A hermeneutical circle of practical theological reflection of four distinct but interrelated moments of reflection enabled interdisciplinary conversation among sources of theological reflection. In this study, one moment of reflection was on the present situation, practices, and perspectives of lay and clergy leaders. Analysis of the social and cultural contexts of the two research sites was a second moment of reflection. This engaged the history of the Black church, urban history of the communities in which the congregations were situated, and sociological theories of the transformation of the Black church since the social movements of the 1960s and the early 1970s. A third moment, reflection on biblical and theological traditions, engaged biblical images of pastoral ministry, the theological traditions of Methodists, and Black and Womanist Liberation Theologies. These moments of reflection recognize the inherent complexity of practices which "themselves contain history, tradition, theology and social experiences and expectations."[3] The fourth moment, formulating revised practices, suggests new transformative practices. In doing this, practices suggested by the field research were correlated with models of leadership in African American as well as Anglo churches.[4] The revised practices emerging from my

---

[2] Dwight N. Hopkins, *Introducing Black Theology of Liberation* (Maryknoll: Orbis Books, 1999), 47.

[3] Swinton and Mowat, *Practical Theology and Qualitative Research*, 16.

[4] This four-step model, which I learned from James Poling, is based on the hermeneutical circle of the pastoral cycle and helpfully relates qualitative research methods and its

grounded theory research was expressed in the form of "tales of transformation" that I constructed and strategies of transformation that emerged from the research.

However, my initial research idea was more narrowly conceived. I initially selected a male pastor of a large and growing congregation to discover methods of evangelism and church growth. The suggestion of a faculty mentor in the department of sociology to "include a woman in my study as it would make it more interesting," provoked reflection on my own inherent sexism which was expressed in my evolving plan to study "Pastoral Leadership in the Black Methodist Church" without consideration of a decision to only study an exemplary male pastor reflected my own ambivalence about the role of women clergy. Indeed, despite being partially blinded by the sexism deeply embedded in Black churches of which I am a part, I came to agree with Hopkins that African American women's experience is an indispensable source for doing Black theology as they make up "at least 70 percent of black churches and over half of the African American community."[5] Too often, African American women's experiences are neglected by male scholars as well as male church leaders.

The decision to broaden the research from one case to two cases was more challenging to balance within the flow of my life and work; however, as a result, it became possible to conceive a grounded theory study comparing the two contrasting cases of pastoral leadership: a male pastor and a female pastor, a large church and a small church, a full time pastor and a bi-vocational pastor, and a church in a middle-class Black community and a church in a poor and gentrifying community.

One of my cases was of the ministry of Rev. Walter Harrison, the pastor of Christopher Temple Christian Methodist Episcopal Church (C. M. E. Church), a well-established congregation of over 3,000 members in a solid Black middle-class community of a northern US city. In the tradition of the Methodist traveling ministry, this full-time pastor had been appointed by bishops to six previous pastoral assignments in his first 17 years of pastoral ministry. After a pattern of moving with his wife and children to serve churches for no more than three years at a time, Harrison was appointed to Christopher Temple, a leading church of the C. M. E. denomination. At the outset of my research, this denominational leader and community activist had served as pastor of Christopher Temple for 15 years. Over his pastoral tenure, the membership had grown from 1,200 members on roll with about 400 active to 3,000 members

---

relationship to theological dimensions of practical theological research. Swinton and Mowat, *Practical Theology and Qualitative Research*, 94–7.

[5] Hopkins, *Introducing Black Theology of Liberation*, 44–5. Hopkins identifies six important sources in a Black theology of liberation: the Bible, the African American church, African American women's experiences, a faith tradition of struggle for liberation, Black culture, and radical politics. See ibid., 42–6.

on roll with about 2,000 active. With a theological commitment to church growth and to developing leaders, Harrison had received at least 100 new members into the C. M. E. Church in each of the last 20 years of his ministry and had helped 25 women and men develop their ministry as clergy in the C. M. E. Church. Rev. Harrison began his pastoral ministry in the late 1960s, completed his seminary education in the early 1970s and had served as a national leader of Operation P. U. S. H. (People United to Serve Humanity). Besides framing this congregational study as a case of evangelistic growth and leadership development, I began to see Christopher Temple as an example of the transformation of a traditional denominational church by pastoral leaders whose social consciousness and theology was shaped by the Civil Rights and Black Power movements.

Sociological perspectives of the Black church were a critical conversation partner in my analysis of each case study. In an article arguing that the contemporary Black church is a product of the social movements of the 1960s, Cheryl Townsend-Gilkes asserts that new pastors influenced by the civil rights movements and Black power generation consciousness were capable of transforming "silk stocking" churches and drawing many new members precisely because of their ability to transform their churches wisely applying the critical lessons of these social movements.[6] In his study of the Civil Rights Movement, Aldon Morris argues that the Black church has been a key institution for transmitting the protest tradition, the Black community's response to a persistent and pervasive context of racial oppression. Utilizing Max Weber's theory of charismatic movements, he analyzed interviews of civil rights leaders and reveals qualities for effective pastoral leadership in the Black church and community and the sources for that development. His analysis provided theories of the qualities, practices, aptitudes, and kinds of education and preparation existing in social movement leaders.[7] These sociologically derived theories were examined in relationship with the data of my study.

The other case that I "complexified" and explored was the ministry of Rev. Dr Carol Evans, one of the persons received and developed under Rev. Harrison's ministry at Christopher Temple. She was appointed to her first pastorate by Bishop Isaiah Douglas to serve as pastor of Isaiah-Matthews C. M. E. Church, a product of the merger of two fledgling congregations. At the time of her appointment, seven years prior to the beginning of my study, one of the churches had burned down. The other church, she described, as having been "run down." One church had never had a woman pastor. The other grieved the loss of a beloved woman pastor. Tackling this set of challenges, Dr Evans learned

---

[6] Cheryl Townsend-Gilkes, "Plenty Good Room: Adaptation in a Changing Black Church," in *The Annals of the American Academy of Political and Social Science* 558:1 (July 1998), 107.

[7] Aldon Morris, *The Origins of the Civil Rights Movement: Black Communities Organizing for Change* (New York: The Free Press, 1984), 7–12.

to "manage the messes" that she encountered and successfully managed a quarter of a million dollar renovation of the burned out church facility. Under her leadership, the congregation grew from 31 on roll to over 200 members on roll. During the course of her ministry at Isaiah-Matthews, she wrote a Doctor of Ministry project paper to develop a methodology for renovating the facility and redeveloping the ministry. Despite the growth and development of this congregation, situated in a poor and gentrifying community, the church could not support full-time employment. Thus, one of her burdens was maintaining a full-time secular position of employment while attempting transformative ministry.

I saw Dr Evans as a particular case of the broader challenge to the Black church posed by the growing presence of gifted, committed, well-trained female clergy in the Black church, which is still dominated by male clergy leadership. In 1968, the year that Carol Evans began preaching, the denomination that she would later embrace, the C. M. E. Church would be only two years from voting to give women the right to be ordained. The social forces of the 1960s and early 1970s that radically impacted American culture also impacted the Black church's official stance with respect to women clergy. Yet, the Black church, even at the outset of the twenty-first century is just beginning to address sexism as a serious concern. I came to see Evan's story as one that might offer insight and inspiration to other Black women who struggle against the forces limiting women to entry level or token appointments.

Furthermore, Townsend-Gilkes identifies a pattern of women, like Evans, who formerly functioned as "highly visible church workers who functioned as leaders of the female infrastructure that was the proverbial backbone of the church" discovering new callings as pastors independent of husbands.[8] Like many other Black clergy-women that I have known, she carved out a minis try as a "second career." Formed in ministry in Pentecostal churches, I see Dr Evans also as an example of how some Black Methodists are reclaiming the Holiness-Pentecostal heritage, long neglected in denominations formed in the Wesleyan theological tradition. Mamiya identifies what he calls the rise of a Neo-Pentecostal movement which reclaims theological emphasis on the work of the Holy Spirit and charismatic expression in worship combined with progressive social outreach.[9]

I initially framed my question one of exploring the question of the possibilities, problems, processes, and principles of transforming leadership in a sister Black Methodist denomination, the Christian Methodist Episcopal Church.

---

[8] Townsend-Gilkes, "Plenty Good Room," 112.
[9] Lawrence Mamiya, "A Social History of the Bethel African Methodist Episcopal Church in Baltimore: The House of God and the Struggle for Freedom," in James P. Wind and James W. Lewis (eds), *American Congregations: Volume I, Portraits of Twelve Religious Communities* (Chicago: The University of Chicago Press, 1994), 262–271.

Political, scholarly, as well as methodological considerations motivated my selection of congregations outside of my own denomination. At the time, the two denominations were involved in serious merger conversations. There were and are many commonalities to these denominational bodies which were birthed out of struggles with American Methodism on the slave question. Methodologically, I thought it best to enter field research as a relative "outsider" in order that I might use my marginality to "make the familiar strange," pushing me to probe beyond my assumptive knowledge of similar A. M. E. Zion churches. My scholarly interests in the praxis of pastoral leadership engaged my prior studies in evangelism, sociology of the Black church, urban sociology, Black and Womanist liberation theologies, and practical theology. Politically, I was aware that it would be difficult for me to research the ministerial hierarchy of which I was an active member.

Overt field research depends on gaining consent and access to sites of research. The selected congregations, Christopher Temple C. M. E. and Isaiah-Matthews C. M. E.,[10] were recommended in independent conversations with ministers familiar with C. M. E. congregations in the area. They were characterized as two "growing" congregations; the rest as simply "holding their own." Furthermore, their ministries were directed not only toward members, but also non-members in the communities. After my initial calls to the mega church pastor went unreturned, I took another approach and called the supervising minister, the presiding elder of both churches, whom I had previously worked with in community ministries as a pastor. Fortunately, Presiding Elder Crider was receptive to my research plans and viewed me as credible. He became the "gatekeeper" to introduce my research plans to both ministers. After my respective presentations to them, they came to see my research as not only benefitting my research aims, but as honoring their ministries. Rev. Walter Harrison, pastor of Christopher Temple C. M. E., played a crucial role of introducing my research interests to his bishop, who embraced my research project as well. Hence, my commitment to the practice of ministry in African American faith communities played an important role in my access to the perspectives of the "hierarchy" of lay leaders, pastors, presiding elder, and bishop.

The ethnographer's biography and social history, vision as well as blind spots, commitment to practice as well as to reading within particular theoretical frameworks, their subjectivity as well as rigorous analysis all contribute to a flexible but disciplined plan of theological research. In his or her exploration of situations in faith communities, the ethnographer/research instrument must be personally reflexive. According to Willig, personal reflexivity involves "reflecting on the ways that our own values, experiences, interests, beliefs,

---

[10] Pseudonyms were used throughout to minimize risk and harm to the persons and congregations studied.

political commitments, wider aims in life and social identities have shaped the research. It also involves thinking about how the research may have affected and possibly changed us, as people and as researchers."[11]

Posing Problems and Answers Relevant to the Communities Studied

Through the course of my research, I came to articulate the "practical problem" as follows: "A new vision of black transformative pastoral leadership is needed at the outset of the 21st Century because of the practical condition of many denominational black congregations, which are struggling to fulfill their traditional priestly and prophetic roles in communities that really need the services that these unique congregations provide. Critical to the C.M.E. aim of a 'transformed church' is a better understanding of my concept of 'transformative pastoral leadership.'" If ethnographic research in the context of ministry takes seriously the goal of not only generating knowledge, but contributing to the faith communities studied, the research problem and process must respond to the actual conditions "on the ground."

As I was in the process of gaining informed consent from the pastors and congregations that I selected for my study of "Pastoral Leadership in the Black Methodist Church" I was encouraged to attend the Tri-State Annual Conference of the C. M. E. Church that summer. As both congregations were a part of the same Annual Conference and both pastors were supervised by the same presiding elder and bishop, I recognized that attendance at the conference would provide an indispensable denominational frame for the subsequent theoretical sampling of activities, accounts, and artifacts that I had planned in each congregation. Theoretical sampling is the term that Glaser and Strauss use to describe the recommended strategy for grounded theory research:

> Theoretical sampling is the process of data collection for generating theory whereby the analyst jointly collects, codes, and analyzes his data and decides what data to collect next and where to find them, in order to develop his theory as it emerges. This process of data collection is *controlled* by the emerging theory . . . . The initial decisions for theoretical collection of data are based on a general sociological perspective and on a general subject or problem area . . . . The initial decisions are not based on a preconceived theoretical framework.[12]

---

[11] C. Willig, *Qualitative Research in Psychology: A Practical Guide to Theory and Method* (Buckingham: Open University Press, 2001), 10.

[12] Barney G. Glaser and Anselm L. Strauss, *The Discovery of Grounded Theory: Strategies for Qualitative Research* (New York: Aldine De Gruyter, 1967), 45.

I was welcomed by Bishop Issac Douglas to this conference and introduced to share my research intentions. Only then did I learn of the C. M. E. Church focus on transforming leadership at that time. I discovered that, in 1998, the chief governing body of the C. M. E. Church adopted as their quadrennial theme, "A Transformed Church: Living in Hope for the Life of the World." A pragmatic thrust of transforming churches was thus related to a theology of hope and the church's ethical responsibility to look beyond institutional survival to participate in God's concern "that they may have life, and have it abundantly."[13] Thus, at all levels of the church—whether the General Conference, Annual Conference, District Conference, or local church, the planned focus of this four-year period was on explicating the need for transforming leadership which actually served life-giving needs of individuals, congregations, and communities. Though I had come to the conference with an interest in exploring the role of church leaders (bishops, presiding elders, pastors, and laity) in fostering transformation as well as in conserving tradition within the systems and structures of the C. M. E. Church, a serendipitous discovery was that my interest in researching transformative pastoral leadership coincided with the interest of this particular denomination.

During my visit to this annual conference meeting, I was struck by the self-critical appraisal of Bishop Douglas as expressed in this excerpt from his sermon:

> Some of our churches are on life support systems. They are clinically dead .... We need to reevaluate the church as leaders .... We must ask the question, "Is your church a transforming church?" Not a transformed church for this implies a finished product .... Are you a transforming leaders or are we stuck in tradition? In Matthew 7 Jesus said, "By their fruits you will know them. A good tree will bring forth good fruit." You will see the evidence of a transforming leader by how they make a difference.[14]

Pressing on to offer his evaluation of the condition "on the ground" of the churches, Bishop Douglas offered some of his "theories" of why some churches are not transforming churches. His first reason might be named a theological one: some people think that the church belongs to them rather than to God. His second reason might be named as sociological: some churches operate on a seniority system and are exclusive clubs. Reflecting a concern felt in mainline churches as well as many African American churches, Bishop Douglas

---

[13] John 10.10 b NRSV.
[14] Sermon excerpt quoted by Jeffery L. Tribble, Sr, *Transformative Pastoral Leadership in the Black Church*, Black Religion/Womanist Thought/Social Justice Series, Dwight N. Hopkins and Linda E. Thomas (eds) (New York: Palgrave Macmillan, 2005), xv.

declared: "We cannot be a transformed church until we let some things die! Some things in the church need to die."

This critical self-assessment by the bishop along with explicit discussion of the critical nature of my practical theological research during the process of gaining informed consent with my research partners assisted me in walking the line between appreciative inquiry and critical assessment of the ministers and their ministries. While the study of African American pastoral leadership was facilitated by my identity as an ordained minister, it also complicated the challenge of producing a critical study. In Crain and Seymour's study of ethnographic research in ministry they argue that "knowing is connected, that mutuality is crucial, and that our efforts at interconnected knowing and mutuality are measured against God's will for a creation based on wholeness and justice."[15] Clearly, Bishop Douglas' sermon suggested mutual interests in a transformed church and that prophetic criticism by church leaders in the field might be enhanced by the contributions of the scholar.

It is challenging to remain in close relationships with pastors and congregational leaders while research and writing a critical and constructive study. Yet, the alternative is for critical theologies to remain divorced from congregational ministry. The Black church, in particular, needs to be empowered not only in its prophetic criticism of outer systems of oppression, but also for prophetic internal criticism. Commenting on this challenge, Wiley writes:

> The ultimate challenge for Black theology is to complete its return to the Black Church without compromising its responsibility not only to affirm the Black Church, but to critique it. It must do this by fostering a "prophetic spirituality" of "internal propheticism" that will constantly challenge the Black Church to be self-critical and to empower the people it serves not only to learn theology, as it is passed down from above, but to do theology from the grassroots up. Similarly, the challenge for the Black Church is not only to provide a space for Black theologians to do their work in a free, uninhibiting, and non-threatening environment, but also to work diligently to close the gap between the Black Church and the African-American community.[16]

Wiley rightly articulates the need for the church to accept both affirmation and critique from theologians, but does not emphasize the mutual accountability of practical theologians toward the faith communities that they study.

Ethnographers make public interpretations of findings that were heretofore private perspectives within the faith community. Wisdom, judgment, love, and

---

[15] Crain and Seymour, "The Ethnographer as Minister," 299.
[16] Dennis W. Wiley, "Black Theology, the Black Church, and the African-American Community," in *Black Theology: A Documentary History Volume II 1980–1992*, James H. Cone and Gayraud S. Wilmore (eds) (Maryknoll: Orbis Books, 1993), 136.

respect for persons and congregations must guide our representations of communities where we, the scholars, are not the only "knowers." In this study, I envisioned myself in relationship with a community of knowledgeable persons with whom I sought to construct knowledge. This community of "knowers"—female and male clergy, lay church leaders, theologians, sociologists, scholars of the Black church in the past and present—are connected in our common concern for discovering truth about the Black church and its ministry in the world.

In this image of a community of "knowers," I borrowed from the image of a "community of truth" explicated by Parker Palmer. He first describes "the objectivist myth" in which there is an "object" of knowledge that is grasped conceptually by "experts" who are better able to discern pure knowledge than "amateurs" who do not contribute to our understanding because of their lack of training and subjective biases. In this view, truth flows from experts qualified to grasp truth to amateurs who are only able to receive truth. Palmer rejects this model and proposes instead the image of a community of truth in which the subject, not the expert, is the center of attention.[17]

With this image in mind, I imagine a communal quest for something that I call "transformative pastoral leadership in the black church." Invited participants to this communal conversation share three important assumptions. First, they care about the health of the Black church, formed from the experience of oppression and marginalization. Second, they believe that the Black church has a critical role to play in the Black community as well as the wider public in light of its history of being the dominant social institution of Black people. Third, they believe that the rise or fall of that church depends on its leadership. Exemplary pastors, bishops, Black theologians, Womanist theologians, sociologists, community activists, and civil rights leaders are invited to represent communal perspectives. The voices of women are heard as well as men. Additionally, voices normally not represented in scholarly discourse are invited: the perspective of pastors in small struggling churches as well as the views of the people in the pews. The perspectives of trustees, stewards, Christian educators, prayer warriors, and Sunday School teachers, who do much of the ministry, shaping the internal congregational culture along with pastoral leaders, must be heard. Dedicated matriarchs and patriarchs with limited formal schooling are crucial to the dialogue because of their depth of faith and commitment as well as their commonsense wisdom.

Through a purposive sampling process, I represented these perspectives in my research of the subject which I call, "transformative pastoral leadership in the black church." A community of truth was summoned to understand this

---

[17] Parker J. Palmer, *The Courage to Teach: Exploring the Inner Landscape of a Teacher's Life* (San Francisco: Jossey-Bass Publishers, 1998), 99–106.

subject as the problem of generating theories of pastoral leadership rests on the general principle that leadership does not occur in a vacuum; it always occurs in a community, in a group, in a social historical context. In this explicit interpretive dialogue, I engage a living tradition in which innovation, adaptation, and transformation is necessary in a new rapidly changing urban context which I describe as post-Christian, post-civil rights, and post-industrial city.

As I reflect on my choice of representing the range of perspectives in this imagined "community of truth" I am aware of how my being shaped by a similar community impacted my epistemological assumptions. While participating in a seminar of Ph.D. students in Congregational Studies and Christian Education at Garrett-Evangelical with my team teaching colleagues, Jack Seymour and Margaret Ann Crain, Jack asked "what is it about those of us who invite 'ordinary people' as partners in our ethnographic research?" To value, and perhaps even privilege, the knowledge of people "in the field" over highly trained "elite" suggests a mutuality with the researcher in the construction of knowledge. Prior to this question, I had not reflected deeply on why this mutuality was a "no-brainer" for me.

The recent history of African American people demanded, for me, this kind of mutuality and respect for people of different levels of formal education. My paternal grandfather, though going no further than the seventh grade, possessed the intelligence to develop a successful business and inspired his sons to be self-employed business owners. My father, though offered a college scholarship, was discouraged from taking it by his high-school counselor who thought it made little sense for a Black man to go to college when he could be employed in the family business. My mother was inducted into the national honor society in high school. As the first member of her family to earn a high school diploma, no one had the vision or financial resources to encourage her to further her formal education. She, instead, got involved in her children's education making sure that all of her four children earned at least a college degree. While working in my father's business and supporting our education, she later earned an associate of arts degree.

Besides my firsthand knowledge of intelligent men and women like my grandparents and parents whose formal education was limited by social and economic constraints, I also was told stories of Blacks who, despite post-secondary educational successes, were restricted from full participation in the fields for which they had trained. I consider myself a part of the first generation of Blacks to benefit from the struggles of the 1960s and 1970s. Affirmative action programs, for me, were simply a mechanism for putting similarly qualified players on the field who, otherwise, would not have even had an opportunity to play in the game. I knew and interacted with too many knowledgeable people that I considered wise in my historically disadvantaged community to restrict my sources of knowledge to "elite" scholars with formal theological education.

If my experiences in my family and professional life were not enough to convince me of the value of the perspectives of lay church leaders at various level of formal education, I am grateful that I was given the assignment of interviewing about 90 church leaders the summer after my first year of seminary. Though I didn't have the training that I have now, this was my first paid "job" in ministry and my first experience of ethnographic listening. Rev. Dr Nathaniel Jarrett, then pastor of Martin Temple A. M. E. Zion Church (later elected a bishop) hired me to assist him in having conversations with church members at a significant juncture of congregational life: the building of a new sanctuary and service facility. Listening to the women and men who volunteered to allow this student minister to "stand on holy ground" by listening to their faith stories and perspectives helped to transform my perspective of congregational ministry. Though the A. M. E. Zion Church has a polity where the perspectives of ordained elders are privileged, this pastor taught me the value of listening to the people and developing ministries according to their interests and gifts. I found that my interviews with "seasoned saints" were moving experiences that evoked historical and theological reflection. Though their commonsense language differed from the sometimes esoteric language of the academy, I saw them as living embodiments of the accumulated wisdom of the race.

As we examine the historical development of the Christian church, all streams of living theological traditions have gifts as well as wounds which are passed down to succeeding generations. It is my judgment that one of the gifts of the living tradition of the Black church is its holistic ministry which is best demonstrated when both the priestly and prophetic functions of ministry are vibrant. I follow Lincoln and Mamiya's positive interpretation of the Black church. Their dialectic model is useful for the task of social analysis of a particular Black church. Describing their model Lincoln and Mamiya write:

Black churches are institutions that are involved in a constant series of dialectical tensions. The dialectic holds polar opposites in tension, constantly shifting between the polarities in historical time. There is no Hegelian synthesis or ultimate resolution of the dialectic. Although this dialectical model is not completely new, we feel that it is time to reassert the dialectical tensions in order to obtain a holistic picture of black churches. The task of the social analyst is to examine the social conditions of any particular black church, including the situation of its leadership and membership, in order to determine what its major orientation is in relation to any pair of dialectical opposites.[18]

---

[18] C. Eric Lincoln and Lawrence H. Mamiya, *The Black Church in the African American Experience* (Durham: Duke University Press, 1990), 11–12.

One of those pairs of dialectical opposites is "the dialectic between the priestly and prophetic functions." Priestly functions involve activities concerned with worship and maintenance of the spiritual life of the membership. The priestly function is crucial to nurturing a healthy congregational culture and is requisite to effective mobilization for social ministry. Prophetic functions involve activities that involve the church in political, economic, educational, and social concerns of the community. Some churches are closer to one end of the dialectic than the other. In my vision of transformative pastoral leadership, the tradition of holding these holistic functions in creative tension, I see as wisdom from past generations that must be passed down to a new generation of leaders.

With this in mind, I posed the research problem as follows:

> By comparing the similarities and differences of pastoral leadership in two research contexts, I am seeking to describe and explain a concept, transformative pastoral leadership in the Black church, and generate grounded theories of this praxis (qualities, practical wisdom, skills appropriate to the context) relevant to the evolving nature and mission of the Black church as we enter the 21st century and to suggest how such leadership might be fostered through education and mentoring.

In their text, "The Craft of Research," Booth, Colomb, and Williams say that the answer to the research problem should be (a) concise; (b) contestable, meaning not self-evident, but needing the evidence of research; and (c) conceptual, explicating concepts central to the research problem.[19] To these dimensions of the answer, I added (d), crafted for the intended audience. The audience that I imagined for my writing was one not only theological and sociological scholars, but also students of ministry and significant laymen. Glaser and Strauss had written that "Our basic position is that generating grounded theory is a way of arriving at theory suited to its supposed uses."[20] Thomas Frank had captured my attention in helping me to envision developing thick rich descriptions of ethnographic research as a form of "poetics." Frank writes:

> Poetics demands a rigor of plain language, of saying what is really here. It is a discipline of accurate description, of simplicity that is the only way to wipe the lens of incarnation . . . . Poetics in congregational life entails a mode of worship, preaching, teaching, and community-making that is first a way of being, not didactic or productive . . . . Poetics offers imaginative resources for fresh understanding of a congregation's culture as well as an enriched vision of congregational presence as a sign and catalyst for God's reign of

---

[19] Wayne C. Booth et al. *The Craft of Research* 2nd edition (Chicago: University of Chicago Press, 2003), 156.
[20] Glaser and Strauss, *The Discovery of Grounded Theory*, 3.

well-being and justice in the world. Poetics names and expresses, reflects and reinforces the soul of the congregation.[21]

Accordingly, I created "storylines"—descriptive stories about the central phenomenon of the study, "transformative pastoral leadership in the black church"—corresponding to each of my cases.

The storyline that I created from the Christopher Temple case study is as follows:

> Rev. Harrison, a student of the C.M.E. system, mentored in the tradition of the Black preacher and influenced by the Black consciousness fostered by the civil rights and Black power movements of the late 1960's and early 1970's is intentionally working towards the transformation of persons, an established denominational church, and a Black middle class community. With a clear sense of history of the Black church and a view of its potential in the ongoing struggle of Black people in this country, the transformative dimensions of Harrison's ministry are spiritual, cultural, political, economic, and social.

Though the ethnographic portraits are particular to the pastoral leaders studied in the context of congregation, community, and denomination, the storyline reveals my attempt to place my portraits in multiple "mattings" or frames of reference shedding light on my emerging insights. These frames included theological, historical, and sociological frameworks.

The storyline that I created from the Isaiah-Matthews case study is as follows:

> Dr. Evans, a spiritually gifted and theologically trained clergy woman, shaped by the experience of her struggle to overcome painful experiences of her past and the burdens of institutional oppression in the Black church, is one of a growing wave of women who is challenging the unofficial tradition of males only leadership in the Black Methodist church by intentionally working towards the transformation of persons as well as her congregation in Isaiah-Matthews gentrifying community. Though the battle for financial survival has limited their community outreach, she transforms the attitudes, beliefs, and behaviors of her inner core of leadership through a nurturing and caring ministry. Though one respondent describes her as "the mother hen of us all," there is a toughness that challenges men as well as women to greater accountability and faithfulness in ministry. There is also a keen

---

[21] Thomas Edward Frank, *The Soul of the Congregation: An Invitation to Congregational Reflection* (Nashville: Abingdon Press, 2000), 25.

business acumen that complements her "radical preaching" and real life-oriented teaching.

I gave each of these confessional "tales of the field"[22] an overarching title, an indigenous figure of speech, that appeared to "fit the data" of how transformation had taken place. Of the value of a "master trope" Hammersley and Atkinson write:

> The ethnographer necessarily uses various figures of speech (tropes). These are used to construct recognizable and plausible reconstructions of social actors, actions, and settings. They are also used to convey many of the analytic themes as well . . . . The reflective ethnographer, then, will need to try out figures of speech: testing them against the data, searching not just for their power to organize data under a single theme, but also for their extensions and limitations. They may be productive of new, often unanticipated insights. The writer of ethnography will therefore need to try out and explore the values of various figures of speech, gauging their relevance to the issues at hand, sensing the range of connotations, allusions, and implications.[23]

My confessional assumption is that God is the unseen social actor in all of the setting and scenes of my study. I titled my thick description of Christopher Temple, "God Did It: A Tale of a Male pastor in a Transforming Traditional Church." The figure of speech, "God Did It," was prominently written on undeveloped property adjacent to the expressway that was acquired by Christopher Temple for community economic development. In an interview with Rev. Harrison's wife of 27 years, I asked about the motivation of this sign. Constance Harrison's response was as follows:

> I believe the reason my husband had that sign posted was because he wanted people to know that Christopher Temple stands as a beacon of light. He wanted people to know that there was no way in the world that man could take credit for what God did in terms of how this property became available through the prayers of the church, the fasting and through the conversation, wanting something to happen on that corner for the children, the next generation . . . . It's a reaffirmation of what God is doing in our lives, not only

22 See John Van Maanen, *Tales of the Field: On Writing Ethnography* (Chicago: The University of Chicago Press, 1988).
23 Martyn Hammersley and Paul Atkinson, *Ethnography: Principles in Practice*, 2nd edition (New York: Routledge, 1995), 245–6.

because of that building, the brick and mortar, but in our lives, spiritually, God is doing it.[24]

I came to believe that the "transformative pastoral leadership" that I observed at Christopher Temple could not be described without attention to a logic in which both divine grace and human responsibility are explained. The insistent and pervasive claim that "God Did It" is an expression of Christopher Temple's theological belief that God is at work in the world, that persons are called as beneficiaries and instruments of God's work, and that God is deserving of "all the glory" as they engage in the practices of religious and social ministry. Similarly, the effectiveness of one faithful pastor (whom I have named as an exemplar of my concept of "transformative pastoral leadership in the black church") must be understood within an inner logic where God's grace is credited as inspiring human innovation and responsibility.

I entitled the portrait of my study of Isaiah-Matthews, "God of a Second Chance: A Tale of a Female Pastor in a Transforming Merged Mission Church." "God of a Second Chance" was the title of a sermon preached by Dr Evans at a women's conference. In this sermon, Dr Evans seemed to use her own life experience as a hermeneutical lens not only for reading her sermon text but also for reading human experiences with a God who offers radical forgiveness and unconditional love. In the introduction to this sermon, Dr Evans signals that she wants the congregation to take seriously the experiences of a woman in the Bible as an interpretive lens for understanding our human fallibility and vulnerability. Dr Evans declared:

> I think we all know that God, because many times you and I have messed up . . . . and we need to know that we serve a forgiving God. Come with me, if you will, to the book of John. I want to tell y'all about a lesson here that we don't like to talk about too much in the church. Some of us in Christendom have not worked it out. And I'm going to try to look at the woman in the 8th chapter, the adulterous woman, a sister if you will, who could be either you or me. The God of a second chance. . . I'm so glad that I know Jesus that He is a God of a second chance, because for years, many of us have been beating ourselves up because we have not been willing to forgive ourselves of stuff that happened in '62, '73, '85 and so on.[25]

In this particular sermonic context, the sermon was inserted between her opening account of her challenging experience as a woman in ministry at Isaiah-Matthews and her closing account of the "second chance" of her own second

---

[24] Quoted in Tribble, *Transformative Pastoral Leadership*, 24.
[25] Quoted in Tribble, *Transformative Pastoral Leadership*, 82.

marriage, which was a culmination of years of healing and growth from an abusive marital relationship. In my "tale of a female pastor transforming a merged mission church" I related the successful merging of two fledging congregations, the renovation of a burned-down structure, the accounts of the impact that Evans has had on the lives of persons, and the potential impact of the church on a gentrifying community as evidence of this faith community's perceived reality that God is indeed a "God of a second chance."

Closing Reflections toward Epistemological Reflexivity

In this chapter, I have offered explanations and personal reflections, methodologically and practically, on what I have done in field research of African American pastoral leadership, how and why I did it, and what I learned that may be of significance to other researchers. It is clear that this researcher is "joined at the hip" to the research process and product. Hence, in the foregoing I have primarily been engaged in personal reflexivity. However, Swinton and Mowat describe epistemological reflexivity as follows:

> *Epistemological reflexivity* requires us to engage with questions such as: How has the research question defined and limited what can be "found." How has the design of the study and the method of analysis "constructed" the data and its findings? How could the research question have been investigated differently? To what extent would this have given rise to a different understanding of the phenomenon under investigation?[26]

As I continue this process of critical self-reflection on how I, as research instrument, have contributed to this particular ethnographic research, I am aware that my representations of pastoral leadership are my own constructions of a complex social reality. The hope is that the project of defining the concept of "transformative pastoral leadership in the black church" indeed offers "hopeful stories and helpful strategies for those who believe that the black church must continue its historic mission of being an instrument of survival, elevation, and liberation for its people" (a claim that I make on the book cover flap). Though "transformative pastoral leadership in the black church" is *my way of naming* a Christian practice discovered and explicated in a complex Black urban context, I do believe that it is a valid interpretation of a complex reality grounded in the sociohistorical experiences of a marginalized people. Furthermore, I believe that I have a posed a problem and answer that is relevant to the communities that I studied.

---

[26] Swinton and Mowat, *Practical Theology and Qualitative Research*, 60.

Following the publication of the book and my presentation of copies to key co-researchers, I was pleased to receive the "2005 Religious Rev. Carrell Cargle One Church One School Religious Leader of the Year Award" from Bishop Henry Williamson, Sr, Founder, and Mrs Phedonia Johnson, National Director. Respecting the informed consent agreement of confidentiality, I was presented this award before a national gathering of C. M. E. Church leaders without public explanation of why I was being honored. Though an unexpected tribute, I am thankful to have been honored by my co-researchers for my interpretation of these faith communities.

No doubt, this study is constrained by the discipline of generating insights from my grounded theory approach to research. In this approach, "theories" were generated from the data of my two cases, although data from other sources were correlated with my field research. "Theories in process" were developed in the form of thick descriptions and explanations of strategies of "transformative pastoral leadership" in particular contexts of congregation, community, and denomination. I selected two healthy congregations that were not conflicted at the time of my research. They had apparently managed to work through the inevitable conflict of working through the transitions of transformation. All field research is, in the final analysis, more "suggestive" than "prescriptive."

In my use of this text for students who are not C. M. E. or Black Methodists, I have been pleased that there is "identification" and "resonance" to other contexts where leaders have similar circumstances.[27] As responsible ethnographers, we attempt rigorous multimethod research methodologies so that we make responsible claims based on evidence in our multiple data streams. Still, claims of "transformation" are audacious even though I explored the meaning of transformation as a complex phenomenon from within multiple fields of reference. In this study, my understanding of the meaning of transformation was constrained by my field research and several streams of literature: evangelism, adult transformative education, congregational studies, and sociology of the Black church. Thus, I attempted to be open to multiple modes of transformation whether "transformation" was the spiritual transformation of persons by conversion to God through faith in Jesus Christ; adult transformative learning which I understood as growth and development of one's thinking process as well as shifts in perspective that results in changes in thinking, attitudes, relationships, and behavior; the change in congregations as open systems which may reflect, resist, or influence urban transformations and other changes in the world; or the sociological perspective of the church's response to social changes and its participations in movements of social change.

---

[27] I'm wrestling here with the problem of generalization of qualitative research, a problem discussed by Swinton and Mowat in *Practical Theology and Qualitative Research*, 46–51.

As each research methodology is a unique construction, there are a myriad of other ways that the research might have been designed. The attempt to recognize, define, and explain the grounded theory, "transformative pastoral leadership in the black church," was a response to possibilities that I saw in the two sites selected for research. As the "theories in process" were embedded in thick descriptions of the situations in the "slices of life" in each of the pastors' tenures, my discussion of "transformative pastoral leadership in the black church" was further constrained by the particular situations that I encountered in my two in-depth case studies. As transformation may be construed as change in a particular direction and is often slow, incremental, and by no means irreversible, an alternative approach would have the option of looking for promising sites where a variety of transformative transitions are in progress. Successful transitions will involve time, learning, and patience. Further, successful transitions may involve conflict, the death of persons or practices, and other messy factors that cannot be determined or controlled. One cannot know if a particular congregation in transition will transition successfully; hence, the opportunity to directly observe congregations in transition would necessarily require a larger sample of congregations, some of which may not experience successful transitions. This is not the type of research that a solitary ethnographer pursues when one is "on the clock" of completing a dissertation or completing research in a tenure driven time frame. Combining the roles of "consultant" working with congregations desiring transformation and "pro-active researcher" would be another way of an ethnographer fulfilling the dual role of understanding and serving ministries. Participant action research is one approach where cycles of congregational teaching and learning might coincide with ethnographic research which educates and empowers.

Chapter 6

The Listening Church: How Ethnography Can Transform Catholic Ethics

Emily Reimer-Barry

I teach courses in Christian Ethics at a Catholic university, and include a section on HIV/AIDS in each Ethics course I teach. I have found that when I spend time in class explaining the statistics of HIV prevalence globally, nationally, and locally, students have difficulty engaging the material. When I assign in-class writing assignments on these days, some students explain that the "numbers don't mean anything," or they feel "numb" by the statistics. They tell me that it is hard to imagine the struggles of 22 million people in sub-Saharan Africa infected with HIV. It is difficult for my students to envision the real people behind those numbers. As one of my former students explained, "It is hard to have compassion for a statistic."

On the other hand, these same students, after having read ethnographic accounts or personal stories, or having watched a documentary film, become animated in class discussion. They ask engaging questions, and more readily offer their personal analysis of the issues in class. In writing assignments students explain that the class feels "practical" and "grounded" when we are talking about "real people." While my students' easy dismissal of large groups of people is troubling, my sense is that young people yearn to make a personal connection to what they are learning about; their ability to feel a personal connection to the course material makes their learning more meaningful. Stories about particular people engage my students in a more holistic way, engaging even their emotions. In reading personal narratives, students are encouraged to walk in someone else's shoes for a bit; inevitably these students begin to think about themselves and their personal values with fresh eyes. Interestingly, grounded attention to the struggles of individual people draws students into reflection on complex social forces; it demands that my students look again at the statistics of global infection rates that had previously so challenged them.

Whether in the classroom or in academic research, a growing number of Christian ethicists are adopting qualitative methods in order to bring the stories of particular people into our ethical deliberation. In my faith tradition, Roman Catholicism, methodology is a hot topic today. Moral theologians in the Catholic tradition approach their scholarly work from a variety of methodological perspectives. All claim to depend on and interpret human experience as a source of moral wisdom, but scholars attend to experience and interpret experience from different anthropological assumptions and toward varying ends.

Use of human experience in ethics is a slippery thing. There is no such thing as generic human experience. Catholic magisterial teachings tend to be suspicious of the use of sociological methods in theological research and often draw sharp distinctions between the authority of church teachings and the opinions of Christian believers.[1] According to this view, sin infects every part of the human condition, including human reason, so the opinions of Christian believers are suspect; church teachings are more reliable because the Holy Spirit will protect the church from error. But in the past 50 years, theologies of liberation have challenged the dominant methods of theological scholarship by attending in a special way to the experiences of marginalized peoples. Liberation theologians, including feminist theologians, have argued persuasively that ethicists must pay attention to find out whose experience is accounted for in authoritative teachings, and how that experience is interpreted. Liberation theologians argue that in order to attend to the complexities of human experience as a source of moral wisdom, scholars of Christian ethics should give special attention to marginalized voices and those voices not typically heard in academic or pastoral contexts.

Ethnography is a valuable and underutilized methodology that has the potential to positively transform Catholic ethics precisely because it can bring new voices, especially marginalized voices, into the conversation. Drawing on my own research, which centers on gender and HIV/AIDS, this chapter defends ethnography as a method that helpfully integrates the wisdom of human experience together with other sources of moral wisdom, including the Bible and Christian traditions. I begin by describing two essential methodological commitments in ethnographic research: empathetic listening and self-reflection. Then I explain how I organized my ethnographic studies and what I learned, and offer some cautions for theologians interested in developing research projects with ethnographic methods.

Methodological Commitments

Broadly stated, ethnography involves immersing oneself in a particular community in order to learn from the experiences of other people, primarily

---

[1] See for example, John Paul II, *Familiaris consortio* (1981), no. 5. Available online at http://www.vatican.va/holy_father/john_paul_ii/apost_exhortations/documents/hf_jp-ii_exh_19811122_familiaris-consortio_en.html. See also *Veritatis splendor* (August 6, 1993), in *Origins* 23/18 (October 14, 1993), 297–334.

through in-person interviews and direct observation. The researcher adopts a stance of empathetic listening. The starting point of empathetic listening is crucial to ethnographic methodology in theology because it communicates to the informant that her experiences *matter*,[2] that her voice is a valuable contribution to the church's discernment.[3] A stance of attentive listening communicates to the informant that she is an expert in the story of her life; she is an authority, and the researcher is the one who needs to learn.[4] While ethnographers might describe their field notes or interview transcripts as data, one should always keep in mind that this data is fundamentally about the human subjects of one's research. Every effort should be made to avoid describing the interview participant as an object to be studied. Instead, ethnography demands a partnership between the researcher and interview participant that is more helpfully described as collaborative.

The starting point of empathetic listening challenges other methodologies in Catholic ethics. Instead of first asking, "What does the church teach?" the researcher asks, "what is going on here?" Thick description[5] precedes normative reflection. By starting with the lived experiences of particular people, instead of magisterial teachings or divine revelation, ethnography can situate Catholic ethics in the complex contexts of the everyday person's struggles of Christian discipleship. The theologian who utilizes ethnography must spend a good deal of time out of her office and away from the university library in order to interact with collaborators in their everyday lives. Some ethnographers have adopted the term "fieldwork" from anthropologists in order to describe this task; ethnographers go out into the field in order to learn from their collaborators. "The field" could be a hospital, nursing home, school, homeless shelter, prison, corporate office, bus terminal, or other location depending on the researcher's specific project.

In my own research I find the commitment of empathetic listening important because it shifts the locus of authority in the research setting. My goal when interviewing a study participant is to understand as much as possible the research participant's worldview and life story; then my task is to describe my collaborator's worldview in a way that offers an empathetic understanding of her worldview for my readers. I have found that the women I have interviewed appreciated the opportunity to share their stories with me. Ethnography gives me the opportunity to honor the uniqueness of each participant's story. Even when one returns to the library or to one's office, the researcher can remember

[2] See Vigen, *Women, Ethics, and Inequality*.
[3] One of my working assumptions is that theological scholarship can contribute to ongoing discernment within the Catholic church.
[4] See Spradley, *The Ethnographic Interview*.
[5] I credit Clifford Geertz with the term "thick description." See Clifford Geertz, *The Interpretation of Culture* (New York: Basic Books, 1973).

and call to mind the images of people she met, the tone of their voices, their smiles, or their tears. Fieldwork can cultivate in the theologian felt solidarity with those who are marginalized; this grounded perspective inevitably shapes the theologian's analysis of the complexity of the moral issues at stake.

I have successfully integrated ethnographic fieldwork in two different research projects. In 2006, while living in Chicago, Illinois, I developed a qualitative study in which I interviewed eight women who self-described as Catholic, HIV-positive, and married or widowed. My goal was to understand their daily struggles and to investigate how their religious formation had helped or hindered their ability to cope with their HIV infection. Few documents from the Catholic magisterium have addressed the special situations in which these women find themselves. My goal was to learn about their experiences and to analyze their stories in relation to official Catholic teachings. The second project took place in the summer of 2009 when I conducted fieldwork in Kenya as part of a larger collaborative study on gender, health, and empowerment. The project brought together women scholars from the United States and Kenya for a cross-cultural symposium on women. As part of our work together we interviewed local women and observed them in their daily activities. In this second project I was able to interview educators, students, nurses, social workers, an elderly woman, and HIV-positive women living in a variety of settings.

These two research projects, while quite different, still share some common themes. Both attend to the experiences of women, including their understandings of their daily struggles, their descriptions of their faith commitments, and the influence of their religious communities in their lives. The methodological commitment of empathetic listening was important in both projects because I needed to communicate to the interview participants that their life stories are valuable and have much to contribute to the academy and to the church community. I wanted to learn from these women and convey the assumption that they are the authorities on their own lives, and I was the one who needed to learn from them.

A second key methodological commitment in ethnography is self-reflection. Self-reflection by the researcher is essential to ethnography because it acknowledges that the researcher herself is an embodied subject whose experience arises out of a specific context. The researcher must reflect on the way that he or she interacts with the research participants and how he or she interprets the interview data.

As part of this self-reflection the researcher should pay attention to the dynamics of power or privilege that may unwittingly shape the contours of the research partnership in problematic ways.[6] For example, as a white, educated,

---

[6] Wayne Fife, *Doing Fieldwork: Ethnographic Methods for Research in Developing Countries and Beyond* (New York: Palgrave Macmillan, 2005), 149.

upper middle-class citizen of the United States, I entered the interview settings with given powers and privileges that the research participants in my studies did not always share. This reality was more obvious in some contexts than in others. When walking through a camp for internally displaced persons (IDP) in Kenya, young children pointed at me, crying "muzungu!"[7] and asking, "How are you?" My interviews with women there were undoubtedly influenced by the mutual awareness of differences, named with such exuberance by the young children. For some of the women I interviewed in Kenya, including women I interviewed in the slums of Kibera and women at the IDP camp, most of the white women they have encountered are missionaries or aid workers. Many thought of me initially as a potential benefactor, so it was necessary for me to take care in explaining my role as a researcher. A lens of critical self-reflection is essential for the researcher who understands that "encounters take place within systems of power and domination."[8] The privileges I have experienced shape my self-understanding and well as my relationships with others—whether I am cognizant of that fact or not.

In addition to thinking about the power dynamics within the interview setting itself, a commitment to self-reflection means that the researcher must interrogate the ways that her own expectations may shape her interpretation of the interview data. While sociologists describe these problems in a variety of ways, I have found it helpful to think of my own self-reflection as an integrated part of my research. That is, I do not simply acquire data and analyze it, and then reflect on it from my social location. Instead, throughout the whole process of recruiting interview participants, building relationships with gatekeepers,[9] developing interview questions, establishing rapport in the interview setting, transcribing, and analyzing data, I must reflect upon what surprises me, what challenges me, or what confuses me. One must strike a balance here; one should not simply be self-referential. It would be improper to constantly insert oneself into the analysis. But neither should the researcher pretend that she can be completely detached or objective in a project in which she is actively involved.

How I Used Ethnography

Most research projects begin with a proposal. Whether one is a graduate student submitting a proposal to one's dissertation committee, or a faculty

---

[7] Muzungu means white person or foreigner.

[8] Heike Walz, "The Beautiful Princess and the Village Girls," in *Feminist Interpretation of the Bible and the Hermeneutics of Liberation*, Silvia Schroer and Sophia Bietenhard (eds) (New York: Continuum, 2003), 137.

[9] Gatekeeper is a common term used to describe the primary contact person who helps the ethnographer gain access to the community to be studied.

member submitting a proposal for a research grant or publishing contract, the proposal of a project incorporating ethnography will look very different from a more traditional proposal in theology. While both kinds of proposals will begin with a description of the topic or problem, and both will likely include a literature review to demonstrate the project's potential contribution to the field, a traditional proposal in the theological disciplines is expected to offer a precise thesis, succinct methodology, and outline of the argument. But the ethnographer cannot offer an outline of the argument at this early stage; instead, the ethnographer can only give the research questions that will guide her work. These will likely be open-ended questions, meant to describe the scope of the project and not meant to be exhaustive. At this early stage the ethnographer is also working to build relationships with potential collaborators. She is determining how she will have access to the community she wishes to study, and she is cultivating relationships with gatekeepers within this community.

A theologian based in the United States who intends to use ethnographic methods must submit a proposal to his home institution's Institutional Review Board (IRB) for project approval before he begins to recruit interview participants for research. This process is not simply a hoop to jump through. The mandate of the IRB is to protect human subjects from exploitation by researchers. The theologian who plans to incorporate ethnographic methods into his research must demonstrate in the proposal of his project that he understands his obligations as a researcher and that he has strategies in place for protecting his research collaborators. The researcher must explain how he intends to recruit participants for research; in some cases the researcher must demonstrate that he has been given permission by gatekeepers at cooperating institutions who will assist him in finding participants who fit the criteria of her study. He must make his research protocol available to the IRB and demonstrate his strategy for ensuring that the confidentiality of her informants will be protected. While preparing the paperwork for IRB submission is time consuming, researchers should not think of this time as a delay of the project but instead as laying the foundation for a successful project. It is a privilege to listen to and interact with research participants, and the regulations enforced by IRB offer some important protections for those participants.

Methods of Recruitment

When I had secured IRB approval, I was ready to begin recruiting interview participants. For the research project on married Catholic women living with

HIV, I partnered with three social service agencies in Chicago.[10] Each allowed me to post information about the study within their offices. I also invited interested case managers at these agencies to pass on information to clients who fit the study criteria. Each participant was screened initially by telephone to confirm that she fit the study criteria. For English-speaking women I accepted the telephone calls on my personal mobile phone; Spanish-speaking women were directed to call the translator whom I hired for this project.

For the project in Kenya I partnered with a field assistant at the Maryknoll Institute of African Studies, who assisted me in scheduling interviews with women in a range of settings based on my own preliminary investigations as well as my field assistant's contacts in the field. I did not use any recruiting documents for the project in Kenya; most interviews were arranged by telephone call.

Language Barriers and Interpretation

Researchers do not always speak the same language as the subjects they wish to interview. While it would always be preferable to learn a new language and to so immerse oneself in a new culture that one would not require the assistance of an interpreter, this is not always possible. But it is possible to use an interpreter in an ethnographic study.

In both research projects I have found the assistance of an interpreter to be essential. When investigating the experiences of HIV+ women in Chicago, I was aware that Hispanic/Latina women are at an increasing risk for exposure to HIV. While I do not speak Spanish, I wanted to include Hispanic/Latina women in this study, so I hired an interpreter to assist me in interviewing Spanish-speaking women. My interpreter, Susana Mate, had previous experience in research settings. She was present in both interviews of Spanish-speaking women, even though one participant, who is bilingual, spoke in English during the interview. In the interview with the Spanish-speaking participant, Susana translated both for me and the interview participant in a method called consecutive interpretation, whereby she would interpret for each of us by summarizing our statements or questions and relaying them to the other. Susana also translated my recruiting documents and consent forms into Spanish, fielded telephone inquiries from Spanish-speaking participants, and created a verbatim transcript of one of the interviews.

---

[10] I partnered with Vital Bridges, Community Outreach Intervention Project, and National Catholic AIDS Network.

I relied on my field assistant, Jedidah Ruhere, for consecutive interpretation when conducting fieldwork in Kenya. While some of the women I interviewed were comfortable speaking in English, many spoke only Kiswahili. Jedidah assisted me in arranging interviews and in interpreting during interviews. In addition, we shared and discussed our field notes with one another after each interview.

The presence of an interpreter in an interview setting is not ideal. The pauses necessary for interpretation break up the conversation between the researcher and participant. There is the possibility for misunderstanding if the interpreter summarizes either's comments in a confusing way, or if by summarizing these comments the interpreter misses some of the nuances of the original speaker's speech patterns (which is inevitable). Consecutive interpretation takes extra time and extra patience for all parties involved. Use of an interpreter also creates a greater risk for breach of confidentiality because an additional person has access to the confidential information of the participant.

Despite these constraints, I decided that it was important in both studies to partner with an experienced interpreter so that I would be able to interview a larger number of women with a wider range of experiences. By partnering with experienced interpreters who had previously worked in research settings and whom I found to be knowledgeable and trustworthy, I attempted to limit any potential problems. Despite the limitations I have described, these interviews were a vital part of the overall studies. To exclude some women from participating because of my own inability to speak Spanish or Kiswahili would have required that I neglect important voices that should be heard.

The Interviews

The primary method of acquiring data for my projects was the open-ended in-person interview. I also took copious field notes after each interview. Open-ended questions allow the researcher to understand and capture the points of view of other people without predetermining those points of view through prior selection of questionnaire categories, as is typical of quantitative research.[11] The researcher must then let additional questions emerge in the process. It is for this reason that sociologist Michael Quinn Patton admits, "qualitative inquiry seems to work best for people with a high tolerance for ambiguity."[12] In these oral histories, the researcher invites the participant to

[11] B. L. Berg, *Qualitative Research Methods* (Needham Heights: Allyn & Bacon, 1989), 28.
[12] Michael Quinn Patton, *Qualitative Evaluation and Research Methods* (Thousand Oaks: Sage, 1990), 183.

share her experiences, beliefs, feelings, and attitudes. Some experienced researchers admit that the open-ended interview is sometimes more of an art than science;[13] that is, aspects of the interview data are imprecise, difficult to measure, or even rooted in feeling or emotion.

The interview partnership depends upon mutual respect, clear communication, and trust between researcher and participant. In any interview context, just as in personal relationships, trust must be earned, not assumed. In order to begin to establish this trust in the interviews I conducted, I began by thanking the participant for being willing to speak with me, by describing the aims of the project, and by securing her consent. I told her that she could stop the interview at any time to take a break, and that she could refuse to answer any question if it became too personal. For example, in the study I conducted in Chicago, I asked each participant a series of questions to help her to feel at ease in the interview. I asked her how she was feeling that day, or asked about a family picture, or thanked her for her clear driving directions. Sometimes for a brief time we talked about the weather. I asked her how she learned about the study (if I had not already asked this during the telephone screening). Frequently that led me to ask about her involvement in that particular social service agency, and we would talk for a short time about AIDS outreach agencies within Chicago, or about the city itself. The point of these initial bits of conversation is to help her feel comfortable so that she can settle into her natural speaking voice. It helped me to see whether we were building a rapport of trust, or whether she had anxieties about the study that we should discuss before getting further along. In reading her body language I sensed whether she was worried or distracted or impatient, or whether she sensed that I was trustworthy, and that my project was organized and valuable and worth her time. To be an effective interviewer requires that one rely on intuition and that one present a demeanor of friendliness. However the message I tried to communicate through these verbal and nonverbal cues was not "I want to be your friend" but rather "I respect you and I want to hear about your experiences. I can be trusted to protect your confidentiality. I will be sensitive to your fears or apprehensions."

For each study I had an interview protocol that served as a general guide for interview questions. Open-ended questions enabled me to invite each interview participant to put everything into her own words. For the study I conducted in Chicago, my protocol included some demographic questions and other facts, including year of diagnosis, number of years married, number of children, and type of drug regimen. But more important were those questions that invited the participant to share her feelings, her descriptions of God, or how she makes sense of her everyday struggles. I would ask, for example: "Tell

---

[13] Fife, *Doing Fieldwork*, 93.

me about the day you were diagnosed as HIV-positive. How did it make you feel? Whom did you tell? Tell me about your wedding day. How did you first meet your husband?" If she began to distance herself from the story or to talk in the third person, saying, for example, "Everyone should use condoms," "It's important to get your name on the ADAP list," or "You've got to pray about it," then I would ask her to describe her own feelings or opinions. I would ask, "Do you and your husband use condoms?" or "How did you get your name on the ADAP list?" or "When you pray, what do you say to God? Do you ever have a difficult time praying to God?"

When interviewing women in Kenya, my interview protocol included a variety of questions about the interview participant's daily life, health concerns, and her perceived role in her family and community. For example, I would ask the informant to tell me about herself and her family, and to describe a typical day in her life. I would ask: "In your community, what things do women typically do? What things to men typically do? Would you say the roles are equal, or do either men or women do more work?" I also asked questions like: "Who is responsible for health in your community? When you are sick, do you go to a doctor or a traditional healer? Do women and children have everything they need for a healthy life? Do they have enough to eat and money for children's school fees?" I also asked the women about their faith and their faith communities. I asked them about how they pray, and what they teach their children about God and (for the women who self-described as Catholic) about the church.

I did not ask all of these questions in every interview, but instead let follow-up questions emerge out of each woman's particular answers. Still, the research protocol indicated the range of questions and the general scope of the interviews. Open-ended interviewing requires some careful direction by the researcher but also requires a willingness to let the interview take shape based on the unique perspectives of the participant.

An additional concern for in-person interviewing is whether the participant's observations and stories are true and accurate accounts of their own lives.[14] While I do not believe that any of my collaborators intentionally falsified information, it is possible that a participant self-edited her own story, or has gaps in her memory. I attempted to avoid these possibilities by asking each woman to describe concrete incidents or details of a given story. Because they had little, if anything, to gain by withholding information or lying, I have no reason not to believe their accounts.

For the interviews I conducted in Chicago, each woman agreed to let me audiotape the interview. Then each interview was transcribed verbatim. While it is true that the presence of the tape recorder can have an effect on the

---

[14] For a discussion of this concern see Robert S. Weiss, *Learning from Strangers: The Art and Method of Qualitative Interview Studies* (New York: Free Press, 1994), 146–50.

participant's comfort level or desire to self-edit, I wanted to be able to listen again to the interviews and secure a verbatim transcript instead of relying only on my own notes. I found also that since it was being recorded, I felt less tied to my notebook and more able to make eye contact and create a posture of openness and listening during the interview. I do think that after a few minutes, each woman became more comfortable within the interview session and that the presence of the tape recorder was not a concern.

For the project in Chicago, I transcribed the English interviews myself; my interpreter, Susana Mate, transcribed the Spanish–English interview. Specific names and place names were removed or renamed in the transcripts so as to protect the confidentiality of the research participants. In transcripts, I cleaned up some language to take out some of the "ums" and "you knows" and to take away some of the false starts and repetitions. The intent was not to formalize the conversation or edit out any vivid speech patterns, but rather to prevent the reader from becoming distracted or confused. My sense is that the woman's voice is more able to come through when the quotations were less choppy. I do indicate pauses, and do try to indicate areas of emphasis, exasperation, changes in tone, emotion, or body language relevant to the meaning of the quotation. Each participant was given 25 dollars at the conclusion of the in-person interview to honor her time commitment. For those who traveled to my office for the interview, this money was a way to reimburse them for their travel expenses. While I do not think that any of the women participated solely to receive this money, each seemed appreciative and all accepted the money. Four women explicitly told me that they would have participated even if I had not paid them.

My research project in Kenya, which shared some similar themes to the project I had conducted in Chicago, was different in other respects. All of the interviews took place in a three-week period. I hired a field assistant to assist me, and she was present for every interview. I did not record the interviews that I conducted in Kenya, and do not have verbatim transcripts from the interviews, but I did write extensive field notes. After each interview I described the interview location in my notes, and recorded quotations from the interview that seemed particularly meaningful. I also read my field assistant's field notes and preliminary analysis, and we had extended conversations after each interview.

In the Kenya project I did not give a stipend to any of the interview participants, although in some cases we did give a gift to the gatekeeper organization. For example, we brought groceries to the women's empowerment project in Kibera and the food was distributed among the members present that day by the directors of the organization. When we interviewed an elderly woman in her home, we brought her a gift of tea and milk to thank her for her hospitality.

Consent and Confidentiality

Theologians who use ethnography should have a clear plan in place to protect research participants from coercion and, when necessary, to protect the confidentiality of respondents. In the research project I conducted in Chicago, I began each interview session by describing the aims of the research project and the kinds of questions that would be asked during the interview so that each participant had full information about the study. Each woman read and signed a consent form indicating that she understood the project's goals and risks and that she freely consented to participate. She was given a copy of the consent form to take home with her, and I took the signed form. To ensure each participant's confidentiality I used a pseudonym for each woman in the project instead of using her real name. I also omitted or changed the identifying names of hospitals or other institutions described by the participant.

For the research I conducted in Kenya, I obtained verbal consent from each participant instead of written consent. Since many of the women in the study were illiterate, they would have been unable to read or sign a written consent form. Written consent forms can also raise suspicion among family members who might worry that the researcher is making a profit from the individual's participation in research. In light of these concerns, and in light of previous studies in the region which have relied on verbal rather than documented written consent, the IRB gave me approval to seek verbal consent instead of written consent. I began each interview by explaining the goals of the project and the method of the interview. Each study participant was given full information about the study, and I told her that she could refuse to answer any question, or she could withdraw from the study at any time. I asked each woman how she would like to be identified in the report, and whether or not I should use her real name. Some women indicated that they wanted me to use their real names, while others asked that I use a pseudonym instead.

Post-Interview Analysis

Data from quantitative research is quite different from data collected in qualitative research because qualitative findings are longer, more detailed, and more variable in content.[15] For qualitative research, the stages of the research process are not strictly linear (i.e. recruitment, data collection, analysis, writing of results) because even in field notes during and after each interview one remarks upon any significant themes that have emerged, and begins the

---

[15] Patton, *Qualitative Evaluation*, 24.

process of comparison between interviews. Thus the beginnings of one's analysis overlap with the stage of data collection.

The method for analyzing the data involves immersing oneself in the data, which can mean listening again to interview tapes, rereading transcripts, and rereading field notes. In doing so, one pays attention to any themes that emerge from the data. I have found it helpful to think of two stages within this process of inductive analysis: recognizing concepts, and discerning patterns.

Sociologist Wayne Fife describes this first stage of analysis as a give-and-take between "micro" and "macro" levels of analysis. The data from oral histories with individual research participants constitute micro-level data, while macro-level data includes the larger environmental context in which that person's story is situated.[16] As the researcher rereads transcripts and field notes, she looks for preliminary themes that seem to stand out.[17] These become the "concepts" in a given transcript; concepts can refer both to the micro-level and macro-level of a participant's story, but an analysis of micro-level information should be given priority.

For the project I conducted in Chicago, the task of analyzing the data at the conclusion of eight interviews was daunting. The data I collected included 180 pages of typed interview transcripts and two wire-bound notebooks of field notes. But some concepts did emerge. In my field notes I had already begun to write some preliminary mapping of relationships between concepts within an individual participant's story, and concepts within multiple participants' stories. My first list of these concepts included: survival, resilience, regret, relationships, responsibility, self-respect, dependence on God, dependence on spouse, friendship, fidelity, dependence on government, denial, poverty, fear, family, communication, fatigue, stigma, shame, violence, trust, prayer, opportunities, empowerment, and justice.[18] While this list was completed after the final interview, many of these themes had been documented in earlier sections of my field notes as I reflected upon each interview and preliminary connections between participants' stories. Sharon Walker explains that with an inductive approach a researcher must feel her way through the interview process.[19] Sometimes in feeling my way through an interview I noticed similarities between stories. I took note of these similarities, as well as any contrasts.

In the second stage of analysis the researcher seeks to discern patterns among concepts. For example, after I had developed a list of key concepts from within each interview transcript, I mapped relationships between these

---

[16] Fife, *Doing Fieldwork*, 120.
[17] Ibid.
[18] Field notes of author, October 20, 2006.
[19] Sharon Walker, *Women with AIDS and Their Children* (New York: Garland, 1998), 66. Walker references I. E. Seidman, *Interviewing as Qualitative Research* (New York: Teachers College Press, 1991).

concepts, and grouped them into related subgroups. For each subgroup I used a different color highlighter and went through every page of the transcripts and field notes, highlighting passages according to the concepts within the passage that fit a theme I had already named within the given subgroup. Then, by reviewing the colored markings I could identify additional relationships between participants' stories.

In my preliminary analysis, I had to resist any urges to make the data fit a single pattern. As Fife explains, sometimes the researcher naturally imposes a theoretical framework on a data set before the completion of data collection. There is a tendency for the same concepts to come up again and again because the researcher becomes predisposed to see in new data concepts that arose in earlier data sets; one cannot help but be influenced by earlier kinds of analysis, which informs the categorizing and analysis one does on later sections of the project.[20] In the studies I conducted, the interviews conducted at the end of the process had slightly different foci than those at the beginning of the process. The research questions had developed, and this development is reflected in the kinds of questions asked and the direction imposed within the interview setting. So, while I may have been predisposed in later interviews to recognize themes that had appeared in earlier interviews, I was also conscious of the ways in which each woman's story was unique. In my analysis I am careful to point out not only similarities between stories but also differences.

The larger conceptual patterns that emerged enabled me to explore relationships not only between interview transcripts but also between the micro-levels and macro-levels. Once I had recognized these patterns, then I had to analyze the patterns themselves. I also came to understand that additional research would be required in order to understand the way that these patterns within the interview participants' stories could be contextualized within broader social, religious, cultural, and economic areas of analysis. For the theologian using ethnographic methods, the first step of analysis is to immerse oneself in the data. But one must always contextualize this data. Then one can begin to interpret the data and offer a theological analysis.

For the project I conducted in Kenya, I was initially overwhelmed by the complexity of the data, including my field notes in three notebooks and interviews with more than 30 women in a variety of settings. I began to note emergent themes in my field notes after each interview. I also had the opportunity to discuss my analysis of these themes and my experiences in the field with my field assistant and with the other scholars in the project, and was able to learn about their experiences of fieldwork as well. Their research complemented mine; similar patterns emerged in the stories they heard. In order to contextualize the individual narratives, I researched related themes and sought data

[20] Fife, *Doing Fieldwork*, 121–2.

regarding statistics of gender-based violence, statistics of HIV incidence, post-election violence, employment trends, and other related topics.

Cautions

There are a number of reasons why many theologians have not (at least not yet) adopted ethnographic research projects. Ethnographic research requires a significant investment of time. The process of building relationships with gate-keepers and research partners can take many months. Furthermore, the data collected in interviews or participant observation field notes can be unwieldy and confusing. The researcher must be comfortable with an open-ended process and the inevitable ambiguity that one experiences in the middle of a complex project. In addition, the power dynamics in interview process can complicate one's interpretation of the informants' stories. There is a risk that the researcher could exploit the stories of her informants to create an argument that fulfills her own agenda without sufficient attention to the informants' own complex stories. And a researcher who takes on an advocacy role can complicate the research partnership and the data derived from research. A more basic problem prevents many theologians from adopting qualitative methods: qualitative research is truly interdisciplinary work, and theologians are rarely trained in sociological research methods. Furthermore, given the ongoing debates on theological methodology, one is very likely to encounter theologians who are suspicious of methods that are nontraditional.

Thus, some cautions are in order. The theologian who wishes to adopt ethnography should seek help from those with experience in the method. One will likely have to take the initiative to find someone with experience in the method. Sometimes sociologists trained in qualitative methods can be particularly helpful resources on our campuses, and especially so if one does not have colleagues in one's department who can offer sound advice. One might also consider starting a writing group to facilitate discussions with colleagues who are working on projects that utilize similar or complementary methodologies.

A researcher who is less experienced in ethnography must take special care to acknowledge the limits of one's method and appropriately qualify, nuance, and contextualize one's claims derived from ethnography. One should make clear in the analysis that each informant speaks only for her/himself, and cannot be assumed to speak for everyone is her/his social group. In addition, one should set up some process to communicate with informants during the analysis stage of the research in order to remain accountable to the research participants. There are different ways to be accountable to the research participants. For example, after completing the study in Chicago I contacted each collaborator to thank her for participating in the study and to give her a printed copy of the final report. I invited each woman to read the study and give me her feedback. I discerned that each woman appreciated the opportunity to share her struggles, to name problems she has encountered, and to offer her experiences in the hopes that others might learn from them. But I am sensitive to the fact that women I interviewed continue to live with the struggles they named a few years ago, and they have benefited very little from my research.

How the Church Could Benefit from Ethnography

Ethnography has the potential to transform Catholic ethics because it demands that Catholic theologians and leaders of the Catholic church begin their deliberations on contemporary ethical questions by first attending to varieties in human experience. Ethicists must first have a clear sense of what is going on before they can presume to know how to respond. Ethnographic methods present a challenge to the methodology of contemporary Catholic moral theology because it requires that the teachers of the Catholic church begin with empathetic listening and descriptive analysis instead of beginning first with normative claims. Analysis of the pope's 2009 travel to Africa may help to illustrate this point.

Before arriving in Cameroon on his first trip to Africa since becoming pontiff, Pope Benedict XVI told reporters that HIV/AIDS is "a tragedy that cannot be overcome by money alone, that cannot be overcome through the distribution of condoms, which can even increase the problem."[21] While the pope's comments were criticized by medical doctors, public health researchers, and government officials around the world, Vatican spokespersons defended the pope; Father Federico Lombardi explained that the pope was "maintaining the position of his predecessors" by opposing condom use and by promoting sexual abstinence and marital fidelity.[22] Instead of emphasizing condoms, Lombardi explained that the church's priorities include education, research, and spiritual assistance.[23]

One of the striking aspects of this recent news story is that the pope made these provocative comments to news reporters while on his plane, before arriving in Cameroon. The first Vatican official to defend his comments

---

[21] "Pope Tells Africa 'Condoms Wrong,'" BBC News Online: http://news.bbc.co.uk/2/hi/7947460.stm (March 17, 2009).

[22] "Vatican Defends Pope's Stand on Condoms as Criticism Mounts," Reuters News Service Online: http://www.reuters.com/article/idUSLI43220920090318 (March 18, 2009).

[23] "Spokesman Explains Church's Fight Against AIDS," Zenit Online News, online: http://www.zenit.org/article-25415?l=english (March 19, 2009).

emphasized their continuity with recent papal teachings. While I hesitate to read too much into the pope's brief comments, the episode raises some important questions about the moral obligation of empathetic listening. Why did Benedict make this statement *before* his trip, and what did that signal to the church members awaiting his arrival in Africa? Why did he not first go to Cameroon and Angola, meet with AIDS-affected Catholics, ask them questions about their daily lives and their concerns, and then speak to those concerns? In order to interpret the firestorm caused by the pope's comments and the remarks of his critics worldwide, one should consider first that this is an issue of moral methodology.

Catholic moral theology could benefit from a sustained engagement with the experiences of everyday Catholics. The Second Vatican Council welcomed the participation of the laity and encouraged lay Catholics to become more active in the life of the church.[24] In my studies I was able to interview Catholic women living with HIV in both Chicago and Nairobi. Their testimonies challenge some aspects of church teachings, even as the women described their abiding faith and their hope in God's providence.

For example, while official Catholic teaching forbids artificial contraceptive use for married couples, the women whom I interviewed in my study in Chicago—women who self-describe as Catholic, married, and HIV-positive—reported that condomistic intercourse can be a vehicle for marital bonding. The sacramental character of their marital relations seemed to have been enhanced not only by their day-to-day acts of emotional support and companionship but also by their sexual love-making. The decision to use condoms was a difficult one, and not one taken lightly by these Catholic women living with HIV; the women reported that they wrestled with feelings of fear, guilt, and vulnerability in their sexual activity. Condoms should not be seen as a "quick fix" solution to the complex problem of HIV; nevertheless, these women did report that they see condom use as necessary in their lives. The perceived tension between condom use and Catholic teaching was a central and consistent theme for these women; in order to live out their marital obligations of mutual love and protecting their spouses from harm, the women explained that they and their partners use condoms in their marital sexual relations. But one should not get the impression that condoms are an easy answer or that condoms solve all of these women's problems. Marriage did not shield these women from fear, stress, or suffering. Indeed, these women tell stories of financial troubles, violence, fear of infecting their spouses, loss of intimacy in sexual loving, greater vulnerability with each other, and fear that they cannot protect their children from grief and harm in the future. When asked to describe the

---

[24] Second Vatican Council, *Lumen gentium*, in *The Documents of Vatican II*, Walter M. Abbott (ed.) (New York: America Press, 1996), nos. 10–13.

purposes of their own marriages, the women described the need to privilege mutual love over procreative ends, particularly at different ages and life stages. They described simple acts of companionship as touchstones of what the marital relationship is all about—accompanying one's spouse to doctor appointments, going to church together, reminding each other to take medicines, caring for the home together.

In my field work in Nairobi I interviewed a group of women who are part of a women's empowerment project in the slums of Kibera. Kibera is the world's largest slum and is home to over one million people. The women I interviewed there face enormous obstacles, including poverty, unemployment, disease, malnutrition, and sexual violence. Most of the women are single mothers, and all of the women I interviewed are living with HIV. Through the empowerment project they have come together to form networks of cooperative care, including home-based care for the sick and dying, as well as child care. The empowerment project also offers job training, programs on HIV prevention and living with AIDS, feeding programs for children, and income-generating cooperatives for the women (beading, fruit sales, salon work, and fish selling).

The women whom I interviewed in Kibera are living with HIV, but their situations are very different from the women I interviewed in Chicago. The women live in one-room shacks shared with their children. They have no beds and no toilets and no running water. They have to pay twice a day when they collect water from the city (5 shillings for 20 liters), and even though waterborne illnesses are rampant, they told me they cannot afford to boil the water because of the cost of charcoal. They had the option to pay 5 shillings to use the community toilet, but most said they could not afford to pay the toilet fee multiple times a day for themselves and their children. Usually the women and their children dispose of the waste themselves (and have coined the term "flying toilets" for human waste that is saved in a bag and tossed out the window).

The women I interviewed have experienced a great deal of stigma because of their HIV-positive status. One woman told me that she had been married for 16 years when her husband died of HIV. His family blamed her and chased her out of the village saying she had brought shame to their family. With six children in tow, she arrived in Kibera to fend for herself in the city. She complained, "If a man dies of HIV, his family can still say it is his wife's fault, even if she was faithful to him. That's what happened to me." Another woman was 27 when her husband left her for his mistress. She and her three kids moved to Nairobi, and for a while she worked as house help for a wealthy family. When that family moved out of the country, she lost her job and couldn't find another job. Thinking she had no other options, she turned to prostitution. She told me: "No one likes prostitution. But when you see your own children hungry and crying you don't have a choice. A mother has to do whatever she can to provide for her children. That's what a mother does. That's what I did." Now she struggles to pay her rent and provide school fees for her children. While she has not yet become sick from her HIV disease, she is worried that she will not be able to provide a stable home life for her children when she becomes sick with AIDS. The women's empowerment project has helped her to have hope because now she is able to make beaded necklaces that she sells, and her children are also able to receive help in the children's feeding program.

In these two very different research projects, I was able to listen to the stories of women living with HIV, and was able to ask them questions about their daily lives and the faith that sustains them. Their stories are complex, and still must be contextualized in even more complex layers of socioeconomic, national, religious, and gendered analysis. Despite the complicated nature of this analysis, a grounded approach to research on the lives of women living with HIV offers a fresh perspective not often seen in Catholic teachings on ethical issues related to HIV/AIDS. Even the Roman Catholic pontiff could benefit from sustained engagement with the complex stories of persons living with HIV/AIDS. Instead, part of the problem with the statements Pope Benedict XVI made prior to his travels in Cameroon and Angola is that they reflect a posture resistant to listening to those most affected by AIDS. The implications of my ethnography with HIV+ women in both the United States and in Kenya are that these women want their stories to be heard, and believe that they have something to teach the wider church community.

Conclusion

One way to attend to human experience in Catholic ethics is to utilize qualitative research methods, but this methodology has not been widely adopted among church leaders. One vocal proponent of sociological methodology in ethics is Todd David Whitmore, who critiques Christian ethicists who practice what he calls "veranda ethics."[25] Such ethicists write about poverty without themselves experiencing it; they write about war from the comfort of their offices far away from any war zones. In a strongly worded critique of the scope of contemporary research in Christian ethics, Whitmore challenges Christian ethicists to reflect anew on Jesus as moral exemplar; in his interpretation, to follow Jesus requires that one take real bodily risks on behalf of solidarity and love of neighbor.[26]

---

[25] Whitmore, "Crossing the Road," 273.
[26] Ibid., 290. Whitmore's own research focuses on the lives of displaced persons. My ethnography did not require such personal risk-taking. His strongly worded critique is likely to be not accepted by all Christian ethicists who do ethnographic fieldwork.

For Whitmore, a Christian ethics informed by such risk-taking will be cura-
tive for the blindness that prevents academics from attending in their writings
to the horrors of human existence that haven't yet been recorded in our academic libraries. When ethicists fail to acknowledge the privileges and limitations of their social locations they risk ignoring real problems of the world that
are outside their own experience. For Whitmore, this is a failure not only of
the discipline but of discipleship. While Whitmore acknowledges that qualitative fieldwork is time consuming, unwieldy, and risky,[27] he encourages his colleagues to pursue this research methodology. His sentiments are echoed by
South African theologian Denise Ackerman who writes, "Theology done at
arm's length from the reality of the context in which we seek to speak theological
words is not worth the paper it is written on."[28] For these scholars, ethnography
offers a method for attending to the messy, complex realities in which the
Christian life is lived.

While in their enthusiasm for this method both Whitmore and Ackerman
may have overstated their case, their intent seems to be to draw attention to
the need for Christian ethicists to think candidly about their own privilege
and social location and how these necessarily limit their scholarship. I would
not argue that theology done "at arm's length" is worthless; indeed my own
project relies on the scholarship of many researchers who did not use qualitative methodologies. Nor does good theological thinking require taking bodily
risk. One does not have to be HIV-positive to understand some of the difficulties of an HIV-positive woman's experience. One need not live in a war zone to
critique the horrors of war. But attention to plural, practical, particular human
experiences can inform Christian ethics in a profound way, both inside the
classroom, as well as within one's scholarship and in the ongoing discernment
of the church community as a whole.

There is something uniquely valuable about a qualitative research method
that invites persons with a particular life experience to reflect on that experience and share it with a researcher. By doing ethics "from the bottom up"[29] the
ethnographer can attend first to the everyday experiences of persons who are
on the margins, persons whose flourishing is thwarted. To attend to their
experiences will require the praxis of listening.[30] Only after such listening can
one return to the documents of the Christian tradition in order to discern the
wisdom of those documents or their applicability to lived experience today.

---

[27] Whitmore, "Crossing the Road," 275, 284.
[28] Denise Ackermann, "From Mere Existence to Tenacious Endurance: Stigma, HIV/AIDS,
and a Feminist Theology of Praxis," in *African Women, Religion, and Health: Essays in Honor
of Mercy Amba Ewudziwa Oduyoye*, Isabel Apawo Phiri and Sarojini Nadar (eds) (Maryknoll:
Orbis, 2006), 239.
[29] Whitmore, "Crossing the Road," 280. Whitmore cites Richard B. Miller, "On Making a
Cultural Turn in Religious Ethics," in *Journal of Religious Ethics* 33 (September 2005), 410.
[30] Ackermann, "From Mere Existence," 231.

The church should be a listening church as often as she is a preaching church; indeed, the praxis of listening should be prior. But for this listening to occur, women must be given safe spaces in which to discuss their experiences, to process their moral reflections. Ethnography is not the only way to create such space for women's voices,[31] but it is at least one potentially helpful method.

---

[31] Haddad, "Living It Out," 135–54. Haddad describes Bible study groups organized in churches in South Africa as "safe sites" for women to resist taboo and name what oppresses them; for Haddad, the ultimate goal is social change but women must first be given the opportunity to name what changes are important and necessary for their flourishing.

Chapter 7

Ethnography as Revelation: Witnessing in History, Faith, and Sin

Robert P. Jones

The standpoint of the Christian community is limited, being in history, faith, and sin.[1]

The task of this chapter is to argue for ethnography as a faithful Christian practice, to offer a theological rationale for the understanding of ethnography as a form of revelation that has the potential to positively influence the church's self-understanding and witness. Theologically, I ground this argument in H. Richard Niebuhr's understanding of "external history" and in James M. Gustafson's development of a doctrine of sin as "contraction of being" that results in limited moral vision. I argue that ethnography as external history may assist the church in enlarging its moral vision by inviting critical self-reflection and exposure to its own unacknowledged biases, thereby contributing to the ongoing task of appropriating and specifying the self-disclosure of God in the world.

I contend that this view is both more theologically attractive and empirically accurate than an alternative view put forward by Stanley Hauerwas, who has long criticized the use of the social sciences in Christian theology. Drawing on Karl Barth in his Gifford Lectures, Hauerwas argued that the principle task of the church is to be "a witness" of the gospel to the world—a task he understands largely if not exclusively in terms of a one-way movement from the church (who has the gospel) to the world (who does not). Against this view, I argue that because the church, to take Niebuhr's phrase above, always acts "in history, faith, and sin," adequate moral vision and witness is only possible when the church is capable of taking in other "revelations" about the world and God's activity in the world in a way that is capable of transforming and even chastening its own "witness." I draw on my own ethnographic research among elite activists in the debate over the legalization of physician-assisted suicide in Oregon in order to demonstrate both the ambiguity of the church's "witness"

---

[1] H. Richard Niebuhr, *The Meaning of Revelation* (New York: Macmillan, 1941), 86.

on this issue and the possibility of understanding ethnography as revelation that might assist churches in their understanding of a complex moral issue, possibly leading to more faithful witness.

Before proceeding, I should clarify what I take to be the relevant task of ethnography for the church. I should also clarify that I am making no claims for the objectivity of any ethnographic perspective. A key part of my argument is that no perspective, whether ethnographic, theological, or otherwise, can escape the particularity of a perspective. In *Analyzing Social Settings*, anthropologists John and Lyn Lofland make the following observation, which I take to be inescapably true:

> All human observations of the world (whether of the social, the biological, of the physical world) are necessarily filtered. Human *perception* is always human *conception*: What we "see" is inevitably shaped by the fact that we are languaged; by our spatial, temporal, and social locations (by culture, history, status; by our occupational or other idiosyncratic concerns; and, especially relevant here, by the scholarly discipline within which our "looking" takes place).[2]

Furthermore, in explicitly normative work, what we select for "seeing" is governed by our prior perceptions of what ethical problem is being addressed. The resulting ethnographic work is not merely arbitrary, however. As Lofland and Lofland go on to point out, the admission of the necessity of selecting and filtering does not imply that the data is merely a created and fabricated fiction, and several methods (e.g. using multiple informants, cross-checking interview data with other written materials) exist to check potential bias.[3] The work that good ethnography can do is to present the reader with another social world; in simple terms, it seeks, with all the caveats noted above, "to document the existence of alternative realities and to describe these realities in their own terms."[4]

Hauerwas has, for the last two decades, contended that to begin with a social-scientific definition of a problem that needs solving is to draw the church away from its primary purpose, which is to demonstrate "what the world is meant to be as God's good creation," and to tempt it to "rely on violence to bring order."[5] He has famously argued that the church does not need a social

---

[2] John Lofland and Lyn H. Lofland, *Analyzing Social Settings: A Guide to Qualitative Observation and Analysis* 3rd edn (Belmont: Wadsworth, 1995), 68.
[3] Lofland and Lofland, *Analyzing Social Settings*, 68.
[4] Spradley, *The Ethnographic Interview*, 11.
[5] Hauerwas, *The Peaceable Kingdom*, 100–1. Hauerwas himself notes that his position is a milder version of the neo-orthodox view of sociology, which sees it as a positivist, secular worldview that has marginalized theology by staking an exclusive claim as interpreter of the "secular" world. For example, John Milbank contends that unless

ethic but that the church is a social ethic. As noted above, in his Gifford Lectures, these sentiments are expressed in his call for the church to recover its sense of "witness" to the world. Moreover, the resources for this task must come exclusively from within the church. For example, Hauerwas makes the bold claim that "only by writing history on their terms can Christians learn to locate the differences between the church and the world."[6]

While I appreciate the force of this statement as a warning shot across the bow of a church he thinks has lost its distinctive communal witness and theological voice, this conception of "the church" does not ultimately square with the messy reality of churches in the real world. That is, any reference to some ideal, monolithic "witness of the church" is problematized immediately by the conflicting witnesses of multiple churches on any concrete issue. The question is not just what Athens has to do with Jerusalem but what the United Church of Christ has to do with Southern Baptists. Furthermore, these divisions do not merely represent conflicting theological interpretations of the gospel, something one might call faithful disagreement. Rather, these disagreements are so severe and so polarized that they cannot all be right, and attempting to defend them all as faithful outgrowths of the same gospel threatens to evacuate that gospel of any meaning. It seems clear that any argument that the "witness of the church" has any real referent in the real world is mistaken. To recall Niebuhr's categories, it places too much confidence in the church's ability to act "in faith" and not enough humility in the church's propensity to act "in history and in sin."

Ethnographic accounts, especially those aimed at illuminating the social worlds of the disadvantaged, may function in the way H. Richard Niebuhr thought what he called "external histories" functioned. He summarized this function as follows:

We have found it necessary in the Christian church to accept the external views of ourselves which others have set forth and to make these external histories events of spiritual significance. To see ourselves as others see us, or to have others communicate to us what they see when they regard our lives from the outside is to have a moral experience. . . . Such external histories have helped to keep the church from exalting itself as though its inner life rather than the God of that inner life were the center of its attention and the

other disciplines are ordered, at least implicitly, by theology, "they are objectively and demonstrably null and void, altogether lacking in truth." See John Milbank, "Theology and the Economy of the Sciences," in *Faithfulness and Fortitude: In Conversation with the Theological Ethics of Stanley Hauerwas*, M. T. Nation and S. Wells (ed.) (Edinburgh: T&T Clark, 2000), 45.

[6] Stanley Hauerwas, *With the Grain of the Universe: The Church's Witness and Natural Theology* (Grand Rapids: Brazos Press, 2001), 234.

ground of its faith. They have reminded the church of the earthen nature of the vessel in which the treasure of faith existed.[7]

Niebuhr later clarifies that the church's task of "[seeing] ourselves as others see us" is in some sense an "effort to see itself with the eyes of God."[8] Furthermore, consistent with my analysis here, Niebuhr claims that what the church sees when it looks through such external histories is not a pure church separate from and with a clear witness for the world, but a "finite, created, limited, corporeal being, alike in every respect to all the other beings of creations."[9] This human institution must take into account the limited, human character of its founders and sustainers, and must make itself see the often unhappy but inevitable connections between such things as Protestantism and capitalism generally and its moral stances and its own class interests specifically. As Niebuhr concludes, "To know itself as the chief of sinners and the most mortal of societies—all this is required of [the church] by a revelation that has come to it through its history."[10]

Recovering Niebuhr's category of external history is a helpful starting point for thinking about ethnography as revelation, a tool for seeing a social world through the eyes of others, which in turn provides an opportunity to see ourselves as others see us and ultimately make an effort to see ourselves through the eyes of God. This approach serves as a more adequate starting point for Christian moral reflection than a notion that the church simply possesses a witness that it should deliver to the world. From this perspective, the task of the church is not simply to "witness" to the world on a given issue, but rather the task of the church is to see where it is already acting in sin in order to see how it might begin to act in faith. Christians cannot be content to see the difference between the church and the world from history written on their own terms; rather, they must be open to alternative histories.[11] These alternative histories, such as the work of ethnography in presenting the richness and real difference of alternative worlds, might serve as revelation that prompts the process of self-reflection, repentance, and faithful action.

---

[7] Niebuhr, *The Meaning of Revelation*, 84–5.
[8] Ibid., 88.
[9] Ibid., 89.
[10] Ibid., 89.
[11] Although I do not have space to pursue this point further, Hauerwas explicitly notes that although he was attracted to the Niebuhr of *The Meaning of Revelation*, he concluded, "[Niebuhr's] distinction between inner and outer history seems to me to cause more trouble than it is worth" (Stanley Hauerwas, *Peaceable Kingdom*, xx). I contend his elimination of the tension between internal and external history, along with the doctrine of sin it implies, is a key reason Hauerwas becomes overconfident in the church's ability to produce a faithful witness.

The Ambiguous Witness of the Church on Physician-Assisted Suicide

Despite widespread assumptions to the contrary (i.e. the myth perpetuated by the media and by PAS proponents that the debate was exclusively between secular liberals and religious conservatives), Christian churches were represented on all sides of the PAS debate, an observation that implies that speaking of the church's singular "witness" on this issue in any simplistic sense is misguided.[12] What is most striking is that the churches largely, but not exclusively, divided on this issue in two ways that divided wider society: along liberal/conservative, ideological pro-choice/pro-life lines and along ethnic and social class lines.

Throughout the debates from 1994 to 1997, Oregon's leading ecumenical organization, Ecumenical Ministries of Oregon (EMO), struggled with the division within its own ranks.[13] Although EMO officially opposed Measure 16 (ODDA) in 1994 and supported its repeal in Measure 51 in 1997, the outward consistency of their position did not accurately reflect the internal dissentions that existed. For example, the 1994 agreement to oppose Measure 16 in 1994 was achieved not by a strong consensus over the issue of PAS itself but over an agreement among the board of directors that Measure 16 was "flawed legislation" on technical grounds.[14]

As Leslie explained, two arguments held sway, neither of which addressed PAS directly. First, the majority report from the Legislative Ministries Commission, the committee charged with forging a recommendation on Measure 16 for the board of directors, focused mainly on criticism of technical aspects of the law, such as the safeguards, which they determined were inadequate. The report charged that Measure 16 was "unwise and dangerous public policy" and

---

[12] For a full examination of the role religion, culture, and class played in these debates, see Robert P. Jones, *Liberalism's Troubled Search for Equality: Religion and Cultural Bias in the Oregon Physician-Assisted Suicide Debates* (Notre Dame: University of Notre Dame Press, 2007).

[13] EMO is a "statewide collaborative partnership of sixteen Christian denominations, bringing people of faith together in unity and renewal through community ministry, advocacy, and education since 1917" ("Ecumenical Board Offers Support to Measure 51" Portland: Ecumenical Ministries of Oregon, 1997). The member denominations are as follows: African Methodist Episcopal Church, African Methodist Episcopal Zion Church, American Baptist Church, Antiochan Orthodox Church, Christian Church (Disciples of Christ), Christian Methodist Episcopal Church, Church of the Brethren, Episcopal Church, Evangelical Lutheran Church in America, Greek Orthodox Church, Presbyterian Church USA, Religious Society of Friends (Quakers), Reorganized Church of Jesus Christ, Latter Day Saints, Roman Catholic Archdiocese of Portland, United Church of Christ, United Methodist Church. Leslie further clarified that EMO is one of 40 state councils of churches with the National Council of Churches (NCC). Also, Leslie clarified that the Roman Catholic archdiocese are not members in all states, and that in Oregon while the Archdiocese of Portland is a member, the Archdiocese of Baker in the eastern part of the state is not (David A. Leslie, Interview by author [Portland, June 23, 2000]).

[14] Ecumenical Ministries of Oregon, *Voter's Guide to 1994 Ballot Measures* (Portland: Ecumenical Ministries of Oregon, 1994).

"bad law" because it did not require mental evaluation or family notification and unnecessarily played on citizens' fears about dying in pain, when in fact "modern means of pain control are extremely effective."[15] While the majority report mentioned the potential for abuse with regard to those who were "poor, elderly, or without access to good medical care," this concern was subsumed under the technical worries and was not elaborated as an independent and substantive worry, nor was it linked to specific social forces that structure these vulnerabilities.[16]

Second, because EMO itself owned and operated Oregon's only residential hospice program, Hopewell House, the board was sensitized to the incompatibility between the end of life views put forward by many PAS advocates and hospice's traditional principle of "neither hastening nor prolonging life." Leslie summarized EMO's 1994 position as follows:

> EMO came out against [Measure 16], probably mostly because we do own and operate a hospice. We felt that there was another reason for us to oppose PAS, because we are in the business of hospice care—pain management, spiritual care, and the idea of interdependence. We're trying to say that some of the arguments some people use for PAS—not that they're invalid, they're operative and real—we're trying to say that there's another way to address those issues.[17]

As Leslie pointed out, however, the Oregon Hospice Association, of which EMO is a member as the owner of Hopewell House, did not take a clear and large role in the debates, which would have helped clarify their own position. Thus, EMO's 1994 opposition to Measure 16 was almost exclusively built upon the technical argument that Measure 16 was "flawed legislation," a position that left EMO without a clear mandate when Measure 51 was considered three years later.[18] As Leslie summarized it, such a technical opposition "begs the [main] question" and leaves open the subsequent response by PAS advocates, "What are the flaws, and if I fix them you'll come on my side, right?"[19]

---

[15] Ecumenical Ministries of Oregon, *Voter's Guide to 1994 Ballot Measures*, 24.

[16] An internal report by the Legislative Commission of EMO made a more substantive argument in opposition to Measure 16, but its arguments did not make it into the majority report. In brief, it argued, based on Ecclesiastes 3.2 (i.e. "For everything there is a season, and a time for every matter under heaven; a time to be born, and a time to die"), that "Ballot Measure #16 attempts to disrupt the natural season and time of death" (ibid.).

[17] David A. Leslie, Interview by author (Portland, Oregon, June 23, 2000).

[18] The minority report of the Legislative Ministries Commission recommended a position of neutrality, a "non-recommendation" that would "appreciate that there are doctrinal and theological differences among us within the faith community." Furthermore, they recognized that many had not yet understood the implications of the 1993 Advance Directive Act and suggested that a study of the existing choices available under this act would be "an appropriate beginning for this decision journey" ("Ballot Measure #16 Attempts to Disrupt the Natural Season and Time of Death [Portland: Ecumenical Ministries of Oregon, 1994], 24).

[19] David A. Leslie, Interview by author (Portland, Oregon, June 23, 2000).

One of the central problems EMO faced was the diversity of moral stances among its own membership, a feature of the religious landscape that advocates of PAS strategically obscured and the media largely ignored. Leslie summarized the situation as follows:

We have the two extremes represented very, very clearly. That is, the Archdiocese of Portland, as an institution reflective of the official teaching of the Roman Catholic Church, is very opposed to PAS. On the other hand, we have the Quarterly Meeting of the Society of Friends and the United Church of Christ, that have positions supportive of PAS.[20] What do you do when you have a divided house? The reality in Oregon was and still is that everybody's house is divided. Even when you have official church positions on either side, the polling data will tell you that there is no consensus.[21]

Furthermore, the disagreements were exacerbated because of a lack of explicit and careful theological reflection on the issue. Leslie summarized his impression of the basic internal disagreement as follows:

On one side of the issue, you have the right to life: "thou shalt not kill." [Also, you have] the idea that the profession is about sustaining life, not ending life. There are those elements both theological and ethical. On the other side, there are the issues of autonomy and individual decision-making; for example, when does life begin and end? But I'll keep coming back [to this point], for some reason there was a lot of rhetoric, but not a lot of thinking through this stuff theologically.[22]

Leslie noted that there were few explicit and substantive links drawn back to each religious tradition, a process that Leslie believes would have changed the quality, and possibly the outcome, of the discussion within EMO.

Thus, the churches in Oregon did not present one "witness" on the issue of PAS but were themselves divided not merely by theological differences but by ideology and class interest in ways that paralleled wider society. For example, in 1994 the following Oregon churches were opposed to the Oregon Death with Dignity Act (ODDA), arguing mainly that it violated the sanctity of life: Assemblies of God, The Church of Jesus Christ of Latter-Day Saints, the Church of the Nazarene, the Episcopal Church, the Evangelical Lutheran Church in America, the Missouri Lutheran Synod, the Roman Catholic

---

[20] In the 1997 consideration of Measure 51, the Central Pacific Conference of the United Church of Christ and the Willamette Quarterly Meeting, Society of Friends (Quakers), both went on record against the majority support of repeal of ODDA.

[21] David A. Leslie, Interview by author (Portland, Oregon, June 23, 2000).

[22] Ibid.

Church, the Southern Baptist Convention, and Muslims in Oregon.[23] In addition to the United Church of Christ and the Society of Friends that Leslie listed above, the following supported ODDA, largely arguing that PAS was a matter of individual freedom and responsibility: the Unitarian Universalist Association, the United Methodist Church (Pacific Conference), and the Presbyterian Church (USA).[24]

In what follows, I briefly examine the ideological and class affinities of the four denominations that supported the legalization of PAS.[25] These denominations, and especially their Northwest regional bodies, generally stake out the left edge of the liberal Protestant block, and have in two things in common: pro-choice ideological affinities and members who are largely upper-middle to upper class. First, each of these denominations supports legalized abortion in some cases, ranging from the more straightforwardly pro-choice Unitarian Universalist position, where "the right to choose" abortion is seen as a key aspect of a constitutional "right to privacy,"[26] to the more cautionary United Methodist position,[27] where the legal option of abortion is approved as a tragic "conflict of life with life," despite a belief in "the sanctity of unborn human life" that makes this approval "reluctant."[28]

Second, membership in these denominations is generally correlated with indicators of higher social class, including education and income level. Following up on Niebuhr's hypothesis about the social sources of denominational

---

[23] Derek Humphry and Mary Clement, *Freedom to Die: People, Politics, and the Right-to-Die Movement* rev. edn (New York: St. Martin's Griffin, 2000).

[24] Gail Kinsey Hill, and Mark O'Keefe, "Church Follows New Political Path," in *Oregonian* (October 16, 1997). The denominational groups listed here are regional groups that supported and opposed PAS in Oregon in 1994. Many but not all of these regional groups held positions consistent with their national bodies, but some took positions in the absence of a national position and some in opposition to the national position. For example, while the Unitarian-Universalist and the United Church of Christ positions were consistent with their national bodies, the PCUSA has deferred discussing a national policy on PAS until 2006. In addition to endorsing ODDA in 1994, The Pacific Conference of the Northwest for the United Methodist Church endorsed the 1991 Washington Initiative 119 to legalize PAS by lethal injection and voluntary euthanasia. The United Methodist national body had no official position until the 2000 General Conference, when they adopted new social principles statement on "Suicide" and "Faithful Care of the Dying," which oppose PAS (United Methodist Church (U.S.) 2000, par.161M, 161L).

[25] I could locate no data for the Society of Friends and have therefore omitted them from the following discussion. The lack of data is partially due to the highly independent nature of Friends meetings, and the Northwest Pacific Meeting is known for inconsistent reporting of its meetings. Although this is regrettable, this group is small and thus would affect the argument little.

[26] Unitarian Universalist Association, *Right to Choose* (1987).

[27] United Methodist Church (U.S.), *The Book of Discipline of the United Methodist Church, 2000* (Nashville: United Methodist Pub. House, 2000), paragraph 161J.

[28] These resolutions are available online. The Unitarian Universalist Association statement can be found at http://www.uua.org/actions/women/87abortion.html, and the evolution of the United Methodist statement on abortion is available from the United Methodist News Service (http://umns.umc.org/backgrounders/abortion.html).

differentiation, Wade Clark Roof and William McKinney note that the major religious constituencies in America "can be ordered fairly easily along a status hierarchy" that is rooted in socioeconomic standing.[29] Among the congregations under consideration here, the Congregationalists and the Presbyterians have been among the top-five elite denominations from the country's founding. Unitarian-Universalists have also long-maintained high class status and comprised the highest status group at the time of Roof and McKinney's study in 1987. Methodism has evolved from a lower-class to a solidly middle- to upper-middle class denomination.[30]

To see the extent of these status differences, consider the difference between the Unitarian-Universalists, who most clearly favored abortion and assisted suicide, and Catholics and Southern Baptists, who clearly oppose these issues, on two key variables: percent of college graduates and family income. Unitarian-Universalists represent the highest status group, with 72 percent college graduates and 52 percent having a family income over $20,000 in 1987. On the contrary, Catholics and Southern Baptists had only 12 percent and 6 percent college graduates with only 34 percent and 23 percent having a family income over $20,000 respectively. In other words, Unitarian-Universalists had over 6 times the percentage of college graduates and over 1.5 times the percentage of families with income over $20,000 as Catholics and Southern Baptists.

These striking differences push us back to Niebuhr's question of whether the differences in the witnesses of these churches is due to some genuine theological difference in interpreting the gospel, or whether the gospel has become captive to class interest. Niebuhr's analysis of previous conflicts, such as slavery and war, pointed to a similar phenomenon, and by my lights, Niebuhr's rebuke on these issues may not be far off the mark here:

> Each religious group gives expression to that code which forms the morale of the political or economic class it represents. They function as political and class institutions, not as Christian churches. . . . [For example, in the case of slavery,] the interests of economic class bent to their will the ethics of the Christian church and it was unable to speak a certain word in the issue of slavery. When the irrepressible conflict came the various denominations, as was to be expected, showed themselves to be the mouthpieces of the economic and sectional groups they represented.[31]

---

[29] Wade Clark Roof and William McKinney, *American Mainline Religion: Its Changing Shape and Future* (New Brunswick: Rutgers University Press, 1987), 109. Roof and McKinney measure status over four indicators: education, family income, occupational prestige, and perceived social class.

[30] Roof and McKinney, *American Mainline Religion*, 110.

[31] H. Richard Niebuhr, *The Social Sources of Denominationalism* (Cleveland: World Publishing, 1964), 24.

I contend that precisely such an accommodation has occurred in the case of PAS. In order to substantiate this evaluation, I now need to identify the often-obscured but crucial class-interest at stake in the issue of PAS. I give this first in quantitative form and then, drawing on my own ethnographic work, in qualitative form—the form that powerfully influenced my own thinking on this issue. Paul Weithman has helpfully identified the key class difference over PAS as a difference between those whose socioeconomic situation makes it likely they will be *overtreated* at the end of life and those who might be *undertreated*.[32] Members of the denominations supporting PAS, as members of upper-middle to upper classes, typically fit the profile of those who are more likely to be at risk of overtreatment and therefore have an interest in PAS as a hedge against this problem. Members of lower status groups, who are more likely to be without large financial reserves and adequate health insurance, have more worries about fighting for adequate treatments than fighting off unwanted treatments.

A brief look at some quantitative data supports this hypothesis. Disadvantaged groups are, not surprisingly, likewise consistently less likely to support PAS in surveys. For example, in an article highlighting the gendered aspects of euthanasia and PAS, Susan Wolf cites telling data from an exit poll following the referendum for 1992 California Ballot Proposition 161, which sought unsuccessfully to legalize both PAS and voluntary active euthanasia.[33] The poll found that the disadvantaged groups in society—women, older people, Asians, and African Americans—showed the least amount of support for the measure, with younger men with postgraduate education and incomes over $75,000 per year showing the highest. Likewise, a Gallup poll of older Americans illuminated this class and racial divide. Only 37 percent of those with incomes under $15,000 thought PAS should be legal compared to 60 percent with incomes over $55,000, and only 15 percent of African-Americans thought PAS should be legal compared to 51 percent of whites.[34]

Given this situation—where churches did not present one witness but multiple witnesses that seemed less linked to some pristine theological position and more to class position—how is it possible to speak of the church simply presenting a witness to the world? As I argue in the next section, this situation

---

[32] Paul J. Weithman, "Of Assisted Suicide and 'The Philosophers' Brief,'" *Ethics* 109 (April 1999), 548–78. Kristen Luker has argued similarly that certain groups of women (lower and middle class) opposed abortion because its legalization, rather than its prohibition, undermined their equality and class interests, which were rooted in their status as mothers. Likewise, upwardly mobile and upper class women supported abortion because their status was linked more to career than motherhood. See: Kristin Luker, *Abortion and the Politics of Motherhood* (Berkeley: University of California Press, 1984).

[33] Susan M. Wolf, "Gender, Feminism, and Death: Physician-Assisted Suicide and Euthanasia," in *Feminism and Bioethics: Beyond Reproduction*, Susan M. Wolf (ed.) (New York: Oxford University Press, 1996), 290.

[34] Larry Seidlitz et al., "Elders Attitudes Towards Suicide and Assisted Suicide: An Analysis of Gallup Poll Findings," *Journal of the American Geriatrics Society* 43 (1995), 993–8.

implies that the church is often in need of other witnesses that might chasten its own, reminding it that it not only acts in faith but in sin. I argue that if the church has a deeper understanding of its propensity for moral shortsightedness, then ethnography, which helps present another reality than is readily apparent, may serve such a function.

Ethnography and Moral Vision

H. Richard Niebuhr's insistence that the church remember both its faithfulness and its sinfulness forms that basic theological cornerstone of a constructive theological argument for the fruitfulness of using ethnography in Christian ethics. I wish to argue against the idea put forward by Hauerwas that the virtues generated by the church are sufficient for sustaining its moral vision. Hauerwas, for example, is unswervingly confident that such Christian virtues can "teach us to see the world without illusions or false hopes."[35]

Because Christians always act in faith but also in sin, however, the role of the church cannot only be to witness to the world in order to show the world that it is the world, for this presumes too much purity of motive and too much reliable self-knowledge. Rather, the church must also be open to allowing the world, especially the poor and oppressed, to show the church how much it has not yet become fully the church.[36] Before demonstrating the power of ethnography with an account of two disadvantaged groups in the PAS debates, I first develop a theological account of sin that demonstrates the appropriateness of ethnography for theology.

James M Gustafson's understanding of the human fault as a contraction of the human spirit informs my diagnosis of the Hauerwas' overconfidence in the church's own pristine witness and ability to "see" straightforwardly the relevant moral aspects of the issue at hand. Gustafson's reinterpretation of the traditional concept of sin as "corrupt rationality" in terms of moral perception merits quoting at length:

> The fault of rationality is not so much a matter of errors in logic as it is in misconstruing that realm of reality that engages us; it is a matter of the wrong depiction and interpretation of the particular "world" that attracts

---

[35] Hauerwas, *The Peaceable Kingdom*, xxiii.
[36] Although I only have space to sketch this point here, one of the roots of Hauerwas' overconfidence in the church's witness is his explicit severing of the tie between H. Richard Niebuhr's conception of the "internal" history (which he retains) and "external" history (which he rejects) of the church. For Niebuhr, the latter always chastens and informs the former, both allowing space for the social sciences to describe the church as a human institution and for external criticisms of the church's self-conceptions. One of the key roles that ethnography could perform is contributing to the external history, and thus self-criticism and reflexivity, of the church.

our attention and that evokes our activity. In accord with much that has previously been written in this book, it is clear that one's place in history, society, culture, and even nature affects what is seen, and how what is seen is construed. There is no possibility of human emancipation from the particularities of a perspective. The bias that naturally occurs, however, has different consequences depending on what it is that one is construing. . . . We cannot be held accountable for our finitude, which is part of our nature. Our rationality, however, is flawed by our refusals to "see" certain aspects of the world to which we are attentive, our refusals to take into account relevant information and explanations, our refusals to be corrected in light of substantial evidences and persuasive arguments. It is corrupted by sloth, the self-satisfaction that makes us content with the level of development of our intellectual capacities we have achieved, and with the sufficiency of our partial perspectives and interpretations so that we do not submit them to criticism and correction by others.[37]

In my judgment, such an understanding of human tendencies must be the cornerstone of any Christian approach to moral issues. It recognizes that all moral positions are heavily influenced by certain interests. Interests themselves are not solely negative, as they are the source of passion and political or moral activity itself; however, persons' unavoidably partial perspectives also tend to narrow the scope of advocacy, especially when they result in what Gustafson identifies as "the resistance to being corrected, the resistance of closed-mindedness."[38]

The problem, then, is a "contraction of the human spirit" that is marked by a conspicuous "not seeing." Borrowing language from Jonathan Edwards, Gustafson explains further that this fault is "becoming more contracted in our being than we ought to be."[39] It is "like some powerful astringent" that narrows our moral vision and results in a shrinking "into a little space, circumscribed and closely shut up within itself."[40] For Gustafson, this contraction applies not only to individual persons but to human communities when policies are proposed that advance the interests of one group at the expense of others, precisely what I argue has occurred with the legalization of PAS. As a result, "imagination becomes stultified by this contraction; we are unwilling to imagine other ways of ordering experience, other ways of relating aspects of knowledge to each other, other contexts in which what we know can be interpreted."[41]

---

[37] James M. Gustafson, *Ethics from a Theocentric Perspective: Theology and Ethics* vol. 1 (Chicago: University of Chicago Press, 1981), 300–1.
[38] James M. Gustafson, *Ethics from a Theocentric Perspective*, 302.
[39] Ibid.
[40] Ibid.
[41] Ibid.

The correction of this human fault can be described predictably as an "enlargement of soul and interests." While Gustafson notes that a conversion to a theocentric perspective that requires one to "relate to all things as appropriate to their relations to God" supports such an enlargement, he also realistically notes that incremental corrections may be made either as a result of events that provoke reconsideration of the contractions on the basis of enlightened self-interest.[42] Corrections may also be made based on the revelation of a previously unrecognized perspective, especially one that exposes one's own convictions as narrow self-interest. My hope is that my attention to the class interest driving many of the churches' policies on PAS may provoke such an enlargement, which may in turn lead to policy that is more consistent with such an enlarged vision.

Social Class and Exemplary Narratives

Hauerwas has long maintained the power of narratives but has remained skeptical about the use of social sciences. I submit, however, that the power of ethnography is precisely its ability to construct narratives of other cultural worlds, narratives that may confirm or challenge the stories Christians tell about themselves. I conclude by presenting three selections from my own ethnographic work that underscore the class interest (i.e. worries about overtreatment versus undertreatment) that underwrites different positions on the issue of PAS. While the quantitative data cited above points in this direction, the qualitative data, as a textured narrative, has greater potential for communicating the real struggles of real people in ways that have more moral leverage for beings who understand themselves largely as storytelling beings.

In my interviews with 31 activists in the PAS debates, I was struck by the emergence of what I call "exemplary narratives" that served as the basis of different positions on the issue. Often, when I would ask informants about principles or virtues that influenced their position, they responded with stories before, or instead of, identifying the abstract subjects of my question. I sketch three of these stories below that demonstrate that the class-driven divide over worries about undertreatment or overtreatment was foundational for the debate.

Quinlan and overtreatment

Most histories of the contemporary Right to Die movement cite the landmark court case regarding Karen Ann Quinlan as providing the impetus for the

---

[42] Ibid.

movement. For example, Peter G. Filene uses the Quinlan case as the herme-neutical key to understanding the "cultural history of the right-to-die in America."[43] On April 14, 1975, Quinlan became unconscious and stopped breathing at a party at a friend's house. When friends found her, her skin was blue and cold, and they began CPR. By the time she reached the hospital, she had been undergoing CPR for roughly an hour, and she still was not breathing on her own. The hospital diagnosed her with a drug overdose and placed her on a respirator to prevent pneumonia. Her eyes were open and blinked but were empty. Throughout the summer she declined, her limbs drawing up and her weight dropping from 115 to less than 70 pounds. By August, her parents had accepted that she had undergone severe brain damage that had left her in an irreversible persistent vegetative state, and, consistent with their Catholic faith, saw the respirator as "extraordinary" treatment that was simply hinder-ing the natural death process and could be removed with moral justification.

When the neurologist at St. Clare's Hospital refused to comply with their request to turn off the respirator on August 2, nearly four months after being placed on it, Joseph Quinlan hired an attorney to have him appointed legal guardian of Karen so that he could be empowered to disconnect the respira-tor.[44] After initially being denied guardianship on the grounds that he could not make "disinterested" decisions on behalf of his daughter as the medical staff could, Joseph was finally awarded guardianship on appeal to the New Jersey Supreme Court on March 31, 1976.[45] Shortly thereafter her father ordered the physicians to unhook her from the respirator, and Karen was expected to die shortly thereafter. Doctors at St. Clare's Hospital, however, ordered that she be "weaned" from the respirator, a process that was completed May 22. She was moved out of intensive care, kept alive with a feeding tube and catheter, and was transferred to a nursing home by June. Remarkably, the situation remained much the same for the next nine years, until, after over a decade of being kept alive with a respirator and feeding tube, in July 1985, Karen Ann Quinlan died of pneumonia.[46]

As Filene notes, "the media's narrative of the Quinlan family had personal-ized modern dying," and had particularly heightened Americans' fears that

---

[43] Peter G. Filene, *In the Arms of Others: A Cultural History of the Right-to-Die in America* (Chicago: Ivan R. Dee, 1998).

[44] Kathleen M. Foley, "Assisted Suicide in the United States" (Washington, D.C.: House of Representatives, 104th Congress, 1996), 11–22.

[45] *In re Quinlan* is a landmark case because it established a constitutional "right of privacy" against intrusion by doctors and the state; thus, it affirmed that the decision to discon-tinue life sustaining treatment belonged to the patient. Second, it allowed in the case of incompetence for substituted judgment in the interest of the patient, realizing that subjectivity always enters into such decision (Filene, *In The Arms of Others*, 88–91). A key but often overlooked insight is that the liberal standard of neutrality in the form of "dis-interested judgment" was the prime cause of the difficulties that resulted from this case.

[46] Filene, *In the Arms of Others*, 161.

they, too, might be subject to the dark side of the development of medical technology.[47] As Kathleen Foley testified in a hearing regarding PAS before the
House of Representatives in 1996, calling the period from the mid-1960s to the
present that "Age of Delayed Degenerative Diseases," the Quinlan case brought
into bold relief a new kind of dying that has accompanied the rapid development of medical technologies.[48] In his account of the history of the Right to Die
movement, Derek Humphry—founder of the Hemlock Society, author of Final
Exit, and arguably the father of the contemporary Right to Die movement—
argues that Quinlan was something of a martyr for the Right to Die cause:

> The results of the [Right to Die] revolution, as many have called it, were
> achieved at the expense of one young life and through the pain, determina-
> tion, and courage of one small-town New Jersey family . . . . Karen Quinlan
> came to symbolize the struggle Americans faced over a death with dignity
> and the dehumanizing advancing role of modern medicine. She gave the
> world a name and a face on which to focus its anxieties concerning the futile
> use of technology. She became famous as the one nobody wanted to be like.
> Hers was the prolonged death everyone wished to avoid. She changed the
> face and practice of medicine forever.[49]

Humphry's interpretation of the Quinlan case, that she was the famous person
that had "the prolonged death everyone wished to avoid," is probably correct on
its face, but it simply assumes the preconditions for this event: the access to this
high level of care and the financial means to sustain such care. For those with
such means, such a case indeed strikes a nerve, and legalized PAS may provide
a rational tool against such overtreatment. For those without such means, however, such as the disadvantaged without health insurance or income levels to
sustain such care, such fears fall flat as my next examples demonstrate.

Elizabeth Bouvia, disability, and undertreatment

One of the strongest and most distinctive voices raised from the perspective of
the disadvantaged were the voices of disabled activists who were affiliated with
the small but active disabled rights group "Not Dead Yet." Ellie Jenny, the key
Oregon spokesperson for the group, is a native Oregonian who has been active
in politics, particularly "pro-life" and disability issues, since the late 1970s. Jenny
knows firsthand the frustrations of navigating the Oregon healthcare system as
a disabled person who is dependent on the state for her health care needs, which
are many. Jenny has been confined to a wheelchair from the age of 14, when she
was struck by a truck while riding her bike with her sister. After obtaining a

---

[47] Ibid., 82.
[48] Kathleen M. Foley, "Assisted Suicide in the United States."
[49] Humphry and Clement, *Freedom to Die*, 86.

bachelor's degree and a master's degree in counseling, Jenny worked as a counselor for six years, before falling out of her wheelchair, which required three surgeries and nine months of confinement to bed. After recovering, she found herself forced to choose between health care and a job.

For Jenny and NDY, the story of Elizabeth Bouvia serves as the exemplary narrative that ties the impetus behind the legalization of PAS not to increased choice but to discrimination against the disabled. In *Bouvia v. Superior Court*, Elizabeth Bouvia, a competent 28-year-old quadriplegic woman petitioned for the right to remove a nasogastric feeding tube that had been inserted against her will. Richard Scott, one of the co-founders of The Hemlock Society was legal representation for Ms Bouvia, and the psychologist who certified that that Ms Bouvia's request was a rational decision, based on the fact that her disabilities prevented her from achieving her life goals, was Faye Girsh, fellow member and future national president of The Hemlock Society USA for 1998.

Not Dead Yet's materials give the following account of Elizabeth Bouvia as the key event in "the history" of the attitude of euthanasia advocates toward the disabled. Not Dead Yet's materials claim that Ms. Bouvia was used as a pawn of The Hemlock Society, USA. Ms Bouvia's downward spiral began with alleged discrimination against her by the graduate program in social work at San Diego State University, where one of her professors reportedly told her she was "unemployable." She dropped out of school, had her wheelchair-lift-equipped van repossessed, and then experienced a string of tragedies: she got married, had a miscarriage, divorced her husband, learned that her brother had drowned and that her mother had cancer. Under significant emotional strain, she checked herself into the Riverside County Hospital psychiatric unit and said that she wanted help to die.

At this point, Scott and Girsh of The Hemlock Society took up Bouvia's case. Not Dead Yet emphasizes that Scott did not take up the cause of fighting the discrimination she had experienced, but rather took up the cause to help her die, arguing that her case was essentially no different from the case of a terminally ill patient.

> Plaintiff should not be denied that same right [to withdraw life-sustaining treatment] merely because she is 26 years of age and does not yet require a machine or machines (other than a wheelchair) to prolong her pitiful existence.[50]

In order to make this argument, Scott needed to argue that Bouvia's request for assistance in dying stemmed exclusively from the fact that her disabilities prevented her from achieving her life goals, not from the emotional experiences of the past two years. The psychologist Scott secured to make this judgment was Girsh.

---

[50] Plaintiff's Memorandum, *Bouvia v. Superior Court 1986*, 14; cited in *Not Dead Yet* (1998).

Jenny's worries about the potential harm to the disabled from legalized PAS derive from this narrative and from her own experience of discrimination. From Jenny's perspective, euthanasia supporters are vehement advocates of choices and rights but fall strangely silent when confronted with those who cannot concretely embody these ideals, either through lack of physical ability or lack of social and economic resources. As Jenny notes, they fail or refuse to see the connection between physical or social conditions and vulnerability, only "hopping in" when the issue is helping people kill themselves.

> I don't see how [they] can say that [the law] is going to protect people who are already so vulnerable under rationed health care and who have needs that are beyond her wildest comprehension and who have to deal with life in a way that she has no idea of. It's totally inappropriate for someone like that to assume legally, because I don't live in a world of legal. I live in a world of economics, of my HMO, that's my world. I don't have a choice about this insurance or that or only breaking a leg once in a life. You know, I'm dependent on health care. I'm dependent on rationed care. These guys have no idea. Most of them are white and wealthy and able. If they were a different minority—minorities don't support this. They see through it . . . .

> It amazes me. It amazes me. I can't say that enough . . . . I don't see why people can't see beyond . . . . Well, I know why they can't. It's because they don't live in a world that's different, they don't. They live in a world that's able and going and doing. It's not thinking about being able to go and do and what you do in between. . . .

> It amazes me that they can't see . . . [51]

Jenny's key claim is that these issues "look different" from the perspective of the disabled. For example, while "professional, white, able-bodied" persons may be worried about being subject to more medical procedures than they desire, many disabled persons have difficulty getting the basic services they need. Jenny fears that the ultimate outcome of the trends she has seen in Oregon healthcare over the last two decades will culminate in the legalization of euthanasia and in "a duty to die" for the most needy and expensive persons in society.[52] Her fear is based not simply on an analysis of the trend itself but on the observation that Humphry and The Hemlock Society in Oregon have

---

[51] Ellie Jenny, Interview by author (Salem, Oregon, August 13, 1999).
[52] For example, the material Jenny gave me from Not Dead Yet included excerpts from John Hardwig's 1997 article in *The Hastings Center Report* entitled, "Is There a Duty to Die?" where Hardwig gives the following "fundamental insight underlying a duty to die," which has dire consequences for the disabled: "A duty to die is more likely when continuing to live will impose significant burdens—emotional burdens, extensive caregiving, destruction of life plans, and, yes, financial hardship—on your family and loved ones."

supported these limitedmeasures directly or indirectly, while openly stating that their ultimate concern is the legalization of euthanasia.[53]

Based on the exemplary story of Elizabeth Bouvia, Not Dead Yet identified on the national level The Hemlock Society, USA, as the main proponent of this discriminatory attitude toward the disabled, due to their support of both PAS and euthanasia not only for the terminally ill but, as Hemlock Founder Derek Humphry often puts it, for the "hopelessly" ill.[54] Thus, both Jenny and Not Dead Yet see the agenda of The Hemlock Society as one that has at its root a discriminatory and fearful attitude that, along with much of society, devalues the lives of the disabled. From their perspective, even when more limited legislation is proposed, such as ODDA, which is limited to PAS for terminal individuals, these limitations are merely political concessions and are intentionally vulnerable to expansion.[55] Thus, a deep-seated cultural aversion to disability, coupled with "current cost-cutting trends in managed health care and rationing" undermines the ability of any "safeguards" to "protect people with disabilities from wrongful death."[56] Not Dead Yet summarizes their opposition to PAS as follows:

> When all the facts are considered, any alleged "benefit" to a few through legalization of physician-assisted suicide is far outweighed by the threat to

---

[53] Both Humphry and The Hemlock Society are clear that they advocate voluntary active euthanasia only, not involuntary active euthanasia. Jenny's worry, however, is that in a society that devalues the lives of the disabled and in a healthcare system driven primarily by profit, this line cannot be maintained in practice.

[54] Derek Humphry, Interview by author (Junction City, Oregon, June 22, 2000).

[55] As Jenny testified in the 1997 legislative session during hearings on the proposed Measure 51, ODDA could be challenged by a disabled person resulting in the law being broadened to include lethal injection. David Schuman, Deputy Attorney General of Oregon, in reply to a query from state Senator Neil Bryant, has subsequently confirmed Jenny's fear, noting that ODDA is vulnerable to a challenge, under both the Oregon Constitution and the federal American with Disabilities Act, that it unlawfully discriminates against the disabled by its requirement that medication must be orally ingested. Schuman explains as follows: "Under judicial interpretations of both Oregon Constitutional law and federal statutory law, when a state law or regulation, on its face, does not discriminate against—or even mention—any particular identifiable minority group, but the law will nonetheless have a disproportionally burdensome impact on such a group, then that law will be treated as though the discrimination were intentional. . . . The Death with Dignity Act does not, on its face and in so many words, discriminate against persons who are unable to self-administer medication. Nonetheless, it would have that effect. . . . It therefore seems logical to conclude that persons who are unable to self-medicate will be denied access to a 'death with dignity' in disproportionate numbers. Thus, the Act would be treated by courts as though it explicitly denied the 'benefit' of a 'death with dignity' to disabled people. This fact, in turn, makes the Death with Dignity Act vulnerable to challenge under both Article I, section 20 of the Oregon Constitution (under which the state must make privileges and immunities available to all classes of citizens on the same terms), and Title II of the Americans with Disabilities Act (which, with certain exceptions, prohibits government from denying benefits or services to disabled persons)" (David Schuman, Personal letter to Oregon State Senator Neil Bryant, Salem, OR, 1999).

[56] Not Dead Yet, "White Paper: Not Dead Yet," 1998.

the many people with disabilities, terminal and not terminal, who live in a society which devalues our lives.[57]

David Holladay, poverty, and undertreatment

In this section, I draw on interview material from an activist involved with Friends of Seasonal and Service Workers (FSSW), Barbara Sarantitis, Director of FSSW in Portland, along with printed documents and public testimony by this organization and its sister organization, Northwest Farm Workers Association (NFWA), before the Oregon Health Sciences Commission. FSSW was formed in 1981 to support Northwest Seasonal Workers Association (NSWA), itself organized in 1976 as "the only successful organizing drives on the West Coast of farm workers, seasonal workers, and service workers, located from Southern Oregon to San Diego."[58] Sarantitis, who left a career in hydraulic engineering to work as a volunteer organizer, shares several of Jenny's basic

[57] Ibid.

[58] Friends of Seasonal and Service Workers, *Friends of Seasonal and Service Workers: History and Mission* Flyer (Portland: Friends of Seasonal and Service Workers, 1999). These groups both have informal ties to the National Labor Federation (NLF), an organization founded in Brooklyn, NY, by Eugenio "Gino" Perente-Ramos. NLF has been characterized as a "cult" by several anti-cult organizations and some relatives of persons who have been recruited as "volunteer labor organizers." *The New York Times* noted, in a correction to their earlier obituary of Mr. Perente-Ramos (born Gerald William Doeden), that "experts on cult activities, a former wife of Mr. Perente-Ramos, and several parents of his followers said yesterday that his labor activities and association with Mr. Chavez had been exaggerated, and that for two decades, he had been the leader of a cult that recruited troubled young people, housed them in communal quarters and 'brainwashed' them into believing they had committed their lives to social justice by collecting food and clothing for the poor" (Editor 1995). After his death, police raided NLF headquarters, where weapons were seized and 28 people arrested. In the 1980s, Mr. Perente-Ramos was also the leader of the Provisional Party of Communists, which was also raided by the FBI on evidence that it had planned a series of violent acts (Perez-Pena 1996). Both NSWA and FSSW are explicitly listed as affiliates with NLF on anti-cult websites (e.g. http://users.rcn.com/) and FSSW distributed NLF materials.

   After two interviews with Sarantitis, and 12 hours of participant observation at a morning clothing and food distribution center, an afternoon door-to-door "labor organizing drive" through a neighborhood housing many migrant farm workers, and an evening at their Portland headquarters attending a "labor college" on healthcare, I too had reservations about their legitimacy. Although I saw nothing I would characterize as "cult" activity, I remained perplexed about how the group proposed to make changes, except for the minor differences they made in the lives of families through their direct benefit services (e.g. I personally witnessed approximately 20 families receiving food and clothing assistance on a Saturday morning in space donated by a local bank). Although their diagnosis was in many places accurate and convincing, a clear and plausible solution was never presented, for example, to the problem of corporate domination of health care. My selection of the group, however, does not depend on their effectiveness nor on their practicality. Indeed, a central part of my argument depends on the fringe nature of the group. My point is that even fringe groups whose credibility is questionable may raise crucial arguments that ought to be considered on their own merits in public debate.

convictions about the opposition to PAS. Sarantitis and FSSW, like Jenny and Not Dead Yet, were originally galvanized not by the issue of PAS but by the issue of healthcare rationing for the poor as proposed in the Oregon Health Plan. What seems remarkable at first glance, for a small organization whose primary purpose is community benefit and labor organization, is its significant investment in issues of healthcare policy. Prior to the Oregon Health Plan legislation, FSSW largely focused its efforts in advocating better access to health care for the poor, but with the advent of the legislation for the Oregon Health Plan, FSSW became focused and vocal opponents of what they termed "death squad medicine."

This striking term was coined after the deaths of two poor children, 7-year-old Adam "Coby" Howard and 2-year-old David Holladay, who died because their families were unable to pay for expensive liver and bone-marrow transplants after the legislature removed transplants from the list of eligible treatments under Medicaid in 1987.[59] These cases were cited repeatedly by NSWA and FSSW as the narrative basis for arguments about the relationship between poverty and undertreatment. In an introduction to a booklet published by NSWA, David Holladay's mother Sheila explains that her son "was a victim of these state policies which denied him a life-saving bone marrow transplant; he was killed by health care rationing." Holladay endorses the position of NSWA and dedicates the publication to "the memory of [her son] David and many unnamed others who have become the victims of this state's policy of medical rationing."[60]

Citing the case of David Holladay explicitly, Jana Clark, Educational Director for NSWA, argued the following during a hearing in Medford, OR:

When the Oregon legislature passed medical rationing into law they determined to pass a death sentence for many hundreds, if not thousands, of poor who will now be denied medical services. . . . We will not allow you to build a false front of public acceptability on a program where a law exists that will require that poor people will die through conscious denial of available medical services. It is legislated murder—capital punishment, if you will, for the crime of being poor . . . .

We irrevocably refuse to participate in this process, unequalled in horror to the thinking man since committees of privileged Jews in the ghettos of Nazi Germany were formed to decide which of their fellows should go to the gas chambers. Let us not be like rats in a cage who simply kill the weaker members to enhance their own chances for survival. That is what the voices

[59] Robert S. Boyd, "Rationing Health Care," in *The Seattle Times*, January 8, 1990, F1.
[60] Jana Clark, "Health Care Rationing," *There Is Only one Answer: Treat the Cause, Not the Symptoms* (Medford: Northwest Seasonal Workers Association, 1989).

of authority are telling us today we have to do, but we cannot accept this as our only choice. We see that it is possible to do more, to do better.[61]

Clark closed her speech will a call for the other participants in the hearing to "take a stand for human decency and the ethics of the medical profession" by walking out on "this death row hearing" (a call that met with little response).[62]

One month later at a hearing in Portland, Julie Cohen, FSSW Operations Manager, sharpened this critique, coining the term "death squad medicine" to refer to the "legislated murder of the poor" and challenging the commission to embrace in plain words what is was in fact advocating.

> If this state wants hangmen, let the state pay them. Let them be voted on, on the grounds of the deaths that they will cause, and let them inform the abandoned citizens that they are indeed being abandoned . . . .

> In this make-believe world of financial Concern [sic] only money counts. You are either on the guest list or on the menu. We are on the menu. That is why we not only renounce but denounce this method as a prelude to mupder [sic]—or more precisely, the enforced euthanasia of the affected.[63]

NSWA and FSSW cited theses cases as evidence of the injustice of the Oregon Health Plan, which rationed care among Oregon's Medicaid population. Although the cases predated ODDA and were thus obviously not about PAS, they were later cited as evidence that the state had taken a hostile stance toward the poor in three ways: by denying life-saving treatments, by legalizing PAS, and especially by redoubling these injustices by including PAS as one of the covered services under the heading "comfort care" in the Oregon Health Plan while other life-saving treatments were excluded. Sarantitis summed up this position in a cover letter that went out to advertise a FSSW-sponsored Wesley J. Smith speaking engagement: "Whatever one's opinion is about [PAS], the reality is that it is more 'cost-effective' to encourage the poor to kill themselves than to pay for their care."[64]

If FSSW was outraged at health care rationing itself, the coupling of PAS as a covered service under the Oregon Health Plan that "flat out [denies] some life-saving treatments to the poor" further strengthened their charge that the

---

[61] Clark, "Health Care Rationing," 2, 8.

[62] Ibid.

[63] Jolie Cohen, *If this State wants Hangmen . . . A Critique of the Oregon Scheme for Health Care Rationing, commonly referred to as Death Squad Medicine* (Portland: Friends of Seasonal and Service Workers, 1989), 1, 3.

[64] Barbara Sarantitis, Interview by author (Portland, Oregon, August 18, 1999).

plan deserved the term "death squad medicine."[65] As they see it, physician-assisted suicide is but an extension of the attitude toward the poor that began with the acceptance of circumscribed rationing of health care solely among the poor.

> Overall, Death Squad Medicine is the political condition reached when profit-driven interests of medical insurance corporations and HMOs work hand-in-hand with the government to install laws, policies, and programs that serve to deny entire categories of health care to anyone unable to pay the price tag that those for-profit interests demand for provision of lifesaving health care services . . . . Many elderly and poor are now faced with the government saying it will not pay for necessary heart and blood pressure or other medicines, but will pay for you to receive a lethal prescription through physician-assisted suicide such as in Oregon. This is no choice at all.[66]

This theme of a lack of real choice is prominent in the perspective of FSSW. Sarantitis also explicitly pointed to the "sham" of "choice" for low-income persons,[67] as explained in one of their 1999 flyers opposing the funding of PAS under the OHP:

> Most [of the reported cases of PAS under ODDA in 1998] chose suicide based on fears of future physical dependence and of becoming economic burdens on their families. What is touted as a question of "individual choice" (for those few who wish for suicide), when institutionalized as public policy, creates a powerful demand on the poor, low-income elderly and disabled, as a class, to fulfill what some callously call their "duty to die."[68]

This insight into the problems of a profit-driven health care system and the lack of real choice for the poor, leads FSSW to the following substantive conclusion regarding PAS, which merits quoting at length:

---

[65] For example, the 1999 update of FSSW's "Community Labor College Manual," a training guidebook for grassroots educational meetings, contains a 33-page section entitled "Death Squad Medicine as a Symptom of Government *in* Crisis Ruling by Crisis" in *Community Labor College Training Manual* (Portland: Friends of Seasonal and Service Workers, 1999). There they explain that the term "death squad" is taken from "the El Salvadorian 'Civil War' whereby a team/squad of government soldiers carried out government orders to murder those who were not in compliance with government policy" (p. 21). Note that this invocation of the imagery of "death squads" would have had more than metaphorical force for the NSWA's constituency, many of whom are immigrants from Central America.

[66] Ibid., 26.

[67] Barbara Sarantitis, Interview by author (Portland, Oregon, August 18, 1999).

[68] Friends of Seasonal and Service Workers, *Oregon Residents Need Comprehensive Medical Care—Not Doctor-Assisted Suicide* Flyer (Portland: Friends of Seasonal and Service Workers, 1999).

In the current atmosphere . . . in which entire sectors of our poor population are actively denied medical care, it is unconscionable to even consider physician-assisted suicide . . . .

The problem with publicly funded and legalized assisted suicide is that the "voluntariness" of the alleged "choice" is always suspect when resources are in short supply. . . . The average cost of drugs needed to terminate a life is ten dollars, making it a financially attractive alternative to long term treatment of patients with serious illnesses. Within this rubric we cannot condone legalizing physician-assisted suicide as a co-called choice for a patient who—isolated, alone, living in constant fear of or actually suffering the effects of not being able to obtain treatment due to their poverty—is pushed to the brink and comes to see suicide as a way out of that avoidable pain and suffering. In this context, to not cover basic medical treatment, but to authorize physician-assisted suicide is a form of murder. And as with all murders, there is a motive: money.[69]

Conclusion

These three perspectives, with their competing exemplary narratives, demonstrate the striking difference in the issue of PAS from the social status perspectives of those who most fear overtreatment at the end of life and those who most fear undertreatment. As I demonstrated above, the division of churches on this issue largely tracked their class location, with higher status churches supporting PAS and lower-status churches opposing it. This was especially true for the churches strongly supporting PAS. What exactly is the work that ethnography might do in this situation?

I certainly am not interested in making overly strong claims about the unilateral power of ethnography to bring about faithful Christian action, which requires a myriad of intact, faithful Christian practices in communities with coherent internal histories, to use Niebuhr's terminology. When values are in tension, however, ethnographic accounts of the perspectives of the disadvantaged may provide the necessary moral leverage—leverage that may be lacking from internal accounts—to allow the church to enlarge its moral vision, repent of its defense of its own class interests, and act more faithfully.

In the case at hand, the key to the answer to this question lies in the following observation. While it may be true most of the churches on both sides were guilty of merely expressing "the caste system of human society," as Niebuhr put it, it is striking that the higher-status, more liberal churches supported PAS

---

[69] *Friends of Seasonal and Service Workers: History and Mission* (Portland: Friends of Seasonal and Service Workers, nd), 27–8.

despite the fact that they are known to have strong social agendas supporting the disadvantaged on other issues. Indeed, this paradoxical fact did not escape Not Dead Yet co-founder Lucy Gwin who—noting that in the abortion debate, the battle lines were drawn generally between "the usual suspects" of liberals versus conservative "right to life" groups—was openly perplexed by the abandonment of their typical liberal allies on the issue of PAS (Willing and Castaneda 1997). Thus, what may have prevented the liberal churches above from realizing the plight of the disadvantaged with regard to PAS may have been the absence of these stories from their deliberations. Absent these, the sobering Quinlan story ruled the day. If these accounts were presented, however, and received as potential sources of revelation, deliberations and perspectives may have been enlarged and the temptation to push for one's own interests at the expense of the less advantaged might have been thwarted.

Chapter 8

Theology and Morality on the Streets: An Examination of the Beliefs and Moral Formation of Street Children in Light of Christianity and African Traditional Religions

Melissa Browning

Some people were bringing little children to him so he might touch them. But his disciples rebuked them. When Jesus saw it, he was indignant and said to them, "Let the little children come to me; don't stop them, for the kingdom of God belongs to such as these. I assure you: Whoever does not welcome the kingdom of God like a little child will never enter it." After taking them in his arms, he laid his hands on them and blessed them.

(Mark 10.13–16, NRSV)

Watoto ni Taifa la Kesho
Children are the nation of tomorrow.

(Swahili Proverb)

In African religions and philosophies, blessing has long been an essential aspect to human flourishing, and children have always been seen as a sign of this blessing. Just as in the biblical story of Isaac and Jacob, a blessing given is a sign of affirmation and inheritance; it transfers the strength of life from one person to another. Whether a rite of passage or a daily ritual, blessing always contributes to the well being of the community and to the continuous nature of life. A person who is not a recipient of blessing is cast-aside and separate from the life of the community. They become part of the frustration of human flourishing, and weaken rather than sustain life.

In Jesus' own lifetime he recognized the importance of children within the community. According to the Gospel of Mark, people were bringing children to Jesus to be blessed, but the disciples pushed the children away. Perhaps they felt Jesus had more important matters to attend to; after all, these were just children, the silent members of so many communities. But Jesus said these children were inheritors of the kingdom of heaven, and he blessed them.

Today on the streets of Nairobi live 50,000[1] children who are more often rebuked than invited to a blessing. Children in Africa have always been seen as a sign of blessing, but what happens when the blessing moves to the street? The streets of Kenya's cities are both home and work to more than 250,000 street children of all ages.[2] These are children who play games and tell stories, but they are also children who are hungry and search for food in garbage dumps. They are children who have been denied a blessing and who have lost their childhood. Their life is hard and the streets are tough, but behind their tattered clothes and the bottle of glue they sniff to numb their hunger, there is a prodigal daughter or son who needs to be welcomed home.

Using fieldwork with street children in Nairobi, Kenya, this chapter asks how we as a global community can seek to do justice to these children who are so often overlooked. Everything in Kenya fits within a framework of community, yet these children exist outside of common community frameworks. This chapter attempts to place street children back in the framework of community through an examination of religious belief and morality, which are considered central to African identity. By utilizing the themes of blessing, life-force, and human flourishing, and by drawing on my own ethnographic research done with street children in Nairobi, I will argue that for these children and their families, morality and faith are always present, yet are redefined in the context of survival and forced choices.

Understanding Street Children

The problem of street children is not just present in Kenya but exists throughout the world in both the global north and the global south. There are currently 100–150 million street children in our world.[3] These children have been displaced because their world has become insecure. Some turn to the streets after being abused, some come to find their freedom, but most are there because they think the streets represent their best chance for survival. For many, the inability of the family to meet basic needs such as food or shelter is the underlying cause of street migration.

In Kenya the problem of street children is complicated by postcolonialism, poverty, and death. After Kenya's independence, those who were once prohibited

---

[1] See Global March, "Worst Forms of Child Labor Data: Kenya" (www.globalmarch.org) and Consortium for Street Children (www.streetchildren.org.uk).

[2] Numbers vary. According to Consortium for Street Children, the number is estimated at 250,000 with 50,000 street children living in Nairobi. See: http://www.streetchildren.org.uk/

[3] While the exact number of street children is unknown, Amnesty International cites the number as being between 100–150 million worldwide. See: www.amnesty.org/en/children

from looking for work in the city soon came in great numbers.[4] These people did not just leave behind a rural way of life, but a community, a support structure, and often with time, the traditional values that sustained community. City life did not turn into the wellspring of opportunity many hoped for; jobs were limited and no governmental support system was present to sustain those who came.[5] This mass migration forced people to search for low-cost housing while looking for employment, giving rise to the slums that now surround Nairobi. Within the slums, individual survival often becomes more important than the spirit of community for which Africa is known. The problem only intensified with the advent of HIV/ AIDS, which now by conservative estimates, claims 400 lives a day in Kenya.[6] This high death rate, coupled with a high birthrate, has left many children as orphans when one or both parents die. Because of these and other factors, 50 percent of Kenya's current population is under 18 years old.[7]

When encountering the family situation in Nairobi, the immense stress of living poor in the slums quickly becomes apparent. Abject poverty often turns to despair and frustration. Nairobi is considered an overurbanized area, meaning there are not sufficient resources to support the large urban population. In addition, 60 percent of urban households are headed by women, and since women are not able to inherit land throughout much of Kenya, and often have less education than men, female-headed households are significantly poorer.[8] The high stress of providing for a family in the city turns children into liabilities rather than blessings. In the process of interviewing children, many said they ran away to the street because of parental abuse, often by a single parent or an extended family member responsible for their care. Other children said they came to the streets because their parents sent them there to beg in order to provide money for the family.

Sending children to the streets to beg is a grasp at empowerment by disempowered people. In Kenya, the lack of governmental infrastructure compounds the problems of poverty. There are few laws in place to protect children and the poor, and those that are present are rarely enforced. The police frequently carry out long shifts and are unequipped to deal with the children, leading to child abuse by those who are entrusted to keep the peace.[9]

---

[4] Alward Shorter and Edwin Onyancha, *Street Children in Africa: A Nairobi Case Study* (Nairobi: Paulines Publications Africa, 1999), 18 and Phillip Kilbride et al., *Street Children in Kenya: Voices of Children in Search of a Childhood* (London: Bergin and Garvey, 2000), 6, 51.
[5] Shorter and Onyancha, *Street Children in Africa*, 18.
[6] *2004 Report on the global AIDS epidemic*, UNAIDS (www.unaids.org).
[7] *At a Glance: Kenya*, UNICEF Country Reports (www.unicef.org). By way of comparison, 24 percent of the US population is under 18 (UNICEF).
[8] Beth Blue Swadener and Kagendo N. Mutua, "Mapping the Terrains of Homelessness in Postcolonial Kenya," in *International Perspectives on Homelessness*, Valerie Polakow and Cindy Guillean (eds) (Westport: Greenwood Press, 2001), 267–8.
[9] Human Rights Watch, *Juvenile Injustice: Police Abuse and Detention of Street Children in Kenya* (New York: Human Rights Watch, 1997), 21–30.

Kenya is a country where 60 percent of its citizens live on less than one dollar a day and the rich–poor gap is widening. Kenya was just ranked the fifth most unequal nation in Africa[10] and is one of the top ten most unequal countries in the world.[11] The complexity of the problem of street children is such that a finger cannot be pointed at any one area to blame for the situation of these children. They are a manifestation of the intense poverty and disease Kenya faces each day.[12] Each child on the street is a child missing out on education, healthcare, adequate nutrition, and proper shelter.

Types of street children

All street children fit in the category of abused and neglected children. They all lack life-sustaining measures of food, shelter, and often love.[13] But within the broad category of street children, some have made the streets their only home, while others come to the street to beg and return home to their families at night.

According to Shorter and Onyancha, street children in Kenya can be classi-fied into three groups. The first group, who can be called *"Children of the streets,"* are homeless, either by their own choosing or by circumstance.[14] These children live, eat, and work on the streets. Many have been on the streets for years, and are connected to street gangs or families. These children often have regular routines of work such as paper collecting, begging, prostitution, or stealing. Some have run away and see the streets as a better alternative to their homes. Others are on the streets because their parents died and they had no one to take them in, or more likely, because they became a financial burden to the relatives who did take them in, which led to abuse and the child feeling unwanted. These children fill the void of family by recreating community on the streets. Most children in this first group have been initiated into "street families" who work and live together. You can find the children gathering together with their street families as it begins to get dark to pool their resources

---

[10] Patrick Mathangani, "Kenya: Education blamed for the gap between rich and poor," in *The East African Standard*, May 20, 2005.

[11] See "Pulling Apart: Facts and Figures on Inequality in Kenya," Society for International Development (SID), 2004, 7.

[12] Shorter and Onyancha, *Street Children in Africa*, 19–20.

[13] See Phyllis Kilbourn (ed.), *Street Children: A Guide to Effective Ministry* (Monrovia: MARC, 1997); Anne Nasimiyu-Wasike, "Child Abuse and Neglect: An African Moral Question," in *Moral and Ethical Issues in African Christianity*, J. N. K. Mugambi and A. Nasimiyu-Wasike (eds) (Nairobi: Action Publishers, 1999).

[14] The terms "Children of the streets, Children on the streets, and Children for the streets" are used by Patrick Shanahan, a missionary working with street children in Accra, Ghana. See Patrick Shanahan, "The Alternative Africa," in *White Fathers-White Sisters* (Issue no. 341, Aug-Sept. 1998), 4–15. Shorter and Onyancha also use Shanahan's terms in their analysis.

and tell stories from the day. They often cook together and maintain a hierarchy where older children act as parents to younger children.[15]

"*Children on the streets*" are different. They come to the streets to beg or find work, but are still connected to a family. Through begging, they provide needed income for their families. These children usually live in one of the slums surrounding the city. Some children are taught how to beg by their parents who will sometimes accompany them to the street.

When I met Otieno[16] he had been on the street for two days. He's only 7 years old but he comes to the streets alone. His mother and siblings live in a slum in Eastlands where Otieno returns each night. His oldest brother is in school, and he has two younger siblings at home with his mom. In the mornings, this small boy boards a bus for a free ride into the city to look for food and beg for money to help his family. Since children are allowed to ride the buses for free, Otieno's mom could not accompany him even if she wanted to since she cannot afford the fare. In my research I found that most children on the street who are still attached to a family unit are not as likely to steal or sniff glue. Some children even see begging as a game or a way to please their parents.

But both groups are at risk of becoming "*Children for the streets*"—children who have so assimilated themselves into street life that they see no other way of life. The longer a child is on the street, the harder it is to reconcile that child to their community. For these children, street life becomes the norm, and survival means doing whatever it takes to get by.[17]

On any given day in Nairobi, you could sit on a street corner and watch the differences between these types of street children. A young child whose mother sends them to beg with a cute smile and tattered clothes receives far more sympathy and money that the child who is older and sniffing glue. I watched this pattern one Saturday morning as two boys stood on the same sidewalk, asking for money. The first boy was about 7 or 8, dressed in a baggy, dirty shirt and asked for money in between sniffs from his bottle of glue, hidden in the sleeve of his shirt. The second boy was only 3 or 4, a bit cleaner, and he laughed and held hands with adults as he asked them for money. The second child persisted in getting a shilling from almost everyone walking by, while the first boy received almost no money and was ignored by foreigners all together.

The same psyche is within us all. With some children it is easier to be moved to compassion than with others. The children with no family on the streets, hiding behind their glue bottles, are often the children who have the greatest need. It is these children who are harassed and picked-up by the police and who are forced to bribe night watchmen with sex or money for a safe place to

---

[15] Shorter and Onyancha, *Street Children in Africa*, 64–70.

[16] The names of all informants in this chapter have been changed to protect confidentiality.

[17] Shanahan, "The Alternative Africa," 4–15.

sleep.[18] They find their food in garbage dumps, and they often steal to find money to buy what they need. While these children also use the money they beg for or steal to buy glue, which makes them high, this action also speaks to survival since glue is cheaper than food and causes them not to feel hunger or cold.

Street children as related to blessing and curse: an analysis of the African life-force

Within African cultures and traditions, blessing is seen when life is strong and when things go well. For this reason, the birth of a child is a sign of blessing.[19] African peoples arrange their lives on the basis of life-giving and life-destroying forces. As long as life continues, blessing is found. Curse is seen as that which frustrates life and flourishing, that which blocks the blessing coming from God.[20] The idea is that life gives life, parents give life to children, older siblings give life to younger siblings, and as life gives life, all life is increased. At any step in this process the flow of life can be blocked. Everything from bad manners to evil spirits can work against community and block the flow of life.

The concepts of blessing and curse are strongly linked in the African mindset. Blessings, like life, are seen to come from God, but evil (always rooted in humanity) can get in the way. If something happens, such as sickness or death, religious specialists such as diviners will look for a cause, which is almost always found in a broken relationship either with the ancestors or with the living community.

The African mindset of blessing and curse parallels the interpretation found in the Hebrew Scriptures. In Deuteronomy 11.24 and 30.19, the choice between blessing and curse is given by God to the people of Israel. "I call heaven and earth to witness against you today that I have set before you life and death,

---

[18] Shorter and Onyancha, *Street Children in Africa*, 46.

[19] While pointing this out, it must also be noted that this concept is not without problems. Women too often suffer when children are not born because they are seen as "cursed" or lacking blessing. (For a full treatment of this see Mercy Oduyoye, "Poverty and Motherhood," in *Motherhood: Experience, Institution, Theology*, Anne Carr and Elizabeth S. Fiorenza (eds) [Edinburgh: T & T Clark, 1989], 23–30.) In light of this, I follow the lead of theologians like Oduyoye who argue that concepts within African culture (such as blessing) must be "retrieved" and "interrogated" to understand how they help or harm women. (For a more detailed explanation see: Isabel Apawo Phiri, Sarojini Nadar, and Mercy Amba Oduyoye, *African Women, Religion, And Health: Essays in Honor of Mercy Amba Ewudzi Oduyoye* [Maryknoll: Orbis, 2006].)

[20] Douglas Waruta, class notes from the Maryknoll Institute of African Studies, June 6, 2001. Waruta's articulation of life-flow is common in African theology and can be seen in the writings of Benezet Bujo, Martin Nkafu Nkemnkia, Laurenti Magesa, and Placide Tempels. Bujo uses the concept of life-force, which is influential to understanding of flourishing in this chapter. Nkemnkia understands the concept as vitalogy, and Magesa sees it as the search for abundant life, and Tempels uses the word "muntu" or living force.

blessings and curses. Choose life so that you and your descendants may live"
(Deut. 30.19, NRSV). Those who chose life were those who chose blessing, but
those who frustrated life and made life weak chose God's curse. Within the
African worldview, the dominating theme is a choice to maintain and
strengthen life. Every breath is an action focused on making life strong.

In relating the concept of blessing and curse to street children, the complexity comes when we look at these children, who some would say exhibit weak
life, or block the flow of life within the community, and wonder if they are part
of the blessing or the curse. To many people these children seem to be more
cursed than blessed. Within African culture stealing and begging are characteristic of weak life. But in both the African and biblical worlds of blessing, we
see that for one to be a blessing, they must first be blessed. Blessing is transferred from the parent to the children and from the children to the grandchil-
dren, always continuing the flow of life. But when children are not blessed—when
they are not taught right from wrong, when they do not see themselves as a
blessing—they have little blessing to give.

Within the biblical record, blessings given also included curses for those
who broke the pattern of blessing. When Isaac blessed Jacob, he ended the
blessing by saying, "Cursed be everyone who curses you, and blessed be everyone who blesses you" (Gen. 27.29c, NRSV). A West African proverb carries a
similar meaning saying, "We do not seek to hurt anyone, but if anyone seeks to
hurt us may they break their neck."[21] Both African and biblical traditions provide instruction for giving blessing for blessing and curse for curse. In the
same way, an underlying current to these passages and proverbs tell us that
one who has not been blessed has a hard time being a blessing to others. Street
children, who are often seen as contributing more curse than blessing, are
themselves children who are not being blessed. A parallel can be seen between
those children who seek to destroy life through theft and drugs, and those
whose own life has somehow been destroyed.

But blessing for blessing and curse for curse is not the only ideology found
in Christian scriptures or in African tradition. In the gospels, Jesus was famous
for blessing the unblessed. In chapter five of Matthew, Jesus proclaims blessing
for the poor, the persecuted, the mourning, and the oppressed.[22] In this tradition, Christians are called to be givers of blessing, especially to those who are
without. In the same way, the concept of returning blessing for curse can also
be seen in African tradition through the use of reconciliation rituals and sacrifice that seek to bring people back into the community.[23] Any effective solution for street children must seek to give blessing in place of curse, restoring
life to those who need it most.

---

[21] Chinua Achebe, *No Longer at Ease* (Nairobi: East African Educational Publishers, 1958), 5.
[22] Matthew 5.3–10
[23] Laurenti Magesa, *African Religion: Moral Traditions of Abundant Life* (Nairobi: Paulines
    Publications Africa, 1997), 175–215.

The Dignity of Street Children

Before the community is able to address solutions to the problems facing street children, they must first seek to uncover the dignity and humanity of these children. When coming face to face with the presence of street children, both Kenyans and foreigners often feel overwhelmed with the lack of solutions available to combat the problem. No one is quite sure of what to do. Some say giving money and food only encourages street children to stay on the street, while others say it is all that saves their lives.

When talking about street children, we must first ask the question of why so many who pass by turn away, attempting to ignore these children. There is something within us that allows us to separate ourselves from other people through our preconceived notions of who they are. In doing so we limit others' potential and rob them of their own voice. Blessings of dignity, which can help street children find their way back into the community, are scarce where prejudice exists.

The fieldwork that forms the basis of this chapter used participant observation and interviews to observe and talk to street children and their parents about faith, morality, and religious beliefs. The goal of this fieldwork was to seek out commonalities between the beliefs and practices of street children and the beliefs and practices central to Christianity or African traditional religions. In seeking out these commonalities, my goal as a researcher was to allow children to speak their stories in the hope that their stories would provide a path for street children to be reintegrated into the systems of community from which they had been separated.

Responses of informants: survival vs. faith

Each child and parent I spoke with expressed a deep belief in God, but their view of God centered less on "spiritual" attributes and more on survival and protection. This is of particular interest, because I found that in Kenya a common response to the problem of street children is street evangelism. Both religious organizations and missionaries, primarily connected to evangelistic organizations in the west, see spiritual, not physical salvation, as the primary need for street children. In a conversation with an NGO informant on street evangelism, I asked if the primary need of these children should be food rather than the gospel. She disagreed, saying, "the gospel should be foremost on everyone's mind." Perhaps it is easier to make judgments once you've eaten your own dinner. A Maasai proverb reads, "The [person] who is hungry will not laugh when you tickle him."[24] By the same token, the child who is hungry will

---

[24] David M. Anderson, *Maasai: People of Cattle* (San Francisco: Chronicle Books, 1995), 19.

not listen when you speak. These children are in such want of basic necessities such as food, water, and shelter, that God is not relevant unless God can supply these things. When a person came to Jesus, he first met their needs. He multiplied bread and fish, he turned water into wine, and told parables of lilies, sparrows, and of begging for bread to remind the people God cared for their physical needs.[25] For children on the streets, faith is another tool for survival.

1. Case study: Rose Wambui

Rose Wambui is a mother of three who lives on the street because she cannot afford to pay her rent. When I asked Rose about her belief in God, her eyes began to shine, her Swahili sped up, and her voice grew louder. She was excited to tell my field assistant and me of her faith, which was still strong despite her hard life. She told us that she remembers all the sacred stories of scriptures. Noah and the Ark and Adam and Eve were familiar memories to her but she admits that she often forgets these stories when the problems of life become too many. Rose said that she teaches her children a new sacred story. The stories of survival have replaced the stories she remembers from scripture. The stories she tells her children are about life, how to live carefully and how to survive. For Rose, her children are her only reason to survive. She believes that God is with her, even on the street, and that God has a purpose in her hardship. She knows that there are rich people in the world, those who have wealth and never need to beg for food, but she said that even these people may not be as blessed as she is. God has given her children, and through this has shown her blessing.

Rose's faith was firm and steadfast, and each time I met her on the street, she wanted to take time to talk. During each of these conversations she reminded me she was hungry. Of course, some would argue that this is why she was so eager to talk to me because we would end our talks at a nearby food stall. After spending time with Rose I would argue that when you spend entire days and weeks sitting on a street corner and thinking of ways to obtain food or money it simply becomes what you ask your God and your friends to give you. Just like everything else in Rose's life, her faith was intertwined with her survival. Strong life and religious blessing are one in the same, and she reaches out for both wherever she can find them.

2. Case study: Teresia Nambura

Teresia Nambura held a similar view on faith in the midst of hardship. She has been on the street for nine years, off and on. She is from Manchakos, a small

---

[25] See: Luke 9, John 2, Matthew 6, and Luke 11.

town about an hour from Nairobi, but now she is renting a small shack in Koragosho slum. She uses the money her children collect on the streets to pay the rent. She and her children come to the streets each morning to search for food and money, but return home in the evenings. Teresia told me she had no one to ask for money, her parents were dead and she is not married so the only place for her to find money is on the streets. This is the story for many Kenyan women who cannot inherit land or compete in patriarchal job markets.

She said she used to be Catholic, but now life is so hard that she finds little time to go to church. She still believes in God, and growing up, church held a big place in her life but now she finds less time or incentive to go. The issue of time is also a concern when she hears people preaching on the streets. She will listen, but she says because she is burdened with concern, she doesn't stay long. At home she still prays, and when she does attend church what she hears there gives her encouragement to continue living and overcome challenges. She knows God watches after her. She believes this because most days they come to the street in the morning hungry, and a "good Samaritan" will come along and give her food and a reason to call the day good. Teresia prays to God to give her work and daily food. The sacred story she tells her children is one of respect, to obey other adults and to never abuse anyone. Teresia knows the stories of the Bible and often sings songs she remembers from church. She hopes that one day she and her children will be off the street and not have to depend on others for food and money.

As with many on the street, both of these street parents exhibited a faith that was linked to their overwhelming needs. The faith of those on the streets is a faith that knows suffering but still speaks strongly of life and prays for survival. Those who have experienced hunger leading to malnutrition know it is all consuming. It is as if the person is diseased with pain, and this hunger, like a sickness becomes all they can think about. Many find it hard to exhibit faith under such stress, while others may feel faith is all they have. The same stresses that hindered faith in the time of Jesus' ministry can be seen with each child and parent living on the streets of Nairobi. True to African Religion, they know God is there, and they believe God cares for them, but as Rose Wambui said, when the troubles of life become too much religion is easy to forget.

3. Case study: Kimathi Kimaru

Every researcher finds a pattern, only to have it contradicted by an exception. My exception was Kimathi. This little boy fell somewhere in-between the two types of street children. His mother lived on the street, yet he also was a part of a small gang of street boys. He became my exception because in him I found a faith seemingly unburdened by life's hardships. Kimathi is perhaps the most religious street kid I have ever met. I got to know him in Nairobi's Uhuru Park one Sunday before the street preaching. Kimathi was quite polite; he came up

and chatted with us without asking for money and we gave him a few Coke bottles to return for some shillings. He told us he was 15, but he didn't look a day
older than 10. He said he was already 12 the day he was born. A comical statement, yet somewhat true for a kid forced to grow up quickly on the streets. If
Kimathi was as old as he said, then due to his size he most likely was showing
signs of stunting from malnutrition early in life.

Kimathi was from Machakos, a town about an hour outside of Nairobi, but
now made his home with his mom in front of Kenya Commercial Bank on the
sidewalk. He said he came to the street with his mother when problems came.
His father passed away, so his mother came to Nairobi to look for work. Kimathi
told us he belonged to "any church" and found time to listen whenever he
found preaching.

On the streets he hangs around with a group of three other boys of all ages.
They are his "gang" but he informed us that he prefers to help out his mom, so
he meets her at "home" in front of the bank each night. He told us he shows
love to others on the street by helping them out, and sometimes even helping
them run away from trouble. He also always tries to help out kids who are new
to the street, because in his opinion, the Nairobi streets belong to these kids.
When asked if he would share his food with other kids on the street, he assured
us that he would. After all, he said, they are just street kids like him. Kimathi
believes that God is always with us, not far away but right here among us. He's
happy to tell you that he is a Christian, and shows up for street preaching every
single Sunday, and some days during the week. He prays with his mother on
the street and they often sing songs they know from church together. Kimathi
looks forward to a day when he can attend school and told us that it didn't matter how far away school was, he would be willing to walk quite far if he had to.
He told us that he was sure that God knew everything and that God is always
there to help. When we asked how God helps him, he reminded us that even
that day, God sent us to give him Coke bottles to return for shillings.

Kimathi believes that this same God helps him wake up each morning and
survive throughout the day. He told us he never steals, even when there's not
enough money for food. If there's not enough food, he will just spend the night
there and wait for morning to find more money. Kimathi told us he prays, but
like most boys his age, he admitted that he didn't pray much! His biggest prayer
was for God to keep him safe each day. Kimathi believes that after he dies he
will go to heaven, and the worst possible sin is abusing someone else.

Responses of informants: analysis of religious belief within Christianity and African tradition

Like Kimathi, most of the children interviewed were eager to talk about faith
and spirituality. They each had very strong opinions on what was right and

what was wrong. The children participating in this research ranged in age from 7 to 16, both boys and girls, both with and without parents on the street, as well as some children who are now off the street. Children were asked questions about God, prayer, morality, the afterlife, sacred stories, and rites of passage, with questions drawn either from African traditional religions, Christianity, or both. This fieldwork, centered in Nairobi, which is predominately Christian, would most likely look different from fieldwork done in a city such as Mombasa, which is predominately Muslim.

Religious affiliation and practices

When beginning my research, some colleagues jokingly asked me to find out if street children were "Baptist" or "Catholic." My field assistant and I laughed at the joke, not knowing how identifiable that question would become in our research. As we begin to ask children and parents questions about their faith, they quickly responded, "I'm Catholic!" We soon realized that these participants were identifying with those who provided the most help and assistance to children and families on the street. They told us they were Catholic because it is the Catholic nuns and priests who have had the greatest impact on street children in Nairobi. They were quick to identify with the church that provided the greatest sympathy toward their situation. While the Catholic Church has exercised a concentrated impact in Kenya, Protestants have been more scattered in their effort, and tend to be harder to identify than those dressed in a habit or clerical collar.

Another substantial influence on these children comes through street preaching. On any given day in Nairobi, street preachers will gather groups of listeners at bus stops, in city parks, under trees, or outside public toilets. On city buses there are signs that prohibit these street preachers from preaching on the bus. Once while waiting on a *matatu* (the public transportation vans that are known for dangerous driving), a man walked up with a Bible and began reading passages of judgment. After rambling in Kiswahili for a moment about the importance of making things right before we die, he hung outside the door of the open and now moving van and prayed for us to have a safe journey. As John Mbiti has said, Africans are "notoriously religious"[26] and in Kenya this can be seen on any city sidewalk. Some informants told us that in Nairobi a van comes around each Sunday to pick up street children and take them to a spot in the park for their own Sunday morning service. This service is geared toward issues street kids face, warning them of the

---

[26] John S. Mbiti, *African Religions and Philosophy* (Nairobi: East African Educational Publishers, 1960), 1.

dangers of sniffing glue and leaving the streets with strangers who may try to harm them.

The children interviewed described God as a creator and a caregiver, the sustainer of life, and always present. Many children and parents said that God was the reason they were still alive and the reason people are able to give them food and money. Several believed God had a purpose in their being on the street, and no one interviewed expressed bitterness toward God for their lot in life. One of our most animate interviewees expressed that God was always with him, right there on the street, not far away in heaven. He went on to say that people are able to pray to God through Jesus and then God sends angels to help with their problems. Other children told us that God was in heaven, and some called God indescribable since God cannot be seen.

Within African tradition, God is seen in similar ways. God is the wind and breath of creation, unseen, and unknowable. God is seen as "essentially good," yet sometimes also associated with calamity that comes.[27] Those on the street who felt God had a purpose in their being there were faithful to their African heritage and did not question God. African theologian Martin Nkafu Nkemnkia describes suffering as having a purpose that is wrapped in mystery.[28] Many informants in this research would have agreed. As for provision, those interviewed believed all good things came from God. Just as the rain in the rural *shamba* (garden) is a gift and blessing from God, so is a loaf of bread given to a child on the street. In the fieldwork, my field assistant and I heard many stories of "good Samaritans" who gave gifts from God.

The children also talked about the importance of prayer. When we asked the children what they pray for, most answers centered on food, shelter, provisions for school, and help getting off the street. One 7-year-old boy told us he prayed that his family would stay together. Each prayer for these children is focused on daily necessities rather than abstract concerns. One NGO worker I spoke with told me these children pray, but they pray for "selfish things" instead of praying for God's will. It is true that these children pray for themselves and their families, but as with most people, prayers always speak the needs that touch most closely. These prayers can hardly be considered "selfish," since survival depends on their prayers being answered.

Within African tradition, a prayer is as natural as a heartbeat. In rural areas, people awake with a prayer escaping their lips, thanking God for the new day, for cows that give milk and for crops that grow. In Africa, prayers are centered on making life strong through health, wealth, and immortality. Health is requested because life is supposed to be strong, and wealth because life should not be threatened by want, and immortality so that life can continue. Health

---

[27] Ibid., 36–7.
[28] Martin Nkafu Nkemnkia, *African Vitalogy* (Nairobi: Paulines Publications Africa, 1999), 113–17.

and wealth are seen through having children and the ability to feed and care for them. Once the first two requests are answered, immortality of the community is assured.[29]

Africa has long been a place of sacred story and song, and the children we interviewed told us about their sacred stories. In Africa, stories and proverbs serve to educate children, as they uphold a moral code for sustaining life within the community. Children whose parents were still with them on the streets, or those who left home later, were more likely to know both biblical and African traditional sacred stories.

The new sacred stories for children living on the street are those of survival. Every child who had a parent living with them on the street told me they didn't steal because their parents told them of what happens when you're caught. Tales of burning children in tires, of mob beatings, and being caught by "witches" emerged as oral traditions learned by these children. These tales were all based on real situations. Mob justice is prevalent in Kenya as a response to theft, and children often die as a result. As for the stories of "witches," children in Nairobi have been abducted and killed in recent memory in what was thought to be ritual sacrifice. Parents and street gangs watch out for younger members through stories that teach them how to survive and how to live on the streets. These stories take on a spiritual nature in that they are life-giving and life-preserving.

In an African worldview, the spiritual world and daily living are deeply intertwined. Laurenti Magesa expresses this view by saying "For Africans religion is quite literally life and life is religion."[30] There is no separation of Saturday and Sunday, every day a person has breath is a day that is holy and set apart for God. In this way, every action a street child takes to preserve his or her own life, apart from those actions that are life-destroying, could be seen as an act of worship and a breath of thanks unto God.

Rituals and rites of passage

While it can be said that many rural traditions have been forgotten by city dwellers, those traditions closest to the core are still deeply remembered. Rituals such as circumcision, initiation, and marriage are still important to children living on the street. While observing street children in downtown Nairobi, I came across a group of children gathered around a pull-cart. Much to my cultural dismay, inside the pull-cart (which was half full of limes) was a boy, about 18, standing in the cart completely naked with his feet and hands tied to the sides. I rushed to the other side of the street and watched from a

---

[29] Waruta, class notes from the Maryknoll Institute of African Studies on June 7, 2001.
[30] Magesa, *African Religion*, 33.

safer area. I was sure the boy was going to be beaten or killed, but those who walked by barely flinched and the boy tied to the cart seemed somewhat happy. I followed the boy in the cart for almost a mile asking questions of those who surrounded me along the way. In my journey I learned that the boy needed to be circumcised and the street children were taking him through town to raise donations for the procedure. I was told this boy was likely to be married soon, which is why he had to be circumcised. Circumcision has long been a rite of passage for some people groups in Kenya and it is one ritual that these children keep.[31]

In the same way, a form of age-mate initiation is also important among members of street families. To belong to a group or gang of children, new children are often required to fight or perform menial tasks for leaders of the group. It is through these rituals that they are accepted and acceptance becomes a blood-bond of fidelity to the group.[32] Acting like families, gangs of street children care for one another deeply. If one is sick, the others will take that child to the hospital and then raise money to pay the bill. One informant told a story of a girl who was raped by another child. The children in her street family took her to a clinic and she received care, but a few days later she became very sick. The children began to worry that she might have AIDS, and knowing little about the disease, feared she may die within the hour. They quickly rushed to a social worker they knew at Undugu Society, and asked for help bringing this girl to the hospital.

Another rite of passage on the street is marriage and having children. Since marriage has been an all-important part of the maturation process in Africa, it retains its resiliency on the streets. These children have no bride-wealth to pay and no parents to tell, but they marry among themselves and many look forward to having children. Marriages on the street takes place young, often when street children are only 14 or 15. One informant said that within these street marriages, looking at a street boy's wife is become the most heinous sin. The informant told me older street boys are very protective of their wives and will quickly fight anyone who tries to speak to her. Many small children now on the streets are second-generation street children as a result of street marriages.

Morality and Human Flourishing

As a part of this research, informants were asked to answer questions morality and understandings community. The questions, geared toward children, were

[31] Kilbride et al., *Street Children in Kenya*, 33.
[32] Shorter and Onyancha, *Street Children in Africa*, 64–70.

simple questions about stealing, sharing and what they considered to be "right" and "wrong." Here, rather than recite their answers, there is one story that is worth retelling. One afternoon my field assistant and I were interviewing a young street mother with three children and a colleague was present with us at the interview. The informant was part of a street gang of five or six kids who were eager to hang around, but the more questions we asked the larger the crowd became. As the interview went long, the children began asking the colleague who was present for food or milk.

Our colleague felt overwhelmed with compassion, and came back with cartons of milk right as we were starting on our second interview with an 18-year-old mother of two who was sniffing glue and breast-feeding as she talked to us. Her 2-year-old child was holding a piece of dung in her hand, probably her own, and her 4 year old was clinging to me, quite interested in the movement of my pen. The mother was still a child, and because of malnourishment she looked more like an 11-year-old boy than a mother of two. This girl had her first child while in prison, and the second on the streets. But this was an interview we never finished. Soon the milk arrived. There was enough for each person there to have their own carton with some leftover, but the children became so anxious to get the milk, a fight soon broke out. They were yelling and grabbing at the bag. After realizing we couldn't restore any order to this situation, we dropped the bag into their hands. The mothers were pulling so hard on the bag that the cartons exploded and we were all covered in milk.

Ruth, the mother we interviewed first, quickly escorted us off the scene and helped us get away from the fight safely. We decided we learned more in that experience than we did from all our interview questions. It was amazing to see the people who had once befriended us to turn against us when they were concerned that there would not be enough milk for everyone. The sad thing being that there was plenty for everyone to have their own carton, but their hunger and desperation caused them to loose all compassion and patience in that moment.

When reflecting on the event with some colleagues, Dr Gerald Wanjohi, a professor at University of Nairobi, walked up and listened in on our conversation. As I retold the story, he told the group that these children behaved that way because they do not have a "concept of plenty." He said that even though we told them repeatedly there was enough for everyone, they could not have understood because they had never experienced enough.

In Africa, having enough is a sign of blessing. This blessing is essential to the flow of life and those without are thought to be under a curse. Within the context of life-sustaining actions, children of the street can be more clearly understood. In Africa, life is all-important. As seen in the analysis of the children's prayers—health, wealth, and immortality are of extreme importance to people living on the street. In Africa, morality is judged by its intentions and by life.[33] Those who have time to ponder lofty thoughts often ask questions of whether or not it is acceptable to steal or to cheat if your child's life depended on it. It is easy to make judgments from air-conditioned classrooms as to what is right and what is wrong, but what about on the streets? I can tell a child it is wrong to steal, but is in not also wrong for me not to give to meet her needs? According to Magesa, within African tradition "greed constitutes the most grievous wrong."[34] When I have plenty and refuse to find a way to share, am I not worse than the one who steals because she has none?

When seeking out morality within the context of life-sustaining actions, we again ask the question of whether these children, at the edge of desperation, are behaving in life-sustaining or life-destroying ways. It is evident that these children are seeking to sustain life and looking for ways to make life strong, even if the end result of their actions is immoral. Within this perspective, their morality should be judged on their intentions. This does not excuse their life-destroying actions, but it understands why they behave the way they do and provides an avenue for reconciliation. In order to be effective reconcilers of street children, we must not only teach them what not to do, but must empower them to find different and better ways to make life strong. We cannot ask them not to steal if we will not teach them how to earn money and we cannot ask them not to sniff glue without bringing enough food to satisfy their hunger.

Reconciliation of Street Children

NGOs and churches working within urban settings are beginning to realize the problem is bigger than just feeding and sheltering street children. These children are not just displaced, but are now entrenched in street life. By providing a way off the street, children are asked to move into a different culture, which sometimes proves too challenging. The children who do not want to leave have found the streets to offer freedom, even safety. It has been said that these children are an "alternative Africa."[35] These children exist within a unique street culture. Magesa calls instruction in childhood "crucial in determining whether these capacities (for strength and intelligence and work) would be exercised in prosperous tranquility or would instead be frustrated and lead to heart-sickness and disorder."[36] Many street children have proven Magesa's point; without this vital instruction, they have become frustrated and have turned to create an alternative society. In this sense, these children are

---

[33] Benezet Bujo, *The Ethical Dimension of Community* (Nairobi: Paulines Publications Africa, 1997), 25.
[34] Magesa, *African Religion*, 64.
[35] Shanahan, "The Alternative Africa," 4–15.
[36] Magesa, *African Religion*, 92.

missing out on the rich culture that is found in community in Kenya. Creative ways must be sought to reconcile these children with their communities. Even though street life is a culture ingrained in these children, it will never be a healthy way of existing.

Reconciliation: a case study

In my research I learned of "an old Kenyan woman" who buys food for a group of street children each day. But this woman has decided if she finds them with glue, they are not allowed to have food. In fact, she exchanges food for glue bottles, warning the kids of the dangers of sniffing. She has found a way to meet the needs of street children while making a statement about their behavior. It may not solve all the problems these children face, but it is a life-sustaining action that contributes to the community.

Samuel Shomba never minds giving up his glue bottle for food. As he told me the story of this "old mama" he smiled and reminded me that what she does is good. Samuel is 12, and although he's only been on the streets for three months, he knows he never wants to leave. He came to the streets because after being beaten frequently by his mother. He told us that his mother was capable to care for them, she had a garden, and his father worked in the Maasai Mara (a large game reserve in Kenya). Even with these resources, Samuel said his mother only beat and neglected he and his brother. There were six children at his homestead, four belonged to his aunt, and Samuel and his younger brother were his mother's only two children. Samuel's younger brother ran away first to Nairobi, joined a gang and learned street life, and then returned for Samuel and the two took a train back to Nairobi. There they rejoined this gang of about 15 children, both young and old. The gang was described by Samuel as "tough," in fact he didn't want us to meet them because he felt they might take advantage of us. In this gang were two older girls, and several "married" couples renting houses in the slums. When we asked Samuel if he wanted to go to school, he told us he didn't because he knew the teachers there would only beat and abuse him. In his short time on the street he has been beaten and chased by police and felt his street family was often his only protection.

Samuel's story finds similarities with the thousands of street children living in Kenya. The lives of those who have run to the streets to escape their families are often characterized by rebuke rather than blessing. While street children like Samuel often do not trust adults, be they parents or teachers, he seemed to deeply respect the "old mama" who brought him food. Through a simple act of exchanging bread for glue, this woman recognized the humanity and life-force with these children. Simple acts that give blessing can hold great potential for reconciliation.

Conclusion

Perhaps the hardest thing in life to see is a suffering child. Jesus knew this well when he invited the children to sit at his feet and receive a blessing. An unblessed child is a child who lacks hope and direction. The knowledge of life is passed from parent to child, yet many children living on the street have missed out on the opportunity to learn life-sustaining ways. Despite the lack of participation in systems of community, children on the street have beliefs similar to those found within African traditional beliefs and Christianity. While those beliefs are present, they are often hidden or crippled by the daily demands of survival.

The responses of street children in this study remind us that the physical and the spiritual cannot be separated. The two are intertwined. Blessing from God and relationship to God is manifested through the continuation of life. The potentials and possibilities these children have are limitless. They represent life and in them lies Kenya's future. There are hidden talents, hidden intelligence, and undiscovered love inside of each child living on the street. As knowers and lovers of the gospel, as hopeful participants in communities of faith, we must make it our pursuit to look more deeply and see the life that lives beneath tattered clothes. We must learn to bless each child we meet.

Chapter 9

Living with Indigenous Communities in Chiapas, Mexico: The Transformative Power of Poverty and Suffering

Andrea Vicini, S. J.

A Feast to Celebrate Service and Commitment

Among the many ways in which we can be introduced to an unknown culture one stands as special and unique: a feast. In 2005, after a quite long drive on a side road on the Chiapas' mountains, in an early December warm day we reached a small hamlet on a hill side in the Bachajón's mission in the diocese of San Cristóbal de Las Casas. Brightened by the sun, the hamlet looked over-crowded with people coming from the surrounding areas, states, and as far as Mexico City. It was still early morning, but you would not have guessed it by looking at the number of busy people. The feast was already in an advanced stage of preparation. We were invited to celebrate with the local indigenous Mayan community, who speak Tzeltal,[1] the many charges and responsibilities that were given to some among them.

Over 15 people were at the center of the celebration. Some of the charges involved leadership roles within the community; others concerned serving the poor, the needy, and the sick; some people were chosen to be catechists. Other roles required work to prepare the next year's feast; during the whole year this implied growing the corn for the *tortillas*, attending and feeding the livestock, cultivating vegetables, overlooking the preparation of the next year's feast and running it by making everything run smoothly. In all cases leadership was for a fixed time; it required extra work for the community, to be added to one's regular labor for one's own family, and it implied accountability to the community.[2]

---

[1] Tzeltal is one of the four Mayan languages spoken in the diocese. The other languages are: Tzotzil, Ch'ol, and Tojolab'al.

[2] The Mexican theologian Alexander P. Zatyrka, S. J., who has an extensive direct knowledge of the Bachajón's mission, named some of these non-ordained ministries in a paper presented at the conference "Local Ecclesiologies in Dialogue," organized by the Jesuit School of Theology (Berkeley, CA), on May 29, 2009. They include: "Community Promoters

Women were preparing and cooking the *tortillas*; cutting, washing, and cooking the vegetables; overlooking the cooking of the meat, and preparing the coffee. Men were cutting the beef in small slices to prepare the traditional meat dish. Dozens of children were running, playing, checking on what everyone was doing and even helping their elders in their chores. A musical group was playing in the church for those who were not involved in preparing the feast, mostly visitors from other indigenous communities and from faraway cities. Finally, some men were fixing the huge tent that we were going to use as open church. There, cantors and musicians were rehearsing. The tent was located on a hillside, in the hamlet's largest flat space available. Its amphitheater shape allowed a good view to all the bystanders for the feast's central event: the Mass during which responsibilities would have been given, the people would have been blessed, and we would have prayed for those who were willing and ready to take their turn in serving the community for the good of all.

To understand the importance of this feast we need to look at what happened a few decades ago. In 1958 the Jesuits began to serve the indigenous communities in that large mountain area in Chiapas. At the beginning they were doing the usual apostolic work: they celebrated the Eucharist, weddings and funerals; administered Baptisms and prepared the people for Confirmation; formed children and adults through catecheses. At the occasion of a second meeting[3] of indigenous communities' delegates, their Bishop Samuel Ruiz García, and the Jesuit missionaries, held to evaluate the current mission work and plan for the future, the Bishop proposed to reflect on the following scenario:

Suppose that tomorrow all the missioners and the bishop travel by plane. And that the plane has an accident and they all die. That would mean no more missioners to accompany you. You would be left alone. Do you think you are ready for that? What do you have to show for more than 15 years of missionary presence among you? Please think about it, discuss it among yourselves and share with us your reflections.[4]

(*¡Koltaywanej*), Catechist Coordinators (*¡Tijwanej*), Community Visitors (*¡Ula'taywanej*), Visit Coordinators (*¡Chahpanwanej*); Catechist Instructors (*Jukawal*), Spiritual Assistants (a sort of Archdeacon, called *¡Muk'ubtesej O'tanil*), and the very important *¡Tojobteswanej*, or Indian Ecclesial Advisor. There are also institutions such as Ethnic Ecclesial Council for Reconciliation" (A. P. Zatyrka, "Emerging Successful Ecclesiologies: The Autochthonous Church in the Bachajón Mission, Chiapas," 5); available at http://www.scu.edu/jst/whatwedo/events/archive/dialogue.cfm (accessed January 21, 2011). For a more comprehensive description, see: A. P. Zatyrka, "The Formation of the Autochthonous Church and the Inculturation of Christian Ministries in the Indian Cultures of America. A Case Study: the Bachajón Mission and the Diocese of San Cristóbal de Las Casas, Mexico" (Dissertation, 2 vols; Innsbruck: Leopold Franzens Universität, 2003); in particular, vol. I: 366–452.

3 The meeting was held in 1975 in Tacuba, "some 60 km west of the town of Bachajón" (Zatyrka, "Emerging Successful Ecclesiologies," 3). For a more detailed account, see: Zatyrka, "The Formation of the Autochthonous Church," vol. I, 253–4.
4 Zatyrka, "Emerging Successful Ecclesiologies," 3.

Alexander P. Zatyrka writes that

none of the missioners or the bishop expected what the Tzeltal delegates answered. Domingo Gómez, one of the Elders (*Trensipal*) from Tacuba was chosen to express their conclusions. It came in these general terms: "We think that perhaps the missioners and the *jTatik*[5] bishop are not doing their job correctly. We know through Scripture that our Lord Jesus Christ taught his followers during three years. Then he was killed on the cross, resurrected and lived among his disciples for another 40 days, at the end of which he left them to go to heaven. But his work is still present among us two thousand years later. However, you have been here for 16 years and we still need your presence to continue in our faith life. What did our Lord do that you are not doing now?" Then he ventured the answer: "Before he left, our Lord Jesus Christ left his Holy Spirit to continue his work. But you have not given us this Spirit. It is true that we receive the Holy Spirit in our Baptism, in our Confirmation, in other Sacraments. But you have not given us the Spirit that builds the community and keeps it united. If you give this Spirit to us, then you will see how your work continues, even if you have to leave us. We want to have our own ministers!"[6]

These indigenous communities were asking about acknowledging concretely within them the Holy Spirit's presence and action through specific ministries, even ordained ministries, and, in particular, the many gifts of the Spirit as community charisms. How could they believe in the Holy Spirit's action without seeing the signs of the Spirit's presence within the Mayan community? Was the Spirit quiet and absent, or gifts where present but they were not yet recognized? Why everything was held by the Jesuits—liturgical celebrations, catecheses, service of the poor and the sick . . . ? Why was the Holy Spirit silent and apparently inactive within the Mayan communities while was so creatively at work within the first Christian communities that were so vivid in the Jesuit fathers' preaching?

The reasonableness, the ethical relevance, the spiritual and ecclesiological depth of these concerns started a process of common rethinking of the apostolic choices and strategies. Together, indigenous communities, Jesuits, and their Bishop began searching to understand what the common good required and entailed. They became aware of the importance that they assigned to community service and shared responsibility for community life. In the form of varied types of ministry, service was well present in the Mayan society long before the beginning of Christianity; service characterized the Mayan

---

[5] In Tzeltal this term indicates respect and it means "our father." See Zatyrka, "The Formation of the Autochthonous Church," vol. I, 253, fn 97.
[6] Zatyrka, "Emerging Successful Ecclesiologies," 3–4.

culture and social life. A strong sense of personal, common, and shared responsibility, as well as a series of well-defined specific tasks and roles aimed at achieving the common good, was culturally and religiously intrinsic to the Mayan culture. They still constitute who the Mayan people are. They also shape who they become as a community. Many of the service roles that were present in the Mayan social structure were also in the Roman Catholic ecclesial structure. It was astonishing to notice the correspondence between the action of the Holy Spirit within the Church, with the different charisms and ministries in the single Christian communities, and within the Mayan social structure.

The feast that we were celebrating was only one of the many feasts that were made possible by that initial Mayan questioning, by the Bishop and the Jesuits' willingness to let themselves be challenged by it, and by the Bishop's readiness to recognize and to incorporate what the Spirit had already prepared well ahead of time. The serious and prolonged commitment to religious and ethical education, as well as to communal discernment that followed, enriched and shaped those local Mayan Catholic communities. They became blessed with a great number of tasks and services aimed at promoting the common good by expressing mercy, compassion, and care for all those in need and vulnerable. It also strengthened participation and allowed for a greater justice in their social and political context marked by discrimination, oppression, violence, and marginalization against the indigenous people.

The celebration started with a very spiritually intense prolonged time devoted to the typical Mayan prayer that connects the people with the ancestors—that is, the beloved and the believers that preceded us—and with the whole creation. It situates us within the universe and history. It strengthens our relationship with the divine present within us, in our relationships, and in creation. It allows us to ask for what we need and what we desire. It is a vocal prayer, uttered out loud, and it is led by the community elder. It is personal as well as public, intimate but shared, so that each prayer can become anyone's prayer.

The moving celebration lasted for a few hours, with a great care given to the different parts of the Mass as well as to blessing the persons assuming the community charges, praying for them, and solemnly giving to them their charges. The liturgy of the Word was special. After over a decade of work of a Catholic and Protestant commission, the Bible was completely translated into Tzeltal and, therefore, the scriptural readings were read in their local language. God's Word was proclaimed in their own tongue, by reading their own Bible.

Two more elements need to be highlighted. First, in the Mayan culture any responsibility and community charge is assumed and shared by the whole family. Hence, the families were gathered around those at the center of the celebration. The personal responsibility of the chosen women and men is assumed and lived out as a familial responsibility, and it involves the synergy, cohesion, and sacrifice of all the family members.

Second, all Mayan communities living in the Chiapas' mountains are extremely poor. They live in wood houses built on the bare ground, very often with only a door and no window, a fireplace for cooking, very limited furniture, and a few belongings. However, it is among them that I experienced, for the first time in my life, what it means and what entails the word "dignity." I was stunned by noticing how they wear with elegance their typical clothes (in particular the women), without forgetting that often they own only two clothes: one for feast days and another for daily life. It is a dignity that manifests itself in the ordinary. It can be recognized by looking at how the women and men walk on the steep hills or on the roads; how they interact among themselves and with others; how, in many villages, they get and carry the water from the only tap that is available; how they endure decades, even centuries of humiliation, injustice, and oppression without losing sight of the justice that is long overdue . . . The dignity that I perceived in them and in their gestures astonished me and, by touching me deeply, transformed me. By being themselves, they were teaching me how to be fully human, how to be myself, and how to be with them discretely and respectfully. By contemplating their dignity—personal, familial, ecclesial, and social—I received from them and I was strengthened in my commitment for a greater justice.

Chiapas is one of the too many corners in our world today where, even as a foreigner, you feel a palpable tension. You are surprised by the extensive presence and control of police and military forces in the territory and you become aware of the violence suffered by the indigenous people in the past and still today. Sadly, as it happens too often, the poor and the vulnerable are not enough protected and are exposed to abuses and violence. In particular, the Chiapas suffers from a war of low intensity, where powerful economic powers and their political and military counterparts aim at gaining the control of the land at the expense of the indigenous people living there. These powers exploit Chiapas' major economic resources—petroleum, uranium, abundant water, rare woods, and so on—and nothing appears to limit their aggressive policy.

As it happens in many other countries in today's world, the dignity of so many people, their culture, their well-being, their own flourishing, and their own existence are threatened by unjust and violent powers. Such awareness, with the suffering and the struggle that it implies, surfaced in the homily and in the prayers of the faithful during the feast's Mass, but it did not spoil the festive ambiance. At the end of the celebration everyone rejoiced with all those gathered there and congratulated the many people who had received a new responsibility. The music played and the goods prepared by so many people completed the feast. Everyone had tasty food in abundance, and nobody lacked it, at least on that day.

On ethnography

There are many ways in which we can reflect theologically about personal and communal experiences, as well as particular and global events. One of these ways is by aiming at being ethically involved, as researchers who are also respectful participants. In the spirit of the whole volume, I attempt a theological ethnographic approach. As the theoretical analytic pages in this volume have previously indicated, two are the relevant elements of any ethnographic work and, I add, of any approach in theological ethics: the *agent(s)* involved and the *context.* Both are situated in history and are shaped by it, by what comes before them, by what happens in the present, and by what is expected for the future. The first agent that I mention is the divine, that is, in a Christian perspective, the Trinity. Then there are all the people with whom there is a direct or an indirect interaction and myself as a theologian—each one marked by ethnic, cultural, and religious backgrounds, with a specific formation and training, with a series of experiences that make us who we are. Finally, the specificity of any context—in this case Mayan and Mexican—reveals itself as a richness that inspires, challenges, confirms, and transforms those who belong to such a context and, probably even more, the moral agents who come from and are rooted in different contexts. A sufficient degree of attraction to diversity—to respect, explore, discover, and appreciate it—is indispensable. Otherwise, one's context becomes a sort of prison from which we cannot venture toward novelty or like the opaque "lenses" that do not allow us to see anything else that is around us and outside ourselves.

As a white, Italian, pediatrician, Jesuit priest, and theological ethicist I interacted with the various Mayan communities in two major ways: with a less active role and a discrete presence, in almost the totality of the accounts that I give in these pages, and with a more active role, as in the case of the Holy Week liturgy that I describe later. Hence, both ways of being ethnographically involved were explored and both were significant and complementary. In a newly discovered culture one might privilege one approach over the other, but when the relationship aims at equality the emphasis is not only on a personal choice. In other words, I personally prefer a low profile approach, but in interacting with the people, in working in that Mayan parish for a few months, the people too have a say on how you live with them, on how you share who you are and what you are able to do with them. You are not behind a desk, protected. You are out there with them, with the desire of getting to know them, of respecting them, and of caring for and with them. Many of the people with whom you interact become dear to you. You like them and love them and they like you and love you.

The ethical and theological relevance of these interactions and how they make vivid God's presence in human relationships can be hardly explained in words, because words seem to be so limited to express the beauty and the goodness experienced. Hence, the ethnographic work might appear mostly evocative of those experiences, and of similar ones that we might have had in our life's journey. Careful and well disposed listening, as well as openness to the lives, experiences, sufferings, struggles, and desires of peoples and of local communities are both part of a theological and ethical move. First, it mimics God's move toward humankind. Second, it confirms what we have already experienced throughout our life journeys and throughout history. Third, it becomes our own virtuous move. In all three instances the result is a personal and collective transformation for the common good and a greater justice. Finally, it dismisses the common view that the study of the "facts" should be our starting point, followed by theological reflection upon the empirical work. A new approach is possible, more integral, more humanly and divinely centered.

Palenque: The Strength of a Suffering Community

There was only a shadow overlooking the whole celebration. It became evident at a second event that took place shortly after, at a three-day gathering (March 13–16, 2006) of the diocese of San Cristóbal de Las Casas. The participants were the 335 ordained indigenous lay permanent deacons and their families, together with the candidates to the deaconate in formation and their families. This gathering, the seventeenth of this type, took place in Palenque—such an important Mayan archeological and historic city in Chiapas. Together with the over 700 participants were Bishop Felipe Arizmendi Esquivel and the Auxiliary Bishop Enrique Díaz Díaz. Those three days were the annual occasion for common formation offered to all deacons.

The opening plenary talk, given by Alexander P. Zatyrka, S.J., who directs the Department of Religious Sciences at the Universidad Iberoamericana in Mexico City, analyzed the current political and social situation in Chiapas and in the whole Mexico. It vividly highlighted the people's struggles and it force-fully indicated what the promotion of justice and the service of faith require from us today. Another plenary talk reflected on the deacon's ministry, by examining its biblical sources and by studying its presence in the early Christian community, throughout church history, and in today's church. In the great hall in which we were gathered, we were divided into the four large language groups (i.e. Tzeltal, Tzotzil, Ch'ol, and Tojolab'al), each one with its own indigenous translator; this linguistic richness confirmed the feeling of diversity lived with intensity, and the people's commitment to know, understand, interact, and dialogue.

It became very clear what saddened all people gathered there. In the recent years, during the term of the now Bishop Emeritus Samuel Ruiz García, the indigenous permanent deacons had gradually become a vital presence in the diocese. Their service in preaching and in taking care of the needy and of the sick had been both important and vital. With the 8,000 indigenous catechists in the diocese, these deacons accompanied, supported, and strengthened the many local Catholic communities spread throughout the Chiapas' mountains. However, the Vatican Congregation for Divine Worship and the Discipline of the Sacraments, in a very brief official letter, had blocked the future ordination of permanent indigenous lay deacons in the diocese of San Cristóbal de Las Casas.[7] With great dignity, desire for understanding, and willingness to be faithful members of the Roman Catholic Church, the Bishops and their people discussed the Vatican decision both in plenary sessions and in small groups. They were suffering for what they could not fully understand. By reading the Congregation's letter, they were experiencing a sort of theological and ecclesial confusion, as if the Second Vatican Council's promotion of autochthonous churches[8] was seen as leading to a sort of autonomous church, neither portraying their Roman Catholic identity, nor their objectives and pastoral strategies.

What characterized the whole diocese was the Roman Catholic way of worshiping, studying, educating, celebrating, growing in one's faith, praying, loving the neighbor, trying to live a virtuous life and being merciful, serving the poor, and struggling for justice. In their diocese all the believers were living fully their Roman Catholic identity with great attention to discerning the gifts of the Holy Spirit within the single communities and the whole diocese. They were attempting to delineate what could characterize the identity and the practices of an autochthonous church, being faithful to the Second

---

[7] Congregación para el Culto Divino y la Disciplina de los Sacramentos, "Carta sobre la ordenación de diáconos permanentes de la Congregación para el Culto Divino y la Disciplina de los Sacramentos," in *Revista Iberoamericana de Teología* 2:2 (2006), 99–100. The letter was written on October 25, 2005. It was signed by Cardinal Francis Arinze, Prefect of the Congregation, and by Bishop Domenico Sorrentino, Secretary of the Congregation. In the letter we read that, for the Congregation, "continua latente en la Diócesis la ideología que promueve la implementación del proyecto de una Iglesia Autóctona" (p. 99). Further, the letter demands "que se interrumpa la formación de más candidatos al diaconado permanente" (ibid.). For a brief analysis, see: A. P. Zatyrka, "Iglesia Autóctona ¿una ideología?," in *Revista Iberoamericana de Teología* 2:2 (2006), 97–8.

[8] "The proper purpose of this missionary activity is evangelization, and the planting of the Church among those peoples and groups where it has not yet taken root. Thus from the seed which is the word of God, particular autochthonous churches should be sufficiently established and should grow up all over the world, endowed with their own maturity and vital forces. Under a hierarchy of their own, together with the faithful people, and adequately fitted out with requisites for living a full Christian life, they should make their contribution to the good of the whole Church" (Second Vatican Council, "Decree on the Missionary Activity of the Church *Ad Gentes*," in *Acta Apostolicae Sedis* 58:14 (1966), 947–90 (n. 6 at pp. 953–4); quoted in: Zatyrka, "Emerging Successful Ecclesiologies," 2, fn 5). For a brief historic overview concerning the autochthonous church, see: A. P. Zatyrka, "The Rise and Fall of the *Ecclesia Indiana*," in *Revista Iberoamericana de Teología* 2:3 (2006), 27–62; J. A. Estrada, "Por un cristianismo inculturado en una Iglesía autóctona," *Revista Iberoamericana de Teología* 2:3 (2006), 5–26. For a more extensive analysis, see: Zatyrka, "The Formation of the Autochthonous Church," vol. I, 118–44.

Vatican Council's teaching. They had never thought of becoming an autonomous church separated from the Roman Catholic Church, nor had their choices and behaviors as ministers and communities ever indicated that.

During the three-day gathering in Palenque, the Bishops[9] as well as the Deacons and Parishes' Counsel[10] wrote their response to the Congregation's letter. Its tone was calm, informative, collaborative, and obedient. The whole audience wondered why they should endure such further suffering and why they were experiencing such a great misunderstanding. They found strength and consolation in Jesus Christ's passion and death on the cross, while longing for the resurrection. They were hoping to ordain more indigenous permanent deacons. Their presence was needed to strengthen further the Catholic believers in their many indigenous communities, to renew the indigenous incorporation into the Roman Catholic Church, and to expand the evangelization by supporting the 8,000 indigenous catechists who operate in the diocese. The deacon's presence and service was not understood and lived as an alternative to priesthood. While praying and waiting for the gift of indigenous priests within their communities, the deacons were indispensable in helping to hold together the believers living on the mountains. They were helping them to grow in their faith.

In Palenque, the shadow that veiled the people's joy to be together and their commitment to serve the church continued to surface while we were lining up for going to the restrooms or for getting the food prepared by the local parishioners; while, at the end of each day, we got ready to lay down to sleep on the conference hall floor or in the nearby local parish meeting rooms. Because the two Bishops were with us for the whole three days, many people could talk directly with them. Each one enjoyed being listened. Each one felt supported and confirmed, humanly and pastorally. The Eucharistic celebrations and the prayer vigil that were organized nourished spiritually the whole community. We felt God's presence close to each one of us, in an intimate but shared way.

I had spent three days with a vibrant and engaged group of people, with so many lay permanent deacons. It was stunning to experience their great love both for their church and for their people. With their adult faith they showed how to deal with an inexplicable prohibition without endangering their faith and their belonging to the Roman Catholic Church. I was edified, renewed, surprised, and in awe. I had experienced one of those ecclesial realities, throughout our world today, that are strong, healthy, and growing. Those communities

[9] Obispos de San Cristóbal de las Casas (Chiapas, México), "Iglesia autóctona y diaconado Permanente," in *Revista Iberoamericana de Teología* 2:2 (2006), 101–6. The letter was sent on March 16, 2006.

[10] Parroquias y Consejo Diaconal de la Diócesis de San Cristóbal de las Casas (Chiapas, México), "Carta a su santidad Benedicto XVI," in *Revista Iberoamericana de Teología* 2:2 (2006), 107–9. The letter was sent on March 24, 2006.

are served with competence, zeal, and abnegation by engaged ministers, and with a hierarchy closely connected to God's people and with a clear vision of their service to the ecclesial community and to society at large. This was quite consoling, as well as ethically and spiritually nourishing.

San Pedro Chenalhó: A Commitment That Makes Extraordinary the Ordinary

The ethical impact of major events and gatherings on ecclesial and social dynamics can be dismissed rapidly by simply noting that those events are self-contained in time and space and that their impact, while difficult to be assessed with any degree of certainty, appears to be quite limited. It is the ordinary that matters and that confirms or leads to dismiss what occurred during any major event. I was stunned by what I had lived in Palenque, by the growing and vital Roman Catholic Church that I met there. It was the Church heir of the Second Vatican Council with laity and hierarchy working together side to side; with open eyes on the social, political, and cultural context; with more than a simply vocal determination of its preferential option for the poor. It was a church of the poor, made of extremely poor people—in economic terms—but so rich in their willingness to work for the common good and for what is just.

I did not want to idealize what I had lived and I was looking for a more prolonged experience. The opportunity came in another area of the same diocese, in the parish San Pedro Chenalhó, also run by the Jesuits, where the indigenous people speak Tzotzil. In the few months I lived there I could participate in a few two-day workshops of formation for the parish catechists—almost 100 women and men at each workshop; visit various villages that belong to the large parish territory, where displaced indigenous community live in extreme poverty;[11] meet the organizations that work for promoting human rights and that support citizens in their strive for justice; help people in need of medical care, medical advice or support; join international college students and their professors[12] in full immersion trips during Spring break to discover Chiapas, by knowing the people living there, the injustice that they suffer, and their struggle for justice.

Among these many different events and experiences, I limit my attention to the monthly gathering for catechists, aimed at strengthening their formation.

---

[11] They were forced to relocate in different areas within Chiapas because of the intimidation, violence, and threats that they suffered. Because of the land's rich resources, multinational corporations control and exploit the land with the help of the army and paramilitary groups. To avoid any hindrance by the indigenous people living in those territories, they repeatedly intimidated, threaten, and use violence against local indigenous communities, forcing them to leave their land and to relocate elsewhere by losing the little that they own.
[12] In that period, the group of students and their accompanying professor were from Boston College (Boston, MA).

While major events can dazzle us, ordinary ones allow us to check out our perceptions, and to have a more accurate appraisal of community life and of the ethical dynamics occurring among the people and within communities. Suffering from injustice, violence, poverty, and other hardships that fill up daily lives, could harden our hearts, nourish our skepticism, and lead us to retrieve from social and ecclesial commitment and participation. Communal cohesion, self-esteem, activism, assumption of community services and responsibilities can be threatened by a social context that does not support individuals and communities or, at worst, that aims at breaking any growth in one's social awareness and political engagement.

The parish of San Pedro Chenalhó, in the diocese of San Cristóbal de Las Casas, organized a very simple parish center in a central area in the large parish territory, easy to be reached from the four parish corners. I got there as all the other indigenous catechists do, that is, with the cheapest and more common public transportation: an open pickup truck where people stand in the back of the truck, in any weather, getting soaked when it rains. The parish center consists of a wood cabin that is the kitchen, a small house that works as a gathering hall, an office, the local church, and a small house where, in separated sections, women and men can sleep in bunks.

At the beginning of our gathering the men worked digging a trench to install a plastic water pipe for getting water from the nearby village to the parish center. Each one had brought his own tools and we worked together successfully. Then, the monthly formation workshop started early in the morning after a very simple breakfast with *tortillas* and coffee. Each day, the formation included: a biblical and a pastoral reflection given by the indigenous parochial vicar; group discussion and sharing; "questions and answers" time to check out the various communities; discussion and decisions on the catechetical goals for the coming month. Each one of the many communities within the parish was represented by at least a couple of catechists, women and men, married or not.

The two-day formation gathering kept busy the almost 100 catechists from early morning to sundown with a couple of coffee breaks and a very simple lunch and dinner with *tortillas*, baked beans, and *quesadillas*. During the breaks, music was played and songs were sung, unveiling the innate musical giftedness of many indigenous people who can play well various instruments, even without having had any formal and structured musical training. The shared commitment to formation and service, as well as the readiness to spend together days of hard work, manifested their moral stature. Their abnegation was authentic, neither forced, nor artificial. They were involved. They were themselves. It was remarkable and praiseworthy to realize the positive impact of their work in their communities. Their fellow believers could benefit from their service and the result was the growth of all in their Christian formation and engagement. Those catechists showed concretely what shared responsibility entails and how this enriches concrete communities. Of course, some catechists were more able than others; some were more experienced and well trained; in the case of some communities, tensions were occurring and they needed to be named, addressed, and sorted out. This is not surprising. It is part of our ongoing and never ending process of conversion and growth. However, it does not undermine the ethical, ecclesial, and social importance of their apostolic work.

At their gatherings, month after month the catechists could share their insights and developments as well as name and address their difficulties. Their service could be renewed and strengthened. All of this appeared to be quite ordinary to them, and it is indeed, but not everywhere. Collaborative dynamics benefit from a minimal but efficient and essential methodology and discipline, with competence, commitment, and even helpful settings. For each catechist, efforts and sacrifices were demanding, but the achievements were remarkable. In such a way, the parishioners, their pastor—Fr. Pedro Humberto Arriaga Alarcon, S. J.—, and their vicars showed their vision aimed at concretely promoting human, ecclesial, and social progress, and at nurturing their Christian life by using ordinary means— like gatherings, formation, spiritual experiences, celebrations, and so on.

The indigenous dignity that had impressed me in so many different contexts and situations—and that could have been considered merely exterior or limited to single persons and their behavior, choices, and life style—appeared to be more articulated. By living with them it appeared ethically consistent. It manifested itself in participatory and collaborative dynamics, as well as in concrete practices.[13] Because of one's gender and position within the social group, quite fixed roles were assigned to each one. Those roles still were both respected and transformed to promote a greater equality, as it was indicated by the fact that a few women were catechists too, that their voices were heard by all, and their insights and advices were discussed with attention.

Every process of social transformation occurs in time. It was encouraging to notice that the goals pursued were quite comprehensive: the good of the people involved; a greater justice in their social environment; the growth and strengthening of their faith experience. Moreover, their way of proceeding as a Christian community aimed at promoting the people's skills, gifts, and qualities. Any of their qualities and capabilities was at the service of the common good of all. Their ordinary lives nurtured the extraordinary rich life of a strong and growing Christian community. Together with them, we can recognize that the "extraordinary" in our lives is made of the ordinary "stuff" that fills up our days, and that depends on who we are and on how we struggle day after day in discerning and in doing what is good and just, while avoiding what is evil—as the whole moral tradition has taught us.

By living in the midst of those indigenous communities, my understanding of virtues and practices was renewed. In our life—both personal and communal—

---

[13] On the theological relevance of collaboration and participation in a specific ethical field, that is, bioethics, see: Lisa Sowle Cahill, *Theological Bioethics*, 43–69.

often we think of virtues solely as a pious invitation, an exhortation to live well, or an ideal that is often considered as unachievable. However, when we experience virtues and practices lived concretely around us, their importance becomes manifest for single individuals, for families, for communities, for the church, and for the whole society. Hence, the authors who today are writing on virtues provide us with a renewed ethical tool for appreciating and for reaching out to virtuous persons, communities, and societies that, in part, embody one or more of these virtues.[14] The ethical witness of these people strengthens our hope, love, faith, and other virtues. Hence, a virtuous ethical approach that promotes collaboration, interaction, participation, and commitment is anthropologically, historically, and sociologically rooted. This is true for specific communities, as in the case of the Mayan communities in Chiapas. It is also true in the case of other communities, more universally.

Moreover, an ethnographic sensibility in theological ethics leads us to confirm both the relevance and the pertinence of fundamental ethical reasoning. It also shows practically and concretely the importance of insights that depend on ethical theories aimed at interpreting human behavior and choices, as well as local and global social dynamics and their historic articulated process. Finally, people can read anew their experience with new ethical "lenses," while ethicists can reflect on the positive impact of their scholarship and their reasoning. New ways of interacting between scholars and local communities will nourish all the ethical agents involved; they will also confirm, disprove, or contribute to ethical reflection, narratives, concrete actions, and practices.

Acteal: The Drama of Violence and the Power of a Transformative Response

Many times we speak too blatantly and rapidly both about suffering in general and about people who suffer. We all know that suffering changes people— others and ourselves—by affecting us deeply in our identity and personality, as

---

[14] For a few examples, see: J. Porter, "Recent Studies in Aquinas's Virtue Ethics: A Review Essay," in *Journal of Religious Ethics* 26:1 (1998), 191–215; J. F. Keenan, "The Virtue of Prudence (IIa IIae, qq. 47–56)," in *The Ethics of Aquinas*, Stephen J. Pope (ed.) (Washington, D.C.: Georgetown University Press, 2002), 259–71; D. J. Harrington and J. F. Keenan, *Jesus and Virtue Ethics: Building Bridges between New Testament Studies and Moral Theology* (Lanham: Sheed & Ward, 2002); J. F. Keenan, "What Does Virtue Ethics Brings to Genetics?," in *Genetics, Theology and Ethics: An Interdisciplinary Conversation*, Lisa Sowle Cahill (ed.) (New York: Crossroad, 2005), 97–113; C. P. Vogt, "Fostering a Catholic Commitment to the Common Good: An Approach Rooted in Virtue Ethics," in *Theological Studies* 68:2 (2007), 394–417; L. Fullam, *The Virtue of Humility: A Thomistic Apologetic* (Lewiston: Edwin Mellen Press, 2009). For an extended attention to current writings on virtue ethics, see: J. F. Keenan, *A History of Catholic Moral Theology in the Twentieth Century: From Confessing Sins to Liberating Consciences* (New York: Continuum, 2010), 216–18.

well as by shaping how we relate to one another and to life in general. Nobody is spared, sooner or later. Quite often we are tempted to affirm that suffering has a transformative power. The ethical risk in making such a bold statement is that often we make the claim when talking about others' suffering. We do it at their place. Whether and whenever this occurs, we deprive them of the possibility of affirming it with their own words, if they will ever recognize it, and when they will want to say it.

However, there is another possibility. We can be touched by the suffering of our neighbors—understood as an individual or as a group, a community, or a people. By contemplating how they endure their suffering, how they react to it, how they affirm life in concrete life choices, we might find ourselves transformed. We are touched and changed by the suffering of people around us, or of those whose ordeal brings us close to them.[15] By contemplating how many people endure their suffering, how they react to it, how they affirm life in their concrete choices and actions, we find ourselves interiorly moved and renewed. The suffering of the other moves us to compassion, stimulates our creative care, strengthens our commitment for justice, and allows us to gather creative energy to help them.

Sadly, today's world and human history are too full of tragic violent events. Each one contains in itself all the others and it amplifies them. At the same time, our hope might be increased in seeing how so many people are compassionate and how they act to strengthen, spread, and promote justice, freedom, peace, progress, for personal and social well-being and flourishing. To look at one of those events, as I do now, does not undermine or forget the others; on the contrary, it could include them and provide ethical insights.

Acteal is a very small village, like so many others on the Chiapas' mountains. The wooden poor houses are located on the hills' slopes, above and below the only road that connects Acteal to other villages and valleys. In the largest flat space we find a wooden small chapel and a parish building, with a few rooms and a kitchen. On December 22, 1997, a paramilitary group, probably trained by the army, or tolerated by it, stormed in the chapel where people were gathered to pray. Children, adolescents, young people, women—among them a few pregnant women—, men, and the elderly were brutally murdered. The rampage started in the small chapel and continued for a few hours in the surrounding areas among houses and trees. Forty-five indigenous people were killed. The barbarous massacre shocked Chiapas, the whole of Mexico, and the world. Many people from the neighboring areas and from afar began to show their

---

[15] A tragic example concerns natural catastrophes (e.g. the earthquake that struck Haiti on January 12, 2010) or events caused by evil purposes (e.g. terrorist attacks; among them, the attack to the World Trade Center in New York on September 11, 2001, is emblematic). The sharing in others' suffering, and the outpouring of solidarity and help to respond to any tragedy, suggest how we are concretely transformed and, hence, how we want to express our compassion and love for all those affected.

solidarity. Many people came to Acteal to support the survivors and, with their presence, to block further violence. Inside the chapel, on the tin roof and on the wooden walls it is still possible to recognize the holes left by the shots. Even the small figure of the Virgin Mary that was standing there, dressed with the local typical clothing of any indigenous woman living in the area, was damaged by the shots. Now she is called "the Virgin of the Massacre."

It was very moving to celebrate Mass in that chapel with the survivors, who still live there, who did not flee their homes and their land, who were helped to resist that tragic intimidation. Around the world there are places where we can feel what happened there, even if it took place years before.[16] We experience the suffering that occurred there by simply standing in silence and by meeting people who suffered that ordeal. There we shiver, our words are broken, we are intimately moved, and tears begin to flow on our cheeks. The disorder, the chaos, and the violence touch us. They enter us. As James F. Keenan points out vividly, we discover that mercy is entering into the chaos of a people, of a community, of a family, of our own lives.[17] And mercy transforms us. Those memories and their tears, as well as those injustices suffered and that reclaim justice, have an impact on our lives. They shape our moral actions gracefully, by moving us to greater love, care, compassion, and to a stronger commitment to work for justice.

Since that tragic day in Acteal, the outpouring of national and international solidarity has helped the people to build structures: a memorial for the victims with their names, pictures, and stories; a place to gather with large groups, that is used for major celebrations; a monument to commemorate those who were killed there and all the victims of violence throughout history everywhere in the world;[18] and a new small chapel to pray and to celebrate together. This praiseworthy support has accompanied the local community by providing concrete resources, with the compassion and care that it reveals.

Concrete signs, like buildings and memorials, are certainly helpful to awaken our consciences and to keep alive the memory of what happened, against any current revisionist attitude throughout the world. Such a memory is essential to work for a better future. Support and solidarity from people everywhere help us to feel that we are not alone and they help us to find the interior energy that is needed daily. It is also astonishing to discover the many ways in which such help allowed the local indigenous community to start new projects. In such a way, they show us how they responded to that

---

[16] Auschwitz and Birkenau are some of the many tragic places with such an intense spiritual presence.

[17] See: J. F. Keenan, *The Works of Mercy: The Heart of Catholicism* 2nd edn (Lanham: Rowman & Littlefield, 2008).

[18] The monument, created and realized, in 1999, by the Danish artist Jens Galshiøt, is called *Columna de Infamia* (The Pillar of Shame).

tragic experience by positively and creatively transforming reality. The people of Acteal, and of the surrounding villages, responded both to the massacre and to the outpouring of help and support by strengthening their peaceful nonviolent association, called *Las Abejas* (The Bees), that was founded in 1992 with the purpose of working together for peace and justice. There is no peace without justice. There is no progress without justice.[19] The perpetrators and those who armed and sent them are not yet brought to justice. For the pacifist members of *Las Abejas* this is not helping the advancement of peace in their area. They add that neither reconciliation nor forgiveness will be possible without truth and justice. But this lack and delay in administering justice did not stop them from continuing to ask for justice. They got together to strengthen one another and to reclaim the arrest and fair trial of the guilty.

The comprehensive understanding of what justice requires and entails led to further achievements that highlight participation and collaboration. The strengthening of a coffee cooperative, *Maya Vinic* (that in Tzotzil means "the Mayan person"),[20] allowed the single farmers to avoid the mediators (called *coyotes*) who buy the coffee produced at a very low price and sell it at high price in order to make great profits, at the expense of the poor indigenous farmers. Then, in 2006, a few women created in Acteal a small cooperative that produces and sells typical indigenous clothing and crafts, to provide extra earnings to their families.

Suffering strains relationships and leads to experience solitude, loneliness, and isolation or, as in the case of these two cooperatives, it can promote a more cohesive dynamic within the community. Religious narratives and practices can be part too of a process of positive social transformation by strengthening the commitment to work for justice and by promoting gradual reconciliation. Churches gather communities of believers and can promote identity, a sense of belonging, a celebration, and an ethical presence within society at large. Narratives, and the virtuous practices that manifest them, can displace other narratives and practices that are ethically problematic. Such a replacement indicates that transformation does not depend solely on single moral agents, or on limited collective agents like families; it stresses the positive role that can be played by communal narratives and practices.

An example indicates how this transformation takes place and what it determines within a community. It concerns the Holy Week celebrations in indigenous

---

[19] As an example, see Paul VI's Encyclical Letter on the Development of Peoples: Paul VI, "Populorum progressio," *Acta Apostolicae Sedis* 59:4 (1967), 257–99.

[20] The coffee cooperative *Maya Vinic* was started in 1992. Its purpose is to gather the organic coffee produced by each indigenous farmer, to manufacture it, and to sell it nationally and internationally. See: *Maya Vinic*; available at: http://www.mayavinic.com/ (accessed January 21, 2011).

communities that belong to the parish San Pedro Chenalhó. Within Christianity and specifically within the Roman Catholic Church, the Easter celebrations are central to the Christian faith experience. The Holy Week begins with Palm Sunday, with the reading of the Gospel's account of Jesus' entrance in Jerusalem, where he is welcomed as a king. It culminates in the Holy *Triduum* that celebrates the Last Supper, the whole Passion, the Crucifixion, the descent to Sheol, and, on Easter Sunday, Jesus' resurrection.

In 2006, eight indigenous communities celebrated that week by welcoming and by accompanying the small statue of the Virgin of Acteal from one community to another. Our celebrations began in Acteal on Palm Sunday, by situating in Jesus' Passion the people's tragedy and their passion, and vice versa. Then the small statue of the Virgin of the Massacre was placed on the back of a pickup truck and, accompanied by a few indigenous women sitting on the truck and by other people following on foot, we started our pilgrimage. At the end of each village a few pickup trucks would drive a few people to the next community, where the whole village was waiting for the arrival of the small procession. We would enter the village on foot, as pilgrims do, welcomed by the local indigenous community at the village entrance. Representatives from the community accompanying the Virgin and the whole welcoming community would celebrate together and then enjoy the meal and the hospitality offered. A small group of about ten people accompanied the statue of the Virgin of Acteal during the whole week, in every community in which we were welcomed; it was composed of indigenous women and men, of a few religious and lay women and men visiting and helping the parish during those months, some coming from other countries. My presence as a priest working in the parish at that time allowed me to pray and to celebrate with them the Eucharist and the specific *Triduum* liturgies, to listen to them, to get to know them better, to share their food, and to sleep on benches in their chapels or on tables in parish halls. We stayed in a different community each day of the Holy Week. Our pilgrimage ended celebrating Easter in Acteal, together with the pastor, the two parochial vicars, and with the large crowd of people gathered there: the whole parish community was represented and it rejoiced.

Such a way of celebrating the Holy Week was not new to those indigenous communities in the parish. They had already celebrated it in similar ways in the previous years. With the help of their catechists and the community elders, they had prepared it once again, ahead of time, and such a preparation made all celebrations a very enjoyable experience. However, a closer look at the specific context in which they were taking place allows us to appreciate them further. In every part of the world, among neighboring communities, it is not unusual to find tensions, even conflicts, explicit or hidden, that separate persons, families, and villages and that often are based on misunderstandings or on events that occurred in the recent or remote past. This is not surprising. To this, we can add the uneasiness and the increased perception of vulnerability that we all experience when we are guests.

Hospitality is gracious, but in poor communities it always implies extra work and sacrifice to welcome the guests. It was very touching to enjoy their exquisite welcome and to notice the positive interaction between the two communities: the one accompanying the Virgin and the other welcoming us. It was moving to look at how we celebrated together, how we prayed, and how we ate together the food prepared. This welcome and our celebrations healed strained and broken relationships among the communities. During that Holy Week we all experienced reconciliation. Old and recent frictions and misunderstanding did not hinder our being together as a parish community. We were healed by what we were experiencing and by how we were doing it.

The small statue of the Virgin dressed with the indigenous typical clothing, damaged by heinous violence, symbolized God's loving presence. It was this love that we were remembering and celebrating in the *Triduum*. It is a love that embodies the memory of everyone and, in particular, of the less well off, the victims, the suffering, and that includes the 45 martyrs in Acteal. Jesus' Passion embraces the ordeal of every person and of humankind. Then in Jesus' resurrection was anticipated each one's resurrection. The simple events and celebrations that took place during that Holy Week touched us deeply and transformed not only the communities involved, but the whole parish. Once again, people and communities did not wither because of unjust and unbearable suffering, but they found ways to grow in it and out of it as a more united parish, like people honoring their beloved, finding ways to strengthen their commitment for justice, and loving concretely one another.

Encounters, hospitality, memory, celebration, and sharing of the food: these are the basic elements of social interaction. We can appreciate them further by focusing on those who live them and on their virtuous practices. This allows us to go beyond a simple analytic and descriptive approach to appreciate the ethical relevance of what happens. In such a way, we are nourished and strengthened. Hence, we can amplify and expand the transformative power of narratives and of practices within our communities and in today's world. While we appreciate what occurred in specific communities, we can reflect on similar dynamics on a larger scale, nationally and internationally. In disagreement with Alasdair MacIntyre, we can highlight how small and separated local communities are not the ultimate context where ethical life can occur and where people can be virtuous.[21] On the contrary,

---

[21] See: A. MacIntyre, *After Virtue: A Study in Moral Theory* 3rd edn (Notre Dame: University of Notre Dame Press, 2007).

small local communities become emblematic of virtuous dynamics that go well beyond the limits of a specific community. These dynamics depend on, and are shaped by, our human condition and by larger social dynamics. In particular, these dynamics depend on narratives and practices that are, at the same time, extremely specific, but largely widespread and shared—if we reflect on their positively transformative impact on justice, the good, and well-being. In other words, because of human and social "rootedness," the transformative component of virtuous dynamics is locally situated and tends toward the universal. It can be traced in different experiences in other communities, in extremely different contexts around the globe and throughout history—as it is well indicated by other contributes in this volume. It also aims at becoming universal inasmuch as it expresses our sense of longing for the expected further transformation of our world in a more just place, where respect and dignity for each human being and for the whole creation characterize the primary ethical goal.

The particular experience that I briefly described with my ethnographic ethical positioning leads me to highlight and to reaffirm another important ethical element besides virtues. Discernment was part of what the small communities and the whole parish had experienced in deciding how to celebrate the Holy Week, by including the pilgrimage of the Virgin of Acteal. Discernment was well present in all the examples that I indicated in reflecting on indigenous communities. In articulating these discernments, and in the decisions at the end of them, the key figures of responsibility within the local communities—the elderly, the deacons, the catechists . . . —played essential roles. In reflecting on these experiences, we are continuing to discern while we describe and re-think them. Even if we were not involved, we can witness them as participants, and not as external and disinterested bystanders. We discern what helped us and them then, and what could help us today in promoting the common good of local communities and of humanity at large. In such a way, narratives and practices can contribute in giving us insights that eventually can reshape our narratives and reform our practices today, with the choices that this requires.

Conclusion

An ethnographic account is forcefully focusing on very specific and limited experiences. However, because we are reflecting theologically and, in particular, ethically, our insights on specific situations, places, events, and actions aim at considering those experiences through ethical "lenses," by situating them within a larger set of ethical concerns. Our reflection is shaped by what people suffer as well as by their goodness and ability to promote what is good, what is just, what strengthens our dignity, and what makes us and our world more and more beautiful. At the same time, a particular situation allows us to highlight what is universal—humanly, socially, and ethically. Moreover, our universal commitments for justice and for the common good can be strengthened by concrete and particular situations.[22]

The ethnographic approach in theological ethics allows us to experience again how our finitude has in itself the greatness of the infinite, of the transcendent. By situating ourselves within concrete experiences, by being with the people there where they live, with caring and fraternal attitudes, as virtuous beings, we expose ourselves to the richness and to the limits of their human and social experience. We are transformed in our way of looking at the world. We are strengthened in what makes their lives and our lives meaningful. By supporting them, we feel supported in our personal and social growth in the many different contexts in which we live. By being exposed to their values, their dignity, and their ethical choices, we are led to reconsider our human, social, and ethical priority and behavior. We are invited to focus on what is essential in our personal, ecclesial, and social life as individuals and as communities.

The transformative power of particular life-stories and social stories has an ethical impact that concerns the persons involved, but that also goes beyond them, because it is part of the ongoing human transformative process. Hence, concrete experiences throughout the world and history strengthen our hope in human and social progress and in the possibility of promoting it universally.

By describing briefly these experiences and by attempting to share some of the lived emotions, it appears how, by meeting the other, by living with cultures that are foreign to us, with a more refined eye and a more vibrant heart we can also perceive better what belongs to our culture and context. Diversity pierces anew our perception, our mind, our memory, and our moral fiber. When we do not raise too impenetrable defenses to the other, and when we are interested in what is new, foreign, and unexpected, we might be transformed by encountering the "other"—persons, communities, peoples, and cultures. This is particularly evident when to cultural and linguistic diversity we add extreme poverty and suffering resulting from unjust social and political conditions. Our longing for justice, that depends on the injustice we suffered, resonates with their experiences. This transformation shapes how we reflect theologically, and how we live and act as persons and as communities. Our ethical discernment, our decision-making process, and our choices can strengthen our moral growth and our virtuous behavior by amplifying our ethical impact.

---

[22] For similar insights concerning the field of healthcare, see: Vigen, *Women, Ethics, and Inequality*, 200–9.

Hence, the transformative dimension associated with ethnographic work is not only a fortunate side effect of reflecting on a nice, maybe adventurous or challenging field experience. It highlights the ethical relevance and the beauty of a theology that is able to leave the safe campuses of our universities and get "dirty" by sharing fragments of the unprotected ordinary lives of the majority of women and men on earth—particularly when poverty, injustice, lack of work, education, and healthcare oppress them. Such an approach warns us against the arrogance of seeing ourselves as having something precious to give to the other, that so often betrays our ethically problematic paternalistic and colonial attitudes. It could also help us to become more and more able to experience relational equality. However, because the ethical imbalance is so vividly shocking, as westerners we should first aim at placing ourselves more and more in positions in which the moral agency of poor people could be more fully expressed and, as such, be promoted and strengthened.[23]

After a specific experience within a concrete community in a well situated context, even with a temporal distance from it, our theological ethical reflection deepens and allows us to appreciate these experiences. It can also compare them with other experiences that we, or others, have lived in different contexts and cultures—as it is indicated by the various contributions in this volume. This should not be solely an academic exercise, targeted at increasing the bulk and the quality of publications due for tenure-track evaluation committees.

While we highlight and praise the ethical beauty of what we have experienced and witnessed, the ethical goal should continue to be our personal, social, and ecclesial transformation for serving and loving the other. When we look at the past, this implies respect, compassion, and love for the concrete persons we met, with whom we lived and whose faces, smiles, and tears are well present in our minds; whose handshaking and embraces still warm our hearts; whose endurance, hope, and goodness still move us to awe. But it is also demanding in the present and in the future ahead of us.

In such a way, by sharing short segments of experiences with the poor and suffering members of God's people around the world and in history, as believers we struggle to grow and we witness the continuing Incarnation of Jesus in these people in our times. By meeting them, by enjoying their presence, company, and friendship, by sharing with them some of their poverty and struggle for justice, we receive from them and we learn from them. The legacy of these experiences and the ethical fruits that this brings in our lives has a beneficial impact in their lives too, while we continue to reflect on how they are transforming us and on how together we should continue to transform our lives and

---

[23] Feminist ethical scholarship greatly helps us in this regard.

our world today. Hence, we can express more and more our gratitude, indebted as we are to them, because we are well aware that the gifts that we receive from other people and from their life experiences help us to become more and more fully human.

Ordinary choices in our lives highlight our responsibility. After having lived with poor people we can reexamine our use of water and energy, the ways in which we waste food, the fair trade that we could support and expand, and so on. Hence, we could discover once again how the local and the global are extremely connected and inseparable in our globalized world.

More ethical work is also needed. One venue concerns the rights of indigenous people. On September 13, 2007, the General Assembly of the United Nations adopted a declaration outlining the rights of the world's estimated 370 million indigenous people and outlawing discrimination against them. It was the result of a long process of reflection, study, and political deliberation that ended more than two decades of debates. The *United Nations Declaration on the Rights of Indigenous Peoples*[24] was voted by 143 states; 11 states abstained and four—Australia, Canada, New Zealand and the United States—voted against the text.[25] As any U.N. declaration, it does not bind the States that signed it. However, its 46 articles should be considered as an important step in acknowledging the individual and collective rights of indigenous peoples, as well as their rights to culture, identity, language, employment, health, and education. Further, the Declaration stresses the rights of indigenous peoples to maintain and to strengthen their own institutions, cultures, and traditions and to pursue their development in promoting their own needs and aspirations. It also prohibits any discrimination against them and it promotes their right to full and effective participation in pursuing their own visions of economic and social development. This is important for the indigenous peoples, but also for humankind as a whole. We all should want to avoid discrimination, marginalization, extreme poverty, and human rights violations.

Finally, in the suffering of some people and in their struggle for justice we perceive those of the whole humankind. Care, compassion, attention to the other in need, desire and willingness to do whatever is possible to promote the other, to strengthen each one, particularly those who are weaker: these are not solely pious desires or Christian expectations. They express our profound

---

[24] United Nations, *Declaration on the Rights of Indigenous Peoples* (A/RES/61/295);online: http://www.un-documents.net/a61r295.htm (accessed January 21, 2011). The Declaration was adopted by the General Assembly on September 13, 2007.

[25] Since its adoption, Australia, Colombia, and Samoa reversed their position and now endorse the Declaration. During the U.N. Durban Review Conference in April 2009, 182 States endorsed the Declaration. See also: United Nations, Office of the High Commissioner for Human Rights, *Outcome Document of the Durban Review Conference* (April 24, 2009); online: http://www.un.org/durbanreview2009/ (accessed January 21, 2011).

hopes. The ethnographic work in theological ethics can also support our growth in discovering the personal and communal dynamics that, everywhere, promote personal and communal growth and that are grounded in our being human and political beings. Hence, with our commitment to justice and to pursuing the common good, we can be part of the ongoing process of transformation of people's world view, priorities, and values.

Chapter 10

Whiteness Made Visible: A Theo-Critical Ethnography in Acoliland

Todd Whitmore

"Do you think it will bother him more for a white man or for a woman to wash his genitals?"
"It does not matter to him. He is dirty and he is hungry. He just wants a bath and food."

Sister Cecilia and I are bathing Santos. We had come upon him a week ago, lying on his side at the door of his mud and thatch home. The dirt colored him a light red-brown. His skin is normally that shade of black that is so dark it seems purple, like a starling. Sister leaned down to ask him how he was. His voice was barely audible. "I am just waiting for my time."

The United Nations World Food Program delivers food once a month to Pabbo Internally Displaced Persons camp in Northern Uganda, but none of it reaches Santo. He is paralyzed from the waist down, has little dexterity in his hands, and is nearly blind. He cannot go to register for the WFP food, let alone pick it up and bring it home. His family cannot either. Santo's wife is dead. His son, Komakec, partakes daily in the early-morning routine of many of the men at Pabbo: he drinks *arege*, the locally distilled cassava brew, from Coke bottles or plastic baggies. Komakec's wife says that there is no way in hell that she is going to take care of two men. Santo is starving.

Now I am bent over him in his shelter. I pause after rinsing his chest and stomach, which now glisten as they should, and make the mistake of taking a deep breath. Santo cannot make it to the trench two huts over from his, so he shits in what is left of a plastic-weave World Food Program bag. He keeps it within reach behind him, a reminder, too, that someone did once bring him food, but that she is dead now. I drop my washcloth in the red plastic basin we brought with us and ring it out, then dip it in the cleaner water of the blue one. I look over to Sister Cecilia and ask her my question. I am asking her, I later realize, whether there really is or can be a situation, however fleeting, where there is "no longer Jew or Greek, there is no longer slave or free, there is no longer male or female." Or is Frantz Fanon right in *Black Skin White*

Masks?: "[Y]ou come too late, much too late. There will always be a world—a white world—between you and us."[1] I realize, too, that I cannot begin to address these questions without asking Santo and the other people of Pabbo.

I am trained as a theologian. Almost no theologians do ethnography. Rather, the discipline, particularly as it is practiced in the United States, is wedded to philosophy as the main conversation partner for its epistemology, social theory, method, and genre. When doing "applied" theology, we supplement by drawing upon and citing the relevant literature in, for instance, political science or quantitative sociology. We engage texts. If our focus is on a topic relating to Africa, we may read texts by African authors, though even here we may be more likely to turn to Jeffrey Sachs than to Thandike Mkandiwire. We read the latter only if the work is written in or translated into English or, perhaps, French. As a result, theology does not hear directly, if it does at all, those people who do not write. UNESCO reports that there are 136 million Africans who are not literate, and the number is increasing. Almost half of the women in sub-Saharan Africa cannot read or write. Not to undertake methodologies that gather the perspectives, judgments, and patterns of life of such people risks—I would even say virtually assures—reinforcing the patterns of dominance that were set into motion over 100 years ago when Europeans began taking an interest in sub-Saharan Africa.

At the same time, few anthropologists writing today do so theologically. The reasons for this are well-grounded: theology has underwritten colonialism, and theological as well as economic aspects of this arrangement, as we will see below, remain. Works encouraging utilitarian appropriation of anthropological methods for the purpose of Christian mission are still being written and published, and their existence raises questions about whether those colonial structures that are still in place are simply remnants of the past. Still, given anthropology's hermeneutical turn since the 1980s, writing not only about but also from within a religious symbol system cannot be ruled out *a priori* without reverting to a positivist reductionism that views religion as simply a "system of control." Some anthropologists now insist on the necessity of doing an "anthropology of theology."[2] Others now term Christianity the critical "repressed" of anthropology and call for an anthropology of Christianity.[3] However, neither do anthropology from *within* Christian theology.

The position from which I write is that of writing anthropology from within Christian theology in a way that reduces neither the former to utilitarian missiological aims nor the latter to functionalist analysis. The result is what I call "theo-critical ethnography," which draws upon theological analysis for

[1] Frantz Fanon, *Black Skin White Masks*, trans. Charles L. Markmann (New York: Grove Press, 1967), 108.

[2] Frank A. Salamone and Walter Randolph Adams, *Explorations in Anthropology and Theology* (Lanham: University Press of America, 1997), 1.

[3] Fenella Cannell, *The Anthropology of Christianity* (Durham: Duke University Press, 2006).

liberative purposes both narrowly and broadly construed. Given the history of colonialism and Christianity, there are few topics calling more urgently for such analysis than that of whiteness.

The Disappearance of Invisibility

"Munno. Bin kany."
White man. Come here.

The man selling sundry items by the roadside wants my attention. It is an easy enough moniker to work. Munno: white man or, more precisely, European. I am one of only two whites living in the camp of over 65,000 people, the other being an Irish nun who has been here for years and who few people like because, as Olweny says, "She is mean."

"An pe atye munno," I reply. "An atye Acoli matar."
I am not a European. I am a white Acoli.

It is good enough for a laugh from the women selling roasted corn for three cents an ear. The man is doubly caught off guard, by the joke and by the fact that I speak some Acoli. Few whites get out their Land Cruisers—a generic term, like Kleenex, that the Acoli use for all SUVs—for more than the couple of hours it takes to deliver foodstuffs and are never the ones lifting the bags. Fewer still attempt to learn the language. The emergency relief director for Catholic Relief Services—a white Californian—has been in northern Uganda for ten months, and does not know a word of the language. She is not apologetic about the fact.

"Icito kwene?"
Where are you going?

He is curious now.

"Ka cuk"
To the market.

A child walks out from behind a tin-roofed building and sees me.

"Munno. Munno. Munno."

It is less a greeting to me than a signal to other children that a white man is in the area if they want to come have a look. He is saying the word like it is a flashing light—each utterance a staccato bark, with the effect of punctuating the pauses in between.

"Munno. Munno. Munno."

Soon eight or nine children fall in behind me as I walk the main road of the camp. When I turn and check a minute or two later, there are over 20. The word now becomes a chant, even a taunt, with the first syllable drawn out and inflected downwards; the second syllable—clipped and accented—shooting up.

"Muuuu-no. Muuuu-no."

Practitioners of critical race theory and white studies often claim that a chief characteristic of whiteness is that it is invisible to those who are white. An abridged version of Peggy MacIntosh's "White Privilege: Unpacking the Invisible Knapsack," is ubiquitous on websites and in edited volumes addressing whiteness, and her view is standard in the literature. "I have come to see white privilege as an invisible package of unearned assets that I can count on cashing in each day, but about which I was 'meant' to remain oblivious. White privilege is like an invisible weightless knapsack of special provisions, maps, passports, codebooks, visas, clothes, tools, and blank checks."[4] James Baldwin articulates this view earlier when he writes, "Being white means never having to think about it."[5]

However, virtually all critical race theory and whiteness studies focus on the situation in the United States. Articles that address whiteness in a global context tend to merely extend, rather than challenge, the claim of invisibility because they attend to the attitudes and statements of Americans who, even by American standards, are in situations of enormous power, for instance governmental and pharmaceutical representatives.[6] Correspondingly, and oddly, postcolonial studies after Fanon has largely ignored race.[7] Alfred Lopez, in a volume intended to address this lacuna, suggests that this may be because of a "simple conflation." In his words, "whiteness in this context may be so closely associated with colonial domination that no further distinction seems

---

[4] Peggy MacIntosh, "White Privilege: Unpacking the Invisible Knapsack," *Independent School, National Association of Independent Schools*, 49:2 (1990), 31–5.
[5] Tim Wise, "Membership Has Its Privileges: Thoughts on Acknowledging and Challenging Whiteness," in *White Privilege: Essential Readings on the Other Side of Racism*, ed. Paula Rothenberg (New York: Worth Publishers, 2009), 133.
[6] See, for instance, Kendall Clark, "The Global Privileges of Whiteness," at http://monkey-fist.com/articles.
[7] An exception would be the work of Homi K. Bhabha. See Bhabha, *The Location of Culture* (London: Routledge, 1994).

necessary or desirable."[8] Whatever the reason, critical race theory, white studies, and postcolonial studies have, for the most part, failed to address adequately how whiteness operates in the global context. The irony is that the simple and perhaps simplistic projection of a conception of whiteness onto the global context—whether from the American context or the perspective of colonial studies—has made on-the-ground whiteness invisible to the theorists of whiteness themselves.

Like for theology, then, the ethnographic methods of anthropology can help white studies overcome this invisibility. Indeed, for the white anthropologist, his whiteness brings a quite visible complication—I am not saying impediment—to the participant observer methodology. In my 12 weeks in Uganda thus far, I have found that I, as a white male, enter into a field of already-set expectations as to my behavior. My task has not been that of making the invisible visible to myself and other whites, but to make what is already visible intelligible. If we are to use a pair of ocular metaphors, then, it is not that of invisibility versus visibility, but of myopia versus focus.

"Will you remember us?"

It is two weeks before I will be leaving Pabbo, so Justin's question at first seems odd to me. Then I figure that he has seen other whites go and not return, not keep up contact. They may not have told the whites back in America what they have seen and witnessed in northern Uganda. Maybe what he is asking me is less that I stay in contact than that I testify in the United States to what is going on here. Certainly the Acoli have suffered enormously since the war began in 1986. The rebel Lord's Resistance Army (LRA) has abducted over 30,000 youths: the males to fight, the females to serve as sex slaves for the officers, both to carry supplies. The LRA has mutilated thousands of others—like Margaret, whom I met at the World Vision reception center—cutting off their noses, ears, and lips, and sending them back to the camps as living warnings.

Justin is a catechist. In a continent where there are 8,000 people for every priest, lay persons are of necessity prime evangelists. Justin wears a dark ballcap and a climate-bleached t-shirt that says, "Angelo Negri: Light in Darkness" around a faded likeness of the bishop. Negri was one of the early Italian Comboni missionaries who began training catechists in northern Uganda in 1915. The LRA has killed 75 catechists in the war. I met the widow of one earlier this week. When she tried to resist the rebels, they set her hands on fire. There is a lot to remember and a lot to tell.

"Yes. I will remember you. And I hope to come back next year."
"Because we catechists have it very difficult."

I nod. Yes. Yes. We are standing under a mango tree just outside the parish compound, on top of, I am later told, a mass grave of Acolis killed by the government army, the UPDF. Although the mangos are not ripe yet, only those at the very top of the tree remain. Hungry children have knocked the rest off with sticks and eaten them green and hard.

> "We earn only seven thousand eight hundred for six months. That is not very much, is it?"
> I hesitate, startled by what seems to be a new line of questioning. I do the computation anyway. It is about four US dollars.
> "No."

The conversation—or, more accurately, my perception of it—begins to shift.

> "Can you find me a friend in America?"

His reaction prompts recollections from my previous trip to Uganda. An assertive young man extended a pad and pen towards me as I walked to Mass in Kyarusozi in western Uganda and asked to exchange addresses. "I have always wanted a friend in America." His letter arrived two months later with a request to sponsor his schooling. Conversation decoded: In discourse between Blacks and whites in Uganda, to "remember" is to fundraise, to "befriend" is to become a benefactor, and to be white is to be constantly reminded that you are the promise of both.

I look up at the mango tree and then at Justin.

> "I'll see what I can do."

Anthropological and other disciplinary study of patronage systems has seen two sea changes in analysis. Research coming out of the 1960s and earlier tends to view the patron–client relationships, however asymmetrical, as mutually beneficial. The client develops a personal relationship with the patron in order to gain political and economic access, while offering service to the patron. The relationship is often unofficial, but is no less formal for being so.[9] The 1970s bring Marxist analysis to the idea of patronage, with the argument that the determinant is class domination. Appeals to the personal nature of

---

[9] Here I am distinguishing the anthropological study of patronage in various cultures from the narrower understanding of political patronage in the United States, where the winner of democratic elections has the right to make political appointments.

the relationship and to its complementarity simply mask its fundamental unjustifiability.[10] In the 1990s, some authors begin to argue that what is often pejoratively called "corruption" is not the result of a failed set of relationships, but rather the well-functioning of what is merely a different kind of system than that of the modern west. While not as uncritical of patronage systems as the earliest research, neither do these studies view patronage systems as necessarily dysfunctional.[11]

The white theologian *cum* anthropologist in Uganda steps off the plane and into a field of interwoven patronage relationships. How he is to understand, assess, and respond to these relationships depends in large part on his previously held empirical assumptions and normative judgments about patronage. Do patronage systems arise only when states fail and unofficial alternative sources of power fill the void? Or are they alternative forms of political, economic, and cultural relationship that can also be legitimate? To shift from the language of anthropology and political science to ethics: Is patronization intrinsically evil? Can one weigh consequences in assessing an act of patronage? Do the evil consequences always outweigh the good ones? More theologically: Can two Christians relate as patron and client? Or do we add, "There is no longer patron or client," to Galatians 3.28?

"I need your help. God has sent you to me."

Orach Otim is a large man—six-two or so, perhaps 210 pounds. Oddly, he looks like he once was larger, though never fat. It is in his face. He looks like Magic Johnson—same large eyes and expressive mouth—but a version of the man who has lost his effervescence and is shot through with sorrow. He was the elected leader of Pabbo when it first became a camp, but his outspokenness got him arrested by the UPDF. Now we are meeting clandestinely in the back room of a store. I give the gawkers at the door some change so that they will go away.

Even shrunken, Orach has a way of taking up the whole of the couch across from me. He leans forward across the coffee table between us and spreads his hands over the papers he has laid out there. I sit on the front edge of my chair to examine them.

"I have kept careful documentation. I have kept a diary for ten years. Everything is there. Names. Dates. You know about the mass grave under the mango tree by the parish compound. I know the commander who did

---

[10] Michael Gilsenan, "Against Patron-Client Relations," in *Patrons and Clients in Mediterranean Societies*, E. Gellner and J. Waterbury (eds) (London: Duckworth, 1977), 167–84.

[11] Patrick Chabal and Jean-Pascal Daloz, *Africa Works: Disorder as Political Instrument* (Bloomington: Indiana University Press, 1999); Akhil Gupta, "Blurred Boundaries: The Discourse of Corruption," *American Ethnologist* 22 (1995), 375–402.

this. I can give you the names of people in the ground."

"What do you want me to do?"

"I want you to be my Charlie Wilson."

"Who is Charlie Wilson?"

"The man who campaigned in the United States on behalf of the *mujahadeen* in Afghanistan. He got Congress to recognize what was going on there. To give support."

"But I am not a lobbyist. I do not know how to go about lobbying Congress. I am an academic. I write things. Articles."

"Look at me. I cannot even make love to my wife. They tied a cord around my testicles and forced me to jump off of a box."

I flinch. I am sure he sees it.

"They kept me in a room with two inches of water for eight days. I had no way to relieve myself except in a bucket in a corner, and they never emptied it. It overflowed. You know it overflowed. There was no way for me to lie down to sleep. Eight days. When my wife first came to the prison, they just said, 'We do not know where he is.' "[12]

Orach is now out on bail after a second arrest and imprisonment on charges of treason. He goes for a hearing to extend his bail next week. If the judge does not extend the bail, Orach goes back in prison. We think—hope, really—that this will not happen, that the purpose of bail is simply to pose the threat of reincarceration, and so keep Orach quiet.

"What do you want me to do?"

"You need to tell them what is going on here. I need a partner to collaborate with me to help get the story out. I need a computer and training how to use it. I need money to support me because I have no job. There are no jobs for me here. I can put all this information on a disk. And I need internet. You can use the information. I need you to tell the people in the United States what is going on."

Orach sits back as a signal that he has completed his appeal. I continue examining the papers on the table to avoid looking at him.

I know the meaning of the word "partner" and its analogues in this context now. Earlier in the week, I met a man while in Gulu buying supplies. He heard me speaking Acoli to the woman in the shop, and turned to me. After initial

---

[12] So far, I have verified Orach's story with two others. For more on the human rights abuses of the Ugandan military, see: Human Rights Watch, *Uprooted and Forgotten: Impunity and Human Rights Abuses in Northern Uganda* (2005), available at www.hrw.org

greetings, he said, in English, "So, we can join together and collaborate on a project to help the elderly in Gulu. There are many elderly in Gulu who need help. It is easy to get money in the United States, yes? We can collaborate."

My attention turns back to Orach. I think first of the more immediate risks, and look up.

"If I write about you, won't the UPDF be angry and come after you?"

He sits forward again, plants his elbows on knees and clasps his hands—the only things that keep him from leaning even further across the table to touch foreheads. As it is, we are inches apart.

"All I have is the truth. They have taken everything else. They can do nothing to me that they have not already done. I am not afraid of death. They have already taken my life. My only hope is in the truth."

Orach and I say our parting words, and agree to continue the conversation. I exit the door and see that the gawkers have returned. The leader among them holds a knotted baggie of *arege*, like a child with a goldfish bag—same beaming sense of chosenness in a missing-tooth smile—only without the goldfish.

Back in the parish compound, the questions flicker in time with the paraffin lamp on my desk: Is altruistic patronage bad *tout court*? Is there such a thing as patronage on behalf of justice? What would it look like?

The Infungibility of Visibility

One of the critiques of whiteness studies is that it does not take into adequate account the socioeconomic basis of racism, and the fact that in a class society, even those who are white-skinned may be considered "white-skinned negroes."[13] In the northern Ugandan context, the transferability of race manifests itself in one key way: there are some people who are more Black—read, "backward," poor, lower in the strata of the patronage system—than other Black Africans. The Acoli are not only on the whole darker-skinned than most southern Ugandans, they are also often described as less modern and more "backward" by others in the country. In part, this is a result of the colonialization process, where the British made Kampala, in the south, the administrative center of

---

[13] Noel Ignatiev, *How the Irish Became White* (London and New York: Routledge, 1996). In the latest edition of his book, George Lipsitz takes into account and incorporates this criticism of earlier editions. See Lipsitz, *The Possessive Investment of Whiteness: How White People Benefit from Identity Politics* (Philadelphia: Temple University Press, 2006).

Uganda, and sought out the Acoli for the soldier-warrior class.[14] Some of the Acoli, in attempting to modernize, further this view themselves. This is the nub of Okot p'Bitek's poem, *Song of Lawino*, which is a wife's lament of her changed husband. *Lawino* is the most widely read Acoli literary work.

> My husband pours scorn
> On Black People,
> He behaves like a hen
> That eats its own eggs
> A hen that should be imprisoned
>   under a basket . . .
> He says Black People are
>   primitive
> And their ways are utterly
>   harmful,
> Their dances are mortal sins
> They are ignorant, poor and diseased!
>
> Ocol says he is a modern man,
> A progressive and civilized man,
> He says he has read extensively
>   and widely
> And he can no longer live with
>   a thing like me.[15]

Ocol does not dispute Lawino's account. In the correlative poem, *Song of Ocol*, he says,

> You Pigmy men
> Skinning the elephant
> With rusty knives,
> I see your children
> Happy, dancing,
> Swinging from branch to
>   branch
> Like naked hairless
> Black Apes[16]

14 Samwiri Rubaraza Karugire, *A Political History of Uganda* (Nairobi and London: Heinemann Educational Books, 1980); Mahmood Mamdani, *Politics and Class Formation in Uganda* (New York: Monthly Review Press, 1976) and *Imperialism and Fascism in Uganda* (Nairobi and London: Heinemann Educational Books, 1983); Thomas Ofcansky, *Uganda: Tarnished Pearl of Africa* (Boulder: Westview Press, 1996).
15 Okot p'Bitek, *Song of Lawino & Song of Ocol* (Oxford: Heinemann Publishers, 1984), 35–6.
16 Ibid., 145.

And elsewhere:

> What is Africa
> to me?

> Blackness,
> Deep, deep fathomless
> Darkness;

> Africa
> Idle giant
> Basking in the sun,
> Sleeping, snoring,
> Twitching in dreams;

> Diseased with a chronic illness,
> Choking with black ignorance,
> Chained to the rock
> Of poverty . . .

> Stuck in the stagnant mud
> Of superstitions,
> Frightened by the spirits
> Of the bush, the stream,
> The rock,
> Scared of corpses . . .

> Mother, mother,
> Why,
> Why was I born
> Black?[17]

That the realities described are not simply in the mind of a poet who died in 1982 is evident in statements Ugandan President Yoweri Museveni made on a trip to Gulu on the occasion of the new auxiliary bishop of the Archdiocese of Gulu, Sabino Oodki Ocan, on October 22, 2006: "We shall transform the people in the north from material and spiritual backwardness to modernity."[18]

If some Blacks are more "black" than others, a select few are more "white." This, too, is Lawino's complaint:

---

[17] Ibid., 125–6.
[18] Chris Ocowun, "Museveni Hails Gulu Archbishop Odama," *New Vision* (October 22, 2006), 1.

And they dress up like white
     men,
As if they are in the white
     man's country.
At the height of the hot season
The progressive and civilized
     ones
Put on blanket suits
And woolen socks from Europe,
Long under-pants
And woolen vests,
White shirts;
They wear neck-ties from Europe.[19]

However, it is Ocol who articulates the core of what it means to be "white" in Africa, and his words—published by p'Bitek in 1966, soon after Uganda's independence and well before the presidencies of Amin and Museveni—are prescient, pointing to what will befall Orach Otim:

We have property

And wealth,
We are in power;

Trespassers must be jailed
For life,
Thieves and robbers
Must be hanged,
Disloyal elements
Must be detained without
     trial . . . [20]

Given the apparent transferability of race in a patronage culture, is it possible to be a white *cum* "black" person allied in solidarity with the Black *cum* "deep, deep fathomless darkness" Black against the Black *cum* "white" and the white? If race is transferable such that Black can become "white" and Black can be made even more "black," what are the possibilities and limits of whites becoming "black" as a way to subvert patronage? If I place my gifts, skills, and advantages at Orach Otim's disposal to serve his ends over against Museveni and the United

---

[19] p'Bitek, *Song of Lawino & Song of Ocol*, p. 45.
[20] Ibid., 142.

States government that continues to back him, can I, as some whiteness studies texts suggest, "disrupt whiteness from within" and "dismantle privilege?"[21]

I am encouraged by the lack of historical stability of the Acoli word, *munno*. Originally, the word meant all people other than Blacks. Blackness was the norm. *Munno* meant non-Black. The word for white people was *otara*, coming from the word *tar* or "white." *Tar* was and is a positive term. For instance, *lak tar* means "white teeth," and is an indication of happiness (one is smiling) and strength (one has good teeth with which to chew food). The Acoli first applied *munno* to the Arab traders and slavers who came south into Acoliland.[22] British explorers did not arrive until 1862. King Mutesa I of Buganda in southern Uganda, where the explorers first arrived, welcomed them as sources of protection against the slave traders, and in 1894, Britain did assume a protectorate over Uganda. When the explorers and missionaries reached northern Uganda, the Acoli began to distinguish between Arabic and European people, first calling the Arabs *muno abac abac* ("neither black nor white") and the British *muno ingelesa* ("English white"). Still later, when the Roman Catholic Comboni missionaries came, the Acoli called them a third name, *muno hartung*, and realized that the latter were not interested in political rule at all.

Being Roman Catholic, then, might help cross the Black–white divide in Acoliland. Except for a few chiefs and men that they made chiefs, the Anglican British bothered little to evangelize the Acoli. Their focus was on the Baganda kingdom to the south. As a result, while a third of Uganda is Roman Catholic, close to three-quarters of the people in the North are. In the hierarchy that is Uganda, Catholics are at the bottom. It helps, then, that the Catholic community is my main entry into northern Uganda. Nuns of the Little Sisters of Mary Immaculate of Gulu introduce me to the Comboni Missionaries, the Director of the Catechist Training Center, and the priest in Pabbo, all of whom put me up during my research. When I want to venture further out in the bush and live in the Lokung IDP camp, the Director of the Catechist Training Center talks to the priest of Padibe parish who relays word to the catechists in Lokung that I am coming. Many in the north view Catholics as particularly dedicated Acoli, as those who have stayed committed to the north throughout the war. In the 20 years of the war, the percentage of people in the north who are Roman

[21] See Jennifer Harvey, Karin Case, and Robin Gorsline (eds), *Disrupting White Supremacy from Within: White People on What We Need to Do* (Cleveland: Pilgrim Press, 2004). The idea that those in the IDP camps are more "black"—that is, lower in social ranking and with less power—than other Ugandans raises the related questions of whether IDP camps are analogous to "ghettos" in the United States and, more sharply, whether certain parts of American inner cities, with their poverty and the lack of mobility of their residents, are analogous to IDP camps. For analysis that interprets the ghetto in terms of prison and thus lack of freedom, see Loïc Wacquant, "Deadly Symbiosis: When Ghetto and Prison Meet and Mesh," *Punishment & Society*, 3 (2001), 95–133. Wacquant interprets prisons as "instruments for the management of dispossessed and dishonored groups." The research is yet to be done on IDP camps and American ghettos, but Wacquant provides a basis upon which to do the analysis.
[22] Alexander Odonga, *Lwo-English Dictionary* (Kampala: Fountain Publishers, 2005), 157.

Catholic has increased due to the fact that large numbers of others have left. To be Catholic and to be in the North, then, is to be in solidarity with the Acoli, the black of the Black.

How far can a white man press his Catholicism to become "black"? Noel Ignatiev's provocative book, *How the Irish Became White*, argues that the Irish in the United States were once religiously, culturally, and socioeconomically equivalent—or at least strongly analogous—to being "black." The book is now a staple in white studies. If it is correct, then it carries with it an interesting possible corollary: perhaps a white person can reverse the process and become, once again, "black."

Gulu town is the urban center of northern Uganda. With a population of about 50,000 before the war, it now has over 100,000 people due to the conflict. If one is upper-middle class, one moves one's family to Gulu; if one is rich, one moves to Kampala. There are whites too—many of them—and here they get out of their cars: NGO field directors, war researchers, and adventure travelers in shorts—considered indiscrete in Acoliland unless one is a child or on a soccer field—and sporting rolled bandana headbands knotted in the back.

Mega FM radio has been announcing the traditional Acoli culture night for over a week. Even the people in the camps are talking about it, though they cannot afford to go. Tickets are 3,000 Uganda schillings for locals, 10,000 for others (read, *munni*). The event is at the Acholi Inn, the hotel of choice for senior UN representatives and high ranking rebel officers who have surrendered and are now under government protection.[23] They are subsidizing the UPDF commander who owns the hotel.

The crowd assembles early. The women attending sport technicolor *agomo*—dresses with puffed-out sleeves—and wear their hair long and straightened, a sign to others that their houses have running water. In the camps, the women shave their heads regularly, and do not let it grow longer than a quarter inch away from the scalp so as to avoid lice.[24] Long, straight hair conveys distance from pestilence, from "darkness." I am reminded of Lawino's words: "They cook their hair/ With hot irons/ And pull it hard/ So that is may grow long . . . / They fry their hair in boling oil/ As if it were locusts,/ And the hair sizzles/ It

---

[23] The term for the ethnic group and language can be variously spelled either Acoli or Acholi. I use the former because in the language, the letter "c" is pronounced "ch," making the "h" in the latter spelling unnecessary. However, continual mispronunciation of the term by persons unfamiliar with the language has led to "Acholi" being the more common spelling. The inn's international clientele means that it must use the adjusted spelling.

[24] Also, though the *agomo* are taken as "African," a generation ago, the Acholi of both sexes in the far north wore nothing until puberty and then wore only loincloths. There is no small bit of irony, then, in the debate in Uganda concerning mini-skirts. The case is argued that the miniskirt is too modern, and that "African" dress is more modest; yet it was the European Christian missionaries, not the Africans, who first made the case that nudity and loincloths were immodest. The *agomo* continue to be the dresses whites buy in the markets of Gulu and Kampala when they want to buy "African" clothes.

cries in sharp pain/ As it is pulled and stretched . . . / It lies lifeless/ Like the sad and dying banana leaves/ On a hot and windless afternoon."[25] The men in the audience at Acoli culture night wear button shirts and pressed trousers, if not coats and ties. It is the whites who dress down. They are, without exception, in t-shirts and with uncombed hair. Playing Africa.

Three Acoli with video cameras go up on stage for closer shots of the dancers. In the next set, I follow suit. The performer is Ajere, a singer songwriter who plays the *nanga*, a flatboard stringed instrument with no neck that backs the Acoli version of the blues. He is special. This video is not for research; it is for me. Though I arrived early and got a first row seat, the other videographers obstruct my view. I go up on stage in front of the side seats, but lie down on my side so as not to bother those who are seated there. Still, one of the women complains, saying something about the presumption of the *munno*. I do not catch everything, but turn and respond to her remarks anyway.

"An pe aloko leb Acoli maber." I do not speak Acholi well.

Again, the surprise of a *munno* speaking Acoli brings laughter. It seems that, for a moment, the boundaries dissolve.

No one is fooled, however. Despite everyone's effort at racial cross-dressing, no one challenges the fact that whites are charged more than three times the Acoli rate for the event. A cartoon in the Ugandan newspaper, *New Vision*, earlier that week depicts two Black Ugandans watching a white man in t-shirt, shorts, and back-pack. One says to the other, "Boy, that *muzungu* is really stinking." The other responds, "Yeah, stinking rich!"

* * *

There are first of all, then, economic limits to the pliability of race in Uganda. Although Museveni may be atop the patronage pyramid in Uganda, the fact remains that more than 50 percent of the Ugandan government's budget is from foreign aid.[26] There is little argument that Museveni is using the money for his own end of maintaining power. Foreign aid decreases the accountability he has to those within his own country and supports his patronage network within it. While such aid has been used to fund national primary education and other reforms, one study has shown that only 13 percent of Uganda's education budget reaches the schools. The rest is "captured by local officials and

---

[25] p'Bitek, *Song of Lawino & Song of Ocol*, 54.
[26] Thomas Ayodele et al., "African Perspectives on Aid: Foreign Assistance Will Not Pull Africa Out of Poverty," *Economic Development* 2 (September 14, 2005), at https://www.cato.org/pubs/edb/edb2.pdf

politicians."[27] The fact of corruption stirs debate over whether foreign aid as a whole is good or bad for the poor in Africa, whether it is reformable so that it can serve the poor or is beyond repair.[28] Still, it remains that as foreign aid exists now, it forms the economic backbone of an international system of patronage in which whites are at the apex. Under this system, Museveni has to make Uganda at least *look* democratic to the whites. The language of freedom is the mask of international patronage, with elections the main marker of progress. When Museveni's failure to end the war in the North combined with his alteration of the Ugandan constitution to allow him to run for a third term as President in a campaign in which he jailed his main opponent, several countries withheld portions of their donations. That the United States government has not followed suit but rather increased its aid is less evidence that it is being used and so is not in control than that it is more concerned about Uganda as a post-9/11 East African ally than about human rights.

At once side-by-side and integrated with the intergovernmental patronage system is that which functions through nongovernmental organizations. Some donors give money directly to NGOs through commercial banks, and do not go through Uganda's central bank. Other NGOs receive their funding not from governments at all, but from charitable donations and foundation grants. In Uganda, this has the effect of increasing the amount of money that government officials can skim because the administration can direct much of the NGO efforts to aid the North, allowing the officials in Kampala in the South to keep more of the foreign assistance that comes from states for themselves.

On the ground in the North, the presence of NGOs means that even those people bypassed by the system that has Museveni's government and ethnic group at the center get pulled into the dynamics of patronage. The literature on development is replete with analyses—some more polemical than others— of the ways in which humanitarian aid increases dependence.[29] The impact on the IDP camps in northern Uganda is most evident in the way that money

---

[27] Ritva Reinikka, and Jokob Svensson, "Local Capture: Evidence from a Central Government Transfer Program in Uganda," *Quarterly Journal of Economics* 119:2 (May 2004), 679.

[28] Ayodele et al. and Mwenda are against foreign aid. For the view that rightly structured aid is still helpful, see David Beckman, "Debunking Myths About Foreign Aid," in *The Christian Century* (August 1–8, 2001), 26–8.

[29] See, for example, Deborah Eade, *Development and Patronage* (London: Oxfam Publishing, 1997); Ian Smillie, *Patronage or Partnership?: Local Capacity Building in Humanitarian Crises* (Bloomfield: Kumarian Press, 2001); Monica Kathina Juma and Astri Suhrke, *Eroding Local Capacity: International Humanitarian Action in Africa* (Uppsala: Nordic Africa Institute, 2003); Michael Maren, *The Road to Hell: The Ravaging Effects of Foreign Aid and International Charity* (New York: Free Press, 2002); Alex de Waal, *Famine Crimes: Politics and the Disaster Relief Industry in Africa* (Bloomington: Indiana University Press, 1998); Fiona Terry, *Condemned to Repeat?: The Paradox of Humanitarian Action* (Ithaca: Cornell University Press, 2002); David Rieff, *A Bed for the Night: Humanitarianism in Crisis* (New York: Simon and Schuster, 2003); Treje Tvedt, *Angels of Mercy or Development Diplomats?: NGOs and Foreign Aid* (Lawrenceville: Africa World Press, 1998).

exchange displaces other forms of relationship. When Sister Cecilia asks Santo's neighbor to rub the floor of his dwelling with a cow-dung mixture so as to rid it of lice, the woman responds, "How much will you pay me?" That evening I return to the parish compound, and Father Charles complains of the "NGO effect": "They do not know the people. They have no other way to relate to them. So when they meet with them, they pay them money. Now when I want to gather the people in my parish, they all expect to be paid."

Though I have made efforts at solidarity—living in the camps, traveling in the back of pick-up trucks with Acoli going to or from the camps and speaking, however remedially, the language—almost all of the Acoli I come into contact with in the camps view me—my whiteness—through the lens of the patronage system structured by international and nongovernmental aid. They watch, study, and assess me even more closely than I them. Often, when I return to the parish from one of my wanderings around the camp, Father Charles greets me with, "I hear you . . . ," and then proceeds to tell me what people reported to him of my walk. I am always also the ethnograph*ee.* Their study yields a variety of approaches. Sometimes they are direct—"I need money for drugs." At other times they are indirect, and engage in a kind of trolling for schillings—"I have not been feeling well. I have pain in all of my joints." Still other times, they misdirect—"Please, come into my house for some tea . . . " Then, when we enter, " . . . and these are the five orphans I have been taking care of." Their requests may be for material goods or for me to speak on their behalf. They do not want me to "disrupt" the system, let alone "dismantle" it. They want me to be a good patron.

The Visible Kingdom of the White God

"It is not enough."
"What?"
"You are stranding me."

Otim James sits across from me in the dining room of the Catechist Training Center. It is well after mealtime, so we are alone. At 16 years old, he is the male head of a family of at least six—there may be more. He wears a white t-shirt and blue basketball warm-up pants with stars going down the sides. They are too long for him and drag when he walks. I tell him that this is in style in the United States, and he smiles.

Otim's father died last year, probably of AIDS. We know this because his mother is in the hospital in Kitgum town for treatment. I have been to two funerals while in northern Uganda; both people died of AIDS. When the men die of AIDS, they do so in silence.

The rebels abducted and killed Otim's older brother when he was riding his bicycle home for school holiday. He was in S6—the equivalent of a senior in high school—and on the cusp of obtaining the virtually impossible in northern Uganda: a diploma in the camps.

The Training Center must seem the equivalent of a resort and spa to Otim. It has running water and—at least most of the time—electricity. He will have his own room tonight with an off-the-ground bed. But that is not why he came. The smile from my sartorial comment does not last long, and shifts into a frown. He has made the journey from Lokung IDP camp, where I had been staying for two weeks, to request—no, demand—his school fees for the next year.

His visit seems presumptuous only to the uninitiated. When I first met Otim, a friend of the family I lived with in Lokung, I gave him a soccer ball. I had fit a dozen deflated used balls and a couple of pumps in a duffel to bring over with me. I gave Otim the last of the balls. To me it was simply a gift. To him it was the beginning of a relationship. The next day he brought over a couple of his friends and made an indirect request, where description of the situation is understood as proposal. "These are my friends Beatrice and Joseph. They are in P7. Next year they will be going to S1 and will have to pay fees." For Otim, the soccer ball signified a familiarity that sanctioned his serving as a broker between his friends and me. Later, Otim would write and direct morality plays that the Christian youth group would perform for my benefit.

Now he is making his own case.

"You are stranding me."

"You asked for 160,000 for school next year. I said that I would give it to you."

"I need to pick up my mother at the hospital and take her home. We need to get home."

A good patron anticipates the needs of his client. Of course Otim needs to get home. He literally has spent his last schilling getting to the Training Center.

"I could not even afford to pay the boda-boda that brought me here. You left me at the mission."

Otim had taken "taxis"—ridden in the back of trucks—to Gulu. He called when he reached Kitgum, about halfway between Lokung camp and Gulu. "I am coming to get you. Don't leave. I didn't have a chance to say good-bye." He spent his remaining schillings on a phone call from Gulu. "Where are you?" I told him, and he hung up before I could give directions. Instead of going to the Catechist Training Center, he went to a mission a couple of miles down the road. I did not know where he was and could not reach him. Finally, he talked to a nun who knows me and made his way to the Training Center. No matter what explanation I try to give him, he considers the fault mine. "You left me at the mission." The words make me recall his earlier comment coming out of the church in Lokung after service one Sunday. He had been working for the International Refugee Council, but, in his account, they let him go when they discovered that he did not have a high school degree. "They abandoned me."

Now the charge is leveled at me, both for not knowing that he got dropped off at the wrong place and for not foreseeing that he needed money for his and his mother's return to Lokung. Strand. Leave. Abandon. These words, too, are part of the patronage system lexicon.

Omniscience, omnipresence, and omnipotence. These are the traits Christians traditionally assign to God. Most of the Acoli I meet in the camps assign them to me. Opira, my host in Lokung camp, tries to explain. "White people bring all these things. This technology. And they work. Like magic. You are like gods. Even educated Acoli do not see that whites also have weaknesses and make mistakes, just like Acoli." Yet even Opira is surprised when I tell him that I do not have enough money to cover both the medical costs and the care of orphans that the woman he has brought to me requests. Opira's hospitality during my stay at Lokung carries with it his role as patronage broker. In the afternoons, when I sit outside of my quarters and write, he regularly brings me potential clients. After the woman unfolds her story, I hand Opira 20,000 schillings.

"This will cover transportation to Kitgum hospital, where she will receive care."

He begins to hand it to her, but then looks back at me in surprise.

"What about the orphans?"
"I do not have enough for them."

I had just come from my daily walk around the camp, towards the end of which I had 30 or so children following me. "Munno. Munno." A man chides, "Why don't you give them all something.' I respond, "There are 22,000 people in Lokung. I cannot give them all something."

Opira keeps his eyes on me for a moment—shock, disappointment—and then turns to hand the money to the woman. My failure is his too, just as my presence increased his stature in the community.

All of the portrayals of Jesus and Mary that I have seen in the north thus far—in murals, statues—are of white people. White people on the cross. White people ascending into heaven. Iconic theology underwrites the economic system. P'Bitek provides an account of an Acoli's conversion to Christianity as his being "taken" by "the white man."[30]

---

[30] Okot p'Bitek, *Religion of the Central Luo* (Nairobi, Kampala, and Dar es Salaam: East African Literature Bureau, 1971), 95–6.

Aya Matina, a traditional Acoli spirit medium agrees to call upon her *jogi* to speak to me. The session takes over an hour of incantation and response. She is sweating, but is refreshed rather than spent. She sends her daughter, Korina Auma, who is also an *ajwaka*, out to get me a bottle of *arege*, and the exchange begins. I pay her 10,000 for her time. Korina returns with the drink to complete the deal, but first adds her own request to the bargain. "Take my daughter, Aya's granddaughter, with you back to America." I assume the girl must be an infant, one too many mouths to feed, but I am wrong. "She is a good girl. Fourteen and in P7. Please." I do not wish to offend her, so I reply that I will need to check with my wife. In the patronage world, equivocation is a polite way of saying no. Over the next several days, Korina's proposal stays with me and is repeated unbidden by others. "Bring me to American with you. I can live with you." They want to be "taken by the white man" too.

That Thursday, Korina performs her own incantations for me, after which she comments, "It will be a long time before this war ends. After that there will be a second war, a war among tribes. It too will go on for a long time." I assume she is functioning as a seeress and that one of her *jogi* has informed her of this future in a dream. However, when I ask her how she knows these things, she answers sociologically. "All the kids know is fighting. The movies they watch are all fighting movies. Chuck Norris. Van Damm."

She is right. Enterprising Acoli bring generators to the larger camps and show action movies. I watch *Rambo: First Blood, Part II* for the first time in the parish mission in Padibe. One of the most frequent poses I get from young boys wanting their picture taken is that of a kung fu fighter in a preparation-to-fight stance—slightly crouched, arms bent, forearms up at different angles, hands straight and ready to strike.

Korina finishes, "And when they play, all they play is war. They pick up long sticks and one says, 'I will be LRA and you be UPDF.' All they know is war."

Korina simply wants her daughter out of extreme poverty and violence. If the white person is God, then the United States is God's kingdom, the city on the hill.

"Do you want to learn to speak Acoli?"

The young man catches up to me after I finish talking to an elder in the market in my broken Acoli and am heading home. He is about Otim James' age, but is shorter and with ragged clothes.

"I already have a teacher."

We walk in silence for a minute or two.

"So you want to learn to speak Acoli?"

Again, "I have a teacher."
"Oh."

More minutes of silence.

"Do you know how someone like me can get a friend in America?"
"No."
"No? You have no friends?"

The bargaining has begun in earnest. I try equivocation.

"I have my family."
"Only your family? That is it? No friends?"

It is not working. It is time for me to be direct.

"What you mean by friend and what I mean by friend are two different things. You mean someone who can pay your school fees."

He nods without any obvious embarrassment. He is not dissuaded.

"How about a friend just to write back and forth? Like in school?"
"I do not know."
"You were not in school?"
"That was a long time ago. I am older than I look."

We walk in silence some more. Peasant farmers pass by in the opposite direction and he teaches me the Acoli words for ax and hoe. A group of children begin following us, shouting, "Cala! Cala!" My picture! My picture! I tell them, "Camera pe"—No camera—and they leave. The young man says to me, "It is a big thing for them to get a picture taken by a white man. They run and tell the others."
My shooing away of the children seems to make him realize that I am not going to be a good source of money. He turns curious.

"Are there many Blacks in America?"
"Yes, about 13 percent of the people; so there are more than 30 million Blacks in America."
"Really?"
"Yes."
"I thought that you had laws where Blacks could not live there."
"No. There are about 30 million Blacks. About 50 years ago there were laws passed where if you had a restaurant you had to serve everyone, and if there is a bathroom, anyone can go there. But there is still prejudice. There are many places where there are almost no Blacks, but other places

in America where there are many Blacks."

"So there are Blacks there. I did not know that."

His lack of empirical knowledge is as common as the interpretation that the United States is an exclusive place. Many Acoli tell me that they did not know that English is the primary language. They thought it was Latin, assuming a link between contemporary American prevalence and historical Roman Catholic mission. It makes sense that the gods must be related. Educated Acoli living in Kampala—one a school teacher and the other a receptionist at a hotel—come to Pabbo for their father's funeral and are surprised when I tell them that a foreigner who marries any US citizen can also become a citizen. They think the requisite is that one marry a *white* US citizen. They are only too aware that only few are chosen for the promise that is America. Those chosen, in turn, are miserly with their fortune. The most frequently spoken perception during my research is that United States law forbids couples to have more than a certain number of children. The assumed number varies—anywhere between two and five—but the idea is the same: Americans do not even let the souls of their own potential children in.

We reach the parish and the young man turns to head back to where he first spotted me.

"It is a shame that you do not have your camera. They run and tell their friends that a white man has taken their picture." If they cannot go to America, the children reason, maybe their image can.

Hate or Hope?: Not a Conclusion

Displeasure at whites and their construal as being in some way divine comes in a number of forms. One is the disappointment when the white person's resources are found not to be endless, and so he is found not to be a very good god. We are then gods who, in Otim James' words, "abandon" the Acoli. We are occasions for lament. At other times, continuous disappointment leads to the realization that whites are not gods at all, and that our representation of ourselves as such—suffering more on the cross for having come to such a hellish place and ascending to heaven for having suffered—is a sham that inflicts severe damage on and even destroys Acoli culture. We have pressed our economic advantage such that the Acoli, according to the poet Christine Oryema-Lalobo, have no choice but to, "eat from charity/handed out/ by the white man/ in deep silence."[31] This is why another poet, Omal Lakana, wrote: *Adok*

---

[31] Sverker Finnstrom, *Living With Bad Surroundings: War and Existential Uncertainty in Acholiland, Northern Uganda* (Uppsala: Department of Cultural Anthropology and Ethnology, 2003), 192.

Too/ Adok Too/ Kono apoto i wi munu. "If I could become Death/ If I could become Death/ I would fall on the white man."[32] Omal became so well known by this poem that he came to be called Adok Too. He was jailed in 1938 by the British for being too vocal in opposition to their presence in Uganda.

I did not experience any directly articulated hatred of this latter sort in the field, though this is not to say that similar animosity was not present. While ethnographic methods do place one in close interaction with those whom one is researching, in many respects, this proximity serves to intensify the refraction of deeply held belief because the subject has no anonymity—or at least remove—that allows him or her to affect stepping momentarily outside of social structures. Speaking directly in opposition to the status quo—as both Adok Too and Orach Otim have found out—carries with it great personal cost. Acoli are not going to risk that until they know more precisely where I am located in the social structure and what I intend to do with the prerogatives that I have. The structure they and I have inherited is a system of patronage based on racially identified economic differences. The most frequent first approach to me on their part, then, is to ask if I, out of my generosity—no less obligatory for its being so—can help them out.

One of the most striking acts of indirection in Acoliland takes place in the Catholic church in Lokung camp. In the mural behind the altar, the Holy Mother floats in Marian blue with arms outstretched. She appears to be painted pinkish-Caucasian, but with there being no electricity and thus no lighting in the building, it is hard to tell. As one walks from the entrance towards the front of the church, her features become clearer. She is white, more or less, but her hair is thick, her brow is heavy, her nose is wide, and her lips are thick. The mural is not a request for patronage, but a protest and a sign of hope from whoever painted it: perhaps even Acoli can ascend into heaven.

---

[32]   Okot p'Bitek, *Horn of My Love* (Nairobi: Heinemann Kenya Ltd, 1974), 13.

Chapter 11

The Cost of Virtue: What Power in the Open Door Community Might Speak to Virtue Ethics

Peter R. Gathje

Ira begins his day at 4.00 a.m. He rises early to start making the coffee that will be served to the hundred plus homeless men and women who by 5.00 a.m. are already gathering in the front yard of the Open Door Community in Atlanta. Ira came to this intentional Christian community as a homeless person. He was in need of a place that would provide him shelter from the streets and that would help him address his addictions to drugs and alcohol. After Ira starts the coffee, he heads out the door for his morning run. Each year he runs in the Peachtree Road Race and he also participates in a number of other road races. In addition to making coffee, Ira has two other main jobs in the community. He is in charge of the clothing room; the place where clothes are distributed to the men and women who come for showers at the Open Door each week. He organizes the clothing and he supervises other volunteers and members of the community who help with the distribution. And, on Sundays, at the Open Door's worship, Ira is always the person who stands and offers the cup during the Eucharist as people receive communion.

For over 15 years Ira, who is African American, has lived at the Open Door. He is a "partner" in the community. As a "partner" Ira has committed himself to stay in the community "for the long haul." What Ira does not do, by his choice, is serve on the leadership team of the Open Door. The leadership team consists of partners in the community. Currently there are no community members from the streets on the leadership team, and this is often the case. Typically the partners who serve on the leadership team are middle class, are well educated (most have at least master's degrees), have never been homeless, and are white.

The Open Door Community is committed to a shared vision of life that is Gospel-centered. They see as integral to that life and vision the practices of hospitality to the poor and political action that offers resistance to policies that harm the poor. They seek in these practices and the structures of their communal life to affirm the human dignity of every person as made in the image of God, and to reject domination based upon race, class, gender, or sexual orientation. They recognize and confess that they struggle to live out this Gospel vision and these practices. Within this community there is continual self-reflection and questioning about the community's structuring of power consistent with its Gospel vision of life. Ira's place in this intentional Christian community and the structure of leadership is an entry into an ethical analysis of power in light of Christian faith. But to do this analysis in relation to a specific Christian community and its vision and practices is to also raise the issue of how "doing" Christian ethics should draw upon particular Christian communities and not be confined to arguments as found in texts.

My interest in both the particular question of power in the Open Door and the issue of how to do ethics are related to my history with Ira and the Open Door Community. I have known Ira ever since he was invited to live in the Open Door Community. I have been associated with the Open Door Community since 1987. I came to the community as a student at the Candler School of Theology. I was doing research for my master's thesis.[1] Influenced by my advisor, Steven M. Tipton, one of the authors of *Habits of the Heart*, I was interested in exploring how this intentional Christian community negotiated the strong cultural currents in American society that include not only a pull toward expressive individualism, but also Christian shaped civic engagement. In particular, I wanted to see how this community's Gospel vision both motivated its involvement in political life and shaped its approach to political action. As part of my research I went to live with the Open Door Community under the social science rubric of "participant observation."[2] As an "outsider," I went to live as an "insider" to see how the community's faith was lived out both within the community and through its engagement in political life.

I quickly saw how the Open Door Community's political activism, such as demonstrations and nonviolent civil disobedience, grew out of their way of life. Their intentional break from societal conventions was meant to embody an alternative to the reigning social and political arrangements. So, the community not only engaged in protest against policies they saw as further dehumanizing and criminalizing homeless persons, they also welcomed into their community life people from the streets and those released from prison. The community not only protested the death penalty, but offered support for families of prisoners and visited on death row. The community not only protested against war and US military support for Latin American dictators, they also lived simply so as to not pay war taxes and they boycotted goods from corporations such as Coca-Cola.

---

[1] My thesis eventually became the book, *Christ Comes in the Stranger's Guise: A History of the Open Door Community* (Atlanta: Open Door Community, 1991).

[2] For an introduction to participant observation see, Kathleen M. DeWalt and Billie R. DeWalt, *Participant Observation: A Guide for Fieldworkers* (Lanham: AltaMira Press, 2001).

In this research and writing about the Open Door Community for my master's thesis, I began a relationship with the community that has now lasted over 20 years. I have continued to occasionally live with the community. I have written articles for the community's newspaper, *Hospitality*, edited a collection of articles from this newspaper, and written an expanded history of the community, *Sharing the Bread of Life: Hospitality and Resistance at the Open Door Community*. I have participated in numerous political actions with the community. I have been arrested in the front yard of the community by a police officer who did not like being questioned by me about his handcuffing of a mentally ill homeless person who was a guest on the Open Door's property. Inspired by the Open Door, I have joined with others in Memphis in opening a place of hospitality for homeless persons and engaged in Memphis in political advocacy with homeless persons.

I have also continued as an academic, a professor of Christian ethics. Within this field, I generally stand within the approach known as virtue ethics.[3] Although there is great diversity within virtue ethics, I think it is fair to broadly characterize this approach as putting an emphasis upon the development of virtues or excellences of character through practices consistent with a vision of life. Christian virtue ethics focuses upon the moral formation of persons within a community of faith that takes place through practice of the community's vision. What I have found strange in this field of Christian virtue ethics is a lack of sustained attention to the practice of actual communities and how that practice does or does not shape persons in virtues consistent with a community's vision. Instead influential writers in the field such as Stanley Hauerwas or Samuel Wells seem to focus on personal biography, literature, or theatre to discuss virtue ethics.[4] Others draw upon the New Testament church or traditional discussions of virtue within Christian ethics.[5]

---

[3] The literature that reflects the virtue ethics approach is broad. For an overview of contemporary philosophical virtue ethics see Roger Crisp and Michael Slote (eds), *Virtue Ethics* (New York: Oxford University Press, 1997). For an overview of contemporary theological virtue ethics see Nancey Murphy, Brad J. Kallenberg, and Mark Theissen Nation (eds), *Virtues and Practices in the Christian Tradition: Christian Ethics after MacIntyre* (Valley Forge: Trinity Press International, 1997); and from a Roman Catholic perspective, Romanus Cessario, O.P., *The Moral Virtues and Theological Ethics* 2nd edn (Notre Dame: University of Notre Dame Press, 2008).

[4] Stanley Hauerwas in, *A Community of Character*, draws upon the novel *Watership Down*, which is a fictional account about a rabbit community to discuss virtue ethics. He also draws upon his own biography as a Texan to explain virtue ethics. See, for example, Stanley Hauerwas, "The Testament of Friends," in *The Christian Century* (February 28, 1990), 214. Samuel Wells in *Improvisation: The Drama of Christian Ethics* (Ada: Brazos, 2004) draws upon the practice of improvisation in theatre to develop virtue ethics.

[5] For examples of drawing upon the New Testament church see Daniel Harrington, S.J., and James Keenan, S.J., *Jesus and Virtue Ethics* (Lanham: Sheed and Ward, 2002); Joseph Kotva, *The Christian Case for Virtue Ethics* (Washington: Georgetown University Press, 1996); and Jonathan R. Wilson, *Gospel Virtues: Practicing Faith, Hope, and Love in Uncertain Times* (Downers Grove: Intervarsity Press, 1998). For examples of drawing upon the Christian

Gloria Albrecht in *The Character of Our Communities: Toward an Ethic of Liberation for the Church*, is a notable exception to this exclusion of study of specific communities in relation to virtue ethics. Interestingly, she also pays attention to the issue of power within Christian ethics. In analyzing Hauerwas' approach to virtue ethics, she calls for more concrete attention to actual communities within virtue ethics. Albrecht argues that the absence of such attention within Hauerwas hides how his ethic reflects a position of white midde- and upper-middle class power and undercuts action for justice. In her argument, Albrecht raises the issue of power in relation to the seeking of justice. Hauerwas' critique of liberal political life has famously led him into a rejection of Christian participation in efforts to seek justice in a liberal society. However, as Albrecht points out, Hauerwas' social location and the "problem" he seeks to address reflects the concerns of white middle- and upper-middle class people with power.[6] As a result, Albrecht contends, "Hauerwas' ethics equates the renunciation of efforts by white privileged class folk to change the unjust structures of society that benefit us with the religious duty to trust patiently in God as a 'risk' of faith. The renunciation of efforts to transform the society that privileges us is rewarded with religious joy."[7] Albrecht argues that Hauerwas avoids the practice of power for the sake of avoiding the use of violent coercion. She sees Hauerwas as reflecting an unhappy dualism within the tradition of Christian ethics in relation to power, "If one unhappy Christian solution to the experience of relative power has been the Augustinian turn to coercion, Hauerwas' equally unsatisfactory response is to deny the social power of white middle- and upper-middle class Christians."[8]

Hauerwas, of course, posits his political action within the formation of a Christian community that stands in resistance to the injustice of the larger society. For Christians, justice is not a virtue that should first be sought in the larger structures of society; rather it should typify the life of the Christian community. As he has famously argued, the church is to be a social ethic rather than have a social ethic.[9] Yet, as Albrecht's critique points out, Hauerwas' description of such a community reflects white middle- and upper-middle class practices and does not attend to power differentials that might exist within that community.[10] And Hauerwas himself admits that his ethic is not grounded in a specific community of practice.[11]

tradition see Romanus Cessario, O.P., *The Moral Virtues and Theological Ethics* 2nd edn (Notre Dame: University of Notre Dame Press, 2008), and Gilbert Meilander, *The Theory and Practice of Virtue* (Notre Dame: University of Notre Dame Press, 1984).

[6] Gloria Albrecht, *The Character of Our Communities: Toward an Ethic of Liberation for the Church* (Nashville: Abingdon, 1995), 52–4, 60–1.
[7] Albrecht, *The Character of Our Communities*, 116.
[8] Ibid., 115.
[9] Stanley Hauerwas, *A Community of Character*, 11.
[10] Albrecht, *The Character of Our Communities*, 117–18.
[11] Hauerwas, *A Community of Character*, 6.

Albrecht at the end of *The Character of Our Communities* encourages attention to actual communities that engage in struggles for justice and to learn from them visions and practices that reflect the liberatory Gospel of Jesus Christ. For her a central question is, "How can we, as part of the dominant, begin to form redeemed communities characterized by both justice and nonviolence?"[12] It is a good question, and she offers some important beginning resources for responding to that question. But it is a question that lingers and that requires ongoing attention to particular Christian communities that have intentionally sought to live a Gospel vision of justice and resistance to the larger society. Albrecht concludes her book by stating that "learning how to use the power of the dominant for the purpose of liberating others from oppression and ourselves from domination is a primary task for Christian ethics."[13] Such learning necessitates drawing upon the experience of those who have in fact tried to do this.

This brings us back to the Open Door Community. The Open Door as an intentional Christian community, seeks to be a social ethic, to live out the Gospel in daily practice in such a way that it resists the kind of "justice" that typifies the larger society. At the same time, this community engages in public actions that seek social change, that bring transformation of government policies that dehumanize the homeless and execute those convicted of murder. Animated by a Gospel vision of human dignity and respect that accepts the differences of race, class, gender, and sexual orientation without making them the basis for domination, the Open Door both wants to use power for the purpose of liberation and learn in its daily life how to embrace difference in ways that affirm dignity within difference and reject domination. In its community life, the Open Door has had to repeatedly, one might say daily, address how the just distribution and use of power are crucial for embodying that vision.

In its practices of power, the Open Door has faced and continues to face a number of factors that show just how challenging it is to practice a liberating power consistent with a Gospel vision. It is quickly evident how the sharing of power and the delineation of how power is exercised are complicated by several factors. First, there is often the presence of charismatic founders or at least community members with differing levels of charisma in such intentional Christian communities. Max Weber's classical work in regard to charismatic power in contrast to traditional and rational-legal power provides some resources for understanding this challenge.[14] Further, there is the variety of starting places from which community members come in terms of their

---

[12] Albrecht, *The Character of Our Communities*, 141.
[13] Albrecht, *The Character of Our Communities*, 169.
[14] Maximillan Weber, *Theory of Social and Economic Organization*, translated by A. R. Anderson and Talcott Parsons, 1947. Originally published in 1922 in German under the title *Wirtschaft und Gesellschaft*.

experience of race, class, gender, and sexuality. The Open Door Community is diverse, and what it means for a Black formerly homeless straight man to enter into the community's shared vision is different from what it means for a white, middle class, lesbian. Finally, the Open Door Community also has the practical demands of organizing a shared life that includes offering hospitality to homeless persons, visitation on death row and other prisons, and political resistance to the death penalty and to policies that harm homeless persons. Not only does the community have to get things done internally for its own life, it also has external relationships and obligations to attend to, and not all of the people or groups the community is in relationship shares its vision of life. We may already see here that the practices of the community are going to be more nitty gritty and require more conversion of life from community members than such Hauerwasian suggestions as taking time to "enjoy a walk with a friend, to read all of Trollope's novels, to maintain universities, to have and care for children, and most importantly, to worship God."[15]

The Open Door Community began over 30 years ago with four founders: Eduard Loring, Murphy Davis, Rob and Carolyn Johnson who came together at Clifton Presbyterian Church in Atlanta. The community grew out of a ministry to homeless persons and persons on death row that had been based in this small urban Presbyterian Church, pastored by Eduard Loring. Sharing in the work of offering shelter to homeless persons, these two heterosexual, middle class, white married couples, sought to "reduce the distance" between those they served in the shelter and their own lives. To this end, they entered into covenant with each other to form the Open Door Community.

They saw their vision of community life as rooted in the traditions of the early Christian community as described in the Acts of the Apostles, in monastic life, in the Radical Reformation, and in the Catholic Worker movement and in the Koinonia Community. Integral to their vision from the very beginning was a commitment to create a community in which the lines of race, class, and gender would not determine the exercise of power within the community. Instead their commitment was to share power, along with other resources in the community, according to a Gospel vision of shared life, mutual respect, and egalitarianism. The same commitment was extended to include sexual orientation not long after the community began. From the outset they sought to include in Open Door members from the streets and prisons. The clear vision of the founders was to create in the community a structure of shared life that did not reflect the power differentials as defined by the larger society along race, class, and gender lines.

They sought to embody this vision in the daily practices of the community's life. A practice of the community from the beginning, that expressed their

---

[15] Stanley Hauerwas, *Christian Existence Today* (Durham: Labyrinth Press, 1994), 257.

hope for inclusivity and shared power, was the joining of hands in a circle for announcements and prayer. In this circle, no one stood out or above the rest, all stood side by side, and each held the hand of the other, white, Black, female, male, wealthy, poor—were joined with each other. One of the founders of the community, Eduard Loring, has stated that the circle is one of the sacred symbols of the community. "We picture it as a circle of disciples holding hands. As Murphy [Davis, another founder of the community] teaches us: the only chain we can stand is the chain of hand in hand."[16] That line, of course, comes from the civil rights era song, "Keep Your Eyes on the Prize."

This practice of forming a circle and holding hands initiated and continues to initiate every significant event or service in the community: a circle forms before community meals, before serving meals to homeless persons, before leaving the house to provide transportation for family members of the imprisoned, before community members depart for join in a protest. Standing next to each other, holding each other's hands, and facing each other, community members embody the vision of an egalitarian community. Likewise, the community's weekly Eucharistic worship, which takes place in the community's dining room where meals are also served to homeless guests, is structured in a circle, with chairs arranged around the shared table. In this worship, leadership roles rotate; men and women, community members from all different backgrounds preach and lead the Eucharistic prayers, and everyone is given opportunity to voice "prayer concerns."

The circle in prayer and worship embodies the community's vision that reconciliation in Jesus Christ breaks down the dividing walls of race, class, and gender, and makes possible the Beloved Community in which all persons live together in the full dignity of redeemed humanity. In the vision of the Open Door, that full dignity necessarily includes a sharing of power that affirms the dignity and provides for the well-being of each community member. These convictions were evident in the second issue of the community's newspaper, *Hospitality*, in August 1983. A front-page headline "Christ Himself Has Brought Us Peace," quoted from Ephesians 2.14 and the authors of the article, Eduard Loring and another community founder, Carolyn Johnson, wrote,

God sent Jesus into the world that we might be reconciled to God and to each other . . . . Our bodies must be with the victims . . . . As we minister to the poor—as we share our food, our clothing, our money, our churches, our homes—we are transformed. In sharing there is the transformation that makes reconciliation possible.

---

[16] All quotations from community members come from personal interviews conducted by the author unless otherwise noted.

Nearly 20 years later, Murphy Davis, also writing in a May 2004 *Hospitality* article, drew from another of Paul's letters and also from Dorothy Day's Catholic Worker emphasis upon the Mystical Body of Christ, and one of the founders of the Koinonia Community, Clarence Jordan, to express a similar conviction that the community's unity seeks to overcome the wall of separation based on race, class, and gender.

> In the Mystical Body [of Christ] the "dividing wall of hostility" has already been broken down because of the courage of Jesus of Nazareth in confronting the power of death and oppression with life and hope. We receive the gift of unity and community because of this life of "hope in scorn of the consequences." (Clarence Jordan)

Another practice that the community began with and continues with to this day is the rotation of work. Preparing meals, washing dishes, cleaning tasks of various kinds, and the many different tasks necessary for the running of the shared household and offering hospitality are not permanently assigned to any one person or group of persons. Instead, such tasks rotate through the community on a daily or weekly basis. Men and women equally join in the work of the community, as do persons who came to the community from the streets or those who came from other circumstances. No one is "too good" or "too important" to not also engage in such tasks as mopping floors, taking out the trash, or cleaning toilets.

Through such daily practices the community gives concrete expression to their vision of shared power. However, it is in the practices of membership and authority, that the community has both sought to give structural expression to this vision and has encountered the biggest challenges. In these practices of membership and authority, the community has desired to form one circle in Christ through a sometimes complex braiding of three different strands of membership and related expressions of power. Through this circle and the different strands of membership, the community recognizes how race, class, gender, and sexual orientation are locations of power, and that such power can be used and has been used to deny human dignity. At the same time, the community seeks to embody and practice a sharing of power that is based upon a Gospel vision of reconciliation and a just sharing of power.

As mentioned earlier, when the Open Door began, there were four founders, consisting of two white men and two white women who formed two heterosexual married couples. All four of these founders were college educated, and all four also had advanced degrees, including one Ph.D. All four were Presbyterian, and two were ordained Presbyterian ministers. Though none of them came from great wealth, all four were solidly middle class. They described the formation of the community in good Presbyterian language of "covenanting together" for what they called "the long haul" and in egalitarian fashion they called themselves, "partners." This constituted the first strand of membership and power. Together they formed the vision of the community and its initial practices.

Part of the power here also included the charisma of the founders. In particular, Eduard Loring and Murphy Davis were the most powerful in this regard. Their charismatic power in relation to the structure of the community's sharing of power has been an enduring challenge to the vision of shared power. Their ability to powerfully speak of the community's life and their ongoing life-time commitment to that life has over the years meant that their power was immense. Despite many efforts on their part to structure shared power, they have continued to deeply shape the life of the community.

The second strand of membership and power began shortly after the community's founding. The original group of founding partners invited homeless persons and persons formerly imprisoned to join in community life with them. For these members invited in from the streets and prisons there was less of a degree of commitment to the community's vision of life and thus also less power within the community. Those in this second strand of membership were initially called, "houseguests."

Not much later, a third strand of membership took shape as persons from more secure economic backgrounds, mostly white, and mostly college educated, joined the community for varying amounts of time. Invited into the community after some period of mutual discernment, these members were called "resident volunteers." Since their way of entry into the community was also through a type of invitation, and since their level of commitment was also less than the partners, the resident volunteers also had less power.

Through this initial structure of membership, the community began to address the responsibilities and accountability needed for life together. It was through different types of membership that the community sought to order its life, both in terms of daily decision-making and setting long-range policy for the community. The community's founders wanted to have a sharing of power that respected the dignity of each member, but that also recognized that people entered into the shared life of the community under different circumstances, for somewhat different reasons, and for different lengths of time. The founders also wanted a sharing of power that would consistently provide an order necessary for the community's two main practices of hospitality: serving homeless persons through a variety of means such as meals, showers, clothing, and serving imprisoned persons through such things as visitation, transportation of family members for visits, letters, and financial support.

Some of the early struggles within the community around power reveal that simply having these three strands of membership was in tension with the stated vision of shared power. One such struggle is still regarded as a defining moment for the community's structuring of power. The community had been receiving government surplus cheese from the Atlanta Food Bank and using it in meals served to homeless persons. A change in federal regulations meant that to continue receiving the cheese a number of bureaucratic requirements would have to be met, such as tracking numbers of persons served, who was served and how many times, specific amounts of cheese used in meals, how much was lost to spoilage, and temperatures that were used to preserve the cheese.

The partners believed that meeting these requirements would fundamentally alter the hospitality they envisioned the community offering, and that the record keeping would also drain away energy from the direct serving of meals. The partners believed it was better to forego the cheese than lose this vision of hospitality that was at the center of the community's life. Some of the resident volunteers strongly disagreed. They saw the requirements as harmless and thought it best to adjust the community's hospitality to take advantage of getting the cheese.

Murphy Davis saw both the overall vision of the community and the practice of power in relation to that vision as at stake in this issue. She observed that this was "a time to reflect on how we make decisions, who is included in the decision-making process, and which principles of our common life and discipline are not simply up for a democratic vote." In this power struggle, the partners held to their vision and the community stopped using the cheese. Some of the resident volunteers left the community over this decision.

What emerged from this dispute was that the partners more explicitly recognized and affirmed the need for organizing the exercise of power within the community around levels of commitment to the ongoing life of the community and its vision. Experience with life in the community, and familiarity and acceptance of the vision of the community, in essence its collective wisdom or tradition, were now openly recognized and stated as foundations for power within the community. In this structure, the partners retained the power to set the basic vision and practices of the community. Resident volunteers and houseguests would have the limited power of being consulted through regular community meetings called "house meetings" and certain issues could be resolved at those meetings. But other issues involving vision and long range policy would not be resolved there but rather in the partners' meetings. Additionally, power was shared through a "weekly ministries meeting" in which partners and resident volunteers met to discuss and decide the workings of the house, including the making of the work schedule, but again, no addressing of basic vision or long range policies. Murphy summarized the partners' view of this arrangement of power:

We had reached a point of realizing people bring a variety of agendas to the Open Door; and most of them leave after a while. So while we were not going to be mean and harsh, we needed to be realistic. The partners are the only ones committed to being here next year and beyond. Therefore there are some things we could not sit up all night debating.

This structure lasted for about the next five years. There were some continuing tensions, but nothing intense enough to constitute a serious challenge to the arrangement. Then several events occurred that required a revisiting of the structure and the distribution of power in relation to the community's vision. First, Carolyn and then Rob Johnson, two of the original founders, left the community. Their decision to leave reflected two concerns that they had with power in the community. The first concern was their perception that even among the partners there was not enough egalitarian sharing of power. The charismatic power of Eduard and Murphy overshadowed them within the community and also in terms of outside community relations. Further enhancing that charismatic power, especially in relation to outside community relations, was the fact that Eduard and Murphy were both ordained by the Presbyterian Church, but Carolyn and Rob were not. The second concern was that the community's structure was not bringing into shared power those who were houseguests or resident volunteers.

This concern was echoed by some of the houseguests who also chafed under the community's power structure. And here the power dynamics of race were clearly evident. While all the partners and almost all resident volunteers were white, most of the houseguests were African American. One African American houseguest stated in a house meeting, "I don't know how you can have a real community when half the people here [the houseguests] have no decision-making position."

Murphy responded by emphasizing that the house meeting was a decision-making body. But she also stressed that it was not the only decision-making body and that power in the house differed according to the level of commitment to the life of the community.

> House policy is formed out of the common discipline embraced by the partners and resident volunteers in response to the call of Jesus Christ. Decision-making authority comes out of that shared commitment. Since houseguests do not share this commitment, they cannot fully share in the authority of the house.

Several houseguests, both African American and white, expressed agreement with Murphy. They saw that since most of the houseguests were struggling with addictions to drugs and/or alcohol and with transitioning from the streets into a place to live, they really did not want further power and responsibilities. One stated that he saw the Open Door as "a kind of sanctuary from the powers that beat us down, that put us on the streets and kept us there. I need rest more than I need responsibility right now."

Shortly after this house meeting, Eduard shared with me a theological reflection on the community's commitment to the vision of one circle around a common table and the need for ongoing conversion and conversation within the community about authority and power.

One of the ways I'm impressed with the power of evil is that after so many tries, and so many struggles, class structures still remain. I used to be embarrassed about the class distinctions between me and Jay [an African American houseguest who later became a partner in the community]. But as I see what is going on in this society, it is radical that Jay and I eat at the same table, that Jay and I worship the same God. That's about as good as you can discover in North American society today. That doesn't mean I'm giving up and settling for that—I pray, I work, I try to repent of the privilege and class-mindedness in my own life. But I'm not thinking, as I was five, six, or seven years ago, that we're going to pull off a kind of equality and mutuality inside this house that we can't do outside this house. The world is too much here.

Eduard continued by emphasizing the need for ongoing confession of sin and conversion in order to move toward an egalitarian circle within the community.

We have often confessed that the Open Door is not a place to come for those seeking a way out from the sins and demonic powers of modern America. For inside reside the same racism, sexism, classism, greed, desires for comfort, and hunger for short cuts that feed the evil and oppression outside. The difference . . . is not in the presence or absence of sin and iniquity, but in our response to its presence and power in our lives. First comes confession. We are sorry: our hearts are broken. We repent. We commit our lives to being about the long, slow, error-prone process of undoing these sins. Secondly, we have a practice that encourages courage and frightens the Evil One. We often say to each other, "There is no such thing as a stupid question. Ask, ask; keep on asking."

By the fall of 1988 that "asking of questions" in relationship to power and its exercise in the community led to several changes. First, the community participated in an "Undoing Racism" workshop, and recognition in the community of the ongoing power of racism became the focus of discussions and daily life. Naming the power of race to shape perceptions and actions was one way the community sought to intentionally address how race shaped the community's life and its practice of power.

Second, the community began to draw upon the experiences and wisdom of other intentional Christian communities with regard to issues of power. Here the community recognized that their internal power dynamics needed some degree of outside accountability. The community saw that in their practice of power within the community they should also answer to another body. Related to this change was the creation of an advisory board for the community consisting of friends of the community from the larger public. This advisory board was another way for the leadership of the community to have outside accountability. Third, out of those two practices came specific changes to the power structure within the community.

The first change ended the use of the term "houseguests" and began the use of the rather cumbersome appellation, "community members from the streets or prisons." The new term was intended to affirm a deeper belonging to the community by those who entered from the streets or prison. At the same time, the new terminology made explicit that people enter the community and become community members from different social locations, and that this difference makes a difference in the structure of the community's life. In effect, this was an effort to be more transparent or honest about differences that affected the community's life and power within the community. The hope was that such openness would help the community continually face those realities and continue to negotiate ways to address them through attention to how power was shared in the community.

The second change was more substantial and concrete. Some of the resident volunteers and some of the community members from the streets or prisons were invited to become partners. Three resident volunteers and six community members from the streets or prisons accepted the invitation and became partners. Among the partners there would be a "leadership team" that assumed administrative powers within the community. A partner could opt to be or to not be on the leadership team. Partnership thus became not simply a community decision-making role but could also mean recognition of one's long-haul commitment to the life of the community. In this, there was an acceptance of how for various reasons not every partner would want to engage in the administrative work of the "leadership team" even though the community would turn to them for advice based upon the wisdom they had gained in their years of community life.

A third change was the end of the weekly ministries meeting that had excluded members from the streets or prisons. Taking its place was a weekly "calendar check" meeting which involved everyone in the community. In this meeting, everyone together set the work schedule for the week and other basic community work planning was done. Partners, resident volunteers, and community members from the streets or prisons equally shared in this meeting and its decision-making.

A fourth change involved the important community role of being on "house duty." The person on "house duty" essentially runs the house and exercises the most immediate decision-making power to apply the policies of the house. Originally restricted to partners and resident volunteers, members from the streets or prisons were now also invited to "be on house duty." Those who did house duty also began to have a weekly meeting to address issues specific to that work.

These changes brought a stronger sense of shared power within the community. With greater shared power came a deeper sense of commitment to the community. However, some tensions certainly remained. One community member from the streets evaluated the changes saying he still saw divisions of class and that "A new resident volunteer has more say than a guy from the streets who's lived here for over a year." Still, he saw some significant difference with the changes even as he affirmed the ongoing power of difference.

> There can't be equality. People are different. At least here when you're different, you're still valued. You're still treated like a person. The virtue of this place is that it shows we can live together—Black and white, poor and privileged—if we respect each other and give each other a chance. It isn't perfect. No place is. But it's better than any other place I've been.

Another community member from the streets, Ralph Dukes, who became a partner, was also realistic but expressed what he thought the changes meant for his standing in the community. "Being called a partner might just be a change in words. But to me it means I've survived and I'm living, and this is home for me."

One of the resident volunteers who became a partner saw a change in her way of viewing her relationship with those who had been houseguests but were now partners. She attributed this change to both the change in practice and the power of faith.

> I have lived and worked with [a number of the houseguests] for three years, yet I hadn't recognized fully their partnership with me; I hadn't seen completely how they were my family. Acknowledging their partnership publicly was my first step towards sight, and now I know that I had been blinded by the things that make me different from these new partners: my education, the color of my skin, my comfortable existence, and the privilege to choose to come to the Open Door. But with the eyes of faith, given to us by our brother Jesus, we can see Jesus in everyone, and so recognize our partnership together.

This particular structure of power endured for the next 15 years. The ways in which power within the community were shared or not shared were more clearly and openly delineated. The original vision of a completely egalitarian community was made more eschatological, a hope that inspired and to some extent informed the community, but that "realistically" could not be fully embodied. Its partial embodiment remained in the daily shared power of decision-making regarding the work of the community, along with such practices as the prayer circle and the rotation of work. And out of that shared power, both members from the streets and prisons and resident volunteers sometimes aspired to become partners.

The tensions that remained, however, eventually came to require further change. Within the community's life, the dynamics remained largely of white middle-class resident volunteers while members from the streets or prisons came from poverty and were mostly African American. On occasion a white resident volunteer would say or do something in a position of leadership, such as while being on house duty, and an African American member from the streets or prisons would see what took place as racist. The African American community member would raise the issue in a personal confrontation or in a community meeting. Such confrontations were difficult and sometimes led to members of the community leaving. It is rarely easy for a white person to hear and accept an accusation of racism. And perhaps this is even more so for a white person who has come to an interracial community motivated by a faith commitment to equality of persons. Likewise, if a white partner called an African American member of the community to account for some action, the partner would also sometimes be accused of racism. How to negotiate these power dynamics?

Further complicating the power dynamics was the reality that most of the persons coming to the community from the streets or prisons also struggle with addiction to drugs and/or alcohol. The discipline and structure needed to confront addiction and maintain sobriety inevitably led to conflict and questions about trust. With the maintenance of that structure remaining mostly in white and middle-class hands, the challenges of negotiating power intensified.

Further challenges to the community's life and its exercise of power also began to emerge in the late 1990s. Murphy was diagnosed with cancer and began a long battle with that disease which has continued to the present. This has significantly affected her and Eduard's ability to remain as engaged in the daily life of the community. The community also began to face the realities of an aging leadership as several partners entered their sixties and a few entered their seventies. During this same period, several African American partners decided to leave the community, even as there has been increased African American participation as resident volunteers. These changes affected the racial dynamics of the community. The last ten years of community life have brought all of these issues to the forefront and the structure and practice of power within the community are shifting once again.

At present the two remaining original founders, Eduard Loring and Murphy Davis, have left the leadership team even as they remain partners. Their charismatic leadership over the years deeply shaped the vision and life of the community. As is the case with many intentional Christian communities, the question of how to structure power in the absence of charismatic founders presents a significant challenge. How the community will adjust to their reduced role remains to be seen.

At the same time, new leadership is emerging with new community members and a changing of the community's structure of offering hospitality. Perhaps most notable is the combining of house duty meetings with community wide meetings in which a wide range of issues are discussed and decided in addition to setting the work schedule for each week. In some ways the community has returned to its original practice of a weekly meeting making more decisions.

One way this sharing of power has been able to work is that the community has also become more intentional about the formation of community members in the vision of the community. Each new community member is assigned a "pastoral friend" to help guide the new member through the life of the community. The pastoral friend and the new community member meet each week to discuss how life in the community is going and to address any issues that arise. In this there has been a growing acceptance of the necessity for some differences in power being based upon differences in experience and commitment within the community. This is evident in the convergence of views of those who live in the community around this issue. A resident volunteer who came to the community from the streets stated,

> The people with the most experience generally dictate what's going to happen: which they should. The people with the most at stake here should be the ones who make the decisions. The Open Door was here before I came to live here and will be here after me. There's a reason you don't make decisions right away.

Likewise, a resident volunteer who came to the community from a middle-class way of life stated,

> When I came here I wanted to make decisions, but I had no idea what it means to live with someone who is recovering from addiction and someone who has been homeless. Particularly as resident volunteers [from middle-class backgrounds], we're used to having lots of privilege and lots of authority because that's our experience. We come from privileged leadership backgrounds, but we don't know what its like to live here. The folks who are here for the long haul need to make the decisions that shape the long haul life of the community. It is so important to have the folks who are bearing the consequences of decisions over the long haul and who have experienced the larger vision to be making the decisions.

What does an analysis of the place and practice of power within the Open Door Community contribute to intentional Christian communities committed to a Gospel vision of life? Two major conclusions may be drawn. First, the story of the Open Door in relation to power shows how the structure and practice of power within an intentional Christian community with a Gospel vision of shared life will need constant reevaluation and renegotiation. The complexities of dynamics such as charisma, and differing experiences of race, class, gender, and sexual orientation require continual recognition, discussion, discernment, and experimentation with different forms of structuring power. How power is structured and practiced within a community reveals a great deal about how the community is living out its vision. How power is structured and practiced must be openly faced and negotiated if a community is to live into a Gospel vision.

Second, a structure of power that takes into account different levels of experience and commitment to the community's vision of life is necessary for sustaining the community. The ways in which power is structured and practiced in the community are accountable to the community's vision of life. This necessitates attention to formation of community members in that vision, and ongoing reflection upon the vision. It also means that though the vision provides a basis for how power is to be practiced in the community, the vision also needs ongoing appropriation and attention. Such appropriation and attention will need to be guided by those who have the most experience within the community. Wisdom in relation to the vision is thus a basis for power. Yet it is not enough to rely upon such wisdom internally, there is also the need for both outside accountability.

What might this analysis of power within the Open Door Community contribute to virtue ethics? First, attention to "story" or "vision" that does not include attention to real Christian communities engaged in the difficult work of negotiating shared power among diverse peoples simply contribute to patterns of power within the church and larger society that are oppressive and exploitative. Albrecht's critique of Hauerwas may well be extended to virtue ethics more broadly in that virtue ethics has paid scant attention to the dynamics of power in relation to the formation of a vision of life and the formation of persons in such a vision. When attention is paid to those dynamics of power, then the ways in which race, class, gender, and sexual orientation shape vision begin to surface and must be attended to.

Second, there needs to be attention to power not only in relation to the formation of a vision of life, but also in relation to the practice of that vision. It is in the practice of power that what I have called elsewhere "the cost of virtue" will necessarily be faced.[17] The creating of a countercultural Gospel vision of life within contemporary Christian virtue ethics is an exercise in what might be called "cheap virtue" unless it attends to the practice of that vision in real life by real people in real communities. Since it is a goal of contemporary

---

[17] Peter R. Gathje, *The Cost of Virtue: The Theological Ethics of Daniel and Philip Berrigan* (Ann Arbor: University Microfilms International, 1994).

Christian virtue ethics to help create communities of virtue set in resistance to the existing institutional order and its rival conceptions of the good, then it is important to pay attention to those communities that have in fact tried to do this. In paying attention to such communities the cost of virtue for white middle- and upper-middle class people in terms of difficult conversion away from privilege and dominating power and toward shared risk and solidarity with those marginalized by the current structures of power will become evident. Without such attention and conversion, virtue ethics becomes another version of what Dietrich Bonhoeffer called "cheap grace" in which there is a Gospel vision that does not include the cross, and thereby does not include the possibility of a radically new life in Christ.[18]

---

[18] See Dietrich Bonheoffer, *The Cost of Discipleship* (New York: Macmillan, 1960), 35–47.

Part Three

Method

Chapter 12

Benedictions: For Those Willing to Give Ethnography a Try

Collectively, the chapters in Part One explore important histories, debates, and method related to ethnography and theology. However, the methodological discussion is more on the analytical side than practical. Part Two offers thought-provoking, concrete examples of theological ethnography and, along the way, points to some specific methodological designs. You might be the sort of diligent reader who has plowed through the chapters from start to finish. But you may also be the sort of person who has, either by choice or by assignment, turned straight away to this last section that focuses on the "nitty-gritty," more pragmatic discussion of methods. However you got to this point, we now offer some benedictions for those wishing to take up, or deepen their practice of, ethnographic research. Benedictions are "good words," words of sending for those transformed by the Word and Sacrament present for them at the heart of Christian worship. Here, we hope to send those transformed by the powerful and compelling witness embodied especially in the exemplars found in Part Two. And our "good words" for sending you highlight the basic outline of a research project, along with commentary and references to additional reading you may find helpful.

Formulation of a Research Question

At a number of points along the way we have discussed differences between qualitative and quantitative research, and their divergence begins here, at the outset, when one begins formulating a question that the process of research might answer. Robert P. Jones, who wrote Chapter 7 above, does religions survey research in Washington D.C. In this work he can be quite focused in his questions as he begins the process.[1] For instance, in a 2009 study he wanted to

---

[1] See http://www.publicreligion.org. For another prominent example of quantitative research in the areas of religion, public opinion, politics, and various demographics, see

get comparative data on clergy views of homosexuality across denominations. He could ask how many clergy thought homosexuals ought to have the right to marry, be ordained, or enjoy protection against discrimination in the workplace. Such a report gives a broad snapshot of how clergy at a moment in time report on personal convictions. The report found, for instance, that roughly two-thirds of mainline clergy support some legal recognition for same-sex couples (65%), passing hate crime laws (67%) and employment nondiscrimination protections for gay and lesbian people (66%). A majority (55%) of mainline clergy support adoption rights for gay and lesbian people.[2]

However, to understand *how* people come to their convictions regarding homosexuality and religion, and *what* people do on the basis of those beliefs, one needs to at least do interviews, and likely spend time participating in the context of their daily lives. Dawne Moon did just this in her book *God, Sex and Politics*. Whereas survey research can find out what people admit to believing, Moon took a classically ethnographic approach. "I ask," Moon writes, "given that members of these congregations believe in God, what do they do with that belief? How is it that members can purport to believe in the same God and yet have such very different theologies" when it comes to homosexuality?[3] Ethnographic studies go beyond reporting the facts of "what is" found through research to paint a fuller picture what these facts mean in the lives of a person or community. In other words, they are better at getting at "how" and "why" kinds of questions that shape individual and social decisions, activities, and practices.

In terms of practical counsel, we would advise that while an orienting research question is needed at the outset in an ethnographic project, it should be fairly open-ended or at least open to revision as the learning process in the field progresses. Mindy Fullilove explains that ethnographic research is a "feel-forward" approach meaning that the researcher cannot know or identify all of the relevant questions or issues at the inception. Instead, s/he needs to be open to the possibility that the initial questions turn out to be not the most helpful ones for learning from the field.[4] Thus, it is good to identify a basic question or set of questions that one brings to the study. Doing so is vital for crafting a cogent and manageable focus. Yet, this framework should not be heavy handed or overdetermined. There is a necessary fluidity at work

---

the Pew Research Center: http://pewresearch.org/. In October 2010 for example, Pew published an illuminating (if sobering) report on what Americans know about religion, see: http://pewresearch.org/pubs/1745/religious-knowledge-in-america-survey-atheists-agnostics-score-highest (accessed October 11, 2010).

[2] See the Mainline Protestant Clergy Voices Survey at http://www.publicreligion.org/research/published/?id=167 (accessed October 11, 2010).

[3] Dawne Moon, *God, Sex and Politics: Homosexuality and Everyday Theologies* (Chicago: University of Chicago Press, 2004), 4.

[4] Fullilove, *The Little Handbook*, 9.

here—the central research questions may shift as the ethnographer immerses her/himself in the context and learns from it.

Finally, recalling Spradley's insights mentioned earlier in Part One, before the formal ethnographic work begins, we think it is worthwhile to take time to discern what the most pressing issues are for a given place or people. Again, this understanding may indeed shift once the ethnographic portion begins or deepens—the researcher may be decidedly mistaken in what s/he thinks these needs are. Yet, whenever possible and appropriate, there is real merit in attempting to align one's research with the actual needs of others from the outset.

Research Design

The orienting question one begins with, then, sets in motion choices about each of the aspects of the research process that follow. The questions imply, if you will, kinds of evidence required in order to find answers, and therefore set a direction toward particular kinds of research. This volume, in advocating ethnography, imagines the fruitfulness for theology and ethics of following the sorts of "how" questions asked by Dawne Moon. To ask about clergy beliefs regarding homosexuality, one need not leave one's office; constructing a survey to mail out to pastors does require layers of work, but it does not actually require talking to any pastors or visiting any congregations. However, if one seeks to see *how* people's lives in community are shaped by shared belief in God while holding to divergent views of homosexuality, one needs to go and be with them.

While research designs vary widely, a common thread pulls together the various things we include under the term ethnography—that thread might honestly be named "mucking around." While this quite pedestrian term may not immediately strike you as helpful or attractive, it means to point out the difficult and often messy work of actually going out to join in the life of people where they live. This might, as with Whitmore's work, require learning the tribal language of the people and living in difficult circumstances in a huge Ugandan refugee camp. Such vivid writing and close to the bone reflection about the theological and moral issues at stake only arise from the messiness of his fieldwork in the midst of the people. Yet such "mucking around" might also, as with Reimer-Barry, require long hours of careful listening to women's lives. Such listening cannot simply be structured by a narrow set of predetermined questions but, as she notes, open-ended interviews that let questions emerge in response to the salient points raised by the person interviewed. Often such interviews take narrative form, allowing the multilayered unfolding of life lived.

Yet the basics of research design can be unpacked in more detail, and the sections to follow indeed do just that. One must, for example, choose a site for research that balances the need for access with the prospect of rich experiences related to one's research question. One must plan with some flexibility the duration and details of the research, and its potential and complex effects for those studied. Specific plans for use of core techniques of research must be thought through: participating and observing what, how, for how long, with which methods of recording; interviewing which sorts of people with what general questions; combining focus groups with individual interview or not; using a participatory action model or not; how much, and what kind of, historical, sociological, and other kinds of contextual data are needed to supplement the ethnographic materials and so on.

In general, the rule of triangulating data is important to consider. This means one has at least three overlapping but distinct angles of vision on a given project, each offered by virtue of a different method (interviews, observation, participation, document analysis). It also means that as a whole, a research endeavor often relates ethnographic data to relevant quantitative sources of information (e.g. Census data, health/healthcare statistics, poverty indexes, historical documents or narratives of a community, nation, or place. Resourcing quantitative sources of information can help to contextualize what one hears and sees through the ethnographic study. For example, as Paul Farmer shows in his work in Haiti, if one wants to understand fully the challenges and suffering that Haitians describe, one needs to know a good deal about the legacy of US foreign (political and economic) policy in Haiti.[5]

In summary, in choosing a research design for your project, the research question plays a central role: if in the end I hope to know more about my question, how might this design process offer a plan that leads to such a conclusion for me and for those participating in the research? How does the basic question inform how I organize my study? How can I best learn what I hope to learn? What kinds of information do I need? In other words, "form follows function"—the form of the study should correlate with the kinds of questions one hopes to pursue.

Site Selection and Sampling

Obviously, choosing where and with whom to do your "mucking around" is crucial to the overall outcome of the research process. Yet the truth is that even this process is often a great deal messier than cleaned-up and after-the-fact reports show. For starters, research site selection (where the research is carried out) and sampling (a way to talk about who one recruits for interviews, for example) are often shaped by the research question itself.

---

[5] See Paul Farmer, *Pathologies of Power* and also Tracy Kidder, *Mountains Beyond Mountains*.

Take Jones' work as an example. Seeking to understand the contours of Christian voices on the issue of Physician-Assisted Suicide (PAS), Jones turned to Oregon as the site for research because they were the first state to pass a law making such a procedure legal. Within Oregon, he took stock of the landscape and worked towards meeting and conducting interviews with leaders from each of the main points of view within the Oregon Christian community. The choice of Oregon was straightforward, but it took some care and initial background reading and preliminary conversations to discern with whom he ought to seek interviews.

On the other hand, there are times when one's own circumstances provide the entre. In Vicini's case, his work as a priest in the Chiapas region of Mexico exposed him to dynamics that he wished to explore more systematically, turning to ethnography as a disciplined means to understand the life of the communities where he lived and worked. Similarly, Gathje connected first with the Open Door Community through his desire to connect to their powerful witness to reconciliation, and as part of this process of deepening involvement in their community he turned to the discipline of ethnographic research as a means to take stock of the situation in all its fullness. This is not to say one can simply "count" one's daily life in this or that context as ethnography, as Stevens (see Chapter 2 above) does. For starters, one has specific ethical responsibilities when moving from ordinary life to the role of researcher, whether one is part of an institution in which research is regularly carried out or not.

Proposals/Ethics/Institutional Review Boards

Once the research question, design, site selection and sampling characteristics are clearly in mind, a pause is in order before plunging into the work. Here, as Reimer-Barry notes, a process of ethical accountability increasingly includes a formal Institutional Review Board (IRB) that requires clear acknowledgement of one's plans from start to finish. This step includes asking questions about the risks and benefits of participants in the study, a touchy question in her case given that she interviewed women living with HIV. However, the level of obvious risk does not fully account for what is at stake here. It is also a moment to gain outside feedback and perspective on a research plan, a process that may raise ethical concerns or may simple provide wisdom for the process from others who have experience. Reimer-Barry's chapter includes helpful discussion of this process and some of the issues that must be faced before getting to the research proper.

Moreover, responsibility only begins with formal IRB approval. Beyond having any requisite permissions in place from authorizing bodies, researchers are profoundly accountable to those from whom they learn. Even with IRB certification in hand, it is possible to act in ways which disrespect, and even obscure, the realities and people the ethnographer hopes to illumine. As discussed in several places in Part One, ongoing, critical self-reflection about assumptions, descriptions, and what one does with the research (and how one benefits) are crucial dimensions to any study. We need ways to "check ourselves" throughout the process. And we need to demonstrate a kind of accountability that continues well beyond the period of ethnographic study itself.

A challenging question in this regard has to do with the question of benefit. To whom does benefit from the study accrue? This can be fairly unproblematic, as in Jones' research with public leaders in the PAS debate. Their outspokenness in public meant they told Jones little that was not already public. He made no promises that his research would help any particular side in the debate. He did close a loop with participants, however, checking with them before presenting or publishing materials from interviews so that each person could feel accurately represented. However, even there Jones had a deeply theological and ethical aim undergirding his work, and his hope that such research might have a positive effect in Oregon and elsewhere is a key aspect of what motivates people do undertake such study in the first place. Browning's study of street children in Kenya intensifies the tension between the discipline required to listen, watch, and learn as much as possible about those one studies and seeking to have such work matter for their good. Such profound tensions do not go away, and are not easily resolved.

Entry/Permission/Reflexivity

Nonetheless, tensions are part and parcel of the plunge into research. As one moves from the stage of fully fleshing out the proposal and getting various formal approvals, getting into the research site looms. In order to gain entry, even entry within one's own world of context and competence—as was the case with Tribble, an African Methodist Episcopal Zion (AMEZ) pastor seeking to research with fellow AMEZ pastors—permission ought to be sought for the sake of transparency. When Tribble began his research, he sought the permission and help of the leadership in the AMEZ, and they in turn helped him gain access to the pastors he wished to include in his study.

In gaining this entry via the AMEZ leadership, however, Tribble learned that the Bishop had chosen to focus on transformative leadership, a theme central to his research. This circumstance then meant his work was of direct interest to his research partners, and this brings into focus the question of reflexivity. One changes the circumstances of one's study, and careful attention to this fact is a key part of entering the research. While one may welcome this, it ought to be a place of disciplined reflection rather than a background factor one ignores, or worse, covers up. Whitmore's and Browning's painful face-to-face encounters with acutely suffering people caused them to reflect on the complexity of privilege they inhabit, and the responsibilities it holds for the research relationships that develop over one's project.

Participant Observation

A key element of almost every ethnographic research project, participant observation might be also described as "going to see for oneself." But it is more than this, for one can go and see for oneself as a curiosity-seeker, with no intention of doing more than fulfilling a desire at the moment to find out more. One can, as well, be a journalist who goes to see and learn more with an aim to share what one has found. But participant observation as part of ethnographic research is, as we discuss in Part One of the book, "untimely." Not captive to personal whim or the latest news cycle, this sort of participation can take time to dwell, listen carefully, and wait, if necessary, for the insights and experiences that help make sense of people's lives in a particular place. Gathje's long association with the Open Door, including a time living and working in the community, gives him much deeper and more careful information about how power functions in the community than any casual visitor or reporter calling for comment on a deadline would every accomplish.

A key aspect of such participant observation is, not surprisingly, recording one's thoughts, reactions, observations, wonderings, and so on. This is often done through what many call "fieldnotes." While this is mostly a background reality in the research process, it is absolutely essential. It is, in a way, a memory aid. While of course one might use photography, video and audio recording, or other techniques, nothing really replaces the discipline of notes. It is helpful if one is able to jot some notes in the midst of any given event or experience, but regardless, within a few hours of finishing for the day, one ought to spend the time to recount the experiences as fully as possible. The key here is narrative detail, and if a reactive judgment arises it can be placed in a margin and set aside so that the narrative focuses on giving as disciplined a picture of what transpired as possible. Throughout his years of immersion in the Chicago boxing gym, Loïc Wacquant returned every night and sat up at his desk writing about the day.[6]

However, this is not to say one must adhere to the classical model of ethnography—living in an unfamiliar culture for a year or more—as Wacquant's and other similar studies suggest. Some of our case chapters portray quite a variety of on-the-ground research, from relatively brief visits to longer immersions in the local context. These ethnographic exemplars did not all require

---

[6] Wacquant, *Body and Soul.* Also see the excellent "how-to" by Robert Emerson, Rachel Fretz and Linda Shaw, *Writing Ethnographic Fieldnotes* (Chicago: University of Chicago Press, 1995).

time living somewhere; they did, however, as in the case of Jones' work in Oregon, require patient listening and directed but open-ended interviewing. One might also point to the "empathetic listening" Reimer-Barry reports doing with the women in her study.

Interviewing

As we've already begun to describe, interviewing also has a key role in ethnographic research. One might say that when one "goes to see for oneself" part of that process is asking questions of those one goes to see. Of course in the process one might have many conversations, and these informal encounters are all of value. Yet interviewing in a formal sense usually includes general questions or topic areas about which one wants to know. These questions, and key follow-up questions that work to press for further detail or clarity, are the meat (or tofu) of the process, allowing for focus and care in hearing out those one seeks to learn from. While one-on-one interviews are most typical, group interviews are not uncommon. They are not synonymous with focus groups, however, which are more like an opinion survey done in person and at slightly more depth than the typical phone, internet, or mail-in survey questionnaire.

Interviews are difficult, and not least because they require both careful listening and very effective modes of asking questions—both opening questions and various sorts of follow-ups. Odd as it may sound here in a discussion of how to do research, having a handle of one's own issues, and being spiritually grounded oneself, is of great help in the process of research generally and interviewing particularly. One can easily slip into either judgment or attempts at fixing (which incidentally amount to the same thing). While this might be the goal with in conversation with a friend, here the goal is to hold one's own judgments and temptations to fix troubles without being cold (of course, a person falling into a pool of tears does not need the next question, but a momentary pause and supportive presence before continuing). Books and mentors do indeed help with interviewing strategy and still the best teacher is reflective practice, interviewing over and over and over, with critical evaluation of one's efforts via the transcript.

Equipment

In order to have a transcript of an interview, of course, one must either have a fantastic memory and write as much as can be remembered down immediately after, or record the interview and transcribe it. Neither is fool-proof, naturally, but the discipline in either case is rooted in deep respect for what the other has to say. The equipment that allows one to record the event or interview—whether a recorder or an old-fashioned pen and notebook, allows that respect for the other's words and experience. If one is recording, getting permission ahead of time, and offering clarity about how the interview may be used, is appropriate. One might do this when recruiting someone to the research project, or do it just before the interview. Some IRBs will require a formal consent form that all participants sign.

The use of video and photography equipment is complicated. Certainly using them can provide stunning visuals to accompany printed text and/or oral presentations. They can provide helpful context—what the area looks like or what the dynamics of day life appear to be just from seeing the place. They can similarly add greater dimension by putting faces and names to statistics— showing how various issues play out in embodied people's lives. Such a photographic or video portrayal, especially of those who feel ignored, can be a means to confer dignity and even a sense of identity. João Biehl's beautiful ethnography *Vita: Life in a Zone of Social Abandonment* includes stunning photography by Biehl's colleague, Torben Eskerod, that have an ethical argument in some ways parallel to the text itself.[7] In a similar fashion, Barbara Myerhoff's short documentary *Number Our Days*, accompanying her book of the same name, captured and publicized the beautiful but fragile life of a community of very elderly Jewish immigrants in Santa Barbara.[8]

Yet, as the Preface and other places in Part One indicate, they are also often a tool in commodification—turning a human subject into an object for consumption by others. Paul Farmer notes that graphic images do not always lead to meaningful intervention and cites the genocides in Rwanda and Sudan as a case in point.[9] Indeed, when such violent and shocking images are coupled with only passing attention and apathy, they can become, in a sense, pornographic.

Similarly problematic and discussed in Part One, sometimes readers conflate the image with a more complex reality and person. Images can reveal part, but never the whole truth. In sum, their use merits serious reflection. Why does the researcher want to video or take photographs? What purpose do they serve? What are the dangers of doing so? How might collaborators be affected by their use?

In a pragmatic vein, setting up or using a camera can be off-putting to those interviewed. Fears about publicity or confidentiality can arise. Moreover, when a researcher uses and publishes the image of another it can raise questions

---

[7] Biehl, *Vita*, 42.
[8] Barbara Myerhoff, *Number Our Days: A Triumph of Continuity and Culture among Jewish Old People in an Urban Ghetto* (New York: Touchstone, 1980).
[9] Farmer discusses both the powerful place, and limits, of the use of images in: Paul Farmer, "Never Again?," see especially pp. 161–4. "The Rwandan genocide was among the world's most reported and photographed of mass killings. But abundant documentation, visual or otherwise, had virtually no role in halting that genocide" (ibid., 164).

again about benefits. In all, we would caution against the use of video and film equipment unless the researcher is both critically self aware about such use and is completely confident that doing so will not get in the way of building trust and rapport with the people with whom s/he hopes to speak. Asking people if they mind being photographed or filmed can help, but is not a guarantee. Sometimes people can be timid about indicating their feelings to someone they do not know well or have only just met.

Analysis

Typically, one does not wait until the research is over to begin analysis. In fact, when one enters into a research project with one's question(s) in mind, the analysis begins right away. This happens informally as questions arise as to what this or that comment or observation shows about the situation. There are disciplined methods of identifying themes (often called codes) that allow looking at patterns across multiple interviews. Yet even before coding, simply attending to the discipline of research often leads one to begin to see key issues, common patterns and important new insights. When this happens during the unfolding of research, it is important to note this and begin to test how the insights hold up as further interviews, participant observation or other study unfolds. Some approaches argue for deriving themes directly from the participants' own words and lives, but other times the themes derive from the research question itself, or from theoretical frameworks one is exploring within a particular context. Whatever specific method one chooses or creates for tracking relevant themes and insights, it is crucial that a spirit of openness to surprise be present. As noted above with the initial research question, there needs to be room for taking stock of how what one thought would be the central themes or conclusion turn out to be off base or in need of substantive revision. Learning deeply and authentically from the field is a central commitment of ethnographic study.

Moreover, while this thematic analysis is certainly important to do in relation to one's accumulating data, it is also a place for key collaboration so that one is forced to present findings to others and hear their reaction. One possibility, obviously, is the student thesis or dissertation that would have a faculty committee with whom to have these conversations. But another key possibility is that a collaborative research project could be designed and carried out. This is much more common in the natural and social sciences, and ought to become more standard in theology and ethics. The complexity of the world today—and the accessibility of so much information—make the limits of one researcher much more pronounced. Paul Rabinow and George Marcus, in their book on an anthropology of the contemporary, commend a "co-laboratory" or "studio" model in which the whole process—from generating concepts and questions through publication—is shared.[10]

Publication

Finally, ethnography—writing culture, literally—must turn to the task of writing what one has learned. In what we have written thus far, we hope it is clear we do not endorse the privileged position of the scholar who studies and then writes an authoritative depiction of another's culture. Ours is a more humble and self-critical stance, and in moving to writing, this complexity rushes to the forefront. Perhaps Whitmore's chapter in this volume grapples most vividly with the complicated politics and privilege of moving from research to writing. Yet exactly because of his grappling in the context of ethnography as a form of theology, he can see the ways his writing functions both as an instance of his own discipleship and therefore as a witness to the suffering of those with whom he lived in Uganda. Writing about the research does not leave the participants behind but holds them in its horizon as key stakeholders in the dissemination of knowledge gained through the process. Writing, to put it differently, circles back to the ethics of research and one's accountability to those with whom the research was carried out and ultimately to that One in whom all things have their being.

Ethnography as theology stays close to the ground, telling the specific stories of those with whom one has done the research. Yet putting such diverse fields as ethnography, theology and ethics into conversation is a complicated task. The lines and boundaries blur. Often the research goes into unanticipated directions and takes surprising, even unsettling turns. As the writing progresses, the narrative can read like a textual cacophony, rather than a well-orchestrated symphony. Such complexity and even moments of chaos can lead some to lose heart—to give up on the process and go back to more familiar ways of doing, and conceiving of, theology and ethics. This book represents an attempt to bolster courage and to equip people with both a rationale for going forward along with helpful guideposts that might help to navigate the new terrain.

Even more, we are bold enough to suggest that some of the best work comes from "messy" projects where the relevant categories are not overly predetermined, when the researcher feels awkward and at times even ill-prepared, when even a conflicting and raucous collection of voices is heard in the narrative. The noted political scientist, Iris Marion Young, has called for fully attending to such differences rather than glossing over them. She contends that

---

[10] Rabinow and Marcus, *Design for an Anthropology of the Contemporary*, 83.

democracy depends on such wide-ranging participation where all are respected in their unique identities and communities.[11] In a similar vein, bell hooks observes that cultural studies—and we would add ethnography, Christian theology, and ethics—must be committed to "a 'politics of difference' that recognizes the importance of making space" where the sort of mutually respectful listening can overcome traditional divides between us. hooks continues,

> Drawing from a new ethnography, we are challenged to celebrate the polyphonic nature of critical discourse, to—as it happens in traditional African-American religious experience—hear one another "speak in tongues," bear witness, and patiently wait for revelation.[12]

These references to religious experience—and even revelation—lead us to conclude with the conviction that our efforts to both respect and listen to difference within a polyphonic dialogue is rooted in our very understandings of God. Important Trinitarian theologians have shown us that such relationality—self-giving communion within difference—is the essence of God's own life, and the life therefore of our lives in this wild and precious creation.[13] May it be so for us and for the readers of this volume. May we find the tenacity, humility, hope, and courage to attend to the complexity and richness of particularity and to trust—patiently and even impatiently at times—that revelation will come and dwell among us.

---

[11] Iris Marion Young, *Justice and the Politics of Difference* (Princeton: Princeton University Press, 1990).

[12] hooks, *Yearning*, 133.

[13] See especially Catherine Mowry LaCugna, *God for Us: The Trinity and Christian Life* (San Francisco: HarperSanFrancisco, 1991); John D. Zizioulas, *Being as Communion: Studies in Personhood and the Church* (Crestwood: St. Vladimir's Seminary Press, 1985); John D. Zizioulas, *Communion and Otherness: Further Studies in Personhood and the Church* (New York: T & T Clark, 2007).

Bibliography

Achebe, Chinua. *No Longer at Ease*. Nairobi: East African Educational Publishers, 1960.

Ackermann, Denise. "From Mere Existence to Tenacious Endurance: Stigma, HIV/AIDS, and a Feminist Theology of Praxis." *Festschrift M.A.E. Oduyoye*. Maryknoll: Orbis Books, 2006.

Adams, Nicholas and Charles Elliott. "Ethnography is Dogmatics: Making Description Central to Systematic Theology." *Scottish Journal of Theology* 53 (Autumn 2000): 339–64.

Albrecht, Gloria. *The Character of Our Communities: Toward an Ethic of Liberation for the Church*. Nashville: Abingdon, 1995.

Ammerman, Nancy. *Congregation and Community*. New Brunswick: Rutgers University Press, 1997.

Amnesty International. *Children and Human Rights*, www.amnesty.org/en/children (accessed June 3, 2010).

Anderson, David M. *Maasai: People of Cattle*. San Francisco: Chronicle Books, 1995.

Anzaldúa, Gloria. *Borderlands La Frontera: A New Mestiza*. San Francisco: Aunt Lute Books, 1987.

Archibold, Randal C. "Judge Blocks Arizona's Immigration Law." *The New York Times* (July 28, 2010), online http://www.nytimes.com/2010/07/29/us/29arizona.html (accessed October 15, 2010).

Asad, Talal (ed.). *Anthropology & the Colonial Encounter*. Atlantic Highlands: Humanities Press, 1973.

Ayodele, Thomas, et al. "African Perspectives on Aid: Foreign Assistance Will Not Pull Africa Out of Poverty." *Economic Development* 2 (September 14, 2005). https://www.cato.org/pubs/edb/edb2.pdf (accessed June 8, 2010).

Bachelard, Gaston. *Le Nouvel Espirit Scientifque*. Paris: PUF, 1949.

Barnes, Michael H. (ed.). *Theology and the Social Sciences*. Maryknoll: Orbis, 2001.

Barth, Frederik et al. *One Discipline, Four Ways: British, German, French, and American Anthropology*. Chicago: University of Chicago Press, 2005.

BBC News. "Pope tells Africa 'Condoms Wrong.'" (March 17, 2009). http://news.bbc.co.uk/2/hi/7947460.stm (accessed June 6, 2010).

Beauchamp, Tom L. and James F. Childress. *The Principles of Biomedical Ethics* 5th edn. New York: Oxford University Press, 2001.

Becker, Penny. *Congregations in Conflict: Cultural Models of Local Religious Life*. New York: Cambridge University Press, 1999.

Beckman, David. "Debunking Myths About Foreign Aid." *The Christian Century* (August 1–8, 2001): 26–8.

Behar, Ruth and Deborah A. Gordon (eds). *Women Writing Culture*. Berkeley: University of California Press, 1995.

Bell, Catherine. *Ritual Theory, Ritual Practice*. New York: Oxford University Press, 1992.

Bellah, Robert N. *Tokugowa Religion: The Cultural Roots of Modern Japan*. New York: The Free Press, 1957.

—. *Beyond Belief: Essays in Post-Traditional Religion*. New York: Harper, 1970.

—. "What is axial about the axial age?" *European Journal of Sociology* 46 (2005): 69–89.

—. "The Ethical Aims of Social Inquiry." In *The Robert Bellah Reader*, edited by Robert N. Bellah and Steven Tipton. Durham: Duke University Press, 2006: 381–401.

Bellah, Robert N. et al. *Habits of the Heart: Individualism and Commitment in American Life*. Berkeley: University of California Press, 1985.

Berg, B. L. *Qualitative Research Methods*. Needham Heights: Allyn & Bacon, 1989.

Bhabha, Homi K. *The Location of Culture*. London: Routledge, 1994.

Biehl, João *Vita: Life in a Zone of Social Abandonment*. Berkeley: University of California Press, 2005.

—. *Will to Live*. Princeton and Oxford: Oxford University Press, 2007.

Biehl, João, Byron Good, and Arthur Kleinman (eds). *Subjectivity*. Berkeley: University of California Press, 2007.

Boas, Norman. *Franz Boas 1858–1942: An Illustrated Biography*. Mystic: Seaport Autographs Press, 2004.

Bonhoeffer, Dietrich. *The Cost of Discipleship*. New York: Macmillan, 1960.

Booth, Wayne C., Gregory G. Colomb, and Joseph M. Williams. *The Craft of Research* 2nd edn. Chicago: University of Chicago Press, 2003.

Bourdieu, Pierre. *Outline of a Theory of Practice*. New York: Cambridge University Press, 1977.

—. *Language and Symbolic Power*. Stanford: Stanford University Press, 1991.

Bourdieu, Pierre and Loïc Wacquant. *An Invitation to Reflexive Sociology*. Chicago: University of Chicago Press, 1992.

Bouvia v. Superior Court, 179 Cal.App.3d, 1127 (Cal. 1986).

Boyd, Robert S. "Rationing Health Care." *The Seattle Times*, January 8, 1990, F1.

Brown, Delwin et al. *Converging on Culture: Theologians in Dialogue with Cultural Analysis and Criticism*. New York: Oxford University Press, 2001.

Browning, Don. *A Fundamental Practical Theology*. Minneapolis: Fortress Press, 1996.

Browning, Melissa D. et al. "Listening to Experience, Looking Toward Flourishing: Ethnography as Global Feminist Theo/ethical Praxis." *Practical Matters* 3 (2010): 1–25.

Bujo, Benezet. *The Ethical Dimension of Community*. Nairobi: Paulines Publications Africa, 1997.

Bunzl, Matti. "Boas, Foucault, and the 'Native Anthropologist.'" *American Anthropologist* 106:3 (2004): 435–42.

Cahill, L. Sowle. *Theological Bioethics: Participation, Justice, and Change.* Washington, D.C.: Georgetown University Press, 2005.

Cameron, Helen et al. *Talking about God in Practice: Theological Action Research and Practical Theology.* London: SCM Press, 2010.

Cannell, Fenella. *The Anthropology of Christianity.* Durham: Duke University Press, 2006.

Cessario, Romanus, O.P. *The Moral Virtues and Theological Ethics* 2nd edn. Notre Dame: University of Notre Dame Press, 2008.

Chabal, Patrick and Jean-Pascal Daloz. *Africa Works: Disorder as Political Instrument.* Bloomington: Indiana University Press, 1999.

Christ Comes in the Stranger's Guise: A History of the Open Door Community. Atlanta: Open Door Community, 1991.

Clark, Jana. *Health Care Rationing. There is Only One Answer: Treat the Cause, Not the Symptoms.* Medford: Northwest Seasonal Workers Association, 1989.

Clark, Kendall. "The Global Privileges of Whiteness." http://www.kooriweb.org/foley/news/story30.html (accessed June 6, 2010).

Clifford, James and George E. Marcus (eds). *Writing Culture: The Poetics and Politics of Ethnography.* Berkeley: University of California Press, 1986.

Cohen, Jolie. *If This State Wants Hangmen . . . A Critique of the Oregon Scheme for Health Care Rationing, Commonly Referred to as Death Squad Medicine.* Portland: Friends of Seasonal and Service Workers, 1989.

Cole, Douglas. *Franz Boas: The Early Years 1858–1906.* Seattle: University of Washington Press, 1999.

Congregación para el Culto Divino y la Disciplina de los Sacramentos. "Carta sobre la ordenación de diáconos permanentes de la Congregación para el Culto Divino y la Disciplina de los Sacramentos." *Revista Iberoamericana de Teología* 2:2 (2006): 99–100.

Consortium for Street Children. *Street Children Statistics.* http://www.streetchildren.org.uk/_uploads/resources/Street_Children_Stats_FINAL.pdf (accessed June 3, 2010).

Copeland, M. Shawn. "The New Anthropological Subject at the Heart of the Mystical Body of Christ." *CTSA PROCEEDINGS* 53 (1998).

—. *Enfleshing Freedom: Body, Race, and Being.* Minneapolis: Fortress Press, 2009.

Cose, Ellis. *Color-Blind: Seeing Beyond Race in a Race-Obsessed World.* New York: Harper Perennial, 1997.

Crain, Margaret and Jack Seymour. "The Ethnographer as Minister: Ethnographic Research in Ministry." *Religious Education* 91:3 (Summer 1996): 299–315.

Crisp, Roger and Michael Slote (eds). *Virtue Ethics.* New York: Oxford University Press, 1997.

Darnell, Regna. *And Along Came Boas: Continuity and Revolution in Americanist Anthropology.* Amsterdam: John Benjamins, 1998.

de Waal, Alex. *Famine Crimes: Politics & the Disaster Relief Industry in Africa.* Bloomington: Indiana University Press, 1998.

DeWalt, Kathleen M. and Billie R. DeWalt. *Participant Observation: A Guide for Fieldworkers.* Lanham: AltaMira Press, 2001.

Eade, Deborah. *Development and Patronage.* London: Oxfam Publishing, 1997.

Ecumenical Ministries of Oregon. *Ballot Measure #16 Attempts to Disrupt the Natural Season and Time of Death.* Portland: Legislative Commission of Ecumenical Ministries of Oregon, 1994.

—. *Voter's Guide to 1994 Ballot Measures.* Portland: Ecumenical Ministries of Oregon, 1994.

—. *Ecumenical Board Offers Support to Measure 51.* Portland: Ecumenical Ministries of Oregon, 1997.

—. *Letterhead.* Portland: Ecumenical Ministries of Oregon, 1997.

Editor. "Correction: Obituary Omitted Key Facts on Labor Organizer." *The New York Times,* March 21, 1995.

Emerson, Robert et al. *Writing Ethnographic Fieldnotes.* Chicago: University of Chicago Press, 1995.

Estrada, J. A. "Por un cristianismo inculturado en una Iglesía autóctona." *Revista Iberoamericana de Teología* 2:3 (2006): 5–26.

Fanon, Frantz. *Black Skin White Masks* (1952). Translated by Charles L. Markmann. New York: Grove Weidenfeld, 1967.

Farley, Margaret. *Just Love: A Framework For Christian Sexual Ethics.* New York: Continuum, 2006.

Farmer, Paul. "New Malaise: Bioethics and Human Rights in the Global Era." *Journal of Law, Medicine, and Ethics* 32 (2004): 243–51.

—. *Pathologies of Power: Health, Human Rights, and the New War on the Poor.* Berkeley: University of California, 2005.

—. "Never Again? Reflections on Human Values and Human Rights." The Tanner Lectures on Human Values. Salt Lake: The University of Utah, 2006.

Fife, Wayne. *Doing Fieldwork: Ethnographic Methods for Research in Developing Countries and Beyond.* New York: Palgrave Macmillan, 2005.

Filene, Peter G. *In the Arms of Others: A Cultural History of the Right-to-Die in America.* Chicago: Ivan R. Dee, 1998.

Finnstrom, Sverker. *Living with Bad Surroundings: War and Existential Uncertainty in Acholiland, Northern Uganda.* Uppsala: Department of Cultural Anthropology and Ethnology, 2003.

Flyvberg, Bent. *Making Social Science Matter: Why Social Inquiry Fails and How It Can Succeed Again.* Translated by Steven Sampson. New York: Cambridge University Press, 2001.

Foley, Kathleen M. "Assisted Suicide in the United States." Washington, D.C.: House of Representatives, 104th Congress, 1996.

Ford, David F. *Self and Salvation: Being Transformed.* New York: Cambridge University Press, 1999.

Frank, Arthur. *The Wounded Storyteller.* Chicago and London: The University of Chicago Press, 1997.

Frank, Thomas Edward. *The Soul of the Congregation: An Invitation to Congregational Reflection.* Nashville: Abingdon Press, 2000.

Friends of Seasonal and Service Workers. "Death Squad Medicine as a Symptom of Government in Crisis Ruling by Crisis." *Community Labor College Training Manual.* Portland: Friends of Seasonal and Service Workers, 1999.

—. *Friends of Seasonal and Service Workers: History and Mission* (flyer). Portland: Friends of Seasonal and Service Workers, 1999.

—. *Oregon Residents Need Comprehensive Medical Care—Not Doctor-Assisted Suicide* (flyer). Portland: Friends of Seasonal and Service Workers, 1999.

Frontline. *The Age of AIDS*. PBS Frontline, 2005.

Fulkerson, Mary McClintock. *Changing the Subject: Women's Discourses and Feminist Theology*. Minneapolis: Fortress Press, 1994.

—. *Places of Redemption: Theology for a Worldly Church*. New York: Oxford University Press, 2007.

Fullam, L. *The Virtue of Humility: A Thomistic Apologetic*. Lewiston: Edwin Mellen Press, 2009.

Fullilove, Mindy. Unpublished handbook for qualitative research for classroom use, *The Little Handbook*, edited by Mindy Thompson Fullilove, created for the use of the Qualitative Research Methods (QRM) 101 class, Mailman School of Public Health, Columbia University, New York, 2001.

Gathje, Peter R. *The Cost of Virtue: The Theological Ethics of Daniel and Phillip Berrigan*. Ann Arbor: University Microfilms International, 1994.

Geertz, Clifford. *The Interpretation of Culture*. New York: Basic Books, 1973.

Gill, Robin. "Churchgoing and Christian Ethics." *New Studies in Christian Ethics* 15. New York: Cambridge University Press, 1999: 13–30.

Gilsenan, Michael. "Against Patron-Client Relations." In *Patrons and Clients in Mediterranean Societies*, edited by E. Gellner and J. Waterbury. London: Duckworth, 1977: 167–84.

Glaser, Barney G. and Anselm L. Strauss. *The Discovery of Grounded Theory: Strategies for Qualitative Research*. New York: Aldine De Gruyter, 1967.

Global March. *Worst Forms of Child Labor Data: Kenya*. http://www.globalmarch.org/worstformsreport/world/kenya.html (accessed June 3, 2010).

Gordon, Deborah A. "Writing Culture, Writing Feminism: The Poetics and Politics of Experimental Ethnography." *Inscriptions* 3/4 (1988): 7–24.

Gossett, Thomas. *Race: The History of an Idea in America*. New York: Oxford University Press, 1963.

Gupta, Akhil. "Blurred Boundaries: The Discourse of Corruption." *American Ethnologist* 22:2 (May 1995): 375–402.

Gustafson, James M. *Ethics from a Theocentric Perspective: Theology and Ethics*. Vol. 1. Chicago: University of Chicago Press, 1981.

—. "The Sectarian Temptation: Reflections on Theology, the Church, and the University." *Catholic Theological Society of American Proceedings* 40 (1985): 83–94.

Haddad, Beverley. "Living It Out: Faith Resources and Sites as Critical to Participatory Learning with Rural South African Women." *Journal of Feminist Studies in Religion* 22:1 (2006): 135–54.

Hammersley, Martyn and Paul Atkinson. *Ethnography: Principles in Practice* 2nd edition. New York: Routledge, 1995.

Hardwig, John. "Is There a Duty to Die?." *The Hastings Center Report* March/April 1997.

Harrington, D. J. and J. F. Keenan. *Jesus and Virtue Ethics: Building Bridges between New Testament Studies and Moral Theology.* Lanham: Sheed and Ward, 2002.

Harvey, Jennifer. *Whiteness and Morality: Pursuing Racial Justice through Reparations and Sovereignty.* New York: Palgrave Macmillan, 2007.

Harvey, Jennifer, Karin Case, and Robin Hawledy Gorsline (eds). *Disrupting White Supremacy from Within: White People on What We Need to Do.* Cleveland: The Pilgrim Press, 2004.

Hauerwas, Stanley. *A Community of Character: Toward a Constructive Christian Social Ethics.* Notre Dame: University of Notre Dame Press, 1981.

—. *The Peaceable Kingdom: A Primer in Christian Ethics.* Notre Dame: University of Notre Dame Press, 1983.

—. *Christian Existence Today: On Church, World and Living In-Between.* Durham: Labyrinth Press, 1988.

—. "The Testament of Friends." *The Christian Century* (February 28, 1990): 213–16.

—. *In Good Company: The Church as Polis.* Notre Dame: University of Notre Dame Press, 1995.

—. *Sanctify Them in Truth: Holiness Exemplified.* Nashville: Abingdon Press, 1998.

—. *With the Grain of the Universe: The Church's Witness and Natural Theology.* Grand Rapids: Brazos Press, 2001.

Hauerwas, Stanley and Charles Pinches. *Christians among the Virtues: Theological Conversations with Ancient and Modern Ethics.* Notre Dame: University of Notre Dame Press, 1997.

Healy, Nicholas M. *Church, Word, and the Christian Life: Practical-Prophetic Ecclesiology.* New York: Cambridge University Press, 2000.

Heyward, Carter. *Touching Our Strength: The Erotic as Power and the Love of God.* San Francisco: Harper and Row, 1989.

Hill, Gail Kinsey and Mark O'Keefe. "Church Follows New Political Path." *Oregonian,* October 16, 1997.

Hobgood, Mary. *Dismantling Privilege: An Ethics of Responsibility.* Cleveland: Pilgrim Press, 2004.

hooks, bell. *Yearning: Race, Gender and Culture Politics.* Boston: South End Press, 1990.

Hopkins, Dwight N. *Introducing Black Theology of Liberation.* Maryknoll: Orbis Books, 1999.

Human Rights Watch. "Uprooted and Forgotten: Impunity and Human Rights Abuses in Northern Uganda." *Human Rights Watch* 17:12A (September 2005) http://www.hrw.org/en/node/11614/section/1 (accessed June 8, 2010).

Human Rights Watch Children's Rights Project. *Juvenile Injustice: Police Abuse and Detention of Street Children in Kenya.* New York: Human Rights Watch, 1997.

Humphry, Derek. Interview by author. Junction City: June 22, 2000.

Humphry, Derek and Mary Clement. *Freedom to Die: People, Politics, and the Right-to-Die Movement* Revised and updated edition. New York: St. Martin's Griffin, 2000.

Ignatiev, Noel. *How the Irish Became White.* London and New York: Routledge, 1996.

In Re Quinlan. 70 N.J. 10, 355 A.2d 647 (1976).

Jenkins, Timothy. "Fieldwork and the Perception of Everyday Life." *Man, New Series* 20:2 (1994): 433–55.

—. *Religion in English Everyday Life: An Ethnographic Approach. Methodology and History in Anthropology, vol. 5.* Oxford: Berghahn Books, 1999.

Jenny, Ellie. Interview by author. Salem: August 13, 1999.

John Paul II. "The Church Family in the Modern World." *Familiaris consortio.* November 22, 1981. http://www.vatican.va/holy_father/john_paul_ii/apost_exhortations/documents/hf_ijp-ii_exh_198111122_familiaris-consortio_en.html.

—. "*Veritatis splendor* August 6, 1993." *Origins* 23:18 (October 14, 1993): 297–334.

Jones, Robert P. *Liberalism's Troubled Search for Equality: Religion and Cultural Bias in the Oregon Physician-assisted Suicide Debates.* Notre Dame: University of Notre Dame Press, 2007.

Juma, Monica Kathina and Astri Suhrke. *Eroding Local Capacity: International Humanitarian Action in Africa.* Uppsala: Nordic Africa Institute, 2003.

Jung, Patricia Beattie and Aana Marie Vigen (eds). *God, Science, Sex, Gender.* Urbana: University of Illinois Press, 2010.

Karugire, Samwiri Rubaraza. *A Political History of Uganda.* Nairobi and London: Heinemann Educational Books, 1980.

Keenan, J. F. "The Virtue of Prudence (IIa IIae, qq. 47–56)." In *The Ethics of Aquinas,* edited by S. J. Pope. Washington, D.C.: Georgetown University Press, 2002: 259–71.

—. "What Does Virtue Ethics Bring to Genetics?" In *Genetics, Theology, and Ethics: An Interdisciplinary Conversation,* edited by L. Sowle Cahill. New York: Crossroad, 2005: 97–113.

—. *The Works of Mercy: The Heart of Catholicism* 2nd edn. Lanham: Rowman & Littlefield, 2008.

—. *A History of Catholic Moral Theology in the Twentieth Century: From Confessing Sins to Liberating Consciences.* New York: Continuum, 2010.

Kerr, Fergus. "Simplicity Itself: Milbank's Thesis." *New Blackfriars* 73 (June 1992): 306–10.

Kidder, Tracy. *Mountains beyond Mountains: The Quest of Dr. Paul Farmer, a Man Who Would Cure the World.* New York: Random House, 2004.

Kilbourn, Phyllis (ed.). *Street Children: A Guide to Effective Ministry.* Monrovia: MARC, 1997.

Kilbride, Phillip, Collette Suda, and Enos Njeru. *Street Children in Kenya: Voices of Children in Search of a Childhood.* London: Bergin and Garvey, 2000.

Kleinman, Arthur. *Illness Narratives.* New York: Basic Books, 1989.

Kotva, Joseph. *The Christian Case for Virtue Ethics.* Washington, D.C.: Georgetown University Press, 1996.

Kuper, Adam. *The Invention of Primitive Society: Transformations of an Illusion.* London: Routledge Press, 1988.

LaCugna, Catherin Mowry. *God for Us: The Trinity and Christian Life.* San Francisco: Harper, 1991.

Leslie, David A. Interview with author. Portland: June 23, 2000.

Lewis, Herbert. "Boas, Darwin, Science and Anthropology." *Current Anthropology* 42:3 (2001): 381–406.

Lincoln, C. Eric and Lawrence H. Mamiya. *The Black Church in the African American Experience.* Durham: Duke University Press, 1990.

Lincoln, Yvonna S. and Norman K. Denzin. *Turning Points in Qualitative Research: Tying Knots in a Handkerchief.* Lanham: AltaMira Press, 2003.

Lipsitz, George. *The Possessive Investment of Whiteness: How White People Benefit from Identity Politics.* Philadelphia: Temple University Press, 2006.

Lofland, John and Lyn H. Lofland. *Analyzing Social Settings: A Guide to Qualitative Observation and Analysis* 3rd edn. Belmont: Wadsworth, 1995.

Loury, Glenn C. *The Anatomy of Racial Inequality.* Cambridge, MA and London: Harvard University Press, 2002.

Lopez, Alfred J. (ed.). *Postcolonial Whiteness: A Critical Reader on Race and Empire.* Albany: State University of New York Press, 2005.

Luker, Kristin. *Abortion and the Politics of Motherhood.* Berkeley: University of California Press, 1984.

Luther, Martin. "The Estate of Marriage" (1522). *Luther's Works, American Edition, Volume 45*, translated by Walther I. Brandt. Philadelphia: Fortress Press, 1965.

MacIntosh, Peggy. "White Privilege: Unpacking the Invisible Knapsack." *Independent School* 49:2 (Winter 1990): 31–5.

MacIntyre, A. *After Virtue: A Study in Moral Theory* 3rd edn. Notre Dame: University of Notre Dame Press, 2007.

Magesa, Laurenti. *African Religion: The Moral Traditions of Abundant Life.* Nairobi: Paulines Press Africa, 1997.

Mamdani, Mahmood. *Politics and Class Formation in Uganda.* New York: Monthly Review Press, 1976.

—. *Imperialism and Fascism in Uganda.* Nairobi and London: Heinemann Educational Books, 1983.

Mamiya, Lawrence. "A Social History of the Bethel African Methodist Episcopal Church in Baltimore: The House of God and the Struggle for Freedom." In *American Congregations, Volume I: Portraits of Twelve Religious Communities,* edited by James P. Wind and James W. Lewis. Chicago: The University of Chicago Press, 1994: 221–292.

Marcus, George and Michael M. J. Fischer. *Anthropology as Cultural Critique: An Experimental Moment in the Human Sciences.* Chicago and London: University of Chicago Press, 1986.

Maren, Michael. *The Road to Hell: The Ravaging Effects of Foreign Aid and International Charity.* New York: Free Press, 2002.

Mathangani, Patrick. "Kenya: Education Blamed for the Gap between Rich and Poor." *The East African Standard,* May 20, 2005.

Maya Vinic. Available at http://www.mayavinic.com/ (accessed January 21, 2011).

Mbiti, John S. *African Religion and Philosophy.* Nairobi: East African Educational Publishers, 1960.

Meilander, Gilbert. *The Theory and Practice of Virtue.* Notre Dame: University of Notre Dame Press, 1984.

Mellott, David. *I Was and I Am Dust: Penitent Practices as a Way of Knowing.* Collegeville: Liturgical Press, 2009.

Merleau-Ponty, M. *Phenomenology of Perception.* New York: Routledge, 1962.

Milbank, John. "Enclaves, or Where is the Church?" *New Blackfriars* 73 (June 1992): 341–52.

—. *Theology and Social Theory: Beyond Secular Reason, Signposts in Theology.* Oxford: Blackwell, 1993.

—. "Theology and the Economy of the Sciences." In *Faithfulness and Fortitude: In Conversation with the Theological Ethics of Stanley Hauerwas*, edited by M. T. Nation and S. Wells. Edinburgh: T&T Clark, 2000.

Miller, Richard B. "On Making a Cultural Turn in Religious Ethics." *Journal of Religious Ethics* 33:3 (September 2005): 409–43.

Mitchell, Jon P. "Patrons and Clients." In *Encyclopedia of Social and Cultural Anthropology*, edited by Alan Barnard and Jonathan Spencer. London and New York: Routledge, 2002.

Mohrman, Margaret. *Attending Children*. Washington, D.C.: Georgetown University Press, 2006.

Moller, David. *Dancing with Broken Bones*. Oxford: Oxford University Press, 2004.

Moon, Dawn. *God, Sex and Politics: Homosexuality, and Everyday Theologies*. Chicago: University of Chicago Press, 2004.

Morris, Aldon. *The Origins of the Civil Rights Movement: Black Communities Organizing for Change*. New York: The Free Press, 1984.

Moschella, Mary Clark. *Ethnography as Pastoral Practice: An Introduction*. Cleveland: The Pilgrim Press, 2008.

Murphy, Nancey, Brad J. Kallenberg, and Mark Theissen Nation (eds). *Virtues and Practices in the Christian Tradition: Christian Ethics after MacIntyre*. Valley Forge: Trinity Press International, 1997.

Mwenda, Andrew. "Foreign Aid and the Weakening of Democratic Accountability in Uganda." *Foreign Policy Briefing* 88 (July 12, 2006). http://www.cato.org/pub_display.php?pub_id=6463 (accessed June 9, 2010).

Myerhoff, Barbara. *Number Our Days: A Triumph of Continuity and Culture among Jewish Old People in an Urban Ghetto*. New York: Touchstone, 1980.

Nasimiyu-Wasike, Anne. "Child Abuse and Neglect: An African Moral Question." In *Moral and Ethical Issues in African Christianity*, edited by J. N. K. Mugambi and A. Nasimiyu-Wasike. Nairobi: Action Publishers, 1999.

Nichols, Aidan. "Non Tali Auxilio: John Milbank's Suasion to Orthodoxy." *New Blackfriars* 73 (June 1992): 326–32.

Niebuhr, H. Richard. *The Meaning of Revelation*. New York: Macmillan, 1941.

—. *The Social Sources of Denominationalism*. Cleveland: World Publishing, 1964.

Nkemnkia, Martin Nkafu. *African Vitalogy*. Nairobi: Paulines Publications Africa, 1999.

Not Dead Yet. White Paper: Not Dead Yet, 1998.

Obispos de San Cristóbal de las Casas (Chiapas, México). "Iglesia autóctona y diaconado Permanente." *Revista Iberoamericana de Teología* 2:2 (2006): 101–6.

Ocowun, Chris. "Museveni Hails Gulu Archbishop Odama." *New Vision* (October 22, 2006): 1.

Odonga, Alexander. *Lwo-English Dictionary*. Kampala: Fountain Publishers, 2005.

Oduyoye, Mercy A. "Poverty and Motherhood." In *Motherhood: Experience, Institution, Theology*, edited by Anne Carr and Elizabeth S. Fiorenza. Edinburgh: T&T Clark, 1989: 23–30.

Ofcansky, Thomas. *Uganda: Tarnished Pearl of Africa*. Boulder: Westview Press, 1996.

Oladipo, Caleb Oluremi. *The Development of the Doctrine of the Holy Spirit in the Toruba (African) Indigenous Christian Movement*. New York: Peter Lang, 1996.

Palmer, Parker J. *The Courage to Teach: Exploring the Inner Landscape of a Teacher's Life.* San Francisco: Jossey-Bass Publishers, 1998.

Pandemic: Facing AIDS. Moxie Firecracker, 2002.

Parroquias y Consejo Diaconal de la Diócesis de San Cristóbal de las Casas (Chiapas, México). "Carta a su santidad Benedicto XVI." *Revista Iberoamericana de Teología* 2:2 (2006): 107–9.

Patton, Michael Quinn. *Qualitative Evaluation and Research Methods.* Thousand Oaks: Sage, 1990.

Paul VI. Encyclical Letter on the Development of Peoples. *"Populorum progressio." Acta Apostolicae Sedis* 59:4 (1967): 257–99.

p'Bitek, Okot. *Religion of the Central Luo.* Nairobi, Kampala, and Dar es Salaam: East African Literature Bureau, 1971.

——. *Horn of My Love.* Nairobi: Heinemann Kenya Ltd., 1974.

——. *Song of Lawino and Song of Ocol.* Oxford: Heinemann Publishers, 1984.

Perez-Pena, Richard. "Group's Leader is Said to Have Used Cult Tactics." *New York Times,* November 13, 1996.

Phiri, Isabel Apawo and Sarojini Nadar (eds). *African Women, Religion, and Health.* Maryknoll: Orbis Books, 2006.

Porter, J. "Recent Studies in Aquinas's Virtue Ethics: A Review Essay." *Journal of Religious Ethics* 26:1 (1998): 191–215.

Rabinow, Paul. "Representations are Social Facts: Modernity and Post-Modernity in Anthropology." In *Writing Culture: The Poetics and Politics of Ethnography,* edited by George Marcus and James Clifford. Berkeley: University of California Press, 1986.

——. *Making PCR: A Story of Biotechnology.* Chicago: University of Chicago Press, 1997.

——. *French DNA: Trouble in Purgatory.* Chicago: University of Chicago Press, 2002.

Rabinow, Paul (ed.). *The Foucault Reader.* New York: Vintage, 1984.

Rabinow, Paul and Hubert L. Dreyfus, with Michel Foucault. *Michel Foucault: Beyond Structuralism and Hermeneutics.* Chicago: University of Chicago Press, 1983.

Rabinow, Paul et al. *Designs for an Anthropology of the Contemporary.* Durham: Duke University Press, 2008.

Rasmussen, Larry L. *Moral Fragments and Moral Community: A Proposal for Church in Society.* Minneapolis: Fortress, 1993.

——. *Earth Community Earth Ethics.* Maryknoll: Orbis Books, 1996.

Reason, Peter and Hilary Bradbury (eds). *Handbook of Action Research: Participative Inquiry and Practice.* Thousand Oaks: Sage Publications, 2001.

Reding, Nick. *Methland: The Death and Life of an American Small Town.* New York: Bloomsbury Press, 2009.

Reimer-Barry, Emily. "In Sickness and In Health: Towards a Renewed Roman Catholic Theology of Marriage in Light of the Experiences of Catholic Married Women Living with HIV/AIDS." Unpublished doctoral dissertation, Loyola University Chicago, 2008.

Reinikka, Ritva and Jokob Svensson. "Local Capture: Evidence from a Central Government Transfer Program in Uganda." *Quarterly Journal of Economics* 119:2 (May 2004): 679–705.

Reno, William. *Warlord Politics and African States.* Boulder: Lynne Rienner Publishers, 1999.

Reuters News Service. "Vatican Defends Pope's Stand on Condoms as Criticism Mounts."March 18,2009.http://www.reuters.com/article/idUSLI43220920090318 (accessed June 6, 2010).

Rieff, David. *A Bed for the Night: Humanitarianism in Crisis.* New York: Simon and Schuster, 2003.

Roof, Wade Clark and William McKinney. *American Mainline Religion: Its Changing Shape and Future.* New Brunswick: Rutgers University Press, 1987.

Rosenbaum, Art. *Shout Because You're Free: The African-American Ring Shout Tradition in Coastal Georgia.* Athens: The University of Georgia Press, 1995.

Ross, Susan A. "Like a Fish Without a Bicycle?" *America* 181:17 (November 17, 1999): 10–13.

—. "Liturgy and Ethics: Feminist Perspectives." *Annual of the Society of Christian Ethics* 20 (2000): 263–74.

Salamone, Frank A. and Walter Randolph Adams. *Explorations in Anthropology and Theology.* Lanham: University Press of America, 1997.

Sarantitis, Barbara. Interview by author. Portland: August 18, 1999.

—. Personal Letter to Announce Wesley J. Smith Speaking Engagement. Portland: 2000.

Scharen, Christian. "Ideology, Ritual, and Christian Subjectivity." *Worship* 70 (September 1996): 406–22.

—. "Lois, Liturgy, and Ethics." *The Annual of the Society of Christian Ethics* 20 (2000): 275–305.

—. "Experiencing the Body: Sexuality and Conflict in American Lutheranism." *Union Seminary Quarterly Review* 57:1–2 (2003): 94–109.

—. *Public Worship, Public Works: Character and Commitment in Local Congregational Life.* Collegeville: The Liturgical Press, 2004.

—. "'Judicious Narratives': Ethnography as Ecclesiology." *Scottish Journal of Theology* 58:2 (2005): 125–42.

Schuman, David. Personal Letter to Oregon State Senator Neil Bryant. Salem: 1999.

Second Vatican Council. "Dogmatic Constitution on the Church." *Lumen gentium,* November 21, 1964.

—. "Decree on the Missionary Activity of the Church *Ad Gentes.*" *Acta Apostolicae Sedis* 58:14 (1996): 947–90.

Seidlitz, Larry et al. "Elders Attitudes Towards Suicide and Assisted Suicide: An Analysis of Gallup Poll Findings." *Journal of the American Geriatrics Society* 43 (1995): 993–8.

Seidman, I. E. *Interviewing as Qualitative Research.* New York: Teachers College Press, 1991.

Shanahan, Patrick. "The Alternative Africa." *White Fathers-White Sisters* issue no. 341 (Aug-Sept 1998).

Shorter, Alward and Edwin Onyancha. *Street Children in Africa: A Nairobi Case Study.* Nairobi: Paulines Publications Africa, 1999.

Smillie, Ian. *Patronage or Partnership?: Local Capacity Building in Humanitarian Crises.* Bloomfield: Kumarian Press, 2001.

Society for International Development. *Pulling Apart: Facts and Figures on Inequality in Kenya.* Nairobi: SID, 2004.

Spohn, William C. *Go and Do Likewise: Jesus and Ethics.* New York and London: Continuum, 2007.

Spradley, James P. *The Ethnographic Interview.* New York: Holt, Rinehart, and Winston, 1979.

Stevens, James H. S. *Worship in the Spirit: Charismatic Worship in the Church of England. Studies in Evangelical History and Thought.* Carlisle and Waynesboro: Paternoster Press, 2002.

Stocking, Geroge W., Jr. *Race, Culture, and Evolution: Essays in the History of Anthropology.* New York: The Free Press, 1968.

Stringer, Martin D. *On the Perception of Worship: The Ethnography of Worship in Four Christian Congregations in Manchester.* Birmingham: The University of Birmingham Press, 1999.

Swadener, Beth Blue. "Religion as a Source of Oppression or Resistance: An Analysis of the Kenyan Situation." In *Culture, Religion, and Liberation,* edited by Wimon S. Maimela. Pretoria: Ecumenical Association of Third World Theologians—EATWOT, 1991.

Swadener, Beth Blue and Kagendo N. Mutua, "Mapping the Terrains of Homelessness in Postcolonial Kenya." In *International Perspectives on Homelessness,* edited by Valerie Polakow and Cindy Guillean Westport. Santa Barbara: Greenwood Press, 2001.

Swinton, John and Harriet Mowat. *Practical Theology and Qualitative Research.* London: SCM Press, 2006.

Tanner, Kathryn. *Theories of Culture: An Agenda for Theology.* Minneapolis: Fortress Press, 1997.

Terry, Fiona. *Condemned to Repeat?: The Paradox of Humanitarian Action.* Ithaca: Cornell University Press, 2002.

Tipton, Steven. "A Response: Moral Languages and the Good Society." *Soundings* 69 (1986): 165–80.

Toulmin, Stephen. *Cosmopolis: The Hidden Agenda of Modernity.* New York: The Free Press, 1990.

Townes, Emilie M. *Womanist Ethics and the Cultural Production of Evil.* New York: Palgrave Macmillan, 2006.

Townsend-Gilkes, Cheryl. "Plenty Good Room: Adaptation in a Changing Black Church." *The Annals of the American Academy of Political and Social Science* 558:1 (July 1998): 101–21.

Tribble, Jeffery L. Sr. *Transformative Pastoral Leadership in the Black Church.* New York: Palgrave Macmillan, 2005.

Tvedt, Treje. *Angels of Mercy or Development Diplomats?: NGOs and Foreign Aid.* Lawrenceville: Africa World Press, 1998.

UNAIDS. "2004 Report on the global AIDS epidemic." http://www.unaids.org/bangkok2004/GAR2004_html/ExecSummary_en/ExecSumm_00_en.htm (accessed June 3, 2010).

—. *AIDS Epidemic Update 2009.* Geneva, Switzerland: WHO/UNAIDS, 2009.

UNESCO. *Literacy in Africa* (2006). http://portal.unesco.org/edication/en/ev.php-URL_ID=31032&URL_DO=DO_TOPIC&URL_SECTION=201.html (accessed May 23, 2010).

UNICEF. *Kenya.* http://www.unicef.org/infobycountry/kenya_statistics.html (accessed June 3, 2010).

Unitarian Universalist Association. "Right to Choose." General Assembly and Board of Trustees of the Unitarian Universalist Association, 1987. http://www.uua. org/socialjustice/socialjustice/statements/14499.shtml (accessed June 7, 2010).

United Methodist Church (U.S.). *The Book of Discipline of the United Methodist Church, 2000.* Nashville: United Methodist Publishing House, 2000.

United Nations. *Declaration on the Rights of Indigenous Peoples* (A/RES/61/295). http://www.un-documents.net/a61r295.htm (accessed January 21, 2011).

United Nations, Office of the High Commissioner for Human Rights. *Outcome Document of the Durban Review Conference.* http://www.un.org/durbanreview2009/ (accessed January 21, 2011).

Van Maanen, John. *Tales of the Field: On Writing Ethnography.* Chicago: University of Chicago Press, 1988.

Verhey, Allen. *Reading the Bible in the Strange World of Medicine.* Grand Rapids: Eerdmans Press, 2003.

Vigen, Aana Marie. "To Hear and To Be Accountable Across Difference: An Ethic of White Listening." In *Disrupting White Supremacy from Within: White People on What WE Need to Do,* edited by Jennifer Harvey et al. Cleveland: The Pilgrim Press, 2004.

—. *Women, Ethics, and Inequality in U.S. Healthcare: "To Count Among the Living".* New York: Palgrave Macmillan, 2006.

Vogt, C. P. "Fostering a Catholic Commitment to the Common Good: An Approach Rooted in Virtue Ethics." *Theological Studies* 68:2 (2007): 394–417.

Wacquant, Loïc. "Deadly Symbiosis: When Ghetto and Prison Meet and Mesh." *Punishment & Society* 3:1 (2001): 95–133.

—. *Body and Soul: Notebooks of an Apprentice Boxer.* New York: Oxford, 2004.

—. "Carnal Connections: On Embodiment, Apprenticeship, and Membership." *Qualitative Sociology* 28:4 (Winter 2005): 445–74.

—. "Habitus as Topic and Tool: Reflections on Becoming a Prizefighter." In *Ethnographies Revisited: Constructing Theory in the Field,* edited by William Shaffir, Antony Puddephatt, and Steven Kleinknecht. New York: Routledge, 2009: 137–51.

Walker, Sharon. *Women with AIDS and Their Children.* New York: Garland, 1998.

Walz, Heike. "The Beautiful Princess and the Village Girls." In *Feminist Interpretation of the Bible and the Hermeneutics of Liberation,* edited by Silvia Schroer and Sophia Bietenhard. New York: Continuum, 2003.

Waruta, Douglas. Class Notes. Maryknoll Institute of African Studies, Maryknoll: June 6–7, 2001.

Weber, Maximillan. *Theory of Social and Economic Organization.* Translated and edited by A. M. Henderson and Talcott Parsons. New York: Free Press, 1947. Originally published as *Wirtschaft und Gesellschaft,* 1922.

Weiss, Robert S. *Learning from Strangers: The Art and Method of Qualitative Interview Studies.* New York: Free Press, 1994.

Weithman, Paul J. "Of Assisted Suicide and the Philosopher's Brief" *Ethics* 109 (April 1999): 548–78.

West, Traci, C. *Disruptive Christian Ethics: When Racism and Women's Lives Matter.* Louisville: Westminster John Knox Press, 2006.

Whitmore, Todd David. "Crossing the Road: The Case for Ethnographic Fieldwork in Christian Ethics." *Journal of the Society of Christian Ethics* 27:2 (2007): 273–94.

Wiley, Dennis W. "Black Theology, the Black Church, and the African-American Community." In *Black Theology: A Documentary History Volume II 1980–1992*, edited by James H. Cone and Gayraud S. Wilmore. Maryknoll: Orbis Books, 1993: 127–138.

Williams, Rowan. "Saving Time: Thoughts on Practice, Patience, and Vision." *New Blackfriars* 73 (June 1992): 319–26.

Williams, Vernon. *Rethinking Race: Franz Boas and His Contemporaries*. Lexington: University of Kentucky Press, 1996.

Willig, C. *Qualitative Research in Psychology: A Practical Guide to Theory and Method*. Buckingham: Open University Press, 2001.

Willing, Richard and Carol J. Castaneda. "Protesters See No Mercy in Assisted Suicide." *USA Today*, January 9, 1997.

Wilson, Jonathan R. *Gospel Virtues: Practicing Faith, Hope, and Love in Uncertain Times*. Downers Grove: Intervarsity Press, 1998.

Wise, Tim. "Membership Has Its Privileges: Thoughts on Acknowledging and Challenging Whiteness." In *White Privilege: Essential Readings on the Other Side of Racism*, edited by Paula Rothenberg. New York: Worth Publishers, 2009: 133–7.

Wolf, Susan M. "Gender, Feminism, and Death: Physician-Assisted Suicide and Euthanasia." In *Feminism and Bioethics: Beyond Reproduction*, edited by Susan M. Wolf. New York: Oxford University Press, 1996: 282–317.

Woolf, Virginia. *A Room of One's Own*. Orlando: Harcourt, 1929.

Young, Iris Marion. *Justice and the Politics of Difference*. Princeton: Princeton University Press, 1990.

Young, Michael W. *Malinowski: Odyssey of an Anthropologist, 1884–1920*. New Haven: Yale University Press, 2004.

Zatyrka, A. P. "The Formation of the Autochthonous Church and the Inculturation of Christian Ministries in the Indian Cultures of America. A Case Study: the Bachajón Mission and the Diocese of San Cristóbal de Las Casas, Mexico." Dissertation, 2 vols. Innsbruck: Leopold Franzens Universität, 2003.

—. "Iglesia Autóctona ¿una ideología?" *Revista Iberoamericana de Teología* 2:2 (2006): 97–8.

—. "The Rise and Fall of the *Ecclesia Indiana*." *Revista Iberoamericana de Teología* 2:3 (2006): 27–62.

—. "Emerging Successful Ecclesiologies: The Autochthonous Church in the Bachajón Mission, Chiapas." http://www.scu.edu/jst/whatwedo/events/archive/dialogue.cfm (accessed January 21, 2011).

Zenit Online News. "Spokesman Explains Church's Fight Against AIDS." March 19, 2009 http://www.zenit.org/article-25415?1=english (accessed June 6, 2010).

Zizioulas, John D. *Being as Communion: Studies in Personhood and the Church*. Crestwood: St. Vladimir's Seminary Press, 1985.

—. *Communion and Otherness: Further Studies in Personhood and the Church*. New York: T & T Clark, 2007.

Index

Made in the USA
Lexington, KY
25 January 2012